E Duret

Practical Household Cookery

Containing 1000 Original and Other Recipes

E Duret

Practical Household Cookery
Containing 1000 Original and Other Recipes

ISBN/EAN: 9783744788175

Printed in Europe, USA, Canada, Australia, Japan

Cover: Foto ©Andreas Hilbeck / pixelio.de

More available books at **www.hansebooks.com**

PRACTICAL HOUSEHOLD COOKERY.

CONTAINING

1000 ORIGINAL AND OTHER RECIPES.

BY

E. DURET,

EX-MANAGER OF THE ST. JAMES' HALL, ETC. ETC.

LONDON AND NEW YORK:
FREDERICK WARNE AND CO.
1891.

PUBLISHER'S PREFACE.

THIS is a practical book, by a practical man, written for practical people. It covers the whole range of culinary effort, and gives a wide choice of meals for every day in the year. There is much that is new in it, more especially with regard to the Italian and other provincial dishes. A strong feature is made of soups and boiled meats and other inexpensive preparations, there being not only a good selection, but the distinctions being well marked. The directions have been carefully revised. They are precise and clear, and there is not a recipe in the book which has not been practically tried and found to be satisfactory. It also contains a number of instructive and valuable remarks on the different products of this country used in cookery.

CONTENTS.

	PAGE
INTRODUCTION—REMARKS ON MEAT IN GENERAL, AND SKETCHES OF SIDES OR HALVES OF BEEF, VEAL, AND MUTTON, SHOWING JOINTS THEREFROM.	1
REMARKS ON NEW ZEALAND MUTTON AND AMERICAN BEEF.	8
REMARKS ON BOILED MEAT.	9
WHAT SHOULD BE HYNDY ON THE KITCHEN TABLE AND LARDER.	11
BOUQUET GARNI OR BUNCH OF DRY HERBS.	11
CARAMEL OR BURNT SUGAR.	12

CHAPTERS

I.	SOUPS—GRAVIES—MACARONI AND PASTE OF ALL DESCRIPTIONS—RICE—RISOTTO—AND ORDINARY JELLY	11
II.	SOUPS FOR CONVALESCENTS AND CHILDREN	76
III.	SAUCES—MELTED BUTTER—ESSENCES—JELLIES.	80
IV.	PURÉES OF VEGETABLES FOR GARNISHING—EGGS—OMELETS—PANADAS—BREADINGS	108
V.	FORCEMEAT—GARNISHING IN GENERAL—SALPICON	124
VI.	FRYING—BATTER PASTE—HOT AND COLD HORS-D'ŒUVRES.	142
VII.	TRIPE—LIGHT ENTRÉES—SAUSAGES	159
VIII.	BOILED MEAT	176
	FISH AND CRUSTACEANS	181
IX.	BEEF	235
X.	VEAL	248

CONTENTS.

CHAP.		PAGE
XI.	MUTTON—LAMB AND KID	259
XII.	PORK—HAM—SUCKING PIG—WILD BOAR	271
XIII.	VENISON—HARE—RABBIT	284
XIV.	POULTRY	289
XV.	GAME	329
XVI.	HOT AND COLD MEAT PIES—PUDDINGS—GALANTINES AND POTTED GAME	342
XVII.	VEGETABLES—SALADS—SANDWICHES	356
XVIII.	PASTE—PASTRY—SWEET DISHES—ICES	387

PRACTICAL HOUSEHOLD COOKERY.

INTRODUCTION AND PRELIMINARY OBSERVATIONS.

SINCE cookery was discovered to be a science and classed, as well as cultivated, as an art by epicures of renown, many more or less valuable books have been written on the subject by professional cooks, as well as by amateurs of all descriptions in the mysteries of gastronomy. The aim of these has, no doubt, been to educate the palate and enlighten the readers as to the different modes of preparing good and tasty food at nominal cost; but the majority of the books are either copies of others, or have been written with a very limited culinary knowledge; with few exceptions, they give neither quantity, measure, nor weight, nor the time needed for following out their numerous and perplexing recipes, and thus afford but very little help to the uninitiated.

This frequent want of explicitness in these works, combined with the growing taste for novelties, has induced me to offer herein the knowledge I have gathered during an experience of many years; and in doing so I shall be content if I succeed in simplifying the directions without producing confusion, and at the same time give in all cases the correct weight and measure, as well as the exact time for cooking each recipe, besides suggesting economical reform in the kitchen and encouraging the use of good and nutritious food. Although steps have of late been taken towards education in culinary knowledge by the so-called schools of cookery, there is still plenty of room for improvement. Cooking ought to be studied as a science and practised as an art in every young ladies' school, as well as in every home, and for the benefit of the nation at large, I sincerely hope that the day will come when every girl, rich and poor, will have the proper means, and I may say further, be compelled to learn its rudiments, so that when she is her own mistress, she may, in due course, not only be able to give her order in a practical manner, and compose her *menus* according to her means and fancies, but be able also, if necessary, to cook *for herself*, and by so doing be less dependent on her cook.

Abroad, and especially in France, the culinary art is far better cultivated than it is here. There men as well as women of every station seem to take a pride in the knowledge of cookery, without in any way interfering with the rights or self-esteem of their cooks; on the contrary, the latter are far more attached to their employers, and also more attentive to their duties, well knowing that their services could be dispensed with at any moment, without causing the slightest inconvenience to their mistresses, should they attempt to show such independence and temper as they so often do in this country.

Having thus far expressed my views on the present knowledge of cookery, I will at once proceed. As our senses were made for our enjoyment, so were the good things in the world. The different products imported into England afford proofs of bounty which it would be unreasonable and ungrateful to reject; in fact, it would be a sort of impiety were we not to avail ourselves of them and turn them to their very best account. In endeavouring to bring before the public their proper use, I take the opportunity of advocating a branch of the culinary art which is not so well known as it ought to be, and is consequently very little cultivated—I mean the pure Italian cookery. Whoever has travelled through that land of fine art and poetry must have indulged, more or less, in its national dishes, and brought back with him sweet remembrances of its palatable, appetising, and nourishing food. My experience as a restaurant manager and caterer of long standing enables me to write with a certain amount of authority on this subject, as whenever and wherever I have introduced some of those specialities, I have always found that they were appreciated and relished. Rice and paste of all descriptions, such as macaroni, spaghetti, tagliatelli, vermicelli, ravioli, &c., &c., play a great part in the ordinary Italian cookery; and as they are all cheap items, nutritious, wholesome, digestive, and can be prepared in so many different ways, it is my intention of expatiating on them, trusting that my efforts will be appreciated by both the middle and working classes, for whose instruction and benefit this part of the work is more particularly intended. There is an old saying which may be appropriately quoted here; that "if you have a favour to ask of a man, ask it of him after he has had a good dinner." There is a great deal of truth in this, and I should very much like to impress its moral on my fair readers, who, if my instructions are properly carried out, will soon discover its truth, and reap the benefit of their industry and culinary knowledge. It is a well-known fact that the Englishman is fond of his home; add to it the comfort and enjoyment of a good dinner, and contentment, harmony, and happiness will reign supreme in the family; herein lies the great bliss in your married life, as well as your recompense.

But in order that culinary duties should be properly performed and easily discharged, and at the same time a source of comfort and pleasure to the performers, it is of the greatest importance that the kitchen arrangements, ventilation and light—combined with the necessary utensils and appliances required for cooking successfully (a list of which I give at the end of this work)—should be studied in a more practical manner and provided for with greater liberality than is actually found, even, I am sorry to say, in some of the wealthiest houses of this country.

Families with limited means are generally very fond of accumulating and shelving innumerable knick-knacks, in their different rooms that are quite worthless for domestic comfort, although very pleasing to the eye as ornaments; but they will disregard and neglect the furnishing of proper stewpans and other appliances, really necessary for providing satisfactorily and successfully for their daily wants.

Cleanliness is one of the most essential conditions in all cooking operations. Vessels and utensils of every description used for such purpose should be kept—the inside even more than the outside—in a constantly bright and polished state, without which no cooking should ever be attempted. Many failures in sauces and dinners spoiled have been attributed to the want of cleanliness. Copper pans should often be examined, and as soon as they are found to redden inside, should at once be sent to be retinned, as nothing is more unwholesome to the food or prejudicial to the colouring of sauces, &c., than a badly tinned pan.

Cleanliness must also be applied to the different dressers, tables, shelves, and sinks, which should be scrubbed daily with soap and boiling water, and then properly rinsed and wiped. The floors of the kitchens, as well as the larder and yard, should also receive their proper attention and be scoured as often as wanted. These recommendations are not to be considered as a luxury but a necessity, and ought to be the fundamental rules in every household.

Special attention must also be paid to the hands and nails, and no food touched with them unless perfectly clean.

INTRODUCTION.

The next thing in order, and which is of no less importance, is, that you should possess a good drawing kitchener; keep it clean and free from soot; make yourself well acquainted with the object of its different keys and dampers, so that you be able to regulate the heat in the ovens as wanted; otherwise all your efforts at cooking and baking will partially be lost. Gas-stoves are simple, clean, and very handy in their way, as far as boiling and roasting is concerned, but will not answer for middle-class families, and therefore I cannot recommend them. French kitcheners or closed ranges are the best constructed in the world for usefulness and economy of fuel.

Remarks on Meat in General.

The knowledge of the quality of meat, as well as the different parts and cuts of the animals, is absolutely necessary to all who have to cater for the public or buy for their own private use.

I therefore give sketches of sides or halves of beef, veal, and mutton, showing from which part of the animal each cut comes.

BEEF.

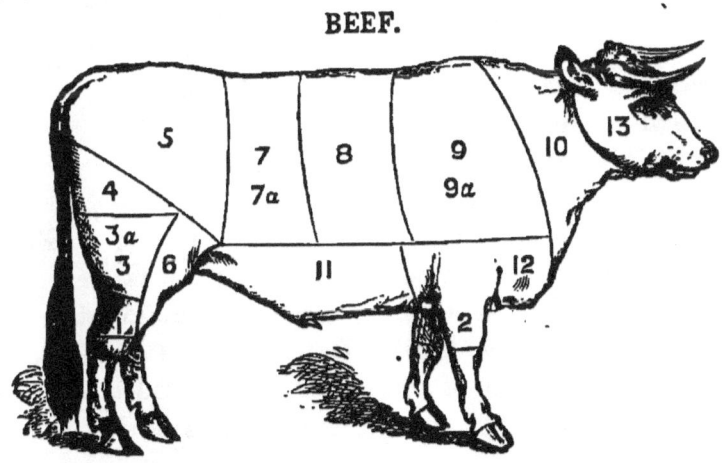

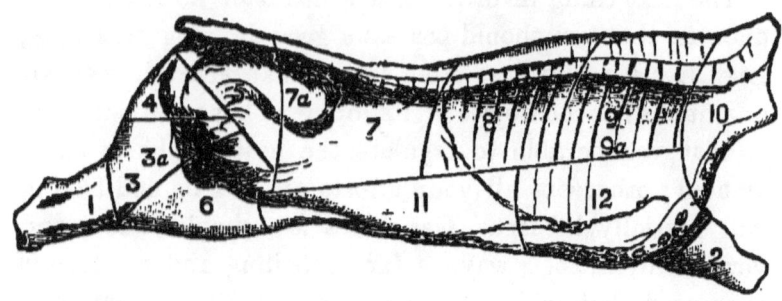

By the above sketches it will be seen that the side of beef is divided into fifteen parts, besides the head and tail, viz:—

1 and 2. Leg and shin, for boiling.

3 and 3a. The top side and silver side, two distinct cuts; the former is used for beef-steaks, and the latter can be braised, but is generally salted.

4. Shows aitch-bone, a roasting joint.

5. Rump, for rump-steak.

6. Thick flank for beef-steak and braising.

7 and 7a. Sirloin with fillet or under-cut, the best joint for roasting, and the kidney for stewing.

8. Fore-ribs, a joint of six ribs for roasting.

9 and 9a. Middle ribs, a joint of six ribs, for roasting and stewing, and shoulder for stewing and braising.

10. Neck, for stewing and boiling.

11. Thin flank, for salting and braising.

12. Brisket, for salting.

In selecting a piece of beef, see that it is of a bright red colour and not coarse in the grain; the fat must be of a light yellow appearance, nicely intermixed with the lean and soft to the touch. Its flavour and quality will depend, as a matter of course, entirely on the breed and food of the animal; but in either case it is advisable that a joint should be hung some days in a cool draughty place before cooking.

Beef of a brown and dull colour, with flaccid fat, but firm and hard to the touch, must be avoided, as these marks are true indications of inferior quality meat.

VEAL.

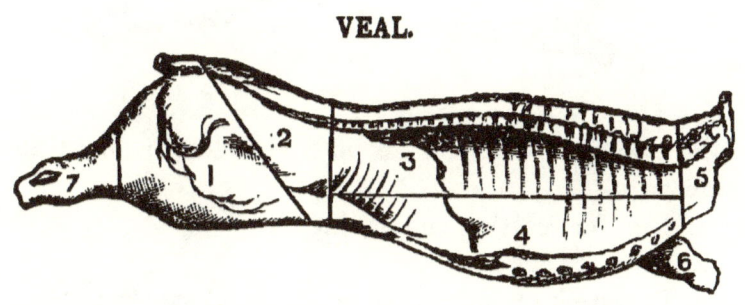

Veal is divided into seven parts, besides the head, tail, and feet—

1. Leg of veal, from which cushions and scallops are cut, otherwise called fillets, and is the best part of the veal for braising and stewing.
2. Loin and kidney, for roasting.
3. Cutlets, for broiling.
4. Breast, for stewing and roasting.
5. Neck, for stewing and boiling.
6. Shoulder, for stewing and boiling.
7. Knuckle, for boiling.

Veal must always be chosen of a light colour; the fat must be perfectly white and transparent. Veal of a reddish tint and lean should be rejected, as it is of an inferior quality. For the same reason avoid coarse flesh and big joints of veal, as these are sure signs that the animal was an old one when killed (see the chapter on veal).

MUTTON.

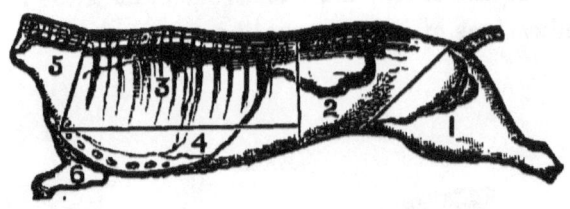

Mutton is divided in six parts, besides the head and kidneys:—
1. Leg, for roasting and boiling.
2. Loin, for chops.
3. Best neck or cutlets, for broiling and stewing.
4. Breast, for stewing.
5. Neck end or scrag, for boiling and stewing.
6. Shoulder, for roasting.

The quality of mutton is known by the same signs as good beef: its flesh must be of a bright red colour, with white transparent fat; in a like manner, prime mutton depends, for quality and flavour, on the breed and feeding; sheep with black legs and heads yield the best mutton.

Mutton of a dull red colour, with yellow and opaque fat, is of an inferior quality.

Remarks on New Zealand Mutton and American Beef.

There is a general prejudice among the well to-do classes against buying fresh meat imported from America and Australia. This, however, ought not to be, as both are equal in taste and quality to the ordinary English-bred meat; and if the consumers would only waive their fancies, they would soon find that it is a very difficult task to tell one from the other, even amongst would-be connoisseurs.

How many hundred legs of New Zealand mutton are sold daily in Great Britain as English, bred and fed, is beyond my power to tell. Suffice it to say, that out of the several thousand carcasses imported weekly into this country from Australia, not the half of that number is sold as such. What becomes of the others? That is the question; and if you cannot guess, I am afraid your butcher will not be able to tell you, for the very simple reason that he does not keep it himself—at least so he will say. The same thing applies to Australian and American beef.

Only first quality New Zealand mutton and American beef should, however, be bought; and in either case the meat must be hung for a few days in a cool and draughty place, previous to cooking.

Remarks on Boiled Meat.

There is also a general idea prevailing in England that boiled meat is not so nutritious as roast meat. This is a great mistake, as it is the only kind of cooking by which you can obtain the full value of your materials, and is not only the most wholesome and easily digested, but the cheapest and most profitable form by which food can be prepared for the working classes, as it has been clearly demonstrated beyond a doubt that the roast joint will lose in weight twice the amount of the boiled one; and as the broth derived from the latter must also be taken into consideration, it will at once convince you, I am sure, that this is the most economical kind of cooking. It forms, I may say, part of the daily bill of fare of almost all classes in other countries.

Mr. Buckmaster, who has studied this point in a most practical manner, and ought to be considered an authority on the subject, says in his valuable little book on Cookery, that "persons who cook their food in water do it more economically, and derive from it a greater amount of nourishment, than those who employ the direct action of heat, as in baking and roasting." I thoroughly agree with him.*

* To cook satisfactorily by boiling, however, a slow and steady fire is required, as the cooking cannot be expected to hasten by indiscriminately heaping up fuel; all excess of heat is wasted when the boiling-point is once reached, and the benefit of a progressive cooking lost without expediting it.

But to boil down or reduce gravy and sauces, a brisk fire, producing quick evaporation, is absolutely indispensable; the contents would lose appearance and flavour if reduced too slowly. It is therefore of the utmost necessity that proper attention should be paid to the different simmering and boiling expressions used, such as gently, very gently, or on a slow fire and a brisk fire, in order to succeed in obtaining the desired effect and taste.

CHAPTER I.

SOUPS—GRAVIES—MACARONI, ETC.

What Must Always be Handy in the Kitchen and Larder.

A SEASONING-BOX, containing salt, white pepper, peppercorns, cloves, nutmeg, cinnamon, mace, cayenne, and allspice, should always be handy on the kitchen-table. A bottle each of olive-oil, white vinegar, and caramel or burnt sugar, a ball of string, and a perforated box of powdered or castor sugar on a shelf. Garlic and shalots in a small drawer by itself; onions in a basket. All fresh vegetables should be kept in a cool place. Flour, eggs, butter, rice, macaroni, and all paste should be kept in the larder, as well as all tinned preserves, such as peas, French beans, mushrooms, tomato sauce, and truffles; also jams, marmalade, syrups, preserved fruits, pistachios, saffron, curry, parmesan cheese, capers, gherkins, vanilla, chocolate, coffee, lemons, orange-flower water, sago, tapioca, semolina, oatmeal, pearl barley, lard, bacon, ham, &c., which should be brought to the kitchen as wanted. The following dry herbs should also be hung in a dry but not too hot place:— Thyme, sage, marjoram, bay-leaves, rosemary, basil, laurel-leaves, chives, and burnet.

As "bouquet garni"* will often be required in the process of cooking, I will give here the proper mode of preparing one, say, for a family of six or eight persons. Take a small handful of parsley weighing about one ounce

---

* "Bouquet garni," a bunch or faggot of dry aromatic herbs.

and wash it clean, add one ounce of thyme, the same weight of bay-leaves and marjoram, and one clove of garlic; roll the dry herbs into the parsley; fold over each end; and tie the bundle round with a small string.

CARAMEL OR BURNT SUGAR.

Caramel can be prepared in the following manner:—Take a small and very clean stewpan, put one pound of loaf-sugar in it, set the stewpan over the fire; stir it continually with a wooden spoon till the sugar is thoroughly melted, then boil it very slowly for fifteen minutes, giving it an occasional stir, when the sugar is seen coming to a dark-brown colour; add gradually one pint and a half of cold water, stirring the while, and letting it again boil slowly for another twenty minutes; then let it cool, strain and pour it into a clean bottle, which must be kept corked. It will keep thus for years.

1. ORDINARY STOCK.

Stock or broth is the principal element of good cooking, as well as the foundation of all soups, and of many sauces. No household should be without it; and as soup is also the first course served at a dinner, I will at once proceed with the mode of its preparation.

In order to study economy, all bones from previously cooked meat should be collected, broken, and put in a stock-pot, together with any skin, gristle, and trimmings of fresh meat, as well as the remnants of cooked chicken and game bones that may be had. Add to these four or five pounds of leg of beef and a knuckle of veal; cover the lot with cold water, say four quarts, and throw in a tablespoonful of salt; boil gently for three or four hours, carefully removing all scum and fat from the top with a skimmer at the beginning of the ebullition, otherwise it will partially re dissolve and spoil the clearness and flavour of the stock; then strain the liquor through a fine sieve into an earthenware pan, and remove to a cool place till next day.

The above stock may be improved a great deal by adding two or three pennyworth of vegetables and ingredients, as in the following recipe, when a broth good enough for soup can be obtained.

2. BROTH OR CONSOMMÉ.

Take five pounds of the shin of beef, tie it with a string to keep it together; add from one to two pounds of knuckle or leg of veal; put these into a stock-pot with the stock made out of bones the previous day, to which a quart of cold water can be added. Should there be, however, no ordinary stock made, pour in four quarts of cold water and a tablespoonful of salt; set it over the fire till it nearly boils, when the scum must be removed most carefully by frequent skimming; add at intervals about a gill of cold water, which will check the ebullition and help the scum to rise. When the scum is all removed, peel two ordinary-sized onions (not Spanish), stick in each three cloves, and drop them in the stock-pot; wash two leeks and a small head of celery, tie them together; scrape two carrots of average size, slit into four and two inches in length; peel two turnips and cut them into four; and then make a "bouquet garni" (page 11), and season with a teaspoonful of pepper-corns. These items should all be put in separately, in order to keep the contents of the stock-pot at the same temperature. Skim the liquor for the last time; after which let it simmer gently by the side of the fire for about three hours; then take the meat out, skim off all the fat, and put it by in a basin; so that, when cold, it can be used for frying or other purposes.

A small cabbage cut in quarters, properly cleaned, as well as a few potatoes, cut in four and added two hours after the other vegetables, will be an improvement to the broth as well as a garnish to the meat.

If proper attention is paid to the skimming and simmering of the stock-pot, the clarifying of the broth will not be required; but should there be a failure in carrying out accordingly the instructions, the best thing to do is to take the whites and shells of three eggs; crush the shells well in the hands or in a mortar; mix them with the whites and a quarter of a pint of cold water, whisk these well together in a basin for a few seconds, add half a pint of boiling broth, still beating the mixture, and pour it into the stock-pot; stir the stock briskly till it boils; then remove the pot by the side of the fire; let it remain there for a few minutes or till the whites of the eggs rise to the surface; after which strain carefully, and the broth will be perfectly clarified.

Pour some of the broth into a soup-tureen in which some thin slices of toasted bread have been previously placed; add part of the cooked vegetables from the stock-pot. Nicely shred and serve. This is the real *pot-au-feu*, and considered the standard dish in France.

Should the broth be preferred of a golden colour, pour a few drops only of caramel in a soup-ladle or spoon; dip it into the soup-tureen and stir three or four times.

Broth should be strained as follows:—Take an earthenware pan or basin of a size large enough to hold the quantity of broth made; lay over it a clean cloth and a fine hair sieve at the top of the cloth, pour on to it the contents of the stock-pot, and remove the strained broth to a cool place free from dust. A piece of muslin gauze may be placed over it, but never cover it entirely, nor at any time pour hot broth into the cold, as the reaction will turn it sour.

Stock can be kept fresh and good for several days in cold weather, but during the summer it is advisable to boil it on the second day and every day afterwards. Storms and thunder will also turn broth sour; and to prevent this, you should boil beforehand.

If any particles of fat remain at the top of the broth, they can easily be removed in a solid state when cold. Blotting or kitchen paper laid on the surface of the broth will also remove all globules of fat.

Note.—When the broth is properly made it will turn into jelly when cold.

The boiled beef and veal taken out of the stock-pot will be found delicious if eaten hot with the remainder of the cooked vegetables and gherkins. I mention this because I know of several instances where it has been thrown away for want of knowledge.

3. ORDINARY FAMILY STOCK.

Broth made out of beef is always the best; nevertheless, in country places where that meat can only be had with difficulty, mutton can be substituted, and by so doing make what is generally called mutton broth; veal may also be added, when the broth will be all the richer.

Take four pounds of neck or scrag of mutton and two pounds of leg of veal (if no veal, six pounds of mutton), put the meat in a stewpan with one ounce of butter, and brown nicely for about twenty minutes; then pour in three quarts of cold water and add two onions; let the liquor come to the boil slowly. Skim as carefully as in No. 2, then add two turnips cut in quarters, one carrot sliced in very small dice, and one ounce of pearl barley previously blanched for ten minutes; let the contents simmer for two hours; after which take the meat out, skim off the fat, then add a little parsley chopped fine, season to taste with salt only, and pour the broth into a soup-tureen with the carrots, turnips, and barley.

Should some of the meat be desired with the soup, cut in small dice about half a pound of the lean mutton, add it to the soup; mix well and serve.

4. ORDINARY STOCK FOR GRAVY AND SAUCES.

Put into a saucepan six pounds of shin of beef, two pounds of leg of veal, two carrots sliced, one onion, and half a head of celery cut in two; brown the lot with two ounces of butter for about twenty minutes; then add three quarts of stock No. 1 and an old fowl. Boil, and skim in the usual way, then let it simmer gently till the broth is reduced by one-half, then strain it into a pan.

To further improve this stock, which will serve afterwards as a foundation to all brown sauces, add a piece of rabbit or an old partridge previously browned either before the fire or in the oven.

Note.—No salt must be put in this stock.

5. GRAVY SOUP.

Put into a stewpan three rashers of bacon, two slices of ham, four pounds of lean beef (silver side or top side is the best), an old fowl, two pounds of leg of veal, two carrots cut in slices, one onion with three cloves stuck in it, half a head of celery, two leeks, two turnips, and a "bouquet garni." Pour in it one quart of No. 1 stock, reduce it by a sharp boiling of half an hour's duration, often stirring the contents with a wooden spoon to prevent burning. Then add four quarts of a similar stock and boil it gently, when proper attention must be paid to the skimming; after which draw it by the side of the fire and simmer for three hours. Meanwhile take about three pounds of leg of mutton, roast it half through and put it into the stewpan, continue the simmering till the mutton is properly cooked, then take all the meat out; let the broth boil again for a few minutes, add about an ounce of sugar, a glass of sherry, and then strain in the usual way.

This broth or gravy is very rich, and is generally served plain.

6. VEAL BROTH.

Take four pounds of either shoulder or leg of veal; put it in a stewpan with two ounces of good fresh butter, and brown it nicely all round for half an hour. Meantime boil two quarts of water in a saucepan; put the veal in, together with an onion having two cloves stuck in it, one carrot sliced, two leeks, and about one pound of lean beef cut in slices, which will add strength and taste to the broth; skim in the usual way, add one fowl, and simmer gently for two hours; then take the meat out, strain the broth, and serve.

This broth is delicious, and can be recommended to invalids as well as to healthy persons.

7. CHICKEN BROTH.

Take two old fowls, killed the previous day, and put them in a saucepan with two quarts of cold water and about one pound of shin of beef; cut in small pieces, let the liquor boil, skim carefully, then add separately an onion with a clove stuck in it, half a head of celery, one carrot, and a "bouquet garni" composed of half the quantity given in the recipe, but no garlic. Then draw the saucepan by the side of the fire and let the broth simmer for two hours and a half or three hours, with the saucepan closely covered. Then take the meat out, clarify the broth if necessary and strain it as in No. 2, taking care to remove all particles of fat before serving. A similar broth can also be made with a turkey, goose, or two ducks; but special care should be taken with it, as the broth made from either of these birds is heavier, and consequently not so digestible.

8. RABBIT BROTH PROVENÇALE.

The meat of young rabbits is generally tender; it consequently possesses all the necessary qualities to make an excellent broth, and yields in no way, as far as taste and nourishment are concerned, to broth made out of chicken.

Take two young rabbits, skin and clean them properly; cut into quarters and place in a stewpan with four tablespoonfuls of olive-oil, a clove of garlic minced fine, two rashers of bacon, one carrot, two onions, two leeks, and half a head of celery, all sliced as in No. 2. Add a "bouquet garni," and brown the lot for about fifteen minutes, stirring meanwhile with a wooden spoon to prevent burning; then pour in three quarts of cold water, boil, skim, and simmer for two hours, sprinkle salt and pepper to taste; strain and serve. A glass of dry white wine will much improve this broth.

9. PARTRIDGE BROTH.

Broth made with partridges is both warming and nourishing.

Put two quarts of cold water into a saucepan, with two old partridges, cleaned and dressed as if for roasting, and two pounds of knuckle of veal; boil and skim, add a similar quantity of vegetables and "bouquet garni" as in No 2; simmer gently for four hours, then strain in the usual way.

This broth is even preferred for strength and quality to the chicken broth, and can be strongly recommended to weak and convalescent persons.

10. GAME BROTH À LA CHASSEUR.

Small game-birds, such as snipe, thrushes, quail, larks, &c., make an excellent broth. Pluck and clean two or three birds of each sort (the more the better), put them into a good-sized stewpan with half a pound of ham cut in small dices, two quarts of cold water, and boil them three hours. Take the birds out; add one pint of boiling water to the broth; season with salt and white pepper to taste, and a little grated nutmeg; boil for another quarter of an hour. Skim off both fat and scum, and pour into a souptureen.

This broth is rather expensive, but very warming and nutritious.

11. GAME BROTH.

Put two ounces of good fresh butter into a saucepan, two carrots, one onion, two leeks, and the head of half a celery, all shred fine; brown the lot for eight or ten minutes; then add three partridges, prepared as in No. 9, but from which the fillet must have been previously cut; an old fowl; and all the bones or meat of cooked game or chicken that may be handy; pour half a pint of good stock over these, reduce it by a gentle simmering for twenty minutes; give it an occasional stir to prevent burning; then pour over it a glass and a half of sherry; continue the simmering for a few minutes longer, then add three quarts of No. 1 stock, and let it boil on a good fire for half an hour; after which draw by the side of the fire, add a "bouquet garni," two cloves, a dozen pepper-corns, and the flank of a hare properly browned; let the broth simmer for two hours and a half, when the fowl and partridges will be cooked; then take them out, strain the broth nicely, remove all particles of fat; pour the broth into a soup-tureen, and serve.

12. A REFRESHING BROTH.

Put into a stewpan four pounds of shin of beef, two pounds of knuckle of veal, and an old fowl; brown these in two ounces of butter for twenty minutes, with two carrots, one turnip, half a head of celery, and an onion, all cut in slices; also the hearts of four lettuces and half an ounce of chervil; pour the lot into a small stock-pot with three quarts of cold water; cover the stock-pot closely, and make it airtight with a border of paste all round made of flour and water.

Put the stock-pot into a large saucepan or bain-marie, fill the latter three parts full of boiling water and let it boil for six hours; adding, as required, boiling water to the bain-marie; then strain the broth, skim the fat as in No. 2, and serve.

This broth may be served as beef tea or soup, to weak, fatigued, or consumptive persons, being wholesome, nourishing, and refreshing.

13. HOW TO MAKE BROTH IN A FEW MINUTES.

Mince two pounds of lean beef, half a carrot, a little celery, and an onion; put the lot in a stewpan with three pints of cold water, and salt to taste. Boil, skim, and strain.

Should there be, however, a wish for this broth to be improved, add at the same time as the other ingredients two ounces of rice or vermicelli in a muslin bag, and when cooked pour the contents of the bag into a soup-tureen with the broth, and serve.

14. JULIENNE SOUP.

Slice four carrots of ordinary size so as to leave the middle or heart part out; shred the other parts into small fillets or strips of about an inch and a half long; add also in the same manner three turnips, one onion, one head of celery, and four leeks; dry and mix the lot well together; put them into a stewpan with one ounce and a half of good fresh butter; fry them to a nice brown colour; then add two branches of endive, a small lettuce, and a little chervil, all shred very fine. Mix well again, and pour two quarts of No. 2 broth, together with six leaves of sorrel previously blanched * and cut small. Boil gently for twenty minutes or until the vegetables are perfectly well cooked; skim carefully; add about half an ounce of sugar; salt to taste; then pour into a soup-tureen with a few small crusts of bread fried in butter, and serve.

15. SPRING SOUP.

This soup, as its name implies, should only be made when the vegetables are fresh and tender; and to make it a success it is essential that all the following items should be cut fine. This will give a good opportunity to the cook to show his or her skill in shredding and cutting the said vegetables in artistic and decorative forms which are always pleasing to the eye.

* Scalded or parboiled in salt water.

Take one carrot, one turnip, the heart of a small cabbage, half a head of celery, about two ounces of French beans, the same quantity each of green peas and asparagus-points; boil the lot in salt water (asparagus apart) till properly cooked; then strain the water and pour the vegetables into a sauté-pan in which two or three spoonfuls of either chicken or beef gravy have already been placed; simmer for a few minutes; then add one quart of No 2 broth; salt to taste and two lumps of sugar; boil, pour it into a soup-tureen, and serve.

16. CONDENSED BROTH OR GLAZE.

Put into a stock-pot six pounds of shin of beef, eight pounds of leg of veal, an old fowl, two old pigeons, the same quantity of vegetables as in No 2, but first browned with butter; pour enough cold water to cover the whole (no salt nor bouquet). Let it boil; skim properly; cover the stock-pot closely, and let it boil gently for six hours; after which, strain through a fine cloth. Return the broth to a stewpan; add a quart of boiling water, skim off all fat, and simmer till the broth is reduced to a gelatinous substance, stirring meanwhile the contents with a wooden spoon, till the gravy is thick enough to remain attached to the said spoon. Then pour it into an earthenware jar, the inside of which must be previously greased with either fresh butter or fine olive-oil; let it get cold. Then lay flat at the top a sheet of white paper properly greased or oiled, and cut to the shape of the jar; then place another cover, made of brown paper, over it, and tie it around with string. Put the jar on a shelf in the larder, as it is now ready for use. When it is wanted, remove the string and paper, and cut with a knife the glaze or condensed broth as required.

17. BRUNOISE SOUP.

Cut in small dice the red part of three carrots, two turnips, one head of celery, two leeks, and half an onion. Blanch the lot in boiling salt water; strain through a colander, and pour them into a stewpan with an ounce and a half of fresh butter. Fry gently for five minutes; then add three pints of No 2 broth; simmer gently for twenty minutes; skim and pour the soup into a tureen with a few slices of bread, and serve.

Two or three spoonfuls of green peas properly blanched can also be added with advantage to the other vegetables.

18. CHICKEN GRAVY.

Take two quarts of chicken broth and boil in a stewpan. Meantime melt a quarter of a pound of fresh butter in another stewpan; add a similar weight of flour and three ounces of ham cut in slices; fry all to a brown colour; pour the boiling broth over and stir with a wooden spoon till it comes to the boil; then draw the stewpan by the side of the fire, and simmer for one hour, stirring the contents about every ten minutes to prevent burning; after which, skim and pass it through a sieve into a small earthenware pan or basin.

This gravy must be nearly white, thick and smooth, and can be used either with purées made of chicken or vegetables, or with soups made of yolks of eggs. A similar gravy can also be made with veal broth, and is more economical.

19. GAME GRAVY.

Take two quarts of game broth, and follow the same recipe as No. 18. This gravy ought to be of a nice brown colour, and can be used for strengthening game soups when required.

20. FISH GRAVY.

Brown some flour in butter as in No. 18; then add one quart of fish broth; let it boil, skim, and strain as above.

21. VEGETABLE GRAVY.

Proceed in the same way as for fish gravy.

22. POLISH SOUP.

Bake eight large potatoes in the oven, peel, and put them into a stewpan with two ounces of butter and one pint of chicken broth. Set the stewpan on the fire, and stir with a wooden spoon until the potatoes are well mashed; then pass them through a sieve into the stewpan again with three pints of hot chicken broth; simmer and stir gently for a few minutes. Meantime put in a basin the yolks of four eggs, two ounces of fresh melted butter, half a pint of cream, a little grated nutmeg, salt to taste, a tablespoonful of grated parmesan cheese and the same quantity of powdered sugar; mix these well together with a whisk, and pour them into a soup-tureen with four spoonfuls of tagliatelli (see Paste) previously cooked in beef gravy; then pour the thick boiling broth over it, stir till well mixed, and serve.

23. CONDÉ SOUP.

Put two pounds of coloured haricot beans if fresh, or one pound if dry, into a stewpan, together with one partridge, a slice of gammon, and three pints of chicken broth properly seasoned with salt and pepper. Set it to the boil, and after an hour or so of boiling take the partridge and ham out; pass the beans through a sieve by rubbing with a wooden spoon; put it in the stewpan again with the broth; let it simmer for five or six minutes longer; then pour it into a soup-tureen with three spoonfuls of croûtons * fried in butter or quenelles.

Note.—If dry beans are used, take care to soak them in water at least ten hours previous to boiling.

24. PURÉE CRESSY SOUP.

Fry for ten minutes in a stewpan with two ounces of butter, eight ordinary-sized carrots, one onion, and two heads of celery, all shred fine; also a pint of fresh haricot beans; after which, add one quart of good broth; salt and pepper to taste. Let it boil for an hour and a half; then pass the vegetables through a fine sieve by rubbing in the usual way; pour the purée back to the stewpan with the remainder of the broth, to which another quart must be added, and about an ounce of sugar. Let it again boil gently for half an hour, without forgetting to stir the purée; then pour it into a soup-tureen, with a few slices of bread cut thin.

If this soup should be required "maigre," † use plain water instead of broth, and before serving take the yolks of four eggs and two ounces of butter; whisk these well, and pour it into the soup-tureen as in No. 22.

25. FISH BROTH.

Fish with plenty of bone (the flesh of which is generally firm) is the best for soup; and the greater the variety used

---

* Croûtons are slices of crumbs of bread cut in small dice and fried in clarified butter to a nice golden colour.

† "Maigre" means food made without meat of any kind.

the better the broth. Fry in a stewpan with two ounces of butter until nicely browned, two carrots, one onion, and half a head of celery, all sliced fine; then add the different sorts of fish previously cleaned and cut into pieces four inches long, with three pints of boiling water; salt and white pepper to taste. Boil fast on a good fire for about forty minutes; skim carefully all fat and scum from the top, and pass the broth through a fine cloth.

This broth must be clear and of a golden colour. Should it not, however, be so, it can easily be clarified with about a quarter of a pound of uncooked fish (the flesh only) and the whites of two eggs whisked, &c., as in No. 2 broth; and if wanting in colour, pour a few drops of caramel and stir well before serving.

26. ANOTHER FISH BROTH.

Prepare everything as in No. 25; but instead of using plain water, take the water in which any vegetables may have been cooked (the more vegetables the better), and clarify in the same manner if necessary.

27. FROG BROTH.

I know well beforehand the expressions of disgust that will be felt in reading the heading of this broth; nevertheless, do not be led astray by an uneducated palate or a prejudiced opinion. Frogs are considered a delicacy in France, are quite as much appreciated in Italy and in Germany, and are reared on a very large scale in America; therefore, why should they not be cultivated and eaten in Great Britain?

The mode of preparing this broth is as follows:—Put two ounces of fresh butter in a stewpan and fry to a nice brown; two carrots, two onions, three spring onions if in season, and the head of half a celery, all shred finely; also two pounds of fresh frogs properly skinned and cleaned. When the whole is nicely brown pour three pints of boiling water over it; salt and white pepper to taste; boil gently for forty minutes; then pass the broth through a fine cloth, and serve with a few croûtons fried in butter.

Whoever partakes of this broth will ask for it again.

28. FROG PURÉE SOUP.

Take the flesh of two pounds of frogs, dry nicely with a cloth; roll the pieces into some flour and fry them slowly in a stewpan with two ounces of butter till well done; after which, pound them in a mortar, mixed with half a pint of Bêchamel sauce; then put the mixture into another stewpan; dilute the purée with a quart of hot frog broth, stir occasionally, and boil for five or six minutes; then pass it through a sieve and back again to the stewpan, with a little grated nutmeg; salt and pepper to taste; add more broth or water if required; set it to the boil; pour it into a soup-tureen with croûtons or quenelles, and serve.

29. CRAYFISH BROTH.

Brown in butter the same sort and quantity of vegetables as in No. 27. Meantime wash well in two waters thirty live crayfish; place these in a saucepan with half a handful of parsley, two onions, the head of a celery, and two carrots, all shred fine; pour enough cold water to cover the lot; add a handful of salt; cover the saucepan and boil fifteen minutes; strain the water through a colander, and as soon as the crustaceans are cold take the meat out of the shells with your fingers; place the meat from the claws and tails on a plate; pound the shells, with the inside residue, in a mortar with two ounces of fresh butter, and mix it with the fried vegetables; fry this for a few minutes longer; then pour three pints of boiling water over it; season with salt and pepper; stir and simmer gently for ten minutes; skim off the butter and place it on a plate apart; pass the broth through a sieve and let it get cold; then pour it into the stewpan and boil till reduced by one-third; after which, strain it through a cloth into a soup-tureen, and serve with the meat off the claws and crayfish-tails, keeping the butter to season sauces when required.

30. VEGETABLE BROTH.

Clean and scrape four carrots; peel six turnips, three leeks, three onions, and two small heads of celery; slice the lot in fours and sixes, and brown them in a stewpan with three ounces of fresh butter, first the onions and leeks, and afterwards the other vegetables; and when all are nicely coloured add about an ounce of sugar, half a pint of boiling water, and salt to taste. Cover the stewpan and let simmer for ten minutes; then pour in three pints of boiling water; add a handful each of dry mushrooms and peas, which will give it a good flavour, and boil again gently for half an hour; then strain through a sieve and a cloth into a soup-tureen in which some croûtons have already been put; and serve.

This broth can also be clarified with the whites of three eggs whisked, &c., as usual; and if preferred, the vegetables can also be served with the broth; in that case do not strain it.

31. ANOTHER VEGETABLE BROTH.

Boil for five minutes in plenty of salt water one dozen each of new carrots and turnips, four onions, six leeks, and three heads of celery; then strain through a colander, and pour the vegetables into a stock-pot or large stewpan, together with two pounds of dry peas; add salt, white pepper, and grated nutmeg to taste; also twelve cloves, three ounces of butter, and three quarts of boiling water. Let the contents boil till the peas are cooked; then strain the broth through a sieve, and serve with slices of bread fried in butter.

In this case, as in the previous number, vegetables can be added to the soup-tureen if liked.

32. HERB SOUP.

Blanch two lettuces, one handful of sorrel, and a little chervil dried and shred; place them in a stewpan with half a pint of broth; simmer for a few minutes; add one quart of broth, and boil for half an hour; stir nicely; add salt and pepper to taste; pour into a soup-tureen with a few slices of bread, and serve.

33. CLEAR ASPARAGUS SOUP.

Cut the green part of a bundle of fifty asparagus, not too large, into points; boil them in salt water for twelve or fifteen minutes; strain through a colander, and pour them into a stewpan in which a quart of broth has already been set near to the boil; let the contents simmer for five minutes only; add salt and pepper to taste, and serve.

34. CABBAGE SOUP.

After having cut a cabbage (savoy preferred) in quarters and washed it carefully in salt water, blanch it with the head of a celery, and let it get cold; then put the pieces into a stewpan with a good slice of ham, a rasher of bacon, and one quart of broth; boil for forty minutes; then take the ham and bacon out, add one pint of broth if required;

salt and pepper to taste; boil, and pour it into a soup-tureen with some slices of bread.

This soup can also be made "maigre" by substituting butter for ham and bacon, and water instead of broth; in that case, soak the slices of bread with half a pint of boiling milk in the soup-tureen before serving.

35. CABBAGE SOUP, MILANAISE.

Fry to a nice colour in a stewpan, with two ounces of butter, half an onion, half a carrot, and half a head of celery, all shred fine; moisten the whole with a good broth, and boil for ten minutes; pass this through a sieve; pour the liquor back into the stewpan, with two tablespoonfuls of tomato sauce, two small savoys cut in fours, after having been blanched and the water squeezed out of them; also two rashers of bacon cut in dice, one sage-leaf, a little minced parsley, two quarts of broth, and a piece of bacon-rind cut in small dice. Let the contents boil for three-quarters of an hour; add one ounce of grated parmesan cheese; salt and pepper to taste; then pour all into a soup-tureen with some slices of bread, and serve with an ounce of grated cheese on a plate apart.

36. TURNIP SOUP.

Cut six turnips into dice, and brown them in a stewpan with two ounces of butter and a slice of ham; after which, cook the contents well with a pint of good broth and two spoonfuls of tomato sauce; boil till done. Then take the ham out, and skim off all the fat. Meantime have ready in a soup-tureen half a dozen slices of bread soaked in one quart of good boiling broth, a handful each of green peas and asparagus-points (properly cooked apart); salt and pepper to taste; then pour the turnips with it, mix well, and serve.

37. TURNIP PURÉE SOUP.

Put eight turnips cut in quarters into a stewpan with two spring onions, two heads of celery sliced, two ounces of fresh butter, half a pint of chicken gravy, one pint of white haricot beans; salt and pepper to taste; simmer and stir gently for a few minutes, without browning the contents; then pour one quart of veal broth over, and boil gently for an hour and a half; pass the vegetables through a sieve by rubbing with a wooden spoon; return the purée to the stewpan together with the remainder of the broth; stir well in order to dilute the purée; add another quart of white broth; stir again; add a piece of sugar the size of a walnut; skim off the fat; boil it for another half-hour; give it an occasional stir to prevent burning; then pour it into a soup-tureen with a few croûtons, and serve.

38. LEEK SOUP.

Cut six leeks an inch and a half long and sliced into fours; fry them in a stewpan with one and a half ounce of butter till of a nice brown; then pour one quart of broth on it; boil for fifteen minutes; add one tablespoonful of gravy; salt and pepper to taste, and serve with croûtons. This soup can also be made "maigre" by using water instead of broth; in that case add two ounces of butter before serving.

39. MANOR-HOUSE SOUP.

Put into a stewpan half a pint each of fresh shelled peas, French beans, and haricot beans, the red part of a carrot, one head of celery, one turnip, and two leeks, all cut in the form of almonds; also twelve shalots, the heart of a small cabbage cut in four, the hearts of two small lettuces cut in halves, a few leaves of sorrel, a little chervil, an ounce of sugar, and grated nutmeg; salt and pepper to taste; add two quarts of good broth; boil for three-quarters of an hour; pour the contents into a soup tureen with a few slices of bread, and serve.

Note.—It is advisable, whenever a soup is made of different kinds of vegetables, to add a piece of sugar the size of two walnuts in order to remove the sour taste from the broth which is invariably given by vegetables.

40. GREEN PEA SOUP.

Boil in plenty of salt water two pounds of fresh shelled peas (the larger the better); meantime blanch apart the hearts of two lettuces cut in quarters and a few leaves of sorrel; dry well and place these in a stewpan with half a pint of gravy; simmer till the lettuces are nicely glazed and the gravy nearly reduced; then add three pints of good broth, and set it to the boil. When the peas are properly done strain the water through a colander; throw the peas into the stewpan with the broth; add a small piece of sugar; skim, set to the boil, and serve with croûtons fried in butter.

41. NEW CARROT SOUP.

Cut in dice twelve fresh carrots; blanch them in the usual way, strain the water through a colander, and let them cool; meantime pour one quart of good broth into a stewpan with a piece of sugar; set it to the boil; and when the carrots are quite cold add them to the broth, together with salt, pepper, and a little grated nutmeg to taste; boil till the carrots are done, and serve with a few slices of bread fried in butter.

This soup can also be made "maigre;" in that case, boil the carrots with half milk, half water, and add two ounces of butter before serving. This broth is very refreshing, and strongly recommended to persons suffering with jaundice, having cured the writer when a boy.

42. LETTUCE SOUP.

Blanch in the usual way six or eight lettuces; dip them afterwards in cold water; press and get them quite dry; put each separately into a sauté-pan in which has already been placed a slice of ham, a bay-leaf, a little thyme, half an onion with a clove stuck in it, and half a carrot sliced; moisten the contents with a good broth; cover the sauté-pan and let simmer till the lettuces are nicely glazed; then add one quart of broth; boil till done; take the lettuces out with a flat strainer, cut them in halves, place in a soup-tureen, strain the broth over, and serve with croûtons.

Half a pint of chicken broth, if handy, will greatly improve this soup.

43. STUFFED LETTUCE SOUP.

Blanch the hearts of twelve lettuces cut in halves; dip them in cold water and squeeze them well; place afterwards these lettuces separately on a board; lay on each a spoonful of stuffing composed of quenelles of chicken with a little chervil minced fine. Fold the lettuces in oblong shape, so as to enclose the stuffing; transfer them one by one into a stewpan already containing half a pint of gravy, a slice of ham, and vegetables, as in No. 42. Simmer gently for a few minutes; then add one pint of chicken broth; let it boil for fifteen or twenty minutes; place the lettuces one by one into a soup-tureen; pour the gravy over, after having strained it, together with one quart of boiling broth properly seasoned, and serve.

44. CLEAR SORREL SOUP.

Clean and shred about two pounds of sorrel, the hearts of two lettuces, and a little chervil; fry the lot in a stewpan with two ounces of clarified butter, and pour over it a quart of boiling broth, with a piece of sugar; salt and pepper to taste; let boil for twenty minutes; skim, pour it into a soup-tureen, and serve with croûtons fried in butter.

In order to make this soup "maigre," after having added water instead of broth, take the yolks of four eggs, whisk them well into a basin; then add half a pint of the boiling soup into it; stir; pour another half-pint of broth; keep stirring; and just before serving pour this mixture into the stewpan with two ounces of butter; mix well; set near to the boil, and serve as No. 43.

45. THICK SORREL SOUP.

Put the yolks of six eggs into a basin with an ounce of fresh butter and half a pint of hot broth; whisk these well and pass it through a sieve; after which, pour it gradually into a stew-pan in which a purée of sorrel and other vegetables, as in No. 44, has already been made and diluted in a quart of boiling broth; stir with a wooden spoon, in order to mix the contents well together; let it come as near as possible to the boil; add an ounce of butter, salt, pepper, and a little grated nutmeg to taste; pour it into a soup-tureen, and serve with croûtons.

46. ENDIVÉ SOUP.

Blanch about one pound of endive; dry, shred, and fry it in a stewpan, with an ounce of fresh butter; add one quart of broth, and boil gently for twenty minutes. Meantime whisk the yolks of four eggs with half a pint of the hot broth, and pour it into the stewpan; mix this well; add two spoonsful of brown sauce (No. 151); salt and pepper to taste, and when nearly boiling serve with either quenelles of chicken or croûtons.

47. CLERMONT SOUP.

Slice six or eight onions, and brown in a stewpan with two ounces of clarified butter; take them out, dry them properly with a cloth, and pour into another stewpan with a quart of good broth; boil for fifteen or twenty minutes; then add a little pounded marjoram; salt and pepper to taste, and serve with croûtons on a plate apart.

48. POTATO AND CHERVIL PURÉE SOUP.

Peel and cut in quarters six large potatoes; boil them in salt water for five or six minutes, in order to remove all sourness; strain the water; pour the potatoes into a stewpan with one quart of broth, two leeks, and half a head of celery; boil till the potatoes are quite done; then pass the whole through a sieve; return the purée to the stewpan, with the remainder of the broth; add some more if required; also a little grated nutmeg, half a pint of cream, an ounce of fresh butter, and a little blanched chervil chopped very fine; set the stewpan on the fire, stir the contents well, in order to dilute and mix the purée properly with the last-named ingredients; and when near the boil pour it in a soup-tureen, and serve with croûtons on a plate apart.

This soup can be made cheaper by substituting plain water for broth and milk instead of cream.

49. CHANTILLY SOUP.

Take one quart of lentils; boil them in salt water till well done; strain the water and pass the lentils through a sieve by rubbing; put the purée back to the stewpan; add in proportion one-third of chicken purée to one quart and a half of good broth, and set to the boil; stir occasionally to prevent burning, and serve with croûtons or quenelles of chicken.

Note.—Lentils must be washed and soaked for at least four hours previous to cooking.

50. GREEN PEA PURÉE SOUP.

Boil three pints of green peas in plenty of salt water; meantime fry in a stewpan, with one ounce and a half of butter, one carrot, half an onion, half a head of celery, and two leeks, all shred fine, as well as a slice of ham. When these items are nicely browned add one quart of broth, and let the contents boil for half an hour.

When the peas are properly cooked strain the water and rub the peas through a sieve in the usual way; strain also the broth through a fine sieve or cloth, mix the purée with it in the stewpan, boil and simmer for a few minutes; then add a piece of sugar and salt to taste. Skim, and serve with small croûtons fried in butter.

If dry peas are used, soak them in water the previous night. This soup can be made with water instead of broth, and either can be improved by adding two ounces of cooked rice instead of croûtons.

51. CHESNUT PURÉE SOUP.

Peel the first skin off about fifty chesnuts and put them in a stewpan with enough boiling water to cover the lot;

boil for five or six minutes; strain the water through a colander; take off the second skin and put the chesnuts in the stewpan with one quart and a half of good broth, one bay-leaf, two cloves, and a slice of ham; boil these for twenty minutes; strain the broth through a colander into a basin; throw away the bay-leaf and cloves; place the ham with half of the chesnuts apart, and keep hot the other half; pound them through a sieve and put the purée back in the stewpan with the broth; dilute the purée well; boil and stir to prevent burning; add salt to taste, with a little grated nutmeg; and after a few minutes' boiling pour it into a soup-tureen in which the other half of the chesnuts, as well as the ham cut in small dice, have already been deposited, and serve with a few croûtons fried in butter on a plate apart.

52. LENTIL PURÉE SOUP.

Put two pounds of properly soaked lentils into a stewpan, two tablespoonfuls of salt, a small carrot, one onion, one head of celery, two leeks, and two quarts of water; boil gently till the lentils are done, gradually adding during the boiling three gills of cold water to swell the lentils and accelerate their cooking; then strain the water through a colander; take the vegetables out and pass the lentils only through a sieve, by rubbing in the usual way with a wooden spoon; moisten now and then with a little hot broth to facilitate the passing of the purée. When this is done, return it to the stewpan; stir well in pouring gradually three pints of boiling broth; let simmer for about twenty minutes, giving it an occasional stir to prevent burning; then skim, add salt and pepper to taste, and serve with croûtons fried in butter.

This soup can also be made "maigre" by using the water

in which the lentils were cooked, instead of broth, and by adding two ounces of butter before serving.

53. WHITE HARICOT BEANS PURÉE SOUP.

Prepare this purée in the same manner as the lentils or green peas; but take care not to cook the beans too much, and before pouring the purée into the soup-tureen melt an ounce of fresh butter with it, and serve with small croûtons.

54. MODENA SOUP.

Blanch one pound of spinach; dry, shred, and fry it in a stewpan with an ounce of fresh butter; salt to taste, and stir till nicely glazed; then let it get cold; after which, add two eggs and a little grated nutmeg, well beaten together; pour the lot into a quart of boiling broth; cover the stewpan with a hot lid, put a shovelful of embers on the top of it, and draw by the side of the fire for a few minutes, during which time the eggs will form a kind of smooth crust at the top of the broth; then pour it into a soup-tureen with croûtons fried in butter, and serve.

55. TRIPE SOUP MILANAISE.

Put two pounds of cooked calf's tripe in a saucepan, with three quarts of boiling water; simmer for ten minutes, and immerse it in cold water; after a few minutes drain and wipe it with a cloth, then shred it an inch and a half long by a quarter of an inch thick. Meanwhile put in a stewpan one ounce and a half of butter, with the same quantity of fat bacon cut in small dice, and fry a shred onion to a nice brown colour with it; then add the shred tripe and fry five minutes longer; after which moisten with three pints of broth; simmer gently for two hours; then add a few sprigs of parsley, half a head of celery, a carrot slit in four, and two leaves of sage, all tied together; simmer again for another hour; then skim off the fat, throw away the bouquet, season with salt and pepper; pour it into a soup-tureen, and serve with croûtons and grated cheese on a plate apart.

56. SOUP À LA ROMAINE.

Melt three ounces of fresh beef marrow in a small stewpan and pass it through a fine strainer into a basin: break two eggs, beat and mix well with the marrow; then add five ounces of bread crumbs which must have soaked in a pint of broth for at least half an hour; season with salt and grated nutmeg to taste; mix the lot well together, and pour it in a stewpan on the fire to simmer till dry, taking care to stir it the while; then sprinkle two tablespoonfuls of flour and one of grated cheese; stir and mix well for two minutes longer, then turn it over on a dish and let it cool; when cold, turn the compound into small balls, hazelnut size, put them in a quart of boiling broth to poach five minutes; then pour the contents into a soup-tureen and serve.

Note.—Butter can be substituted for marrow.

57. SOUP À LA VENITIENNE.

Put in a stewpan the yolks of six eggs with a few drops of lemon juice, and add gradually a quart of cold broth over it, beating the contents meanwhile with a whisk; then let it boil, giving it an occasional stir, and when near ebullition season with salt and pepper; pour it into a soup-tureen with a few slices of bread, and serve.

58. LOMBARDO SOUP.

Take half a pound of chicken stuffing (see Stuffing), divide it into three equal parts, flatten each surface with a knife and lay smooth on each separate part, first, two tablepoonfuls of Bêchamel sauce; second, four tablespoonfuls of green peas purée; and on the third, two tablespoonfuls of crayfish or lobster butter, previously mixed with the yolk of an egg well whisked, having by this means three different colours, white, green, and yellow. Meanwhile have three pints of good broth in a stewpan boiling and with a teaspoon form the three compounds in as many little quenelles as there will be teaspoonfuls; throw them in the boiling broth to poach five minutes by a slow ebullition, then pour into a soup-tureen which already contains two dozen asparagus-points and three tablespoonfuls of green peas separately cooked in salt water, as well as three spoonfuls of croûtons fried in crayfish or lobster butter, the tails of about a dozen crayfish, or the tail of half a small lobster cut in very small dice, a gill of sherry; and serve.

59. ROSSINI SOUP.

Clean and dress four quails and cook them in a stewpan with a pint of game broth, or better still, game gravy; let them get cold in their own liquor; after which, bone and cut them in small fillets, put them in a soup-tureen with a shred carrot and a few chickens' kidneys previously fried and browned in butter, as well as half a dozen button champignons and same number of truffles cut in the shâpe of small olives. Meanwhile have a little game forcemeat (No. 273) diluted with a quart of boiling broth ready, pour it into the soup-tureen, properly seasoned, and serve.

60. EGG SOUP.

Whisk eight eggs and mix it well with a pint of cold broth; then put the liquor into a bain-marie * on a good fire; boil till the eggs are hard; then take the compound out with a spoon, and place it in a soup-tureen in which some slices of bread are already soaking in a quart of boiling broth nicely coloured, and serve.

61. À LA REINE PURÉE SOUP.

Boil a young turkey or two nice chickens in three quarts of white broth; when well cooked skim and remove the fat from the birds; cut all the meat off from the bones and sinews, mince and pound it well in a mortar; put the purée in a stewpan with a pint of Blanquette sauce (No 178), dilute the contents with half a pint of white broth, and pass it through a fine sieve into the stewpan again; boil, and stir. Add a pint of Blanquette sauce if too thin, or white stock if too thick. Season with salt and pepper, mix well together by stirring with a wooden spoon on the fire, let simmer for five or six minutes, then pour it into a soup-tureen with or without three spoonfuls of well-cooked rice or croûtons fried in butter, and serve.

62. ARTOIS SOUP.

Make a purée of green peas (No. 50); meanwhile fry in a stewpan, with an ounce of butter, a handful of croûtons and about two ounces of pickled ox-tongue cut in small dice; mix these with the purée when made, boil, stir, and serve.

* A saucepan put into a large vessel or a larger saucepan with boiling water in it.

63. NAVARIN SOUP.

Make a purée of green peas as described above; pour it into a soup-tureen with one dozen small poached quenelles of pheasant, one dozen pieces of eels boned and fried in butter, the tails of twenty crayfish, and two ounces of green peas cooked in salt water, and serve.

This is one of the most delicious and best soups that can be put on the table, but it is also one of the most expensive.

64. GAME OR CHICKEN PURÉE SOUP.

Cook all the remnants of game or chicken that may be had in a quart of broth, with vegetables, in proportion, as in other soups; when well done strain the broth into a basin, scrape all the meat from the bones, and pound it in a mortar with three spoonfuls of cooked rice; put the purée into a stewpan and dilute it with the broth just made; after which, pass the lot through a fine sieve; return it to the stewpan; add, if required, some more broth, season with salt and pepper, boil, and pour it into a soup-tureen with croûtons fried in butter.

65. MOCK TURTLE SOUP.

Bone and blanch for ten minutes the half of a calf's head (which must be fresh and young); put it in a large stewpan or stock-pot with a good slice of ham cut in dice, about two pounds of leg of veal, two carrots, two turnips, two leeks, half a head of celery, an onion with two cloves stuck in it, two shalots and a "bouquet garni," as well as a bay-leaf; add three quarts of cold broth and boil. Skim properly, and boil for about two hours, or until the calf's head is well cooked and made tender; then strain the broth into a stewpan, put the calf's head apart on a dish, and let the broth boil. Meantime brown two ounces of flour with one ounce of butter in a small stewpan; stir well with a wooden spoon, and when of a dark-brown colour pour gradually over it a quart of the boiling broth, stirring the while; and when properly mixed pour it back with the other broth, stir it well, and boil for a few minutes longer; skim off all the fat and scum; add two glasses of sherry, the juice of a lemon, salt and pepper to taste. Cut part of the calf's head into small dice, put these into a soup-tureen, pour the soup over it, and serve.

This soup is also made clear; in that case no flour is needed. In other respects, proceed as above; but especial care should be paid to the clarifying of the broth before serving.

66. OX-TAIL SOUP.

Cut at the different joints two ox-tails, so that the pieces are as nearly as possible of the same size; soak them afterwards in cold salt water for about an hour or two to remove the blood, then wipe the pieces with a cloth and fry them in a stewpan with two ounces of butter to a nice brown; after which, add two quarts of stock, an onion with two cloves, and a "bouquet garni." Boil, skim, and simmer for three or four hours, or until the pieces of ox-tail are well cooked. Meantime cut a carrot and a turnip in small dice, shred an onion very fine, fry these in a stewpan with one ounce of butter till nicely browned, then moisten with a little broth, and simmer till well done. When the pieces of ox-tail are properly cooked skim off the fat, and pour the meat and broth into the soup-tureen with the vegetables cooked apart. This can also be made thick by adding flour prepared in the same way as mock turtle (No. 65).

67. HARE SOUP À LA SUSINOISE.

Cut in dice of medium size the fillet as well as the most fleshy and tender part of a hare, cook it in a quart of good broth, and when done strain the broth through a fine sieve; put it back into the stewpan; add more broth, if required, and boil. Meantime put the pieces of hare into a soup-tureen with four spoonfuls of big haricot beans, one turnip, one carrot, the heart of a small cabbage, and half a head of celery all shred fine, well cooked, and soaked in game gravy; pour the boiling broth over, and serve.

68. HARE SOUP (ENGLISH STYLE).

Cut in small parts the half of a hare; fry the pieces in a stewpan with three ounces of fat bacon cut in dice, and the same quantity of butter; when the pieces of hare are browned let them get cold in the stewpan; then add two tablespoonfuls of flour, half a bottle of claret, one quart of broth, a small "bouquet garni," one dozen small button mushrooms, an onion, a little cayenne, two cloves, a little grated nutmeg, and salt to taste. Boil, skim, and simmer for about an hour; after which, take the pieces of hare out, bone them, put the meat back into a clean stewpan with a dozen small quenelles of chicken; strain the broth in which the hare was cooked over the meat and quenelles, add some more hot broth if required, boil, and serve.

69. RICE QUENELLES SOUP.

Prepare a good risotto (see Risotto) with four ounces of rice; lay it on a dish to get cold. Meanwhile take half a pound of chicken breast or lean fillet of veal and two ounces of either chicken or calf's liver; hash this fine and brown it well in a stewpan, with two ounces of butter; then pound it in a mortar with the risotto; mix the contents well together with three whisked eggs, a little grated nutmeg, and salt to taste; pass the lot through a sieve into an earthenware pan, moisten with a little boiling broth or water, stir till nicely soft and firm; if too thick add a little béchamel, or if too clear the yolks of a few eggs; mix well; then take a teaspoon in each hand, and with them shape the compound into small quenelles, put them in a buttered sauté-pan, and ten minutes before serving pour over them a quart of boiling broth, boil for six or eight minutes before pouring it into a soup-tureen, and serve.

70. VEGETABLE QUENELLES SOUP.

Boil three pints of green peas in plenty of salt water and a little mint; when well cooked strain the water, put the peas in a stewpan, and mix them well with an ounce of fresh butter, a spoonful of Béchamel sauce, a little grated cheese and nutmeg, and salt to taste. Let it get cold; then proceed to make a dozen quenelles as in No. 69, boil these in the same way, and serve.

By the same process, quenelles can be made with lentils, white haricot beans, and carrots.

71. POTATO QUENELLES SOUP.

Pound in a mortar six ounces of cold potato purée with the boned meat of half a cooked fowl; add salt to taste, a little grated cheese and nutmeg, two eggs, and the yolks of two more; mix these well together, and pass it through a sieve. Having thus a thick purée, turn it into small quenelles, poach these in a quart of boiling broth for fifteen minutes, and serve.

72. GAME OR CHICKEN QUENELLES SOUP.

These quenelles are prepared with either game or fowl stuffing (see Stuffing), and when made, boil them, as above in a quart of good broth, and serve.

73. VENITIAN QUENELLES SOUP.

Brown in a stewpan with two ounces of fresh butter, a similar quantity of flour, then add one ounce of grated cheese and a gill of good broth; work the contents to a paste (on the fire) with a wooden spoon, then draw the stewpan away from the fire, add the yolks of six eggs, stir again till well mixed, and let it get cold; then make the quenelles as before; poach them in a quart of boiling broth for a quarter of an hour, season with salt and pepper, and serve.

74. GERMAN QUENELLES SOUP.

Proceed with these quenelles as in the foregoing, with a mixture of six ounces of calf's liver and three ounces of bacon cut in dice, the same quantity of bread crumbs, two ounces of butter, three eggs, and a gill of cream; pound the lot well together in a mortar, and pass it through a sieve; make the quenelles and boil them for fifteen minutes in a quart of broth, and serve.

75. À LA REINE QUENELLES SOUP.

These quenelles are made with a mixture of ten ounces of either the raw or cooked flesh of a fowl, two ounces of fresh butter, three of potato purée, and the yolks of three eggs; the whole well pounded, seasoned, and mixed together, and poached in a quart of broth as before.

76. SWISS POTATO SOUP.

Peel and boil in salt water one pound of potatoes; let them get cold, then pound them in a mortar with a piece of well-cooked meat hashed fine, with two ounces of fat bacon, one of butter, four eggs, a pinch of pounded aromatic herbs, and salt to taste; when well pounded and mixed together, turn it into small balls the size of small nuts, drop them into a quart of boiling broth to poach for a few minutes, and serve.

If preferred, these balls may be fried in butter and served in boiling broth.

77. DAWN SOUP.

Whisk the yolks of ten eggs with two ounces of melted fresh butter, two spoonfuls of velouté (No. 153), and a little grated nutmeg. Boil three pints of broth; when boiling, pour the half of it gradually over the egg mixture, taking care to stir the while. When properly mixed and diluted, pour the contents back with the other broth over the fire, still stirring; and as soon as it boils, pass it through a sieve into a soup-tureen; add a glass of Marsala or sherry, and serve with croûtons fried in butter.

78. ONION SOUP À LA LYONNAISE.

Peel four medium-sized onions, shred, and fry them in a stewpan with two ounces of butter till nicely browned; then sprinkle two tablespoonfuls of flour; continue frying and stirring for three minutes longer; after which, pour three pints of boiling broth, season with salt and pepper; stir and mix all well together, and simmer for ten minutes. In the meantime put eight dry or toasted slices of bread into a soup-tureen, with a handful of grated cheese at the top, pour the boiling soup over, sprinkle another handful of grated cheese over the broth, and place the soup-tureen in a moderately heated oven for a few minutes before serving.

79. ONION SOUP "MAIGRE."

Proceed with the frying of the onions and flour as in the previous number. Substitute boiling water for broth, and simmer ten minutes; whisk the yolks of four eggs in a basin; mix this well together with a pint of the boiling water, and just before serving pour it back into the stewpan with one ounce and a half of butter; stir well, season with salt, pepper, and a little grated nutmeg, and when nearly boiling pour it into a soup-tureen, garnished (as in No. 78) with bread and cheese, and put in the oven for a few minutes before serving.

80. SHEEP'S HEAD SOUP.

Take a sheep's head, split in two, pick the brains out and put them in a basin to steep in cold water; soak the head in boiling water for five or ten minutes, wash it well, then put it in a stewpan with two quarts of cold water; boil; skim it very carefully, then add the same quantity of vegetables and "bouquet garni" as in No. 2 broth; simmer for about three hours, put the head on a hot dish, skim off the fat, strain the broth through a sieve, and serve with a few slices of bread and some of the vegetables, or better still, with some pearl barley or rice cooked in a muslin bag with the broth.

The sheep's head is very good eaten hot with either a sharp or tomato sauce.

Remarks on Macaroni and Paste of all Descriptions, and how to Cook It.

All pastes such as macaroni, vermicelli, spaghetti, tagliatelli, &c. &c., can be served with broth, and one can always obtain a good soup with them at a few minutes' notice. Likewise paste can also be served as a luxury by different modes of preparation.

The custom in Italy is that, whenever paste or rice is served as a made dish, it takes the place of soup.

Although, as I have said before, paste can be served in many different ways, the mode of its cooking is always the same. Amongst the several sorts and qualities imported to this country, those from Naples and Genoa are the best; and for boiling purposes (that is to say, for soups) those from the latter place are preferred. The time taken for cooking varies according to the age and size of the paste; vermicelli from Naples may be cooked in five minutes, while Genoa macaroni (if old) may take half an hour.

The only way of boiling paste is to plunge it in plenty of boiling salt water, and never on any account soak it beforehand.

As a future guidance in boiling all kinds of paste, I will describe the proper mode of cooking, say, one pound of macaroni. Put three quarts of water and a tablespoonful of salt in an ordinary saucepan, on a good fire. When the water boils fast, immerse the macaroni, and cover the saucepan for ten minutes; after this take the lid off and try now and then if the macaroni is cooked by a slight pressure between finger and thumb; as soon as it yields to the pinch, stop the boiling at once by pouring a pint of cold water into the saucepan; strain the water through a colander, as the macaroni is now cooked and ready for use.

Note.—All descriptions of paste should be eaten as soon as cooked.

81. PLAIN MACARONI SOUP.

Cut in pieces of about two inches long half a pound of macaroni cooked and strained as described in the previous remarks, and put it in a soup-tureen, then pour one quart of boiling broth over, and serve with grated cheese apart.

Shred carrots, haricot beans, french beans, green peas, or any other vegetables can also be added in small quantities to this soup, provided they have been properly cooked in salt water and glazed in a stewpan with good gravy beforehand.

The mode of preparing other kinds of plain paste soup is exactly the same as this.

82. MACARONI SOUP (SARDE).

Peel and slice an onion in small dice; put these into a stewpan with one ounce and a half of butter and two ounces of leg of veal, also cut in small dice. Fry the lot to a nice brown colour, then add five ripe tomatoes, previously peeled and passed through a sieve; moisten with three pints of good broth; season with salt and pepper, and boil for half an hour. Meantime cook and strain as described one pound of macaroni; put it in a stewpan with an ounce of fresh butter and one and a half of grated cheese; toss this up well together on the fire; then pour it into the other stewpan with the broth; stir, and serve.

This soup can be varied by using other kinds of paste, and substituting chicken, mutton, or game for veal.

83. MACARONI SOUP (PALERMO).

Put into a well buttered stewpan three slices of gammon, one pound of lean beef, the same quantity of knuckle, one fowl, the same quantity of vegetables as if for a soup, and half a pint of good broth; set the lot to simmer, and when nicely browned all around add three pints of boiling broth; simmer for one hour and a half, then take the meat and vegetables out, skim, clarify, and strain the broth through a fine cloth, and put it back again into the stewpan by the side of the fire. Meantime cook one pound of macaroni as indicated, strain and cut it in pieces three inches long, put it into the broth, and boil slowly for a few minutes. Prepare and mix in another stewpan on the fire the yolks of four eggs whisked and passed through a sieve, with a gill of cream, half an ounce of grated cheese, one ounce of butter, salt and a little white pepper to taste. When the butter is melted and the lot well whisked together pour it over with the broth, give it a good stir so as to mix well the contents, and when near the boil pour into a soup-tureen, and serve with grated cheese on a plate apart.

84. MACARONI SOUP À LA REINE.

Pound in a mortar the breast of a chicken not too much cooked, mix it with a gill of suprême sauce (No. 188), pass it through a sieve, and keep it hot in a bain-marie. Meanwhile cook one pound of macaroni when drained, place it in a sauté-pan with two ounces of fresh butter, three or four spoonfuls of grated cheese, and as many of chicken gravy. Toss this up well in the sauté-pan, then add the hot purée of chicken to it, and toss again so as to mix the lot well together. When this is done and the compound made quite hot dress it up on a dish, and serve with one quart or three pints of boiling broth in a soup-tureen apart.

85. MACARONI SOUP (MONGLAS).

Cook and strain one pound of macaroni; put it in a sauté-pan with two ounces of fresh butter divided in five or six parts, and placed in as well as over the macaroni; move the sauté-pan over a slow fire, sprinkle half an ounce of grated cheese over it, then place in the centre the fleshy part of half a cooked fowl, properly boned and cut in small dice, also a few slices of truffles, two spoonfuls of foie-gras, a few mushrooms sliced fine and slightly seasoned with a velouté sauce (No. 153). When these are nicely warmed up turn it into a hot dish, and serve with three pints of boiling broth in a soup-tureen apart.

86. MACARONI SOUP (CARDINALE).

Prepare (after cooking) the tails of twenty-four or thirty crayfish; put them apart with a little hot broth in a small stewpan by the side of the fire, to keep them hot. Pound the shells well and make a crayfish butter (No. 169); mix three spoonfuls of suprême sauce (No. 188) with two of purée of mushrooms. Cook and strain one pound of macaroni, put it in a sauté-pan with the two ounces of crayfish butter just made; add two ounces of grated cheese, the purée of mushrooms and suprême sauce, mix well together by tossing it up whilst over the fire, and when properly warmed dish it up on a hot dish; then strain the crayfish tails and place them nicely one by one over the macaroni as a decorative garnish, and serve with three pints of boiling broth in a soup-tureen apart.

87. MACARONI SOUP (DOMINICAINE).

Soak in lukewarm water for a few minutes about three ounces of dry mushrooms; then drain and put them in a stewpan with one pint of fish broth, an onion, a carrot, a bay-leaf, and a few sprigs of parsley. Simmer these for an hour on a slow fire, strain the broth and return it to the stewpan, save the mushrooms; soak three ounces of bread crumbs in water, strain and press the water well out of it; put the bread with the cooked mushrooms into the stewpan with the essence just strained; let these simmer and dry; stir, and when well reduced and the bread crumbs as well as the mushrooms are crisp, pass them through a sieve. In the meantime cook and strain one pound of macaroni, put it in a sauté-pan with a gill of olive-oil; add the bread crumbs and a little anchovy paste with it; keep the sauté-pan over the fire, stir the contents well, and when very hot pour it into a soup-tureen with three pints of boiling fish broth properly seasoned.

This soup is thoroughly "maigre," and is generally served to Roman Catholics on fasting days.

88. PLAIN MACARONI CHEESE.

Cook and strain one pound of macaroni; put two ounces of fresh butter into a stewpan, and when melted pour the macaroni over with three tablespoonfuls of grated cheese; toss it up till well mixed and made hot; season with white pepper only, turn it into a hot dish, and serve with a little grated cheese and nutmeg sprinkled on the top.

89. MACARONI (ITALIAN STYLE).

Put one pound of cooked and strained macaroni into a stewpan with two ounces of butter, three spoonfuls of tomato sauce, and as many of beef gravy; toss up the lot on the fire so as to mix and warm it well together; then sprinkle two handfuls of grated cheese over it, season with a little white pepper, toss up again and turn it into a hot dish, sprinkle again a little grated cheese on the top, with three tablespoonfuls of good beef gravy, and serve.

90. MACARONI (CITIZEN STYLE).

Boil one pound and a half of macaroni; strain, and put it in a stewpan on the fire with two ounces of butter, one pint of good broth; salt and pepper to taste. Boil it; sprinkle over two ounces of grated cheese, add a little more butter, toss it up gently, pour it into a hot dish, sprinkle a little more grated cheese and two or three tablespoonfuls of hot roast-beef gravy or brown sauce over it, and serve.

91. MACARONI À LA NAPOLITAINE.

Cut one pound of leg of veal in thin slices of about six inches long by two wide, prepare about a quarter of a pound of veal or chicken stuffing (see Stuffing), and place it with a teaspoon in the centre of each slice of veal; roll the slices round so as to enclose the stuffing, flour these and put them in a sauté-pan with two ounces of clarified butter, together with a calf's brains properly blanched and sliced; fry the lot to a nice colour, then moisten with half a pint of good broth or gravy, and simmer till cooked and tender. Meantime break one pound of macaroni in short pieces, boil and strain in the usual way; put it in a stewpan with half a pint of good broth or gravy, simmer till nearly reduced; then add a little butter, two handfuls of grated cheese, and a little grated nutmeg; stir well, pour it into a hot dish with the veal and brains nicely and alternately arranged at the top; sprinkle the remainder of the gravy out of the sauté-pan over it, and serve with grated cheese apart.

92. MACARONI AU GRATIN.

Boil one pound of macaroni in the usual way for a quarter of an hour or so; strain off the water; return the macaroni into the saucepan with a pint of milk; boil till the milk is absorbed, then add an ounce each of grated cheese and butter; mix well with the macaroni by shaking the saucepan and tossing it up. When well mixed pour it into a gratin-dish, with two ounces more of grated cheese sprinkled over it, as well as a little bread raspings, grated nutmeg, and an ounce of butter divided in five or six pieces. Put the gratin-dish in a well-heated oven till it has attained a nice golden colour and serve in the gratin-dish.

If preferred, the completion of the cooking of macaroni can be made in broth instead of milk.

93. MACARONI (COUNTRY STYLE).

Cut about two pounds of the round or shoulder of beef in three-inch dice; shred an onion and fry it in a frying-pan with an ounce of butter; when the onion is of a nice yellow colour, add the pieces of beef to it and brown them for five minutes; after which, draw the pan away from the fire. Take a good-sized pie-dish and half a pound of uncooked macaroni; break this in short pieces and divide it in three parts; lay one part at the bottom of the pie-dish, nicely buttered; then put the half of the meat and onions on this layer, season well with salt and pepper; make another layer of macaroni, place the remainder of the meat and onions on it, season as before, and cover these with the third part of macaroni; moisten the lot with broth three-parts full, cover the pie-dish closely with a plain flour and water paste, or with another pie-dish turned over it, and put it in a well-heated oven for about an hour; after which, remove the cover, sprinkle a little grated cheese over the top, and serve in the pie-dish.

Note.—The same thing can be done with mutton or veal.

94. MACARONI MILANAISE.

Boil one pound of macaroni, strain, and cut it up in three-inch lengths, put it in a stewpan with three ounces of butter, four ounces of grated Gruyère cheese, a little grated nutmeg, salt and pepper to taste, and half a pint of good cream; set the stewpan over a moderate fire, toss up the whole well together until quite hot, then shake it up for a few minutes to make the cheese spin, and serve.

95. TAGLIATELLI (HOUSEWIFE STYLE).

Put one pound of sifted flour on the paste-board, make a well in the centre, break five eggs in it, add a teaspoonful of salt and about an ounce of butter, with enough lukewarm water to melt the salt, work these well together to a firm smooth paste, and finish it by pressing the paste from you with the palms of the hands. Then cut it into four pieces, and roll it with the rolling-pin to the thickness of about the sixteenth part of an inch, let it dry for a little while, then fold each piece in ribbons of about two inches wide, taking care to sprinkle a little flour between the folds; cut these through crossways into shreds about the eighth of an inch, take them up gently with both hands, to loosen them and prevent their adhering to one another, spread them again on the paste-board, and when all the paste is shred in this way immerse them (a few at a time) in three quarts of boiling salt water; stir, while you drop them in to prevent their getting lumpy, and after five or six minutes of sharp ebullition drain them well on a sieve; put them afterwards in a stewpan with half a pint of broth, two ounces of butter, salt and pepper to taste; let them simmer for a few minutes; then add three ounces of grated cheese, two or three spoonfuls of good beef gravy, and toss the contents whilst over the fire, so as to mix well together, and serve.

96. TAGLIATELLI À LA CHASSEUR.

Prepare a pound of tagliatelli as in No. 95, boil them in salt water for five minutes; strain them on a sieve and put them in a stewpan on the fire with one pint of game broth, a little grated nutmeg, and a pinch of pepper; simmer until the broth is reduced; then add about two ounces of grated cheese, an ounce of butter, and two dozen small quenelles of game previously cooked in gravy; toss the whole lightly over the fire until the cheese is well mixed with the tagliatelli, then pour the contents into a hot dish, sprinkle two tablespoonfuls of hot game gravy over the paste, and serve.

Tagliatelli can be prepared and served in every respect like macaroni.

96a. TAGLIATELLI À LA GENOISE.

Prepare a pound of tagliatelli as described in No. 95. Pound a small clove of garlic, with three ounces of parmesan cheese and a sprig of green basil, in a mortar; moisten these gradually with two tablespoonfuls of good salad-oil, and when well pounded put the contents in a sauté-pan.

Meanwhile have two ounces of dried mushrooms (cèpes) well soaked in boiling water; strain, dry and chop these very fine, and mix them with the pounded sauce.

Boil and strain the tagliatelli in the usual way, and put

it in the sauté-pan with the mixture on the fire, to which add two ounces of fresh butter; toss the contents up till the sauce is properly melted and well mixed with the paste, then serve with some grated parmesan cheese apart.

97. RAVIOLI À L'ITALIENNE.

Ravioli is considered by the natives to be one of the best Italian-made dishes in existence; and to give a fair idea of its repute as well as its national character, I can only compare it to the English Christmas plum-pudding. Its preparation, however, is not so expensive, neither can the making of it be considered difficult or complicated. Make a paste similar to the one for tagliatelli (No. 95), but add half a gill more of lukewarm water to it; when the paste has been properly worked and rolled in four parts, nearly as thin as a sheet of paper, with the rolling-pin, place them apart on the board. Beat the yolks of three eggs, and with a feather or soft brush moisten one sheet of paste with it, then lay on this (two inches apart) a teaspoonful of chicken force-meat (No. 271). When the sheet is covered in the manner directed with the forcemeat, lay over it one of the sheets of paste and press this down with the thumb over the outer row of balls, then cut these out with a small fluted cutter into half-moon shape, and place them on a large dish, slightly sprinkled with flour. Proceed with the other two sheets of paste in the same way; after which, let them dry on the dish for a couple of hours, then drop the lot gently in three quarts of boiling salt water, boil them on a brisk fire for ten minutes, then strain off the water and put the ravioli in a stewpan, in which a quarter of a pound of fresh butter has already been melted to a golden colour; add to it a pint of good broth, and let it boil for five or six minutes; after which, add two ounces of grated cheese, toss the stewpan gently in order to mix the cheese well with the ravioli, without, however, breaking them. When properly mixed and the broth nicely reduced, pour them into a dish; sprinkle a little more grated cheese and three spoonfuls of good hot beef gravy over, and serve.

In the same manner, ravioli can be made with veal or game forcemeat, as well as with fish; in the latter case, a purée of spinach, the yolks of four beaten eggs, and an ounce of grated cheese must be added and well mixed with the fish.

Tomato sauce added at the same time as the broth will also be an improvement.

98. RAVIOLI À LA ROMAINE.

Prepare five or six dozen ravioli in the same manner as in the previous number. Boil them in broth for fifteen minutes, then strain and put them in a stewpan containing about a quarter of a pound of fresh mushrooms, properly trimmed and cut into slices, with a similar quantity of cooked ox-tongue cut in small dice, half a pint of white wine, a gill each of Espagnole sauce and game essence. Boil on a brisk fire; toss the stewpan, so as to mix and warm the contents well together; and when the sauce is nearly reduced, add two ounces of grated cheese, toss the whole well over the fire, and serve.

99. GNOCHETTI WITH BUTTER.

Put a pint of water into a stewpan on the fire with two ounces of butter, a teaspoonful of salt, and a pinch of pepper. When the contents boil draw the stewpan away from the fire, add gradually to it half a pound of semolina or ordinary sifted flour; stir the while with a wooden spoon till it has reached the consistency of a solid paste, then add to it the yolks of four eggs, well beaten, together with three ounces of grated cheese; mix these well with the paste by tossing it with the wooden spoon, then whisk the whites of the four eggs, already used, to a nice snowy froth, and mix it well with the paste; turn this out of the stewpan, flatten it on a slab, cut it in small equal dice, and roll these into the shape of small filberts. Meanwhile boil one quart of broth, drop the balls of gnochetti in it, and let them simmer for twenty minutes, then drain and dry them. Butter the inside of an entrée dish, divide two ounces of butter into small balls; put a layer of gnochetti and sprinkle a little grated cheese, a few pieces of butter, and two tablespoonfuls of good beef gravy over it; continue the layers of gnochetti, butter, grated cheese, and beef gravy to the end, finishing with grated cheese on the top; then put the dish in the oven for five minutes, and serve.

100. POLENTA* À LA PIEDMONTAISE.

Boil in a saucepan three pints of broth or water, to which a dessert-spoonful of salt must be added. When the broth boils take a strong wooden spoon in your right hand, or better still, the half of a broomstick made for that purpose, which must be about eighteen inches long, and with your left hand drop gradually one pound of polenta flour into the saucepan on the fire; stir the while, to prevent the flour clotting; let it boil for half an hour, stirring the paste almost constantly to prevent burning; after which, sprinkle three ounces of grated cheese over it; stir the contents well, so as to mix the cheese with the polenta, which will now be firm and detach itself from the border of the pan; pour the lot into a dish, melt a quarter

* A flour made from Indian-corn, grown on a large scale and much used in Italy.

of a pound of butter in a frying-pan to a frothy heat, pour it over the polenta, and serve.

101. POLENTA À LA NAPOLITAINE.

Prepare a "polenta" as in the previous number; when nearly cooked add two ounces of fresh butter and stir well, in order to mix the polenta with the butter. Meanwhile set a well-buttered sauté-pan on the fire, with half a dozen slices of fat bacon; put on these a dozen small birds (such as larks, &c)., properly cleaned, and a couple of bay-leaves. Fry the birds to a nice colour, then moisten with half a pint of good broth and a glass of white wine; season with salt and pepper to taste; cover the sauté-pan, and simmer very gently until the birds are well cooked, basting them and turning as often as required.

When the polenta is done and the birds ready, dress the former on a dish spread with grated parmesan cheese, place the birds on the top, strain the gravy over, and serve.

Note.—A few thin slices of truffles or fresh mushrooms, cooked either in gravy or butter, will improve the "polenta."

REMARKS ON RICE.

Rice, like paste, can be eaten with as much advantage in soups as in made dishes, and in either case will always be found nourishing, appetising, and refreshing. Its cooking differs but slightly from paste, as rice can be boiled in the soup with which it is intended to be served. It can also be prepared in more than a hundred different ways, and eaten by all classes, from its simplest and cheapest mode of preparation to the most expensive and luxurious made dishes. Rice is good in almost every soup, can be eaten with any meat, fish, or poultry, is made into various puddings, and served as a sweet with any kind of stewed fruit. The best rice to use is the Italian, the grain of which is short and plump. It can be distinguished from others by a slight grey tinge, and, although dearer than the Indian and Egyptian, is, nevertheless, cheaper than either, on account of its swelling propensity and nourishing properties, which are not possessed by others to the same extent. Never attempt to make a "risotto" with a long white-grained rice, as you will fail.

102. PLAIN RICE AND BROTH.

Pour three pints of good broth into a stewpan, and set it to the boil. Meantime wash in a basin, with two or three different cold waters, a pint of rice; when the broth is on the boil throw the rice in, boil for about twenty minutes, season with salt and a little pepper, pour into a soup-tureen, and serve with grated cheese on a plate apart.

Note.—Rice can also be cooked in plain water, drained, and served with boiling broth, in which case it keeps clearer.

103. RICE AND CABBAGE SOUP.

Blanch in salt water for a few minutes the heart of a cabbage cut in eight parts; strain the water through a colander; press the cabbage, and put it back into the stewpan with three pints of cold broth, a small knuckle or ham-bone, and a quarter of a pound of rice, properly washed, as in No. 102; boil for twenty-five minutes, season to taste, take the bone or knuckle out, and pour the soup into a soup-tureen.

This soup can be made "maigre" by using water instead of broth; in which case add two ounces of butter a few minutes before serving.

104. RICE AND POTATO SOUP.

Proceed with the potatoes as for cabbage, described in the previous number, but omit the knuckle or ham-bone.

105. RICE AND VEGETABLE SOUP.

All kinds of vegetables are good for this soup, but must first be blanched in boiling salt water for a few minutes and properly dried; then fry them in a stewpan with butter; soak them afterwards with good gravy in another stewpan, and boil till cooked. Meantime boil three pints of broth; throw half a pint of rice into it, and after twenty minutes of ebullition mix with the vegetables and gravy, season with salt and pepper, stir, pour into a soup-tureen, and serve with a little grated cheese on a plate apart.

Macaroni or any other paste can be added to either of the above soups, provided it has been previously cooked apart.

106. MINESTRONE.

The minestrone is a real Italian national soup. It is composed of a mixture of vegetables and rice, is very much appreciated and considered as a delicacy by the natives.

Vegetables used for this soup should be fresh and tender, and the following are generally the most in request. Take the heart of a small cabbage, one carrot, four potatoes, three leeks, and half a head of celery; shred very fine; blanch these separately; strain and fry them in two ounces of butter with half a pint of kidney beans, half a pint of green peas, and a dozen French beans cut in small diamonds; then take one ounce of fat bacon, mash with a knife-blade the clove of a garlic, and mix it with the bacon, which must be minced as fine as a paste; put it into a stewpan with three pints of broth, boil it with all the vegetables, add one pint of well-washed rice, a slice of bacon-rind cut in small dice, and two mashed fresh tomatoes. Boil for twenty-five minutes, season with salt and pepper, stir well, then pour it into a soup-tureen, and serve with two ounces of grated cheese on a plate apart.

107. RISOTTO* À LA PIÈMONTAISE.

Put three pints of good broth into a stewpan; when boiling throw in three-quarters of a pound of nice clean rice; cook for twenty minutes on a good fire, giving it an occasional stir; then add two ounces of grated cheese, the same quantity of fresh butter and truffles cut in very thin slices, a little grated nutmeg, salt and pepper to taste, *mix well together*, add a little gravy if too thick, and serve on a hot dish.

108. RISOTTO MILANAISE.

Slice an onion and fry it in a stewpan with an ounce of butter and a little beef marrow till of a nice brown colour; dilute with a quart of broth; boil it, strain the broth through a sieve into the stewpan again, and season with salt and pepper; boil it; then add one pint of rice and a small pinch of saffron; cook on a good fire for twenty minutes, often stirring the contents with a wooden spoon to prevent burning; sprinkle two handfuls of grated cheese over it, with a gill of white dry wine; stir and mix well together; boil for another two or three minutes, then draw from the fire, and just before serving add one ounce of fresh butter, divided in five or six parts and put about in the stewpan; cover with the lid for two or three minutes, then pour it

---

* Risotto is the Italian name for all made rice-dishes.

into a hot dish with a little more grated cheese sprinkled on the top, and serve.

109. RISOTTO (ITALIAN STYLE).

Proceed as above, but omit the saffron; add four tablespoonfuls of tomato sauce at the same time as the cheese, and serve after having given it a good stirring.

110. ANOTHER RISOTTO (ITALIAN STYLE).

Shred fine the red part of a carrot and an onion, cut in small dice a rasher of bacon, fry these in a stewpan with an ounce of butter till of a nice brown colour; then add the giblets and combs of two fowls chopped fine, fry for a few minutes longer, then moisten with one quart of broth, season with salt and pepper to taste, and add a small pinch of saffron; boil it on a good fire; when boiling pour in one pint of clean rice; stir and boil fast till nearly cooked, then add four tablespoonfuls of tomato sauce and six of grated cheese, stir the contents well together, add half a dozen mushrooms and one truffle cut in thin slices, stir again to prevent burning, cook for two minutes longer, pour it into a hot dish with a little more grated cheese sprinkled on the top and one ounce of butter divided in five or six pieces and placed at equal distances about the rice; then place the dish in a moderately heated oven for two minutes, and serve.

111. RISOTTO À LA CHARTREUSE.

Prepare a broth of frogs or of crayfish, and proceed as in the first risotto (Italian style); when cooked, pour the rice into a hot dish with pieces of frog's meat, boned and cut in dice, or the crayfish-tails properly mixed with it, as well as a few slices of truffles.

E

112. RISOTTO (SPANISH STYLE).

Put in a stewpan a quarter of a pound of fresh butter with an onion shred fine; brown this nicely; then add four tomatoes cut in small slices, previously peeled, together with half a pound of ham cut in small dice; fry the lot for a few minutes; then pour over one quart of good broth and one pint of rice; boil on a good fire and cover the stewpan for ten minutes; after which, add half a pint of green peas and the same quantity of asparagus, cut in points and blanched in the usual way; boil for fifteen minutes longer, giving it an occasional stir to prevent burning, and serve with grated cheese on a plate apart, as well as some boiling broth in a soup-tureen, if wished for.

113. RISOTTO À LA PORTUGAISE.

Cook the rice apart in water, strain, and put it into a soup-tureen; pour over a quart of good boiling broth, mixed with three spoonfuls of tomato sauce and the breast of a cooked chicken cut in small dice; and serve with grated cheese on a plate apart.

114. RISOTTO À LA TURQUE.

Put three ounces of fresh butter in a stewpan with a few slices of fat bacon cut in small dice and an onion split across; fry till the onion has taken a brown, when it must be taken out, and a nice tender fowl cut in quarters put in its place; season well with salt; cover the stewpan and let it simmer for forty minutes, giving it an occasional stir; then moisten it with three pints of broth, and when boiling add one pound of rice; stir well, replace the lid, and boil slowly for half an hour; after which, dress it on a hot dish, and serve with grated cheese on a plate apart.

115. RISOTTO À LA PONIATOWSKY.

Fry in a stewpan with an ounce of butter a quarter of a pound of gammon cut in small slices; then add one pint of rice and three pints of broth; boil on a brisk fire for twenty-five minutes and stir often; take the slices of bacon out, add two dozen oysters with two spoonfuls of their liquor to it, mix well together, melt an ounce of butter in a frying-pan apart, pour the rice in a hot dish and the melted butter over it; then serve with a quart of boiling broth in a soup-tureen apart, if desired.

116. CREAM RICE À LA RÉALE.

Put a fowl and half a knuckle of veal into a stewpan with a carrot; add half an onion, the quarter of a celery-head, one leek, and two quarts of broth; boil for an hour and a half, take the meat out, skim and strain the broth through a fine cloth; pour the half of it into a stewpan of medium size with half a pound of rice, washed in two or three different waters and blanched apart for a few minutes; let it boil for an hour, stir occasionally with a wooden spoon; after which, pour in the remainder of the broth; mix well, and pass it through a wire sieve, then through a tammy and back into the stewpan on a good fire till nearly boiling. Meanwhile mix in a basin three spoonfuls of chicken purée with the same quantity of rice cream; add gradually to it half a pint more of the cream, stirring the while; then pour it back to the stewpan with the other rice cream, stir and mix properly before serving with croûtons fried in butter.

117. CREAM RICE À LA FRANÇAISE.

Proceed for this as in No. 116, but add to the vegetables before named a little parsley, which must be taken out when cooked; and just before serving, add half a pint of good cream with an ounce of fresh butter; mix all well together, and when nearly boiling pour it into a souptureen in which a few small quenelles of chicken, properly poached, have already been put. Stir, and serve.

118. RICE CREAM À LA CHASSEUR.

Roast a partridge, cut the meat in small dice, and pound it in a mortar; put the bones and carcass in a quart of chicken broth, boil for ten minutes, skim, and pass it through a fine cloth; then put it back into the stewpan on the fire. When boiling, pour half a pound of rice into it and boil for an hour and a quarter; after which, pass it through a fine wire sieve and tammy. Return the cream to the stewpan on the fire, then mix gradually the purée of partridge with it, boil it, give it an occasional stir, and serve with croûtons fried in butter.

119. RICE CREAM WITH PHEASANT.

Proceed for this as in the "Réale," and then add six quenelles of pheasant, well poached, and serve.

120. RICE AU GRATIN.

Pour three pints of good broth into a stewpan, and set it on the fire. When boiling, throw in one pound of clean rice, and let it boil for twenty minutes, giving it an occasional stir; then season with salt and pepper, add a few allspice, sprinkle two ounces of grated cheese and a gill of good gravy, mix the contents well together, and pour it into a pie-dish, the inside of which must be well buttered. Sprinkle the top with a few bread-crumbs, making a hole in the centre with a spoon, fill it with chicken stuffing or financière, place the pie-dish in a moderately heated oven till the top has taken a nice brown colour and become crisp, and then serve with a little grated cheese on a plate apart.

121. RISOTTO À LA MÉNAGÈRE OR HOUSEWIFE STYLE.

Boil in a saucepan three pints of broth, throw in one pound of rice, boil for twenty minutes, stir occasionally, then add one ounce and a half of grated cheese, the same quantity of butter, season in the usual way, pour a gill of hot gravy, mix the contents well together, add a few slices of truffles or fresh mushrooms stewed in butter, pour it into a hot dish; and serve with a little grated cheese on a plate apart.

122. RICE WITH MILK.

Pour three pints of milk into a saucepan, let it boil, throw in one pound of rice, a small piece of sugar, and a bay-leaf; boil for twenty minutes, stir in the usual way to prevent burning, and just before serving mix the yoke of an egg and a little grated nutmeg with it.

123. BISQUE OF CRAYFISH AND RICE.

This soup is as much recommended for its delicacy as for its excellence, and can be obtained in different ways; but after long study, the following is, I believe, the best and easiest mode of all for its preparation:—

Wash in several waters thirty-five or forty live crayfish of medium size, put them in a saucepan with a handful of salt, a pinch of pepper, a bottle of dry white wine, a "bouquet garni," an onion, carrot, and half a head of celery all shred fine; moisten the lot with cold water, cover the saucepan and boil on a good fire for about twenty minutes, then strain the broth into a stewpan, let it boil, and pour a quarter of a pound of clean rice into it, which must boil for about an hour. Meantime take the tails of the crayfish out of their shells with your fingers, put them apart on a plate, pound the shells and inside residue in a mortar with two ounces of butter, put the purée in a stewpan with three pints of good broth, salt and pepper to taste, and let it boil for fifteen minutes. After which, strain it through a fine hair sieve, return it to the stewpan, and set by the side of the fire to let the scum rise, when it must be skimmed off. When the rice is properly cooked, strain, and pour it into a mortar with the half of the crayfish-tails, pound the lot nicely, and add it to thicken the broth with the remainder of the crayfish; boil it; stir and mix well; boil for about ten minutes; then pour it into a soup-tureen with a few quenelles of chicken or croûtons fried in butter, and serve.

This soup can also be made with crawfish or lobster, but in neither will the delicacy and flavour of the above be found.

124. RICE AND CHESNUTS.

Peel and boil one pound of chesnuts as in No. 51. Meantime boil one pound of rice in three pints of broth. When the chesnuts are cooked, strain and mix them well with the rice, salt and pepper to taste, add two ounces of grated cheese and one ounce of butter divided into four or five pieces, and spread on the rice, cover the stewpan for a few minutes, then sprinkle with a little grated nutmeg, pour it into a hot dish, and serve.

This dish can be altered by cooking the rice with milk instead of broth, and by adding half a pint of cream at the same time as the chesnuts.

125. RISOTTO (GENOA STYLE).

Put a gill of fine olive-oil into a stewpan with a carrot, an onion, a little celery, and one clove of garlic, all minced very fine. Fry the lot till nicely browned, then add one pound of rice, previously blanched in salt water for a few minutes, and strained; fry and stir for five minutes longer, pour three pints of good broth over it, season with salt and pepper to taste, boil for ten minutes on a brisk fire, stir often to prevent burning, then add four tablespoonfuls of tomato sauce, or better still, three fresh tomatoes peeled and cut in small slices; stir well, and boil for five minutes longer; after which, sprinkle over it two ounces of grated cheese and two tablespoonfuls of anchovy butter; stir well, cover the stewpan; draw it away from the fire, and after two or three minutes pour it into a hot dish and serve.

I might go on with more recipes, but, after due consideration, I think the number already given will meet the general requirements. On the other hand, it is advisable to give cooks and amateurs in gastronomy opportunities of showing their ability and power of imagination in cooking fancy dishes of their own invention.

126. PEARL BARLEY SOUP.

Put in a sauté-pan one fowl and two pounds of leg of veal, together with two quarts and a half of broth and the usual sorts and quantity of vegetables as for a soup; let it boil for forty minutes; take the fowl and veal out, skim, and pass the broth through a fine cloth, return it to the sauté-pan with a quarter of a pound of pearl barley, stir occasionally with a wooden spoon to prevent the barley sticking together; boil on a slow fire for five hours, then skim off the scum that rises to the surface; after which, add a piece of sugar; and just before serving, dilute in a basin three tablespoonfuls of chicken pureé with a pint of broth by stirring; pour this afterwards in the sauté-pan, mix it well with the barley, and serve, properly seasoned.

127. OYSTER SOUP.

Blanch two dozen oysters in their own liquor, to which add a glass of Marsala. When firm take them away from the foam with a small flat skimmer and place them on a cloth; draw the stewpan to the side of the fire, and let the liquor deposit and clarify itself. Meanwhile boil three pints of fish broth, to which add as soon as ready the clarified liquor above mentioned, and when boiling draw to the side of the fire and skim. Whisk the yolks of three eggs with two tablespoonfuls of Béchamel sauce, a little grated nutmeg, and one ounce of fresh butter; mix well with the broth in the usual way, pour it into the souptureen with the oysters, and serve.

128. BEER AND WINE SOUP.

Fry in butter a few small slices of the crumbs of bread, then pour a bottle each of pale ale and red wine with the peel of half a lemon; shred three cloves and a little cinnamon, and add them to the liquor. Boil for five minutes, and serve.

129. STURGEON SOUP (ENGLISH STYLE).

Cook in good gravy about two pounds of sturgeon; let it get cold, and cut it in small dice. Meantime boil in a saucepan three pints of broth, into which pour a glass of sherry, Madeira, or port; add the usual seasoning, with a little cayenne and two teaspoonfuls of anchovy butter.

When boiling pour it into a soup-tureen in which the sturgeon has already been put, add a dozen small beef quenelles and as many glazed mushrooms, and serve.

130. GOOSE GIBLET SOUP (ENGLSH STYLE).

Blanch in the usual way the giblets of a goose; strain the water through a colander; cut them in dice and fry them in a stewpan with an ounce of butter; add a glass of sherry or Madeira, and let them simmer till nearly reduced; then draw the stewpan by the side of the fire. Meantime boil three pints of broth, add one carrot, the half a head of celery, one leek, six pepper-corns, three cloves, and a "bouquet garni;" boil gently for an hour, then pass the broth through a sieve and back to the stewpan, clarify it with a little raw minced meat, the whites of two eggs, properly whisked and mixed with half a glass of sherry. Put the giblets into a soup-tureen with a few small quenelles of chicken and three tablespoonfuls of Brunoise, pour the boiling broth, when properly clarified, over, and serve.

131. POACHED EGG SOUP Á LA STYRIENNE.

Boil in a stewpan three pints of good broth. When boiling sprinkle three ounces of good semolina flour, a small quantity at a time; keep stirring, to prevent the flour clotting; then poach six or eight new-laid eggs by breaking each separately, and plunge them into some boiling broth set apart for that purpose in a sauté-pan; boil for about two minutes, draw the pan away from the fire, take the eggs out one by one with a flat strainer; lay them carefully on a cloth, trim each nicely round with a knife, and place them in a soup-tureen with half a pound of green peas previously cooked in salt water and two tablespoonfuls of parsley blanched and hashed fine; then pass the broth in which the eggs were poached through a sieve, mix it with the one in which the semolina flour was diluted, stir well, pour slowly into the soup-tureen, and serve with a little grated cheese on a plate apart.

132. POACHED EGG SOUP.

Poach six or eight eggs in boiling salt water as above, but add two spoonfuls of vinegar; take them out and trim them in the same manner, put them very carefully in a soup-tureen, and pour gently three pints of good boiling broth, nicely clarified, over it, and serve.

133. CALF'S TAIL SOUP (INDIAN STYLE).

Cut at the joints two calves' tails, blanch the pieces in boiling salt water, and brown them in a sauté-pan with half a pint of good gravy; after which, soak the lot with broth, let simmer till cooked, then strain the gravy, return it to the sauté-pan and put the pieces of tails in the soup-tureen, whisk the yolks of two eggs and dilute it with the gravy in which the pieces of tails were cooked, together with two teaspoonfuls of curry powder, set the sauté-pan on the fire, stir well, and when nearly boiling pour it over the calves' tails with a few chicken quenelles and a quart of good boiling broth, and serve.

134. SOUP À LA POLONAISE.

Put in a stewpan the half of a roast fowl, six ounces of gammon cut in thin slices, two pounds of breast of veal, three pints of cold water, and two tablespoonfuls of salt. Boil and skim carefully; add the usual vegetables as in soup No. 2. When the meat is properly cooked take it out, pass the broth through a fine cloth, return it to the stewpan, and when boiling throw in three ounces of gruel previously cooked in plain water, let it boil, stir well, and pour it into a soup-tureen, with the chicken-breast, a little of the veal, and part of the gammon, all cut in very small dice; and serve.

135. COCK A LEEKIE SOUP.

Boil a chicken in two quarts of water, with salt, pepper, and an onion stuck with two cloves, for forty minutes, taking care to skim off the scum at the proper time; then strain the broth through a cloth into a stewpan; add a quart of veal stock and boil. Meanwhile cut the white part of six leeks one inch and a half long, slice these in four, lengthways, blanch them in the usual way, drain the water, and pour the leeks into the broth to cook. Meanwhile cut up the chicken meat, free from bones, skin, and gristle, into small pieces. When the leeks are thoroughly cooked and soft add the pieces of chicken, and let them simmer for another ten minutes, then pour into a soup-tureen after having seasoned to taste; and serve.

136. MUTTON BROTH.

Take three pounds of the scrag end or neck of mutton, cut it into several pieces, wash them in cold water and put them into a stewpan with two quarts of cold spring water; set the stewpan to boil, and skim the broth well; then add two turnips cut in slices, a few sprigs each of parsley and green thyme, and a little salt. After an hour and a half of gentle ebullition, skim off the fat from the surface and strain through a fine sieve into a basin, and keep in a cool place ready for use.

CHAPTER II.

SOUPS FOR CONVALESCENTS AND CHILDREN.

137. PLAIN CHICKEN BROTH.

Cut a chicken or young fowl into four parts, wash these well in cold water, and put the pieces in a stewpan with three pints of cold water and a teaspoonful of salt; boil it, skim it well, then add the heart of a lettuce and a handful of chervil, let it simmer for about an hour, and strain it through a fine cloth into a basin.

138. SIMPLE PAP.

Cut in slices some crumb of bread, put them in a stewpan with enough chicken or veal broth to soak, boil it, pass through a sieve by rubbing, and put it back into the stewpan; boil it again, add a few pieces of butter each as big as a pea, and serve.

139. PAP À LA REINE.

Soak in half a pint of hot broth some slices of the crumb of bread, pound in a mortar the meat of half a chicken, previously cooked in white broth and boned, mix this with the bread and pass it through a sieve, put it back into the stewpan, boil it with the quantity of white broth required, and serve.

140. BREAD RASPINGS SOUP.

Pound in a mortar one pound of crust of bread, or grate a one-pound loaf; boil one pint of broth; pour in the bread-raspings, a small quantity at a time; stir well to prevent clotting, and after ten minutes' ebullition draw the stewpan away from the fire, add a few pieces of butter, pass all through a sieve, and serve.

141. VELVETY SOUP.

Dilute one tablespoonful of flour with two of milk, boil a cup of broth, and when it boils pour gradually the diluted flour over it, stir continually, boil for a few minutes, and serve with a few croûtons fried in butter.

142. SAGO SOUP.

Wash in boiling water, strain and boil in broth, the quantity of sago required, and when it has thickened like a hot jelly it is cooked; draw it from the fire, add a little butter, and serve.

Sago can also be cooked with milk, in which case add a piece of sugar.

143. TAPIOCA SOUP.

Boil a tablespoonful of tapioca to each cup of broth for ten minutes, then add a little butter, and serve. The same can also be done with milk, and instead of butter add sugar.

144. POTATO FLOUR SOUP.

Dilute a tablespoonful of fecula or potato flour with two or three of cold broth, then pour it into a stewpan with a pint of boiling broth, stir this well, and after a few minutes of ebullition serve.

145. SEMOLINA SOUP.

Boil a pint of good broth; when boiling pour gradually two tablespoonfuls of semolina into it, stirring it meanwhile, and let it boil for half an hour; add a little butter, and if too thick some boiling broth, stir again, and serve.

146. RICE FLOUR SOUP.

Fry in a stewpan with an ounce of butter two tablespoonfuls of rice flour for ten minutes, then add gradually a pint of milk to it, stir the while to prevent clotting, boil it, and serve.

147. PASTE SOUP WITH BROTH OR MILK.

Put in boiling broth or milk two ounces for each person of vermicelli, stars, or any other small paste, boil for five or six minutes, add a little butter, and serve.

148. BEEF TEA.

Take two pounds of the lean part of the round or beefsteak, remove carefully all fat skin and sinew from it, then cut it in small square pieces of about an inch, put these pieces of beef into a stewpan with three pints of cold water and a dessert-spoonful of salt, set the stewpan on the fire, and when the contents reaches ebullition skim it in the usual way; then remove the stewpan by the side of the fire, let it simmer for about an hour; after which, strain the broth or beef tea through a fine cloth, and serve.

149. SNAIL BROTH FOR OBSTINATE COUGHS.

Take three dozen garden snails, wash them in three or four different waters, then add to them the hind-quarters of two dozen stream frogs, previously skinned; bruise them together in a mortar; after which, put these into a stewpan with two turnips finely chopped, a tablespoonful of salt, a pinch of saffron, and three pints of cold water; set the stewpan on the fire, stir the lot with a wooden spoon until the broth begins to boil, then skim it most carefully, and set it by the side of the fire to simmer for half an hour; after which, the broth must be strained by pressing it through a tammy-cloth into a basin for use.

This broth, from its soothing qualities, often counteracts successfully the straining effects of a severe and obstinate cough, and alleviates (more than any other culinary preparation) the sufferings of consumptive persons.

150. SIMPLE JELLY.

Take an old fowl, with one pound of lean beef and two pounds of leg of veal; cut each in small pieces, put them into a stewpan with three pints of cold water, and salt to taste. Boil them; skim most carefully, add two carrots and two turnips shred finely; cover the stewpan and boil for three hours; then pass the broth through a sieve; press and squeeze well the pieces of meat; let the broth get cold; add to it afterwards the white of an egg, properly whisked, with a gill of broth; set it to the boil again; stir till it comes to a nice thickness without letting it boil; then pass through a cloth into an earthenware jar or pan, and remove it to a cool place, when it will become a jelly, and is ready for use.

CHAPTER III.

REMARKS ON SAUCES, ESSENCES, MELTED BUTTER, AND JELLIES.

WHATEVER the cookery may be, it is absolutely necessary, even amongst private families, to have certain sauces always at hand, the object of which is to perfect and strengthen, as well as to improve and colour, the different made dishes. Cooking, as I have said before, is an art; therefore it can be compared (if I am not too bold) to painting, inasmuch that, however talented an artist may be, he can never paint a picture unless he has the proper colours at his command; but once possessed of the right combinations, he can extend or reduce and alter his tints according to his taste and ideas. The cook must likewise have the necessary ingredients in order to enable him to produce made dishes both tasty and pleasing to the eye, the latter being always a desirable end in cookery; and although the same sauces may often be in request, it does not follow that the flavour will be uniform, as the artist cook, like the artist painter, will be be able to exercise his knowledge and talent by manipulating his sauces, and give them the hue required as well as the flavour expected.

The four principal sauces, which after broth must be considered the foundation of all good and high-class cooking, are the Espagnole (brown), Velouté (fawn, velvety), Béchamel (white), and Allemande (yellow)..

In order to obtain good sauces it is of the utmost importance that the butter should be good and fresh;

that the seasoning should be put in proper quantities; that the liaison (which here means a binding or thickening) be made with the yolks of fresh eggs, well whisked and properly strained; and that the simmering, as well as the skimming, should have the most careful attention of the cook. Let this be well understood, that in no part of the culinary process is attention and care so much required as in the preparation of sauces, as no remedy will successfully remove the mischief caused by a failure.

Note.—All the sauces made of different compounds, especially those of butter, should be kept hot in bain-maries, and these even then not more than twenty minutes; otherwise, on account of their delicacy, they will either turn, get decomposed, or become oily. To remedy this, and bring the butter sauces to their original smoothness, a piece of clean ice as big as a nut should be added to the sauce in summer, or a little cold water in winter, and this should be worked briskly with a spoon by the side of the fire, before serving.

151. ESPAGNOLE SAUCE.

To make this sauce it is essential that the broth should be good.

Prepare a broth as No. 4, then melt in a stewpan two ounces of butter, pour the same quantity of semolina flour, stir well with a wooden spoon till it boils, then draw the stewpan by the side of the fire, and let it simmer for half an hour, often stirring. After this, add gradually some of the hot broth to it, then pour the lot into it, and set it to the boil, stirring the while, when boiling. Let the fat rise to the top; skim it properly; then pass the sauce through a tammy sieve; return it to the stewpan; boil it again, and reduce it till it has reached a nice thick, but soft,

F

consistency, stirring the while to prevent clotting; then pour it into an earthenware pan; lay a piece of kitchen paper at the top, to remove any remaining particle of fat, and place it in a cool place, as it is now ready for use, and will keep several days.

152. ESPAGNOLE SAUCE No. 2.

Butter a stewpan, with an ounce of butter put in it, a shred onion, and about three pounds of leg of veal cut in small slices skinned and the fat removed, also a pound of beef cut in slices, as well as any carcasses of chicken and game that may be had; moisten the lot with half a pint of broth or stock No. 1. Boil on a good fire till the broth is reduced by one-half, turn the meat round so as to glaze it of an even brown colour; when the meat is nicely glazed, draw the stewpan by the side of the fire, cover it, and let it stand for a few minutes. After this, pour in three quarts of stock No. 1, boil it, skim it in the usual way, and add a "bouquet garni," one carrot shred finely, salt and pepper to taste, then let it simmer till the meat is well done, when it must be taken out and the broth strained through a fine cloth; return the broth to the stewpan, and set it by the side of the fire. Meantime put three ounces of butter in a small stewpan, and when properly melted pour a similar quantity of semolina flour with it. Stir it well over the fire with a wooden spoon, and simmer it for a quarter of an hour, giving it an occasional stir. Dilute this with some of the broth, and when properly mixed pour the remainder of the broth over it; boil it, stir it constantly till boiling, then draw the stewpan to the side of the fire and let it simmer for two hours; skim off the fat and scum as it rises, then strain the sauce through a fine cloth into an earthenware pan, and put by in a cool place for future use.

These sauces will, in ordinary weather, keep perfectly well and good for four or five days.

153. VELOUTÉ SAUCE.

Put about two pounds of lean veal, free from skin and fat, into a buttered stewpan, also three slices of ham, half a pint of white stock, two carrots and one onion shred. Simmer the contents very gently, taking care not to colour the meat, and after half an hour moisten with three quarts of veal broth; boil it, skim it, and then draw the stewpan to the side of the fire; add a few shalots, a "bouquet garni," and the cuttings of half a dozen white mushrooms; simmer till the veal is well done; take it out and strain the broth through a fine cloth; put the broth back to the stewpan by the side of the fire. Meantime prepare a mixture of three ounces of butter with the same quantity of semolina flour in a stewpan, as in the Espagnole sauce, but do not brown the flour; dilute this with the white stock or veal broth in the same way as in No. 152, and mix it with the remainder of the stock in the stewpan; stir constantly till it has reached ebullition, let it simmer for two hours, skim off the fat and scum as it rises, give it an occasional stirring, and strain through a tammy sieve into an earthenware pan, and put by in a cool place.

154. BÉCHAMEL SAUCE.

Put in a stewpan six ounces of butter, the same quantity of lean ham cut in thin slices, one pound of lean veal, one carrot, one shalot, a little celery, all shred in the usual style; also a bay-leaf, two cloves, a small "bouquet" of thyme and pepper-corn. Set the stewpan on a moderate fire, let it simmer without browning the meat, and when almost dry sprinkle over three ounces of semolina flour, moisten with three pints of chicken broth and one quart of cream, stir and mix well together; boil it, draw the stewpan to the side of the fire, and simmer gently; stir occasionally, and skim in the usual way; if too thick add a little more broth or cream, and after two hours of simmering strain through a tammy sieve into an earthenware pan, as with the other sauces.

155. ANOTHER MODE OF PREPARING BÉCHAMEL SAUCE.

Pour into a stewpan one quart each of Velouté sauce and fresh cream, a small "bouquet garni," and three thin slices of lean ham; boil these, and stir constantly till the sauce is almost reduced by half, then pass it through a sieve as before.

156. ALLEMANDE SAUCE.

Fry in a stewpan, with two ounces of butter, one pound of mushroom trimmings; when well reduced, moisten this with three pints of Velouté sauce and one pint of chicken broth; boil till reduced by one-third; then add the yolks of six eggs well whisked, stir this for a few seconds, to mix properly with the sauce, boil it again, and pass it through a tammy sieve into a basin.

157. BUTTER SAUCE.

Dilute two tablespoonfuls of semolina flour in a stewpan with three ounces of melted butter; add a gill of cold water, a little salt, grated nutmeg, and the juice of half a lemon; stir the sauce on the fire till it boils; then draw the stewpan by the side, add six ounces of butter, mix it well, pour it into a bain-marie, and keep it hot for use.

Note.—It is absolutely necessary to have good fresh butter to make this sauce, and it is also advisable to make it only when wanted, as, from its particular delicacy, it is liable to get decomposed if left a certain time exposed to heat.

158. WHITE SAUCE.

Fry two ounces of bacon with four of beef fat in a stewpan, together with the half of a carrot and a shred onion, a small "bouquet garni," the juice of half a lemon, a few cloves, and a pinch of pepper; sprinkle a spoonful of flour over it, stir it well, then pour three pints of boiling water over it; salt it to taste, and boil for twenty-five minutes; skim, stir, and pass it through a tammy sieve.

159. MAÎTRE D'HÔTEL SAUCE.

Put in a stewpan three ounces of fresh butter, a spoonful of minced parsley, previously blanched and dried, a little grated nutmeg, white pepper, and the juice of a lemon; stir the contents well together near the fire, and when the butter becomes of the consistency of thick cream and is near ebullition it is ready to be served.

160. CLARIFIED BUTTER.

Put a pound of fresh butter into a stewpan, simmer gently until it is perfectly clear and of a nice golden colour, or till it has finished fizzing, then pass it through a tammy cloth into a basin, let it get cold, then cover and place it in a cool place, ready to be used when wanted.

161. ANCHOVY BUTTER.

Wash and bone six anchovies, pound them in a mortar with three ounces of butter, and rub them through a sieve with a wooden spoon.

162. RAVIGOTE BUTTER.

Take in equal proportions some parsley, chervil, spring onions, shalots, tarragon, and watercress, blanch the lot for two or three minutes in boiling water, drain and press out the water by twisting it in a cloth, then shred and pound the mixture in a mortar, with two properly washed and boned anchovies and three ounces of butter, boil it in a little stewpan, stir and mix well, and then pass it through a fine sieve, and store away for future use.

163. MONTPELLIER BUTTER.

Blanch, drain, and pound in a mortar the same kinds of herbs as in No. 162, together with six washed and boned anchovies, a small clove of garlic, and the yolks of three eggs boiled hard, half a pound of butter, two tablespoonfuls of olive-oil, one of tarragon vinegar, and salt and pepper to taste. When the whole is properly pounded pass it through a fine sieve. This will be found tasty.

164. BEURRE NOIR, OR BROWN BUTTER.

Put in a small saucepan a gill of vinegar with a teaspoonful of salt, a quarter of that quantity of white pepper, and a bay-leaf; boil it; meanwhile put into a frying-pan six ounces of butter to boil till it begins to acquire a dark-brown colour, then add a few leaves of parsley, washed and dried, boil again for a few seconds, then draw it away from the fire altogether; five minutes after, pass it through a pointed strainer into the saucepan containing the vinegar, which must have been reduced a little in boiling, and pour into a glazed basin for future use. When wanted, this has only to be warmed up, without boiling.

165. HORSE-RADISH BUTTER.

Scrape a large horse-radish, or two small ones, pound it in the mortar with a similar quantity of butter, and rub it through a sieve.

166. TRUFFLE BUTTER.

Cut and pound in a mortar four or five small truffles together with the half of an anchovy and three ounces of butter; when the lot is properly pounded and well mixed, rub it through a fine sieve and put it by for future use.

167. PERIGUEUX BUTTER.

Cut in thin slices four or five truffles, put these in a small sauté-pan, with two glasses of sherry or Madeira and two pepper-corns; boil for a few minutes; let it get cold, then pound it in a mortar with three ounces of butter, and rub through a sieve.

168. CURRY OR CAYENNE BUTTER.

Mix on a plate one teaspoonful of curry powder, or as much cayenne pepper as a small pea, with three ounces of butter, and use it without passing it through a sieve.

169. CRAYFISH AND LOBSTER BUTTER.

Cook and shell about thirty crayfish, as indicated in No. 123; pound the shells and claws in a mortar with half a pound of butter; put this purée in a stewpan on a moderate fire, stir occasionally till the butter acquires a nice red colour; then moisten it with a small cup of boiling water, stir again on the fire, and as soon as it reaches ebullition rub it through a fine sieve into a basin, let it get cold, and when firm take it out of the basin in one piece, cut off the sediment which will have settled at the bottom, and replace the good part in the basin, to be cut and melted when wanted.

Note.—This butter should not be kept too long. For lobster butter, proceed in the same way.

170. ESSENCE OF TRUFFLES.

Chop fine about a quarter of a pound of truffles, or if you have any trimmings use them instead, place them in a small stewpan with half a bay-leaf, a sprig of thyme, and a bruised clove of garlic; moisten the lot with a gill of French white wine, let simmer till the liquor is nearly all reduced, then add half a pint of good broth, set to the boil, and simmer for ten minutes longer; after which, pass it through a fine cloth, by twisting it, into a basin, and put by for use, when it will be found extremely useful for flavouring sauces and stews, in which the flavour of truffles should predominate.

171. ESSENCE OF MUSHROOMS.

Peel clean and chop finely half a pound of fresh mushrooms, fry them in a stewpan with an ounce of butter and a little lemon juice for two or three minutes, then moisten with half a pint of white stock, let it simmer for ten minutes, and rub it through a sieve into a basin for use.

172. ESSENCE OF GAME.

Chop up the carcasses of winged game left from the previous day's dinner, place them in a stewpan with four shalots, a bay-leaf, a sprig of thyme, a blade of mace, two pinches of pepper, and two ounces of butter. Fry the lot to a light-brown colour, then moisten them with a gill of French white wine, and let them simmer and stir till reduced to a glaze; then add half a pint of good broth, simmer again for half an hour, skim and strain it through a tammy sieve, and finish it by adding the juice of half a lemon.

173. ESSENCE OF CHICKEN.

Chop up the carcasses of two or three fowls; put them in a saucepan with about one pound of fillet of veal cut in four; moisten this with three pints of chicken broth, add an onion with two cloves stuck in, the half of a carrot, and a "bouquet garni;" simmer for an hour, strain the essence through a fine cloth, by twisting it, into a basin, remove carefully all fat, and put by in a cool place for use.

174. ESSENCE OF ANCHOVIES.

Wash, bone, and clean six anchovies; pound them in a mortar with a tablespoonful of capers and one shalot; put these afterwards into a small stewpan with salt, pepper, a little mace, and two tablespoonfuls of mushroom ketchup; simmer for five minutes; then moisten with half a pint of broth; boil it on a brisk fire till reduced by half, and rub it through a tammy into a basin.

When wanted, warm it up in a bain-marie, and add a few drops of lemon juice before serving.

175. ESSENCE OF FISH.

Clean and cut in pieces a pound each of whiting, gurnard, and soles, or any other small fish; put them in a stewpan with two onions stuck with two cloves, a carrot, a "bouquet garni," four shalots, a pint of French white wine; salt and pepper to taste; boil for five minutes, then add three pints of fish broth, boil again over a brisk fire till reduced to half its original quantity, and strain it through a cloth into a basin and put it by for use.

176. MELTED BUTTER SAUCE.

Put a stewpan on the fire with two ounces of butter, mix with it the same quantity of semolina flour, half a pint of cold water, the juice of a lemon, and salt to taste; boil on a moderate fire and stir well with a wooden spoon the while, to make it soft and without clots; as soon as it boils rub it through a fine sieve or tammy cloth, return it to the stewpan on the fire, add a little grated nutmeg, six ounces of butter, and a few drops of lemon-juice; stir, and serve as soon as the butter is properly melted.

This sauce can be improved by adding the yolks of two or three eggs well beaten, diluted with a little hot water passed through a sieve and mixed with the sauce before serving.

177. BUTTER AND KETCHUP SAUCE.

Mix well in a stewpan two or three tablespoonfuls of ketchup sauce with a teacupful of Velouté sauce; set it on the fire and boil for a few minutes; stir occasionally with a wooden spoon, add an ounce of butter, stir again, and serve.

Note.—This sauce can be made in the same way with any other essence.

178. BLANQUETTE SAUCE.

Melt three ounces of butter in a stewpan; mix with it the same quantity of flour and work it into a paste without browning; moisten with a pint of veal broth; stir with a wooden spoon till it boils; then draw by the side of the fire, add a bay-leaf and two small slices of ham, simmer it for an hour; skim and pass it through a sieve into a basin, to be used as wanted.

179. POULETTE SAUCE.

Stir an ounce of flour with the same quantity of butter in a stewpan on the fire for three minutes; then add a pint of white broth, and continue the stirring for fifteen minutes; after which, draw the stewpan away from the fire, thicken the sauce with the yolks of two eggs, season with salt and pepper, add a dozen champignons, sliced in twos or threes, with a gill of the liquor they have been boiled in, stir the sauce over the fire till near the boil, add a small piece of butter, stir again to melt it, and serve.

180. GOOSEBERRY SAUCE.

Clean and blanch for a few minutes in a stewpan one pint of green gooseberries; strain off the water through a colander, rub them in the usual way through a sieve into the stewpan again, add two ounces of butter, boil, stir well, and serve.

181. APPLE SAUCE.

Peel and cut in slices five or six apples; put them in a stewpan with half a pint of water; when cooked and the water entirely consumed, rub them through a sieve; return the purée to the stewpan on the fire, add about a gill of hot water, an ounce of sugar, and half an ounce of butter to it, stir well, and when the whole is properly melted, and mixed together, serve.

182. EGG SAUCE.

Mix in a stewpan on the fire a teacupful of Velouté sauce with three hard-boiled eggs cut in small dice; add a little white pepper and salt to taste, also a little grated nutmeg, together with the juice of half a lemon and a dessert-spoonful of anchovy butter; mix the lot well together by stirring over the fire before serving.

183. BREAD SAUCE.

Pour one pint of fresh cream into a stewpan on a moderate fire, and as soon as it begins to foam and swell draw the stewpan away; then add three ounces of bread-crumbs, a little salt, pepper, grated nutmeg, and an onion; boil for five minutes, take the onion out, add an ounce of butter, stir well, and serve.

Note.—The above is the proper manner to make a bread sauce, but a similar one can be made (although not so good) by substituting milk for cream.

184. HOLLANDAISE SAUCE (DUTCH).

Mix in a stewpan on a moderate fire the yolks of four eggs with three tablespoonfuls of Velouté sauce, a little grated nutmeg, and six ounces of fresh butter; stir this continually, and as the sauce thickens draw it gradually away from the fire to prevent boiling, without ceasing the stirring. When it has assumed a nice soft compact form, and swelling in the stewpan, pour in it two tablespoonfuls of vinegar, a little white pepper, and salt to taste; stir well and pass it through a tammy sieve, and serve quickly, or into a bain-marie to keep hot till wanted.

185. INDIAN SAUCE.

Mix two tablespoonfuls of Allemande sauce in a stewpan with a very small pinch of saffron, three ounces of curry butter, or simply one tablespoonful of curry powder and two ounces of fresh butter, set it on the fire, stir, and when properly mixed, and made hot, serve.

186. OYSTER SAUCE.

Blanch for five minutes two dozen oysters in a gill of white wine, strain the liquor into a small saucepan, mix with it one pint of Velouté sauce and a gill of fish broth if handy, or the same quantity of white stock; boil, stir, and simmer for ten minutes, then add the yolks of two eggs well beaten, stir the contents well, pass it through a tammy sieve into the saucepan again on the fire, season with salt and pepper, squeeze the juice of half a lemon, stir gently, pour the oysters in, stir again, and serve.

187. FINANCIÈRE SAUCE.

Cut in small dice a slice of gammon of about two ounces, shred an onion, mince a few mushrooms and one truffle, put the lot into a stewpan with two ounces of butter, add a small "bouquet garni" with a few peppercorns, fry for a few minutes; then pour in it half a pint of white claret or sherry, cover the stewpan and simmer till reduced to half the original quantity; pass the liquid through a fine-pointed strainer into the stewpan, and set it on the fire; keep the gammon, mushrooms, and truffle apart, add and mix with the liqour a pint of Espagnole sauce, boil on a brisk fire for fifteen minutes, stir well, and pass it through a tammy sieve. Meanwhile put in a small saucepan a gill of white wine, with three spoonfuls of cut truffles, add it to the gammon, mushrooms, and truffle that were kept back; cover the saucepan, boil till reduced by one quarter, and pour it with the other sauce at the moment of serving.

188. SUPRÊME SAUCE.

Put in a stewpan on the fire a pint of Blanquette sauce; when near boiling mix with it a gill of chicken essence; stir well, simmer till the sauce has reached a nice soft consistency, without, however, getting thick; then add a tablespoonful of cream, an ounce of butter, and a few drops of lemon juice; stir, and see that the butter is well melted before serving.

189. RAVIGOTE BUTTER.

Pour into a stewpan on the fire one pint of Velouté sauce with half a pint of broth; boil till reduced by one-third; stir almost constantly, and pass it through a tammy sieve into the stewpan, to which add three ounces of Ravigote butter; set it by the side of the fire; stir for a few seconds, and serve.

190. ROBERT SAUCE.

Shred four onions in small dice, fry them in a stewpan with three ounces of butter; when the onions are nicely browned sprinkle over them an ounce of white flour, stir the lot, and fry for two or three minutes longer; then pour in a gill of vinegar with half a pint of broth or water and an ounce of sugar, boil for a few minutes, then add salt and pepper to taste; stir nicely, and serve with either boiled meat or grilled fowl.

191. HORSE-RADISH SAUCE.

Scrape and mince fine a horse-radish, put it into a stewpan with two tablespoonfuls of flour and half a pint of cream, boil for half an hour, rub it through a sieve into the stewpan and boil it again, season with salt and pepper, add a little milk if necessary, and serve.

192. GHERKIN SAUCE.

Cut six green pickled gherkins in very thin slices, put them in a small stewpan with a few spoonfuls of vinegar and a pinch of pepper, let this boil quickly for a few minutes, then add a gill of Espagnole sauce and the same quantity of veal broth, stir on the fire till it boils, then draw the stewpan by the side of the fire, skim it, and serve.

193. CAPER SAUCE.

Put a teacupful of Allemande sauce into a stewpan, boil it with two tablespoonfuls of broth and an ounce of fresh butter, stir nicely, and pass through a sieve into the stewpan, then pour in two tablespoonfuls of capers, set on the fire, and when nearly boiling, serve.

194. FENNEL SAUCE.

Wash and mince finely half a handful of fennel, put it in a bain-marie in which a teacupful of Allemande sauce has already been set to the boil; add a gill of chicken gravy, an ounce of butter, and the juice of a lemon; mix these well together, and let the bain-marie boil for a few minutes before serving.

195. D'UXELLES SAUCE AND D'UXELLES.

Wash, chop, and press in a cloth one pound of fresh mushrooms or trimmings of tinned champignons, one pound of parsley, and half a pound of shalots; put these in a stewpan with a quarter of a pound of butter, and season with salt and pepper to taste; fry on a brisk fire for six minutes, stirring the while with a wooden spoon; after which, put it by in a jar for future use.

This mixture is called D'Uxelles. The sauce is made by adding two tablespoonfuls of the mixture to a pint of Espagnole sauce.

195a. FINE HERBS.

Mince very fine three small onions, fry these in two ounces of butter, then add a quarter of a pound of fresh mushrooms, similarly minced; continue the frying until dry, mix in the trimmings of two or three truffles, and two or three minutes afterwards add a tablespoonful of finely chopped parsley, previously blanched; mix this well together, and put by in a jar covered with a buttered paper until wanted.

196. VENISON SAUCE.

Stir and mix over the fire half a pint of Espagnole sauce with a gill of essence of game; then add a gill of port wine, the half of that quantity of good French vinegar, and two tablespoonfuls of black currant jelly; boil this for two minutes, add the juice of an orange, pour the sauce into a sauce-boat, and serve.

197. MUSHROOM SAUCE.

Put into a small saucepan half a pint of Espagnole sauce with the same quantity of gravy, simmer till reduced to nearly half, give it an occasional stir, then add about four ounces of champignons nicely sliced (buttons and stalks), pour a little of their liquor with it, boil again for a few minutes, stir the while, season with salt, and serve.

This sauce can be improved by adding a gill of white claret or sherry before serving.

198. TRUFFLES SAUCE.

Cut about two ounces of truffles in very thin slices, put these into a small saucepan with either a glass of white claret, sherry, or Marsala; boil it quickly till reduced to half, then pour into it half a pint of Espagnole and a small pinch of salt; stir on the fire till it has boiled for two or three minutes longer, and serve.

199. SALMIS SAUCE.

Prepare some game essence; mix half a pint of it with one pint of Espagnole sauce into a stewpan, boil for a few minutes, stir occasionally, then pass it through a sieve into the stewpan, and set it by the side of the fire. Meanwhile pound in a mortar the cooked liver of two or three partridges, grouse, or any other winged game; mix it with the sauce, add an ounce of butter, boil it, stirring the while, and serve.

200. HARE SAUCE.

Pour into a stewpan one pint of Espagnole sauce with half a pint of game essence, boil it and stir the while, add four tablespoonfuls of good French vinegar, salt and pepper to taste, stir on the fire again, and when boiling pass it through a sieve, and serve.

201. DEVILLED SAUCE.

Fry in a stewpan with an ounce of butter, one shred onion, and two small slices of ham cut in very small dice; when the onion is nicely browned, moisten it with a gill of good French vinegar, add a small "bouquet garni" a bay-leaf, and a pinch of white pepper; cover the stewpan, and let it simmer till reduced by half. Meantime mix in another small saucepan one pint of Espagnole sauce with half a pint of tomato sauce and one pint of veal broth; boil; stir occasionally till reduced by about one-quarter, then add half an ounce of sugar and the quarter of a teaspoonful of cayenne; stir this well, and mix it with the vinegar in the other stewpan, and after a few minutes of ebullition pass it through a fine tammy sieve; serve the quantity required, and put the remainder by in a cool place, to be warmed up in a bain-marie when wanted.

202. ONION SAUCE.

Peel and blanch in salt water three onions, cut them in slices and fry in a stewpan with an ounce of butter for two or three minutes; rub them afterwards through a wire sieve into the stewpan on the fire, pour half a pint of milk, salt and pepper to taste; stir well, and when nearly boiling serve.

203. CUCUMBER SAUCE.

Put in a stewpan half a pint of Espagnole sauce and the same quantity of gravy, reduce this to half by a quick boiling, then add a cucumber of ordinary size, peeled and cut in thin slices, which must have been previously soaked in vinegar and salt for at least half an hour; sprinkle over it a little more salt and pepper, stir gently, boil it, and serve.

204. ITALIAN SAUCE.

Put two glasses of French white wine into a stewpan with two or three large fresh mushrooms properly cleaned and minced finely; also a small chopped onion, a "bouquet garni," and half a dozen pepper-corns; boil it and simmer till reduced to half. Meanwhile put in another stewpan one pint of Velouté or Espagnole sauce, with a gill of game broth; boil it, and stir for a few minutes; then pour the wine sauce gradually over this, keep stirring, rub it afterwards through a tammy sieve, and add the juice of a lemon before serving.

205. ITALIAN SHARP SAUCE.

Fry in a stewpan with an ounce of butter one shred onion and three ounces of lean ham or gammon, cut in small dice; add a bay-leaf, a little parsley, and moisten with a gill of French vinegar; boil and reduce it to half its quantity; after which, mix with it a pint of Espagnole sauce as well as three spoonfuls of tomato sauce and a little salt and pepper; boil it for a few seconds, stir the while, pass through a tammy sieve into the stewpan again, and complete the sauce by adding two tablespoonfuls of capers, previously pressed in a cloth and minced fine before serving.

206. VENITIAN SAUCE.

Put in a bain-marie on a brisk fire a teacupful of Allemande sauce, a few tarragon-leaves cut diamond-shape, previously blanched and drained, one tablespoonful of good chicken gravy, a little grated nutmeg, and a teaspoonful of tarragon vinegar; mix well together and boil it in the bain-marie for a few minutes before serving.

207. GENOISE SAUCE.

Fry in a stewpan with an ounce or two of butter two tablespoonfuls of olive-oil and an onion cut in slices; moisten with a glass of claret, add a handful each of fresh mushroom trimmings and truffles, a little chopped parsley, and half a bay-leaf, and simmer for about ten minutes. Meantime boil in a stewpan one pint of Espagnole sauce, with half a pint of veal broth and three tablespoonfuls of fish essence till reduced to one-third; after which, add the contents of the first stewpan to it; mix well, skim carefully, boil it again for a few minutes, then rub through a tammy sieve, return it to the stewpan on the fire, add two ounces of crayfish butter and the same quantity of anchovy butter; stir and mix well on the fire till boiling, and then serve.

208. NAPOLITAINE SAUCE.

Fry in a stewpan with an ounce of butter a shred onion, with three ounces of gammon cut in small pieces; moisten with a glass of sherry or Marsala and a teacupful of veal broth; add a few sprigs of thyme, a bay-leaf, a few peppercorns, three cloves, and the trimmings of a few mushrooms well cleaned; boil it; cover the stewpan, and simmer till reduced by one-half. In the meantime pour into another stewpan one pint of Espagnole sauce, the same quantity of tomato sauce, and a gill of game broth; boil this till reduced to one-third, then add the contents of the first stewpan to it; stir well, boil for a few minutes, and rub it through a tammy sieve before serving.

209. ROMAINE SAUCE.

Melt three ounces of sugar in a non-tinned copper pan, add four tablespoonfuls of good vinegar to it, and dilute both with a gill of broth; then add one pint of Espagnole sauce, and stir on the fire till well mixed. Boil, and serve.

210. LOMBARDE SAUCE.

Pour into a stewpan one pint of Blanquette sauce and half a pint of chicken essence, boil it, stir it occasionally, and after ten minutes of slow ebullition add the yolks of three eggs, well beaten and properly mixed with an ounce of melted butter and the juice of a lemon; stir the contents on the fire well, and as soon as it reaches the boil draw the stewpan away from the fire; add to it half a pint of tomato sauce, mix this well together, then rub it through a tammy sieve, and serve.

211. SICILIAN SAUCE.

Chop separately and fine four shalots, two small truffles, a little parsley, and a dozen ordinary mushrooms; put the lot into a small saucepan with a little thyme, a bay-leaf, one clove of garlic, and a small pinch of cayenne; moisten with two glasses of sherry; set to simmer on a slow fire for ten minutes; then add one pint of Allemande sauce; continue the simmering for a few minutes longer, giving it an occasional stir, then add a spoonful of minced parsley, previously blanched, and the juice of half a lemon before serving.

212. LOBSTER SAUCE.

Cut the fleshy part of a small cooked lobster into very small dice, and put them on a plate; pound in a mortar the spawn and coral of the lobster with two ounces of butter and rub it through a sieve; then put in a stewpan half a pint of Velouté sauce with the lobster butter just made, half a gill of good gravy, and a small pinch of cayenne; boil and stir occasionally, add the pieces of cut lobster and the juice of half a lemon, sprinkle a little pepper, and serve.

213. SHRIMP SAUCE.

Make half a pint of melted butter sauce, then add the coral of a small lobster, pounded and mixed with a small pinch of cayenne, a teaspoonful of anchovy essence, eighteen picked shrimps, and the juice of half a lemon, and serve.

214. VICTORIA SAUCE.

Put four tablespoonfuls of red currant jelly in a stewpan with a dozen cloves, a small stick of cinnamon, the peel of two oranges, a gill of good gravy, and half a pint of Espagnole sauce; moisten with half a pint of red wine (Burgundy is best), boil it and simmer for twenty minutes, then pass it through a tammy sieve, add the juice of two oranges, and serve.

Note.—This sauce is generally served with red-deer or roebuck.

215. RED CURRANT JELLY SAUCE.

Break into shreds one stick of cinnamon and twelve cloves, put them into a small stewpan with two ounces of sugar and the peel of a lemon, which must be perfectly free from the white pulp; moisten with three glasses of port wine, then set the lot to simmer on the fire for a quarter of an hour; after which, pass it through a fine-pointed strainer into a stewpan containing six tablespoonfuls of red currant jelly, boil it in order to melt the jelly, by stirring and mixing well before serving.

This sauce is generally served with venison.

216. BUTTER SAUCE FOR ASPARAGUS.

Prepare a butter sauce as directed, then add a gill of cream with a teaspoonful of French vinegar; mix well on the fire, and serve.

This sauce is also served with cauliflower, seakale, &c., &c.

217. TOMATO SAUCE.

Fry in a stewpan with an ounce of butter two ounces of gammon cut in small dice, with half an onion, half a carrot, and a little celery, all shred finely, together with a bay-leaf, a small "bouquet" composed of thyme, cloves, and pepper-corns; moisten with three spoonfuls of good vinegar, set it to simmer till the liquor is almost all absorbed, then pour in a gill of white claret and half a pint of broth; add seven or eight ripe fresh tomatoes cut in pieces, with the seed and water squeezed out of them; let it boil for about twenty minutes with the lid on the pan, give it an occasional stirring, then pass it, by rubbing, through a tammy sieve into the stewpan again on the fire; mix with it a pint of Espagnole, Velouté, or Blanquette sauce; boil, and stir gently to prevent burning, add a tablespoonful of powdered sugar, one ounce of butter, and the juice of half a lemon, mix well together, and serve.

Note.—I give the recipe of this sauce as a matter of course, but strongly advise the use of tinned tomato sauce, as it will be found both cheaper and better, on account of the superiority and cheapness of tomatoes in France and Italy, where they ripen better under a more genial sun than in the hothouses of this country.

COLD SAUCES.

218. MAYONNAISE SAUCE.

Mix in a round-bottomed basin half a pint of Velouté or Blanquette sauce with the same quantity of melted white jelly (No. 150), salt and pepper to taste and a little grated nutmeg; set the basin in a bucket or saucepan containing some broken ice, then proceed to work the sauce with a wooden spoon without stopping, pouring with your left hand, little by little, half a pint of good olive-oil, stirring the while. When the sauce is nicely mounted and has reached its proper consistency add the juice of two lemons and a few sprigs of finely chopped chervil and tarragon, stir, and serve.

219. ANOTHER MAYONNAISE SAUCE.

Put in a similar basin as in No. 218 the yolks of two eggs with salt to taste, and a few drops of lemon-juice;

proceed to work this sauce in the same manner as above with a wooden spoon and by pouring half a pint of good olive-oil, almost drop by drop, into the basin to begin with, till the half of the oil has been properly mixed, then a larger quantity at a time can be poured in. Keep stirring to and fro without stopping till the sauce assumes its proper consistency, then squeeze the juice of quarter of a lemon, and add gradually a gill of good French vinegar; stir the while, and when the sauce is of a nice appearance sprinkle a small pinch of white pepper, the juice of two lemons, a little grated nutmeg, and a few sprigs of chervil chopped finely; mix these ingredients well together, pour it into a sauce-boat, and serve.

220. MAYONNAISE RAVIGOTE SAUCE.

Blanch in boiling salt water for a few minutes a small quantity each of chervil, tarragon, parsley, the white part of a small head of celery, and one shalot; then let them get cold, and pound them in a mortar with four washed and boned anchovies; add three tablespoonfuls of Velouté sauce, rub the lot through a tammy sieve, and at the moment of serving mix it with half the quantity of Mayonnaise sauce previously made as in the preceding number.

Note.—The above Mayonnaise sauces are generally served as a dressing with any kind of cold fish, lobster, or cold fowl.

221. TARTARE SAUCE.

Mince finely a few sprigs each of parsley, chervil, tarragon, and one shalot, as well as the white part of the quarter of a head of celery, three boned anchovies, half a dozen capers, and the rind of half a lemon; put the lot into a cloth and twist it, so as to squeeze the juice out, then mix the minced substance with two or three tablespoonfuls of Mayonnaise sauce (No. 219), to which add one tablespoonful of mustard flour, a pinch of white pepper, and a few drops of lemon-juice before serving.

Note.—This sauce can be served with hot or cold fish as well as meat.

222. REMOULADE SAUCE.

Blanch a small quantity of tarragon, chervil, burnet, and an onion; then chop and pound the lot in a mortar with the yolks of three hard-boiled eggs, add salt and pepper to taste, a spoonful of mustard flour and a little grated nutmeg; pour all into a basin, and add gradually to it, in small quantities, about a gill of good oil; work the compound with a wooden spoon exactly as a Mayonnaise sauce, then pour two tablespoonfuls of French vinegar, continue the stirring till well mixed, when it must be rubbed through a sieve, and served. Cayenne can also be added if liked.

223. MUSTARD SAUCE.

Pour four tablespoonfuls of mustard flour into a basin with a little salt, dilute it with a gill of boiling water, stir the while to prevent clotting, add two tablespoonfuls of vinegar; stir, and see that the sauce is smooth before serving.

224. HORSE-RADISH SAUCE.

Cut in very small dice the root of an ordinary horse-radish, pound it in a mortar, then mix it with one ounce of powdered sugar and one of grated bread-crumbs, moisten with vinegar, pass through a sieve, put it into a basin, dilute with more vinegar, and serve.

225. MINT SAUCE.

Put in a basin two ounces of brown sugar with two tablespoonfuls of fresh green mint, chopped fine, and half a pint of vinegar, mix well, and as soon as the sugar is dissolved, serve.

226. MAÎTRE D'HÔTEL BUTTER.

Put about two ounces of butter on a plate with a little chopped parsley, pepper, salt, and the juice of half a lemon, knead the lot well together, and serve.

This butter is used for kidneys, steaks, cutlets, broiled fish of all kinds, &c., &c.

227. CALF'S FOOT JELLY (PLAIN).

Scrape, clean, and cut in pieces four calf's feet, put them in an ordinary saucepan with three quarts of water on a good fire, boil for about four hours, pay proper attention to the skimming, then strain through a hair sieve into an earthenware basin, remove all particles of fat with a sheet of blotting or kitchen paper, and place it on a shelf in a cool place. When cold wash the top of the jelly with a clean cloth dipped in boiling water.

This plain jelly may be the foundation of all wine, fruit, and liqueur jellies when gelatine is not used, and can be kept good for a long time if boiled every day.

CHAPTER IV.

PURÉES OF VEGETABLES FOR GARNISHING, ETC.

228. PURÉE OF TOMATOES.

Cut a dozen fresh ripe tomatoes in slices, squeeze the water out of them and put them into a stewpan on a slow fire, with half a pint of broth, a "bouquet garni," and two slices of gammon; simmer till the liquid is nearly consumed, then add a gill of Velouté or Blanquette sauce, stir and mix all well together on the fire, then rub it through a sieve into a bain-marie to be kept hot till wanted.

229. PURÉE À LA SOUBISE.

Peel, cut, and blanch for ten minutes in boiling salt water six medium-sized onions; strain and squeeze the water out of them; place these afterwards in a stewpan with an ounce of butter and three small slices of gammon, fry for five minutes on a slow fire, then add a gill of chicken broth with a pinch of white pepper; let them simmer for half an hour, pour in a gill of Béchamel sauce, stir occasionally, and simmer again for five minutes; after which, rub through a sieve into a bain-marie, and at the moment of serving throw in a lump of sugar.

Note.—Should there be no Béchamel sauce made, a tablespoonful of semolina flour, diluted in a gill of cream, will be a good substitute for it.

230. PURÉE OF VEGETABLES.

Slice the red part of four carrots, two turnips, one onion, two leeks, and two heads of celery; wash and strain the lot properly, then pour them into a stewpan with three ounces of butter, fry till of a nice brown colour; add to it half a pint of broth in which two or three slices of crumb of bread have been soaking, together with a little each of sugar, white pepper, and grated nutmeg; boil on a good fire till the vegetables are well cooked, then pound them in a mortar, and return the purée to the stewpan, with half a pint of Espagnole sauce and a tablespoonful of essence of chicken, boil again for a few minutes, and pass through a sieve in the usual way before serving.

231. PURÉE OF POTATOES.

Peel, wash, and cut in slices two pounds of potatoes; cook them in a saucepan with a little salt water. When cooked, strain off the water through a colander and return the potatoes into the saucepan with four ounces of butter, a little sugar, and half a pint of cream or milk; stir well on the fire, and boil, then rub through a sieve into the saucepan again, add a little more butter, together with a gill of hot chicken gravy, mix well on the fire, and serve.

232. PURÉE OF GREEN PEAS.

Cook in plenty of salt water with a few branches of mint one quart of fresh shelled peas in a covered stewpan. When cooked, strain off the water through a colander, throw the mint away, pound the peas in a mortar or rub them through a sieve, return the purée to the stewpan with two ounces of butter, half a pint of Béchamel sauce or good gravy, and a piece of sugar, mix well, set to the boil, and serve.

233. PURÉE OF DRY PEAS.

Soak in plenty of water a quart of dry peas for about ten hours, strain off the water in which the peas have soaked, boil them as in No. 232, but with less salt, add a "bouquet garni," a piece of sugar, pepper, grated nutmeg, and a slice of the crumb of bread. When well cooked, strain off the water, throw the "bouquet" away, pound the peas and bread in a mortar, return the purée to the stewpan on the fire, add a gill of Espagnole sauce; stir and mix well, set to the boil, pass through a sieve in the usual way, and serve.

234. PURÉE OF LENTILS.

Proceed for this purée exactly as for the purée of dry peas.

235. PURÉE OF TURNIPS.

Fry in butter eight large turnips, cut in small slices, after having been blanched in the usual way for five minutes; then add a gill of veal broth or some good gravy, a piece of sugar, and two slices of crumb of bread, boil gently till well cooked, skim it carefully, and pound it in a mortar; return the purée to the stewpan with half a pint of Béchamel sauce; stir well, and boil, then pass it through a sieve into the stewpan, and just before serving add half a gill of hot gravy with an ounce of butter, stir well on the fire till mixed, and serve.

236.

Celery, Carrots, French Beans, Endive, Cauliflower, and Spinach are made into purées in the same manner as the above.

237. PURÉE OF CHESNUTS.

Cook and peel two pounds of chesnuts in the same way as in No. 51, but finishing the cooking in water instead of broth; then strain and pound them in a mortar, return the purée to the stewpan on the fire with half a pint of Espagnole sauce, stir, and boil; rub the purée through a sieve into the stewpan again on the fire, add an ounce of butter and a gill of cream, mix well whilst on the fire, and when hot serve.

238. PURÉE OF SORREL.

Pick and wash well in two or three waters three pounds of sorrel; drain off the water; melt in a stewpan two ounces of butter, put the sorrel in and cover the stewpan on the fire for a few minutes; stir afterwards with a wooden spoon on the fire till the sorrel is soft or melted, when it must be turned over into a hair sieve to drain. Meanwhile fry in the same stewpan with two ounces of butter an onion shred very fine, till of a nice brown colour; then add a tablespoonful of flour, a little grated nutmeg, a tablespoonful of brown sugar, salt and pepper to taste; stir on the fire for a few seconds; after which, moisten with a gill of Espagnole sauce, add the sorrel from the sieve, simmer till well reduced and the sorrel turned into a purée, taking care to stir it with a wooden spoon the whole time; then rub it through a tammy sieve in the usual way, and serve hot, garnished with croûtons and a spoonful of good gravy poured over it.

239. PURÉE OF JERUSALEM ARTICHOKES.

Proceed for this purée exactly in the same manner as for the purée of potatoes, taking the same quantity of artichokes, substituting them for potatoes.

REMARKS ON EGGS.

New-laid eggs are absolutely necessary for good cooking. They are as nourishing as their equivalent weight in meat, and more digestible, and, like rice, they can be prepared in many different ways. They are served in soups as well as in made dishes, and are appreciated in salads as well as in sweet dishes and omelets, besides being constantly used in sauces, paste, pastry, liaisons, &c., &c.

The freshness of eggs can easily be ascertained by immersing them gently one after the other in a basinful of cold water; those lying flat at the bottom are quite fresh, those remaining perpendicular are not, and the eggs that float or swim are bad. Thus any one can tell the different ages of, say, a dozen eggs without fear of a mistake, and I strongly advise every one to always try them in this way before breaking them.

240. BOILED EGGS.

Place the number of eggs required to be cooked into a ladle in boiling water for three minutes in summer and half a minute longer in winter, and serve in egg-cups.

241. EGGS WITH BROWN OR BLACK BUTTER.

For each couple of eggs required put a piece of butter as big as a walnut into a frying-pan on the fire; let the butter boil, then break the eggs in the middle, by a gentle knock on the border of the pan (after having tried their freshness as indicated), and drop them gently in, without breaking the yolks; sprinkle a little salt and pepper on each, fry for about three minutes and remove them carefully on a dish with a flat strainer, and keep hot; return the frying-pan to the fire with half an ounce of butter (for each two eggs), and fry this butter till it is nearly black; then add a dessert-spoonful of French vinegar for each half-ounce of butter, with a sprig of parsley chopped fine; pour it over the eggs, and serve.

242. EGGS FRIED.

Melt half an ounce of butter in a frying pan, and when boiling break two eggs, drop them gently into the frying-pan; season with salt and pepper, and when the whites get firm and begin to brown, serve on a hot dish.

243. EGGS WITH CREAM AND BUTTER.

Put about a quarter of an ounce of butter in a small flat enamelled pan, on the fire, with a gill of cream, a little salt and pepper for every two eggs broken, as in the foregoing. Meantime have red-hot a salamander or iron shovel, hold it over the pan on the fire for two minutes, so that the contents are being cooked on the top as well as at the bottom of the pan at the same time; and then serve quickly.

Note.—Eggs cooked in enamelled pans should always be sent to the table in them, on plates.

244. EGGS AU PLAT.

Put a quarter of an ounce of butter into a small enamelled pan as in No. 243; let the butter melt on a moderate fire, then break two eggs and drop them into the pan without disturbing the yolks; let them simmer gently till the whites get firm, season with salt and pepper, put the pan in a hot oven for half a minute, and serve.

245. POACHED EGGS.

Put a quart of boiling water into a sauté-pan with a gill of vinegar and a good pinch of salt; when the water boils, break the number of eggs required to be poached and drop gently one by one into the boiling water; as soon as the whites get firm, take them out with a flat skimmer and place gently on a clean cloth, trim the whites with a knife, and serve either on plain toast, anchovy toast, with slices of bacon or purées, minced meat, &c., &c.

246. EGGS AU PLAT WITH TOMATOES.

Peel, slice, and squeeze the water out of a fresh tomato; put half an ounce of butter into a small enamelled pan on the fire; when the butter is melted, break and drop two eggs into it, with the slices of tomato; season well with salt and pepper, cook till the whites get firm, and then put the pan in the oven for one minute, and serve.

247. EGGS À LA TRIPE.

Boil ten eggs for ten minutes, immerse them afterwards in cold water for a few minutes to get cold, take them out, roll each one after the other on the table to break the shells, which remove with your fingers. Cut them in thick round slices and put into a stewpan. Cut two onions in slices so as to leave them in rings; blanch in salt water for a few minutes; strain and place in a stewpan with a gill of veal broth; boil and simmer till cooked; then pour them over the eggs with half a pint of Béchamel sauce, the clove of a garlic chopped very fine, a little nutmeg, salt and pepper to taste, and the juice of a lemon. Set the stewpan on the fire, toss the lot to prevent burning, and as soon as the eggs are made hot, dish up nicely interwoven with the rings of onion and some slices of bread cut the same shape fried in butter, and serve.

248. EGGS BROUILLÉS WITH ASPARAGUS-POINTS.

Break and beat eight eggs into a stewpan with a tablespoonful of grated cheese, three ounces of butter, a gill of cream or milk, and salt and pepper to taste. Set the stewpan on a moderate fire, stirring all the time with a wooden spoon, and occasionally shake and toss the stewpan to prevent the contents from attaching itself to the bottom of the pan. When the eggs begin to thicken draw the stewpan by the side of the fire, add twenty small asparagus previously cooked, strained, and cut in small points; continue to work the eggs and mix with the asparagus-points until the eggs are nicely set, but not hard. Then pour into a hot dish and decorate with croûtons cut triangle-shape, and fried in butter before serving.

Note.—The same thing can be made with chopped parsley, green peas, mushrooms, truffles, tomatoes, bacon and ham cut in small dice, taking care to previously cook the vegetables in the usual way, or to fry the ham or bacon in butter before mixing with the eggs.

249. EGGS WITH SAUCE.

Boil eight eggs in water for ten or twelve minutes, dip in cold water and shell them, cut each egg into halves lengthwise, and place with taste on a hot dish, and put the dish in the open oven. Meanwhile have ready boiling half a pint of either butter, Ravigote, Blanquette, or any other sauce that may be fancied, and pour it over the eggs, and serve.

250. EGGS AU GRATIN.

Boil eight or ten eggs hard; dip them into cold water; shell and cut in slices; put these by on a plate. Put half a pint of Blanquette sauce into a stewpan, boil it and let it simmer for ten minutes, giving it an occasional stir; then add half an ounce of butter, two ounces of grated cheese, a little grated nutmeg, pepper and salt to taste, the juice of half a lemon, and the yolks of three eggs; stir the lot quickly over the fire till it begins to thicken, when the stewpan must be drawn away from the fire. Then take a gratin-dish, put the eggs in close circular rows in it, spread some of the mixture out of the stewpan, over and between each layer, observing that the dishing-up must be in the form of a dome; smooth the surface over with the remainder of the sauce, sprinkle a handful of bread-crumbs mixed with the same quantity of grated cheese over the top; decorate the base of the eggs with triangular croûtons fried in butter, set the dish in a hot oven to gratinate for about ten minutes, and serve.

251. EGGS À LA DAUPHINE.

Boil twelve eggs hard, plunge them in cold water, take the shells off and cut each egg into halves, scoop the yolks out and put in a mortar, place the whites on a dish and keep hot; add to the yolks a quarter of a pound of butter, about two ounces of the crumb of bread soaked in cream, a tablespoonful of chopped parsley, a little grated nutmeg, two ounces of grated cheese, season with salt and pepper, and pound the whole well together. Add one raw egg and the yolks of two others, mix these well together by pounding again, then take this compound with a dessertspoon, and fill up each white part of the eggs with it, and smooth each one over with the blade of a small knife dipped in water. Having thus filled the whites of the eggs, spread the remainder of the mixture on the bottom of a gratin dish, then proceed to build up the eggs in three or four tiers in a pyramidal form. Rub through a wire sieve the yolks of four hard-boiled eggs, by holding the sieve over the dish so that the shreds like vermicelli may fall direct on and around the eggs, or form afterwards a border round the base of the dish with croûtons fried in butter. Set the dish in the oven for about twenty minutes or till the eggs are of a bright yellow colour, then pour a little hot white sauce round, and serve.

252. EGGS À L'AURORE.

Boil ten eggs hard, remove the shells, and cut each into halves lengthwise, take the yolks carefully out and place them on a dish, shred the whites in fine strips, put these into a stewpan with a sauce composed of half a pint of béchamel mixed with a little lobster butter, the yolks of two eggs, a tablespoonful of tarragon vinegar, and a small pinch of cayenne; toss the strips in the stewpan over the fire until quite hot, then put a layer into the centre of a hot dish with a border of croûtons fried in butter, previously stuck round the bottom of the dish, sprinkle a handful of grated cheese over it, and rub the yolks of eggs put apart through a wire sieve, in the same manner as in No. 251; make another layer of the whites and sauce, then shake again a little grated cheese and shreds of yolk, and so on, till the lot is used up, finishing with the yolks of eggs in shreds. Set the dish in the oven till it has attained a bright yellow colour, and serve.

253. PLAIN OMELET WITH PARSLEY.

Break six eggs into a basin; add one tablespoonful of finely chopped parsley, with salt and pepper to taste; beat the contents well with a fork; meantime melt in a clean frying-pan (size, 7 inches) two ounces of butter, and as soon as the butter begins to fritter pour the egg-mixture into it, taking care to beat it whilst it is being poured in; then stir gently on the fire with the right hand, and give an occasional shake and toss to the pan with left; when the omelet begins to get firm and is partially set, roll over the extremity nearest to the handle with the fork, do the same thing on the opposite side, to give it an oval form, allowing it at the same time to acquire a golden colour on the outside, or side touching the frying-pan. When properly cooked, take a hot oval dish with the left hand, turn the omelet over on to it from the pan, which is held by the right hand almost perpendicular against the dish, and serve.

Although omelets are very simple and easily made, nothing but practice, combined with knowledge and attention, will teach the cook how to ensure success in their preparation. A proper omelet-pan should always be kept for the purpose. The eggs should never be overbeaten, as by so doing a watery mixture is produced, which will sometimes destroy the taste as well as the appearance. And lastly, never attempt to make an omelet with more than fourteen eggs; if more are wanted, it is better to make two small than one large, which is generally difficult to cook properly.

254. OMELET WITH HAM OR BACON.

Beat six eggs in the same way as in No. 253, with or without parsley, and very little salt. Then cut in small dice two slices of either ham, gammon, or bacon (if raw, fry in butter for a few minutes). Melt in a frying-pan two ounces of butter, and when boiling pour into it the eggs beaten as above; stir in the same manner. Mix the pieces of ham or bacon with it, and as soon as cooked fold in same style and serve as described in the foregoing.

255. OMELET WITH ONION.

Peel and slice two onions; fry them in a frying-pan with two ounces of butter till nicely browned; meanwhile beat six eggs into a basin, and add salt and pepper to taste. When the onions are properly browned add a little more butter to the frying-pan, then pour the mixture of eggs into it, stir in the usual way, fold, and serve.

256. OMELET WITH TOMATOES.

Peel, cut in slices, and squeeze the water out of three tomatoes, fry them in a frying-pan with two ounces of butter for a few minutes, and sprinkle a little salt and pepper over them. Meantime break and beat six eggs, with salt and pepper, into a basin as before; melt two ounces of butter in the frying-pan, pour the eggs in and stir in the usual way, and when nearly cooked draw the pan away from the fire, spread the tomatoes over the omelet, push the pan over the fire again, fold as before, and serve.

257. OMELET WITH FISH.

Cut in small pieces, properly boned, any cooked fish that may remain from the previous day's dinner; fry it in a frying-pan with a little butter. Meanwhile prepare an omelet in the usual way, mix the fish with it, fold, and serve.

258. OMELET WITH KIDNEYS.

Procure two or three sheep's kidneys; take the skin off and cut them in thin slices; put these into a stewpan, moisten with Espagnole sauce or good gravy, sprinkle with salt and pepper to taste, add half a glass of sherry, and let them simmer till cooked. Meanwhile prepare an omelet with six or eight eggs, spread the kidneys over it when cooked, sprinkle a little finely-chopped parsley, fold, and serve. A few slices of mushrooms added to the kidneys will improve the omelet.

259. OMELET WITH ARTICHOKE.

Blanch and cut in small quarters, the hearts of three or four artichokes, fry them in butter for a few minutes, and proceed to mix with the omelet as for the tomatoes.

260. OMELET WITH CHEESE.

Beat six eggs in the usual way with salt and pepper; add four tablespoonfuls of grated cheese, then proceed with this as in other omelets, and when on the dish sprinkle a little more grated cheese on the top with a spoonful of good gravy, and serve.

261. OMELET WITH CHEESE, No. 2.

Beat six eggs into a basin with a gill of cream; salt and pepper to taste, with two tablespoonfuls of grated cheese; shred very fine two ounces of Gruyère cheese; then proceed with the omelet in all respects like the others, and when nearly cooked draw the pan from the fire, spread the Gruyère cheese over it, return the pan to the fire, fold nicely, and serve.

262. OMELET WITH OYSTERS.

Proceed and finish this omelet in the same manner as the foregoing, merely substituting oysters, prepared as for scallops, instead of cheese.

263. OMELET PIEMONTAISE OR FONDU.

Put the yolks of six eggs into a saucepan; beat them well with a gill of cream and two ounces of butter; cut in small dice one pound of Gruyère cheese, put the half of it into the saucepan with the eggs, set the pan on a moderate fire, stir gently till the cheese begins to melt; then add the remainder of the cheese to it; continue stirring, but very slowly, and do not let it boil. When properly worked and of the consistency of a Béchamel sauce, pour it into a hot dish, and serve with a few slices of truffles spread on the top of it.

264.

Omelets can also be made with spinach, sorrel, peas, asparagus, mushrooms (fresh and tinned), truffles, brains, giblets, &c., &c. The process of their composition is always the same, only varying in the cooking of the different ingredients required to put with it.

Note.—For all sweet omelets, snow eggs, &c., see Sweets.

265. BREAD PANADA.

Soak about half a pound of the crumb of stale bread in tepid water for a quarter of an hour; then put it on a cloth, fold, and wring it tightly to squeeze the water out; after which, turn it into a stewpan with half a pint of white broth, set the stewpan on the fire and simmer till the broth is completely reduced, stirring all the time with a wooden spoon till the contents assume the consistency of a thick paste; then add an ounce of butter, continue stirring for a few seconds, pour it into a plate and store it away in the larder ready for use.

266. RICE PANADA.

Put three ounces of rice into a saucepan, soak it with half a pint of white broth for about fifteen minutes; set it on the fire and boil gently, without stirring, for another fifteen minutes; add an ounce of butter, stir well on the fire for five minutes, rub the rice through a sieve, spread it on a plate, and put it in a cool place for future use.

267. SEMOLINA PANADA.

Put in a stewpan half a pint of white broth with one and a half ounce of butter; boil; draw the stewpan away from the fire, sprinkle into it four ounces of semolina flour, stir gently by the side of the fire till the semolina is nicely dried up, then turn it into a plate and put by, like the previous panada.

268. BREAD-RASPINGS.

Save the pieces of stale bread, put them in a tin dish in the oven over-night to dry until next morning, then pound in a mortar, pass through a fine wire sieve, and put in a tin box for use.

269. BREADINGS.

For breadings, beat two eggs on a plate, and mix well with a tablespoonful of oil and a little salt and pepper. Rub through a wire sieve a few pieces of crumb of stale bread, put it in a tin dish in the oven to dry and get a bright golden colour, and then turn it into a closed box for use.

CHAPTER V.

FORCEMEAT—GARNISHING IN GENERAL—AND SALPICON.

FORCEMEAT is a mixture of fat or lean meat, chicken, game, or fish, and the necessary seasoning, all well pounded together. These are very useful in cookery, and turned to good account for "hors-d'œuvres" and "gratins," as well as for garnishing fish, entrées, &c., &c., when made into quenelles.

270. VEAL FORCEMEAT.

Clean, peel, and cook four potatoes.; put in a stewpan with an ounce of butter, and mash them properly; turn the purée into a dish, and place the dish on the ice if in warm weather, or in a cool place in winter. Meantime cut in small pieces, six ounces of a cushion of veal, and three ounces of the udder of veal. Melt one ounce of butter in a stewpan, and fry these till nicely browned; moisten with a few tablespoonfuls of broth; let them simmer till the lot is cooked and well glazed; add three ounces of chopped calf's liver; simmer for six minutes longer, and draw it away from the fire; let it get cold; after which, pound it in a mortar with one pound of raw flesh of veal, free from skin and sinew and chopped fine; then add to it the mashed potatoes; season with salt and pepper; sprinkle a little grated nutmeg, with one tablespoonful of Béchamel sauce and three eggs well beaten;

PRACTICAL HOUSEHOLD COOKERY. 125

rub the mixture through a wire sieve into a basin, and put it in a cool place ready for use, either for quenelles or stuffing.

270a. ANOTHER VEAL STUFFING.

Chop fine half a pound each, of veal and bacon, both free from skin, gristle, and rind; season well with salt, pepper, a little allspice, and grated nutmeg; add six sage-leaves well chopped, a teaspoonful of marjoram, and four blanched and finely-shred onions; pound these well together in a mortar, and place it in a stewpan with two ounces of melted butter; stir the contents over the fire for about eight minutes, then add the yolks of four well-beaten eggs, and continue the stirring and mixing for two or three minutes longer, when the stuffing is ready for use.

271. CHICKEN FORCEMEAT FOR QUENELLES.

Proceed for this forcemeat as in the previous number; glaze the boned meat of a chicken in the same manner, but add the chicken's liver five minutes sooner; then pound and pass it through a sieve in the same way.

272. ANOTHER CHICKEN FORCEMEAT.

Pound in a mortar half a pound of raw chicken-breast, free from skin and fat; add to it three spoonfuls of cold Béchamel sauce, the white of an egg, season with salt and a little nutmeg, rub it through a sieve with a little panada, and put by ready for use.

273. GAME FORCEMEAT.

Follow the same instructions for this forcemeat as for the veal, but substitute three ounces of fat bacon or ham for the udder and hare-flesh or venison instead of veal, and when browning in butter add a glass of sherry or Marsala and a bay-leaf, which must be taken out of the stewpan and thrown away; when the meat is cooked, then pound it in the mortar, pass it through a wire sieve, and store away as before.

274. CALF'S LIVER FORCEMEAT.

Cut in small slices half a pound of fresh calf's liver, wash in water, and dry them afterwards with a cloth; fry them in a stewpan with an ounce of butter for a few minutes; moisten with veal broth and simmer till the liver is well cooked; pour the contents in a mortar, and let it get cold; then pound it with a truffle cut in dice, half a pound of raw liver, cleaned as aforesaid, one pound of mashed potatoes, the yolks of three eggs and a whole one; salt, pepper, and nutmeg to taste. When well pounded and mixed together rub it through a wire sieve into a basin, and put by in a cool place.

275. RAW FISH FORCEMEAT.

Clean, cut, and bone about one pound of either cod, turbot, sole, whiting, pike, brill, or any other fish that may be had; pound these raw pieces in a mortar, add six ounces of panada, the yolks of four eggs, and a quarter of a pound of butter, and season with salt and grated nutmeg. When the lot is well pounded together rub it through a wire sieve into a basin, then mix it with two tablespoonfuls of Velouté sauce, and put it in a cool place ready to be made into quenelles.

276. ANOTHER FISH FORCEMEAT.

Prepare one pound and a half of fish as in No. 275; fry the half of it in a stewpan with three ounces of butter and two shalots, chopped fine, for six or eight minutes; stir the while to give it a good turn all round; after which, let it get cold. Then pound it in a mortar, with the other half of raw fish, add six ounces of mashed potatoes and one ounce of butter to it, season with salt, pepper, and grated nutmeg, and complete the mixture with an ounce of grated cheese sprinkled over it, and three eggs well beaten. When the whole is well pounded and properly mixed, rub it through a wire sieve into a basin, and keep it in a cool place till wanted.

277. LOBSTER FORCEMEAT.

Shell the meat out of one or two cooked lobsters, cut in small dice, and pound it well in a mortar with two ounces of butter; add four ounces of panada, three ounces of butter, three eggs well beaten, a spoonful of Allemande sauce, a small pinch of cayenne, salt, and grated nutmeg to taste, and about half a pound of mashed potatoes; pound the lot properly, and mix it well in the mortar. Rub it through a wire sieve with a wooden spoon, in the usual way, into a basin, and put it by in a cool place till wanted.

Note.—Forcemeat should be used the same day it is made, especially fish forcemeat.

The proper mode of forming forcemeat into quenelles for soups is as follows:—Make a paper funnel, put some of the forcemeat in it, close the top by folding the paper down, so as to enclose the forcemeat, cut the point of the funnel to the size required to shape the quenelles, and squeeze the forcemeat out upon a sauté-pan previously buttered, taking care to keep some of the forcemeat in the funnel, in order to enable you to put some more stuffing into it, without being compelled to make another funnel. These quenelles, however, must differ in this much, that those made for soups should be smaller and lighter than those intended for garnishing entrées and other dishes.

REMARKS ON GARNISHING IN GENERAL, AND ON TRUFFLES AND MUSHROOMS IN PARTICULAR.

Garnishing in cookery is principally made of vegetables, prepared and cooked in different ways, and like sauces, plays a great part in high-class cookery. In my attempt, however, to give a great variety, the fact must not be lost sight of, that the majority of them are within everybody's reach, as they include vegetables in general use, cooked with the meat and served around it.

The most expensive item in a garnish is the truffle, a kind of tuber very highly appreciated on account of its aromatic flavour. The months in which it is at its best are November, December, and January; but it can, nevertheless, be obtained nearly all the year round.

The best truffles imported fresh into this country are black, and come from Perigord (France), but unless properly surrounded by mould from which they have been dug, they are subject to lose their very fragrance which endears them so much to epicures. The white Piedmontese truffles have a very high reputation for delicacy, scent, and flavour, but (unhappily for English epicures) they cannot bear a long journey or perhaps such a change of climate.

The use of preserved truffles cannot be advocated, as their original perfume is nearly all lost. There are in this country plenty of fresh mushrooms, gathered daily in fields

PRACTICAL HOUSEHOLD COOKERY.

and woods for about eight months in the year, that might be turned to better advantage, and be in many instances a very good substitute for tinned truffles.

278. GARNISH OF CHESNUTS.

Peel off the first skin of fifty chesnuts, boil the chesnuts in water for five or six minutes, strain off the water, remove the second skin, and fry them in a sauté-pan with two ounces of butter for a few minutes; after which, add half a pint of good broth, let them simmer till cooked, giving an occasional toss to the pan, and when glazed all round, serve with a roast turkey or goose.

279. GARNISH OF LETTUCES.

Plainly cooked as well as stuffed lettuces are served as a garnish with or without being glazed. In either case cook the lettuces as directed in soups 42 and 43.

280. GARNISH OF GLAZED ONIONS.

Peel a dozen small onions of a similar size; put them in a well-buttered sauté-pan with nearly a pint of good broth and a little sugar, let them simmer gently by the side of the fire, taking care to often turn the onions over, so as to give them an even colour all round, and when well glazed and properly cooked, serve them with braized meat.

281. GARNISH OF MACEDOINE BÉCHAMEL.

Blanch in the usual way in separate waters two carrots, three turnips, twenty-five asparagus-heads, a good handful each of peas and French beans, and three branches off the top of a cauliflower; strain off the different waters, cut the carrots and turnips in small fancy shapes, the French beans and asparagus in small diamonds; put the whole in a sauté-pan with half a pint of Béchamel sauce, two tablespoonfuls of chicken gravy, two ounces of butter, a piece of sugar, and a little grated nutmeg; set the sauté-pan on the fire, simmer gently till the vegetables are properly glazed, then serve with veal cutlets, &c.

282. GARNISH OF CELERY.

Clean and cut in pieces of about half an inch long, four large heads of celery; blanch these in boiling salt water for five minutes, strain, and immerse in cold water, and lay them on a cloth. When nicely dried put them in a sauté-pan with half a pint of broth, an ounce of butter, a piece of sugar, a little grated nutmeg, and salt to taste; boil, and then simmer for about an hour; add two tablespoonfuls of chicken gravy, see that the celery gets properly glazed, and serve.

Note.—If this garnish is required for poultry, add some Béchamel sauce and a gill of cream.

283. GARNISH OF NEW CARROTS.

Turn into pear-shape a bunch of new carrots, keeping them as much as possible of the same size; blanch for three or four minutes, strain the water, and put them in a sauté-pan with an ounce of butter, a pinch of salt, and a little sugar; moisten with half a pint of good broth; let the sauté-pan boil, simmer to a nice glaze, taking care to roll the carrots in it, and when ready use them to garnish the intended dish.

284. GARNISH OF TURNIPS.

Peel six turnips, cut or turn them into fancy shapes, boil for five minutes in salt water, drain, and when dried throw them into a sauté-pan with an ounce of butter, a pinch of salt, and a small piece of sugar; moisten with half a pint of veal broth, let the pan boil, and when nearly cooked boil quickly down to a glaze, without letting the turnips acquire much colour, and serve as a garnish.

285. GARNISH OF CUCUMBER.

Peel two or three cucumbers; cut them in slices of the thickness of half a crown; put them in a large dish, sprinkle over a tablespoonful of salt, and moisten with vinegar; let them remain in this pickle for about two hours; after which, strain on a sieve and place in a sauté-pan with half an ounce of butter, half a pint of good broth, and a piece of sugar; set the pan to simmer gently for half an hour, then boil quickly to a glaze; when well done, add half a pint of either Béchamel, Allemande, or Suprême sauce, as the case may be.

286. GARNISH OF STEWED PEAS.

Blanch a quart of new peas for five or six minutes, drain and put them into a stewpan with four ounces of fresh butter, a little sugar, a pinch of salt, an onion, and a small faggot composed of mint and spring onions. Set the stewpan, with the cover on, on a moderate fire for the peas to stew, and when cooked boil quickly for a few minutes in order that they may absorb all their moisture; then add a spoonful of Béchamel sauce, with a little butter, and dish them up with any entrée.

287. GARNISH OF ASPARAGUS-POINTS.

Cut the points of as many asparagus as may be required, boil them in salt water and strain through a colander; when dried, throw them in a sauté-pan with an ounce of butter or a spoonful of Allemande sauce, a little sugar, nutmeg, and a tablespoonful of good gravy; toss them gently over the fire, and serve.

288. GARNISH OF BUTTON ONIONS FOR MATELOTTE.

Peel a pint of button onions; blanch in salt water for five minutes; strain and put them in a sauté-pan with two ounces of clarified butter and a little pounded sugar. Set the sauté-pan on a moderate fire, to fry the onions to a light-brown colour, taking care to toss them up now and then, that they may be equally coloured; when they are nearly done place on a sieve to drain the butter off, return them afterwards to a small stewpan with a gill of broth, boil on a brisk fire, and reduce to a glaze before serving.

289. GARNISH OF BROAD BEANS.

Boil till cooked one quart of fresh Windsor beans, peel off their skin and place them in a sauté-pan with a pinch of pepper, salt, and nutmeg, half an ounce of butter, a spoonful of Béchamel sauce, and the same quantity of blanched and chopped parsley; shake and toss the lot well together on the fire, and serve in the centre of an entrée.

290. GARNISH OF FRENCH BEANS.

Cut a pound of French beans in diamond-shape pieces, boil them in salt water, strain, and put in a stewpan with an ounce of butter, a pinch of pepper, salt to taste, a spoonful of white sauce, and a little lemon-juice; toss the lot well together on the fire, and serve as above.

291. GARNISH OF BRUSSELS SPROUTS.

Pick and wash one pint of Brussels sprouts, boil them in plenty of salt water till well done, strain and toss in a sauté-pan with two ounces of butter, a small pinch of pepper, a tablespoonful of white sauce, a little grated nutmeg, and the juice of half a lemon, and serve.

292. GARNISH OF CAULIFLOWER.

Cut the cauliflowers into small heads, dip in salt water for half an hour, then blanch them in the usual way; drain and boil in another saucepan with salt and a little butter, and moisten with white broth.

Cauliflowers for garnishing should not be too much cooked; if so, they break in the dishing-up.

293. GARNISH OF JERUSALEM ARTICHOKES.

Peel a dozen Jerusalem artichokes, cut in fancy shapes, immerse in cold water to wash them well, then strain and put them in a stewpan with half an ounce of butter, half a pint of white broth, a little sugar and salt to taste. Boil for about twenty minutes, reduce down to a glaze, add a spoonful or two of Béchamel or Allemande sauce, toss over the fire well together, and serve.

294. GARNISH OF WHITE HARICOT BEANS.

Take a pint of white haricot beans that have been soaking in water the whole of the previous night; place these in a stewpan with two quarts of cold water and a little salt; let boil, and simmer gently by the side of the fire for about an hour, strain them through a colander, put them in a sauté-pan with an ounce of butter, two tablespoonfuls of white sauce, salt and pepper to taste, the juice of half a lemon, and a spoonful of blanched and chopped parsley; shake and toss the lot well together on the fire, and serve.

295. GARNISH OF BRAIZED CABBAGES.

Trim, wash, and thoroughly cleanse two good Savoy cabbages; cut them in halves and boil them in water for fifteen minutes; immerse them in cold water, then drain and dry them with a cloth; after which, cut the stalks away, season them with salt and pepper, and tie the two halves together with a string; cover the bottom of a stewpan with six slices of fat bacon, place the cabbages on them, with a carrot, an onion stuck with three cloves, and a "bouquet garni;" moisten with enough broth to cover the cabbages, and spread a buttered round of paper over the whole; let the stewpan boil, cover the stewpan with the lid, and let it simmer by the side of the fire for about an hour; then drain the cabbages on a sieve, remove the string, press the cabbages gently with a dish or board so as to make the top flat and enable them to be cut afterwards into square, oblong, round, or oval shapes, according to fancy or taste, and with them garnish the dish it is intended.

296. GARNISH OF STEWED RED CABBAGES.

Trim, wash, and quarter a couple of red cabbages, shred them as if about to make pickled cabbage, then put about four ounces of butter in a stewpan with the cabbages, season with salt and pepper, add half a gill of vinegar, cover the stewpan with its lid, and set it on a moderate fire to simmer gently. Take care to give it an occasional stir with a wooden spoon. When the cabbages have been reduced to half their original quantity moisten with half a pint of ordinary stock; if there is any skimming from the stock-pot, add it to it; then let it again simmer for an hour; after which, drain the cabbages on a sieve, press them in a clean cloth to extract the butter and fat, and use them as a garnish.

297. GARNISH OF SAUER-KRAUT.

Get two pounds of German sauer-kraut, wash it thoroughly in several waters and drain in a colander, then put it in a stewpan with one pound of streaky bacon, one quart of broth, and one pint of the fat skimmed off the top of the stock-pot, with a pinch of pepper; cover the stewpan with its lid, let boil, and simmer for at least four hours—if six, all the better—then drain it and serve with the bacon. If German sausages can be had, put half a dozen of them with the bacon.

Note.—Sauer-kraut is better warmed up than when freshly cooked, and the more it is cooked the better.

298. FRENCH SAUER-KRAUT.

Split the white hearts of four cabbages into quarters, remove the cores, and shred them very fine; wash them thoroughly in several waters, and drain them well in a colander; when properly dried, put the shred cabbage in a good-sized earthenware pan, throw in a good handful of salt, about a dozen pepper-corns, and a pint of good French vinegar; toss, with your hands, the cabbage in this, and let it remain for four hours; after which, take out, wash it well, and drain properly on a sieve; then put it in a stewpan with half a pound of butter, season with salt and pepper, add a gill of good vinegar, a pound of streaky bacon cut in slices and laid on the top; moisten with a quart of good broth, cover the lot with a buttered paper, and set the stewpan boiling with its lid on, let the contents simmer for about three hours, then proceed to strain and serve as above.

299. GARNISH OF TRUFFLES IN GLAZE.

Cut about half a pound of truffles into various fancy shapes, put these into a small stewpan with an ounce of fresh butter, a pinch of salt, and a piece of glaze or a gill of condensed gravy, or same quantity of No. 4 gravy, cover the stewpan with its lid and let it simmer for ten minutes, toss the truffles in the stewpan with their own glaze, and use them to garnish as required by adding a little Suprême or any other sauce.

300. TRUFFLES IN MADEIRA, SHERRY, OR CHAMPAGNE AS A GARNISH.

Cook the truffles in half a pint of the wine selected for five minutes, then proceed as above.

301. GARNISH OF MUSHROOMS.

Clean, peel, trim and cut away the gritty part near the stalk of a pound of fresh mushrooms, which must be white, full, and firm, or simply cut away the gritty part as above of a pint of tinned mushrooms, put them in a basin of cold water, stalks included, rinse well, dry with a cloth, and throw them into a stewpan with an ounce of butter, a pinch of salt, the juice of a lemon, and a gill of broth, boil gently for five or six minutes, then pour the mushrooms into a bain-marie containing half a pint of Allemande sauce to keep hot till wanted.

This garnish is proper for all white entrées, &c. If a brown garnish of mushrooms is required, substitute Espagnole sauce for Allemande, and omit the lemon-juice.

302. GARNISH OF MUSHROOMS WITH WINE.

Mushrooms can also be cooked in wine, in the same manner as truffles, and the sauce completed as in No. 301, to be used as a white or brown sauce.

303. GARNISH OF COCKS-COMBS.

Put one pound of cocks-combs in a stewpan with enough water to cover them; set the stewpan on a brisk fire and stir with a wooden spoon till the skin begins to rise; then pour in some cold water to stop the boiling of the combs and take them out; strip off the skin and trim the part which has been cut from the head, so as to free it of all feathers; soak the combs in salted water for six hours; after which, immerse them in cold water, which must be frequently changed, until they become perfectly white;

then strain off the water, put the combs in a stewpan with a pint and a half of broth, salt to taste and the juice of a lemon, boil till cooked, and serve with the sauce required.

Note.—Be careful not to boil the combs after the skin rises, otherwise the blood will coagulate and prevent them being white.

304. GARNISH OF CHICKEN'S LIVER.

Trim and throw away the bitter part of four chickens' livers, leave these whole, and immerse them in boiling water; take them out of the boiling water at once to put them in a saucepan with some good beef or chicken gravy, a little white wine, a small faggot of thyme and parsley, and season with salt and pepper to taste; boil and let simmer till cooked, when they must be taken out, strained, cut in slices, and served with their liquor reduced to a nice glaze.

305. GARNISH OF PRAWNS WITH CURRY.

Pick the tails of one pound of good prawns and use them as a garnish with three tablespoonfuls of Indian sauce poured over them with or without rice.

306. GARNISH OF MUSSELS.

Scrape and wash in several waters the shells of two quarts of small mussels (the smallest are the most delicate), boil one quart at a time in a pint of French white wine with an onion sliced, three sprigs of parsley, salt and pepper to taste. Cover the stewpan, toss the mussels occasionally, and when the shells open the mussels are done; take them out of the stewpan, throw the second quart in, and boil in the same manner.

The cooking of a quart of mussels at a time is advisable, because, in the first instance, a pint of wine is saved, and the mussels are done more evenly than they would if they were all cooked in the pan at once. Be also careful in not letting them cook after the shells open, as they will only harden and shrink.

When both quarts of mussels are cooked, take them out of the shells with a pointed knife and serve them with a white sauce made hot.

307. SALPICON À L'ITALIENNE.

Chop fine two sweetbreads, one pound of fresh mushrooms, and half a pound of cooked ham free from gristle and fat, then mix this compound well together, with half a pint of Financière sauce.

Salpicon is the culinary name for a mixture of cooked chicken, game, tongue, or fish with truffles, mushrooms, and "foie-gras," the whole cut in small dice, and served hot, either in patties, small bouchées, or made into croquettes.

308. SALPICON À LA PALERME.

Mix with half a pint of hot Napolitaine sauce a quarter of a pound of cooked macaroni cut in small pieces, the breast of a cooked partridge, two or three cocks-combs, the hearts of four cooked artichokes, and two ounces of cooked ham all chopped fine and well mixed together.

309. SALPICON À LA ROYALE.

Mix well together, in equal parts, after being chopped fine, some foie-gras, chicken meat, mushrooms, sweetbreads, a little crayfish or lobster butter, and the necessary Béchamel sauce, which must be boiling at the time of mixing.

310. SALPICON À LA FINANCIÈRE.

Chop fine two truffles, the breast of a cooked chicken, two ounces of cooked pickled tongue, and four ounces of fresh mushrooms; then mix with Financière sauce, and boil for a few minutes.

311. SALPICON À LA TOULOUSE.

Mix in equal parts, with half a pint of hot Velouté sauce, some chicken and goose livers, mushrooms, and cocks-combs all chopped fine.

312. SALPICON À LA CHASSEUR.

Mix with a salmi sauce the fillets of any game cut in small dice.

313. SALPICON OF OYSTERS.

Blanch the oysters for a few minutes, drain, and prepare in the usual way; cut them in two and mix with a reduced Velouté sauce; add a few spoonfuls of the liquor in which they were cooked, and the juice of a lemon.

314. SALPICON OF LOBSTER OR CRAB.

Cut either the cooked lobster or crab in small dice; add these to a Béchamel or Velouté sauce with a little lobster butter; season slightly with pepper, and mix well with a few chopped mushrooms.

315. SALPICON À LA MONGLAS.

Mix with a reduced Velouté or Espagnole sauce the breast of a chicken, chopped up with truffles.

316. SALPICON VALENCIENNES.

Prepare a mixture of hearts of artichokes, mushrooms, the breast of a chicken, one carrot, the tails of two dozen prawns, or part of the tail of a lobster, all cooked; add four tablespoonfuls of cooked rice; chop the lot fine, and mix with a Velouté sauce and a little cayenne butter.

Observation with respect to French Words in Bills of Fare.

I may say here, without prejudice, that I find the greatest difficulty in translating certain culinary names into English. Although my object is to be understood by all classes, I am often compelled to use original French words, being in many instances quite at a loss to express their proper meaning in English. This matter of using French names in "bills of fare" has often been discussed, and as it is still a subject of controversy in the culinary world, I simply give my reason for the practice I have adopted.

CHAPTER VI.

REMARKS ON FRYING.

THERE are two ways of frying in England, the dry method (in French called sauté), as when you fry an onion or an omelet; and the wet method, as when the article fried is immersed in the boiling fat and swims in it.

The former is generally done in a frying, stew, or sauté pan with butter; the latter in a frying-kettle and drainer, with fat or dripping, lard or oil. Fat skimmed off broth and the light-coloured dripping of roast-beef properly clarified, are the cheapest and best items as a fat for frying purposes. When these are running short the following is the proper mode of obtaining some:—Mince and put in a frying-kettle any beef, mutton, veal, and chicken fat that you may have, with a little water, salt, pepper, and a bay-leaf; set the frying-kettle on the fire and let it simmer till the fat is properly melted, taking care to stir occasionally. When the fat is clear enough to enable you to see the bottom of the pan, draw it away from the fire, and pass through a cloth and into the frying kettle again, as it is now ready for use.

For good cooking, oil should always be used for frying fish only, and be kept apart in a special frying-kettle for that purpose, but careful attention is needed in warming it, which should be done on a slow fire for half an hour, to prevent its rising and boiling over.

When the frying fat becomes of a dark-brown colour it

must be clarified, which process is obtained by melting of the fat with water, or strained into hot water, when all the impurities will fall to the bottom of the kettle, and the clarified fat, once cold, can easily be removed in a solid state from the top of the water.

When the fat has nearly attained a black colour, from constant use, it must not be employed again, as it will give bad taste and colour to everything fried in it, owing to its being decomposed, and having lost all its frying properties.

No pains should be spared by cooks in order to thoroughly understand the proper means of frying, for although very simple and easy in its way, it requires a great deal of attention.

Frying is a special feature in Italian cookery, and practised above all others as an art, by the Italians. Their ingenuity and abilities at frying are, I must say, superior to all other nations. In the first instance, it is of the utmost importance that the different degrees of temperature in the fat should previously be ascertained by the cooks, whose attempts at frying will otherwise often turn out failures.

There are many degrees of heat and boiling among the different liquids. Water boils at a temperature of 212° Fahrenheit, and will never reach a higher one. Fat and oil will attain from 500° to 650° before coming to the boiling-point; this is the reason why fat is used instead of water. If the same temperature could be obtained with water as with fat, frying would be better in the former, as there would be no greasy taste.

The different degrees of heat are generally determined by throwing a small sprig of parsley or a piece of crumb of bread the size of a small nut into the fat; if ebullition and fizzing is at once produced and large bubbles rise to the surface, the fat has reached the desired temperature for frying purposes, which will be about 385° Fahrenheit. A too high temperature must be avoided, which will be indicated by smoke rising from the kettle; in that case the articles fried would be blackened and burnt; on the other hand, if the fat has not reached the proper temperature the things intended for frying will be soaked through with fat, soddened, greasy, and of a dirty pale colour, but not fried.

Properly fried things should be of a golden colour, crisp, and free from fat; to obtain the latter, fried articles should be put on a clean cloth as they are taken out of the frying-kettle, and then turned over.

Frying is most successful when a small quantity is put at a time, otherwise the reaction of too many cold things will cause the fat fall below the necessary temperature and spoil the frying process. All articles to be fried should be properly dried between the folds of a clean cloth and passed through a mixture of breadings (if batter is not used) beforehand.

317. BATTER PASTE FOR FRYING.

Batter is a thin paste often required for frying fish, meat, vegetables, and fruit.

Put half a pound of white sifted flour into a basin with a little salt, white pepper, the yolks of two eggs (save the whites), a spoonful of vinegar or the juice of a lemon, and half a gill of olive-oil; work the whole into a double creamy paste, adding in, a spoonful at a time, about half a pint of cold water; when properly worked let it stand by. Meanwhile whisk well the two whites of egg set apart, and mix with the batter a few minutes before it is wanted.

For fritters, white wine or beer can be substituted for water, and add a little pounded cinnamon.

Remarks on Hors-d'Œuvres or Side Dishes.

Hors-d'œuvres, or side dishes, are tasty dainties, the object of which is to stimulate and sharpen the appetite, and they are served and eaten either before or after the soup. These are divided into two parts, the cold and hot hors-d'œuvres; the former are usually prepared and dished up in small oval dishes, decorated with parsley and put on the table by the butler; but in smaller establishments where the duties of that office are discharged by female servants it invariably falls upon the cook to dress up these decorative dishes, which generally consist of salami, a kind of raw Italian or Lyons sausage, fresh butter, slices of ham, sardines, tunny-fish, anchovies, radishes, olives, gherkins, smoked herrings or salmon, melon, foie-gras, caviare, oysters, &c., &c.

The hot hors-d'œuvres are very numerous and far more complicated than the cold ones, the majority of which are more substantial, and in many instances differ but slightly from "entrées." These are served directly after the soup, and are composed of many items, such as patties and bouchées of all description, croustades, coquilles, rissoles, croquets, cromeskis, mixed fritters, such as brains, liver, sweetbread, scollops, &c., &c.

318. PATTIES WITH ANY SALPICON OR FORCEMEAT.

Patties and bouchées are made out of puff paste, and the following is the proper mode of making them:—

Put one pound of sifted flour on the pastry slab; make a well in the centre of the flour, and pour in it one gill and a half of cold water, with half an ounce of salt and the yolk of an egg. Mix these gradually with the flour, and when done, and the paste is about half-mixed, sprinkle in another gill of water, mix all the flour and work it to a smooth paste until it ceases to adhere to the slab or hands; then roll it out to a round piece. Now take one pound of butter, put it in a clean cloth and press it, to extract any milk or water it may contain; lay the butter on the paste, flatten both to a thickness of about two inches, then fold the four sides of the paste to the centre to enclose the butter and form a square piece. Next take a rolling-pin, roll the paste with it to about the length of three feet, fold over one-third of the length, and fold the other third over this.

This is called "giving one turn," and as it constantly recurs in all recipes for making pastry, I deem it advisable to give its meaning.

Let the paste rest for ten minutes on the slab in a cool place, then give it two turns; ten minutes after, two turns more; and five minutes after this, another turn, making in all six turns. Then roll it out to about a quarter of an inch thick. Take a one and three-quarter inch paste-cutter, cut the paste with it into twenty-four rounds; gather the trimmings into a lump, and roll it out to the same thickness as the first; cut it also into twenty-four similar rounds, place these on a wet baking sheet, moisten the surface with a brush dipped in water, and put a small quantity of salpicon or forcemeat, previously made, on each; then take up one of the first cut rounds and reverse it on to the forcemeat, so as to cover it; repeat this till all the patties are covered, press the two pieces of paste lightly together with the top of a plain inch and a quarter cutter, brush them over with the yolk of two eggs well beaten, put them to bake in a brisk oven till they have reached a nice golden colour, and serve.

319. BOUCHÉES À L'ITALIENNE.

Make two pounds of puff paste in the manner described in the previous number, but give it seven turns, wetting the last turn before folding it; then roll the paste out so as to leave it scarcely a quarter of an inch thick, and about three minutes afterwards take a two-inch fluted circular tin cutter, and with it cut the paste into bouchées; but previously to cutting out each bouchée the cutter should be first dipped in very hot water. As soon as the bouchées are cut out place them immediately in rows, two inches apart, on a baking sheet, previously wetted; then egg them carefully all over with a soft brush dipped in beaten eggs, and stamp them in the centre by making a slight incision through their surface with a plain inch and a half circular cutter, which must also be dipped in hot water each time it is used. The bouchées should then be quickly put in the oven and baked of a light colour; when done remove the covers or tops, pick out the inner crumb carefully with the point of a small knife, then fill up each bouchée with a salpicon à l'Italienne, previously made hot, replace the covers at the top, and serve dished up on a folded napkin.

320. BOUCHÉES À LA PALERME.

Prepare the bouchées as in No. 319, and fill them up afterwards with a salpicon à la Palerme.

321. BOUCHÉES À LA ROYALE.

Proceed with the bouchées as described in No. 319, then fill them up with a salpicon à la Royale previously made hot.

322.

Bouchées à la Financière, à la Toulouse, à la Chasseur, with oysters, lobsters, crabs, à la Monglas, and à la Valenciennes are all made in the same manner.

323. CROUSTADES À LA TOULOUSE.

Make a paste with one pound of sifted flour, a pound of butter, the yolks of two beaten eggs, and a pinch of salt, and mix these with about half a pint of water to a softish paste. When quite smooth gather it up in a lump, and let it rest on the ice for an hour; after which, roll it out to the sixteenth of an inch thick, and line eighteen small croustade moulds with it; fill these with flour and bake them; when the paste is done, and has attained a nice straw-colour, take them out of the oven, turn the flour out, brush the inside of the croustades with a brush, and put them in the oven for two minutes longer to colour; then fill them with a salpicon à la Toulouse, pour a little Velouté sauce over each, and place some puff-paste covers on each top, previously made with "seven turns" paste, rolled to a quarter of an inch thick, cut with a two-inch fluted cutter, and baked as before.

Croustades, according to taste, can be varied with any salpicon.

324. COQUILLES À LA CHASSEUR.

The natural shells of scallops, if kept clean, are not objectionable for this hors d'œuvre, but the silver shells or coquilles, as they are called, are to be preferred.

Fill the number of shells required with the salpicon à la Chasseur, sprinkle the tops with fried bread-crumbs, put them into the oven to warm, and serve.

Proceed in the same way with any other sort of coquilles, and if you have any fish left from the previous day's dinner, bone it, cut it in small dice, and mix with a little butter, the juice of a lemon, salt to taste, a little Velouté sauce and essence of mushrooms, fill the shells with this mixture, strew fried bread-crumbs over the tops, set them in the oven to warm and brown, before serving.

325. RISSOLES OF CHICKEN.

Roll out some "six turns" puff paste to a quarter inch thickness, cut out some rounds with a fluted three-inch cutter, lay some chicken forcemeat the size of a walnut on each round, place a round of paste over each forcemeat, till they are all covered, and press the edges so as to stick them together.

Set the frying-kettle on the fire, and when the fat is of the right temperature fry the rissoles in it; then drain and dress them on a dish, on a folded napkin, garnish with fried parsley, and serve.

Any other forcemeat or salpicon can be turned into rissoles by the same process.

326. CROQUETS OF LOBSTER.

Make some salpicon of lobster and lay flat with a knife on a board, previously strewed with bread-crumbs; then divide the mixture in equal-sized parts and roll them with the hand to the shape of a cork; pass them afterwards in breadings, and then in the bread-crumbs.

Set the frying-kettle on the fire; when the fat is hot enough, fry them till they are crisp and of a light-brown colour; drain on a cloth in the usual way; sprinkle each with a little salt, put them on a napkin on a dish, and garnish with a little fried parsley before serving.

Perigueux or Tomato sauce is generally served with croquets.

Whatever kind of croquets may be wished for or required, their process is always the same.

327. CROMESKIS À LA RUSSE.

Chop up the fillets of a roast fowl into very small dice, and put them on a plate with half their quantity of mushrooms and truffles also chopped fine; stir half a pint of Béchamel or Allemande sauce over the fire until stiffly reduced, then throw in the minced chicken mushrooms and truffles; mix the lot well together, then spread it out about an inch thick on a dish and let it cool; after which, cut the mixture into pieces about the size of two walnuts, form these into egg-shapes, and place them on a dish. Meanwhile have ready a calf's udder, previously braized for the purpose, and cut when cold into very thin layers, just large enough to wrap each cromeski with; then dip them in some light batter paste, and fry them crisp, and to a nice golden colour, in plenty of lard, heated to the right temperature for the purpose; dish them up with fried parsley and serve hot.

Note.—Cromeskis can be made in the same manner with any other salpicon.

Mode of Preparing Sweetbread, Brains, Liver, and Scollops of Veal before Cooking them.

Whatever style of serving *sweetbread* may be contemplated, they must always be soaked in water for at least three hours, taking care to change the water occasionally; after which, put them in a saucepan with plenty of cold water, set the saucepan on the fire to boil, and as soon as they become firm and round, without, however, being hard, draw the saucepan away from the fire, immerse them in cold water, then drain on a cloth and press them between two boards or baking tins, with a four or five pound-weight on the top.

Brains must steep in cold water for about an hour, during which time the water must be changed twice, then pick out most carefully all skinny particles from the surface of the brains. Blanch them in boiling water for five minutes and immerse them in cold.

Liver must be of a bright pinkish colour and entirely free from whitish spots. Wash and wipe the quantity of liver required, then cut it into scollops or slices of about a quarter of an inch thick, and roll them in flour before frying.

Scollops are generally cut off from the cushion of leg of veal, previously freed from gristle, fat, and skin; they are cut in the same style and thickness as the liver, and should be flattened with the chopper or cutlet bat, dipped in water, before frying.

328. SWEETBREAD AND BRAINS FRIED À L'ITALIENNE.

Take two sweetbreads and two brains, prepared as indicated above, and cut each in scollops of about an inch thick. Mix well in a dish, a gill of good oil, half a gill of vinegar, and a pinch of salt; soak the scollops in it for about half an hour, then take them out and dip in some batter paste, previously made for this purpose, and drop them separately into the frying fat properly heated, and with a flat skimmer toss up each scollop gently till they become of a golden colour and crisp; then take them out, and place on a clean cloth which will absorb all the fat; sprinkle some salt on each, dress them on a napkin on a dish by placing alternately one brain scollop and one sweetbread, decorate with a little fried parsley, and serve as hot as possible.

329. ANOTHER FRIED SWEETBREAD, BRAIN AND LIVER (ITALIAN).

Cut in the same manner as above one sweetbread and two brains, after having soaked and blanched them as prescribed; cut also half a pound of liver in scollops; pass each in breadings and bread-crumbs. Put a quarter of a pound of clarified butter in a frying-pan on the fire, fry the scollops in it to a light-brown colour, then drain and dry them on a cloth, squeeze the juice of a lemon over them, sprinkle each with salt to taste, dish them up alternately on a hot dish, and serve.

330. BRAINS FRIED (CITIZEN STYLE).

Prepare four brains in the usual way; after which, cut them in slices of about half an inch thick. Beat the yolks of six eggs in a basin, and mix with an ounce of grated cheese, half an ounce of bread-crumbs, a pinch of salt, and a little pepper; whisk the whites of the six eggs to a snow froth. Put a quarter of a pound of clarified butter into a large frying-pan on the fire, mix gently the whites of the eggs with the yolks, and draw the pan away from the fire when the butter is melted. Put the whole of the mixture, a spoonful at a time, properly detached from each other, in the frying-pan; lay well imbedded in the centre of each spoonful of the egg-mixture a slice of brains; set the pan

PRACTICAL HOUSEHOLD COOKERY. 153

on the fire to fry for three minutes, then turn each compound over and fry them for another three minutes; when of a nice golden colour on both sides, dish them with the side of the brain up, sprinkle each with a little salt, and serve very hot.

Note.—Any kind of cooked meat, poultry, or game can be mixed with the eggs as well as the brains. A little minced parsley and garlic mixed with the eggs will give a good taste to the above items.

331. SWEETBREAD OR BRAINS FRIED (MILANAISE STYLE).

Cut either the sweetbread or brains, after having been duly blanched, as in No. 330. Beat six eggs in a basin with a little finely chopped parsley and the clove of a garlic; season with salt and pepper, when well beaten together dip the slices in it, and roll them afterwards in bread-crumbs, and form them in oval or round shapes. Put a quarter of a pound of clarified butter into a frying-pan, and when dissolved fry on a moderate fire, taking care to turn them over so as to give each side a nice golden colour, when they are cooked, and must be served hot.

332. LIVER FRIED À LA MILANAISE.

Take two pounds of calf's liver, cut it in scollops as described, pass these in breadings and bread-crumbs, then fry them in a frying-pan with a quarter of a pound of clarified butter on a moderate fire, turn the pieces over to give them a nice bronzed colour on both sides, and when tender to the touch sprinkle some salt and a teaspoonful of chopped parsley, squeeze the juice of a lemon over, and serve.

333. LIVER FRIED À LA PALERMO.

Scollop two pounds of calf's liver as No. 332, and flour them, then fry in the same manner as in the foregoing, and dress them on a hot dish. Leave the frying-pan by the side of the fire; chop very fine six fresh mushrooms, a little parsley, and a clove of garlic; put these in the frying-pan with a glass of French white wine and a gill of good broth; season with salt and pepper, boil for five minutes, then add the juice of a lemon, stir nicely, pour the sauce over the liver, and serve.

The liver of sheep, chickens, lambs, and pigs can also be fried and garnished in the same way, but substitute a little vinegar for wine.

334. VEAL SCOLLOPS FRIED À LA GENOISE.

Take two pounds of leg of veal, free from skin, fat, and gristle, cut in scollops and fry them in the same manner as in No. 333, but substitute oil for butter; after which, prepare a similar mixture for the sauce, and serve.

Scollops of mutton, beef, and pork can also be fried, and served with a similar sauce.

335. OYSTERS FRIED.

Blanch two dozen large oysters, press them lightly between two dishes till they are cold; then slit them open, without quite severing them, dip in frying batter, and fry in hot fat; drain and pile on a napkin on a dish garnished with fried parsley, and serve with Tomato sauce in a boat apart.

336. FRIED ANCHOVIES.

Steep two dozen anchovies in cold water for about two hours, or till they are easily opened, and bone them; wipe off the scales, by rubbing them with a coarse cloth; trim the anchovy fillets to an even shape and steep in milk for an hour, drain, wipe, and pass them through the breadings; then fry in very hot fat, drain, and pile them up on a napkin on a dish, garnish with fried parsley, and serve with two lemons cut in quarters.

CHAPTER VII.

REMARKS ON TRIPE.

Tripe is a delicious dish when prepared properly, but it must always be cleaned, scraped, and boiled in plenty of water for several hours before any attempt at cooking it can ever be contemplated. This of course only applies to country places, where tripe can only be had in its raw state, but in towns it can always be bought ready blanched.

337. TRIPE MILLANAISE.

Shred fine a carrot, an onion, and one head of celery; fry these in a stewpan with two ounces of butter; when nicely browned moisten them with half a pint of broth, add a "bouquet garni" composed of sage, thyme, and a bay-leaf, simmer gently for half an hour; then rub the lot through a sieve, throw the bouquet away, and return the sauce to the stewpan, with one pound and a half of tripe, previously shred in pieces about two inches long by half an inch wide; add a good rasher of streaky bacon or a slice of gammon cut in small dice, season with salt and pepper, moisten the lot with a pint of broth, and let it simmer for half an hour; stir occasionally with a wooden spoon, then add a ladleful of Espagnole sauce, stir, and when boiling serve on a hot dish, with grated cheese on a plate apart.

338. TRIPE À LA ROMAINE.

Take one pound and a half of cleaned and blanched tripe, cut it in about two-inch squares; put these in a saucepan with a pint and a half of good gravy or condensed broth, season with salt and pepper, add a bay-leaf, and let simmer for three-quarters of an hour on a slow fire, give it an occasional stir, and serve on a hot dish with grated cheese apart.

339. TRIPE À L'ITALIENNE.

Proceed in the same manner as for the Milanaise. Peel two tomatoes; squeeze out the water and rub them through a sieve; add this purée to the tripe at the same time as the broth, and let it simmer for half an hour; then pour in half a pint of green peas, a few fresh mushrooms cut in slices, season with salt and pepper, simmer again for twenty minutes, stir occasionally, and serve with grated cheese apart.

340. TRIPE (CITIZEN STYLE).

Fry in a stewpan with two ounces of butter one onion shred fine, a clove of garlic chopped very fine, and a slice of gammon cut in small dice; when these are properly browned sprinkle over three tablespoonfuls of flour, stir with a wooden spoon, and fry for two or three minutes longer; then add one pint of broth, same quantity of French white wine, a small "bouquet garni," and two pounds of tripe cut in slices, as in the Milanaise. Boil, stir nicely, add salt and pepper to taste, cover the stewpan and let it simmer for an hour, giving it an occasional stir to prevent burning; then take out the "bouquet garni," sprinkle two handfuls of grated cheese over the contents, stir it well, and serve on a hot dish with a little more grated cheese sprinkled on the top of it.

One or two calves' feet properly boiled and boned will improve this dish if added at the same time as the tripe.

341. TRIPE À LA LYONNAISE.

Melt three ounces of butter in a frying-pan, add three onions shred fine, and when beginning to brown put with it one pound and a half of tripe, cut as in No. 340; stir with a wooden spoon, fry for about twenty minutes, season with salt and pepper, and just before serving sprinkle a little finely chopped parsley with a few drops of French vinegar; stir well, and serve on a hot dish.

This tripe when cooked should be crisp and of a light-brown colour.

342. TRIPE AND ONIONS.

Cook six onions in salt water; when done squeeze the water out of them and chop them fine. Meantime boil one pound and a half of tripe (cut as in the foregoing) in a pint and a half of fresh milk, and after an hour's ebullition, having given it an occasional stir to prevent the tripe burning, mix the onions with it, season with salt, pepper, and a little grated nutmeg, boil, stir, and serve.

343. ANOTHER TRIPE AND ONIONS.

Proceed as above, but instead of milk use veal broth.

344. TRIPE FRIED.

Shred in the same shape as in the foregoing two pounds of tripe, dip these in frying batter and fry afterwards in fat, properly heated for the purpose. When crisp and of a nice light-brown colour, drain and serve on a hot dish, with a little tomato sauce in a sauce-boat apart.

345. SHEEP'S KIDNEYS GRILLED.

Slit the kidneys lengthwise, without cutting through the sinew, remove the thin skin which covers them, and run them on a small skewer (two on each), then sprinkle with a little salt and pepper; place these on a grid-iron over a clear fire with the open side downwards. When done brown turn them over, and let them remain three minutes longer; after which, put them on a hot dish, draw the skewer away, and lay on each kidney a little cold maître d'hôtel or cayenne butter, and serve.

346. SHEEP'S KIDNEYS STEWED WITH FINE HERBS.

Split the kidneys as before directed, cut them into thin scollops, sprinkle with salt and pepper to taste, and fry them brown in a frying-pan with a little butter; then add a tablespoonful each of chopped mushrooms and parsley, and two shalots also chopped fine; let the lot fry for a few minutes longer; after which, sprinkle a tablespoonful of flour and moisten with a glass of sherry; let this simmer for three minutes, then add two or three spoonfuls of brown broth or gravy, simmer another five minutes, squeeze the juice of a lemon, toss it up and mix well together, draw the frying-pan away from the fire, form a border of mashed potatoes on a dish, pour the kidneys in the centre, and serve.

347. SHEEP'S KIDNEYS STEWED À LA CLEREMONT.

Scollop and fry the kidney as in No. 346, and when nicely browned draw the frying-pan by the side of the fire. Meanwhile shred two onions and fry them in a stewpan, with two ounces of butter, to a fine yellow colour; drain off the butter, add a pinch of pepper, a few spoonfuls of good broth, and a little Espagnole sauce; boil; skim, and let simmer till properly reduced; then mix it with the kidneys, stir nicely with a wooden spoon, simmer for three or four minutes, and serve with a border of potato croquets.

348. VEAL KIDNEYS STEWED À LA ROMAINE.

Cut a veal kidney in half, remove the fat part and slice the pieces very thin. Melt a quarter of a pound of butter well in a frying-pan on a brisk fire, fry the pieces of kidney in it, when about half-cooked add an onion and a little parsley chopped very fine, sprinkle over, a tablespoonful of flour, season with salt and pepper, continue the frying for a few minutes longer, then add a glass of white wine, let simmer for a few minutes, and just before serving squeeze the juice of a lemon over it, and toss the contents well, and serve with a purée of vegetables.

349. VEAL KIDNEYS BROILED À LA L'INDIENNE.

Cut lengthwise a veal kidney in two, flatten these slightly with the bat, season with salt and pepper, dip each piece in oil, roll them afterwards in bread-crumbs, and broil four minutes each side, on a good fire. Meanwhile prepare a curry butter, garnish the brim of a dish round with plain boiled rice, place the kidneys in the centre, put the curry butter on it, and serve hot.

350. BEEF KIDNEY À LA PIEMONTAISE.

Cut a beef kidney in two, trim it in the usual way, and slice it in thin scollops, season with salt and pepper, dip the scollops in batter, and fry with butter till of a brown colour; then serve with a garnish of fried parsley and tomato sauce in a boat apart.

351. SHEEP'S TONGUES WITH SPINACH.

Take six fresh sheep's tongues; blanch them for five minutes, to enable the white skin to be removed; then trim and put them in a sauté-pan with about a pint of broth, a bay-leaf, a little thyme, season with salt and pepper; set the sauté-pan on the fire to the boil, and let simmer until the tongues are well cooked and nicely glazed; then take them out, cut them lengthways in halves and return them to the sauté-pan. Meantime dish some purée of spinach, previously made for this purpose; decorate the dish with fried croûtons, place the pieces of tongue over the spinach nicely arranged, pour the remainder of the glaze over them, and serve.

352. SHEEP'S TONGUES WITH GHERKIN SAUCE.

Blanch, trim, cook, and dish up six sheep's tongues, as in No. 351, then pour some Gherkin sauce (No. 192) in the centre, and serve.

353. SHEEP'S TONGUES À LA NAPOLITAINE.

Braize and trim the tongues as above, and when cut in halves let them get cold, then pass them through the

L

breadings, flatten them nicely with the blade of a knife and fry them in fat, properly heated for the purpose; drain in the usual way, and dish them up in the form of a close circle, the centre of which must be filled with macaroni (No. 88), and serve.

354. SHEEP'S FEET, WITH OIL AND VINEGAR.

Chop very fine about two ounces of beef suet, and melt it in a saucepan over the fire, and when clear add two ounces of flour, two quarts of water, one onion sliced, a "bouquet garni," two cloves, a tablespoonful of vinegar, and a little salt and pepper; stir the lot over the fire, and when boiling drop in it eight sheep's feet, previously blanched, cleaned, and trimmed; let them boil for about three hours and a half, when they should be done, and tender; then strain, and put them on a dish with a sauce made in the following manner:—Put in a basin a gill of oil, half a gill of French vinegar, a teaspoonful of salt, a good pinch of pepper, half a tablespoonful each of finely chopped parsley and onion, beat the lot well together before pouring it over the cooked feet, and serve.

Sheep's feet can also be served with a Sharp, Poulette, or any other sauce.

355. CALF'S HEAD TOMATO SAUCE.

Select, according to the size required, a white calf's head, cut it in two, dip these into boiling water to clean the ears out, then bone them entirely, cut the tongue out, and put the brains to steep in cold water; soak the head and tongue for a little while also in cold water, then blanch both in boiling water for ten minutes; strain, and take off the white skin from the tongue; put the two halves and tongue in a clean cloth, with two or three slices of gammon, two sliced onions, one shred carrot, one bay-leaf, and a few slices of lemon, fold these together, and put the bundle into a large saucepan with enough cold water to cover it well; season with salt, add a "bouquet garni," an onion with three cloves stuck in, and one head of celery. Let the saucepan boil, and then simmer for about three hours; after which, take the cloth out, stretch the tongue so as to give it its original shape, cut each half in four, keep the ears in square pieces, wipe the inside of these nicely with a cloth, and slit them with a pointed knife into narrow strips, taking care not to run the knife through the ends, but merely from the inner part to within half an inch of the point, so that when the ear is turned down it will present the appearance of a looped frill. Now cut the tongue in half, lengthways, without separating it altogether, dress these on an oval dish on a napkin, with the ears at each end and the pieces of head in the centre, decorate with green parsley, and serve with a pint of tomato sauce in a boat apart.

Calf's head can be served with oil and vinegar as for the sheep's feet (No. 354), in which case add a tablespoonful of capers and two very thinly sliced gherkins, and four hard-boiled eggs cut in two. It can also be served with Italian, Sharp, Ravigote, or Devilled sauce.

Note.—It is customary in this country to serve a piece of boiled streaky bacon with the calf's head. Of this I do not approve; neither can I recommend the parsley and butter sauce served with it, which is far too insipid.

356. CALF'S FEET FRIED, ITALIAN SAUCE.

Remove the large bone of four calf's feet, cut them in halves, blanch for ten minutes, then boil for about two hours and a half in a liquor made as for the sheep's feet; when done bone them, cut each in four, dip these pieces in a batter paste and fry in hot fat, in the usual way; then serve the pieces dished up with some Italian sauce apart.

Calf's feet can also be served à la poulette; in that case, when they are done, do not fry them, but warm about one pint of Poulette sauce, and mix the pieces with it, and serve.

They can also be cut in halves, cooked as in the foregoing, bread-crumbed, and broiled on a slow fire, and served with a Tartare sauce apart.

357. OX-PALATE FRIED.

Blanch in boiling salt water for ten minutes four ox-palates; drain, cool and scrape to remove the white skin; when properly trimmed put them in a saucepan with one quart of broth, two slices of gammon, and a "bouquet garni;" let them boil gently for about three hours; then drain the palates on a sieve and let them get cold. In the meantime put a quart of Velouté sauce in a stewpan on the fire and reduce it to half its original quantity by sharp boiling, then add the yolks of three hard-boiled eggs, scraped into crumbs, a tablespoonful of parsley previously blanched and chopped very fine, salt and pepper to taste, the juice of a lemon, and an ounce of butter; mix these well together, then draw the stewpan away from the fire.

Take the ox-palates and split them in halves lengthways; each of these must be cut across again in two and placed on a large dish or board; put with a spoon the mixture prepared in the stewpan, properly divided on each of the pieces of palate; roll them up in the form of cartridges, pass them afterwards in the breadings, and a few minutes before serving fry them in the frying-kettle with the fat previously heated very hot for the purpose. If the fat is not very hot, the cartridges will open and separate from the stuffing. Dish them up nicely and serve with a little fried parsley.

Ox-palates can also be served with an Italian, Sharp, Tomato, or curry sauce.

358. OX-CHEEK WITH PURÉE OF VEGETABLE.

Bone an ox-cheek, immerse it in cold water for about an hour, blanch in the usual way for five minutes, and dip in cold water; then drain and trim it; put it afterwards in a large stewpan with the bones at the bottom, add the same sorts and quantity of vegetables as for a soup, together with a " bouquet garni," two quarts of water, and a tablespoonful of salt; boil and let simmer for two hours; after which, take the cheek up very carefully with a flat skimmer and press it between two dishes; strain the broth through a fine sieve; remove the half of it to a cool place to be used later on for brown sauces, &c., and boil down the other half to a half-glaze. Meanwhile cut up the ox-cheek in small pieces of equal size, place them in a sauté-pan with the half-glaze, cover the pan with its lid, and simmer for about ten minutes; roll the pieces nicely in their glaze, dish them up in a circle, fill the centre with a purée of vegetable, pour the glaze over, and serve.

359. OX-CHEEK À L'ITALIENNE.

Prepare an ox-cheek in the same manner as in the previous number, but instead of a purée of vegetable as a garnish, use some ripe tomatoes au gratin, as a border, and pour a little Italian sauce in the centre before serving.

360. FRESH OX-TONGUE WITH GHERKIN SAUCE.

Immerse a fresh ox-tongue in boiling water for a few minutes, to enable the white skin to be removed by scraping; then lard it with a small larding-needle in the following manner:—Trim about half a pound of fresh fat bacon two inches long by about three wide, cut this in strips a quarter of an inch thick, soak them for an hour in a pint of white wine, properly seasoned with salt and pepper and a little chopped parsley.

After having wiped the shreds of bacon and larded the tongue with them, place this in a saucepan with four quarts of cold water, two rashers of bacon, an onion and a carrot nicely shred, together with a bay-leaf, a little thyme, three cloves, a teaspoonful of salt, and two pinches of pepper. Set the saucepan boiling and simmer for about three hours and a half (if the tongue is a large one), then ascertain whether it is cooked. When done, take it off the fire and dish it up with Gherkin sauce (No. 192) and serve. Ox-tongue cooked in this way can also be served with Sharp, Italian, or Tomato sauce; you can also omit the larding and serve it with a purée of spinach, macédoine, or any vegetable that may be in season.

361. PICKLED OX-TONGUE. MADEIRA SAUCE.

Get a good pickled ox-tongue from your butcher, wash it in two or three cold waters, put it in a saucepan on the fire with four quarts of cold water; let it boil gently for about three hours, when it must be drawn from the fire, but leave the tongue in its liquor. Meanwhile put three tablespoonfuls of Espagnole sauce in a small stewpan with a piece of glaze as big as a walnut, and half a pint of Marsala, Madeira, or sherry, a little salt, pepper, and grated nutmeg. Boil it, stir it well with a wooden spoon, and reduce it one-third by sharp boiling. Meantime take the tongue out of its liquor, trim it and remove the white skin, put the tongue back into the saucepan on the fire to warm it up. When boiling dish it up, pour the sauce over it, and serve with a purée of potatoes apart, or any other vegetable purée.

If the pickled ox-tongue is to be served cold, cook it in the same way, and leave it in its liquor for ten minutes before trimming; and when still hot pin it on a board in the larder, so as to give it a round shape, and let it get cold, then glaze it in the following manner :—

362. TO GLAZE COLD MEAT.

Put some glaze into a small earthenware pot; put this in a saucepan two-thirds full of warm water; set the saucepan on the fire to bring the water gradually till it boils. When the glaze is well dissolved see that the tongue is well dried; then with a brush varnish the surface, evenly and smoothly, and when cold lay on another coat, also a third if necessary; but let it be well understood that the glazing has not for object the hiding of the article glazed, but to give it only a polished and transparent appearance, in the same way as a polished piece of furniture, which in either case is always pleasing to the eye.

363. SWEETBREADS LARDED À LA MACEDOINE.

Soak and blanch two sweetbreads, as described in Hot Hors-d'Œuvres, drain and press them between two dishes until cold, after which lard them closely with small strips of bacon, without having been soaked, as for the ox-tongue. Put them in a sauté-pan with a pint of good broth slightly coloured with caramel, a "bouquet garni," a bay-leaf, and salt to taste. Cover the sauté-pan with its lid, and boil gently for about half an hour, taking care to add a little more broth if required; take the lid off, and put the sauté-pan in the oven to dry the surface, which should be of a nice light-brown colour. Then dish them up with a garnish of macédoine (No. 281) and serve, after having poured over the remainder of the glaze in which the sweetbreads were cooked.

Sweetbread prepared in this way may also be served with any garnish of vegetables or vegetable purée, as described in this book, as well as with Tomato or Soubise sauce, &c., &c.

364. OX-BRAINS, NEAPOLITAN STYLE.

Soak the brains required in lukewarm water in the manner described in No. 328, then blanch them for a few minutes in salt water, drain, and wipe them with a cloth; when cold, cut these in scollops, pass them in bread-crumbs, then into some well-beaten eggs and bread-crumbs again. Give each scollop a nice form with your hands; after which, place them in a sauté-pan, with a few thin rashers of bacon, half a carrot, the quarter of an onion shred fine, a bay-leaf, salt to taste, half a pint of French white wine, and same quantity of broth; let these simmer for half an hour, then strain and dish the scollops on some croûtons fried in butter, sprinkle over them a little hot Neapolitan sauce (No. 208), and serve.

365. OX-BRAINS WITH MONTPELLIER BUTTER.

Soak and blanch as above two ox-brains, then cook them in good broth, and let them get cold in the broth; after which drain, and put them in a sauté-pan with three tablespoonfuls of olive-oil, sprinkle over them a little salt and pepper, squeeze the juice of a lemon, add a few sprigs of tarragon, and set the sauté-pan on the fire to simmer for a few minutes, and draw the pan from the fire. Put half a pint of Montpellier butter (No 163) into another sauté-pan on the fire, put the two brains in it, and glaze them well. Dish them up, and pour the Montpellier butter over them before sending to the table.

366. BLACK PUDDINGS.

Take one pint of pig's blood, add to it half a pint of boiled cream, half a pound of the inside fat of the pig, cut in small dice, cut three onions also in dice and fry them with two ounces of butter in a frying-pan without colouring them; mix these with the blood, season with half an ounce of salt, a pinch of pepper, a little grated nutmeg, a sprig of thyme, and half a bay-leaf, chopped very fine; mix all these well together and fill the skins (previously cleaned and washed) with this mixture, taking care to allow space for tying them into five-inch lengths. When completed and thus tied, immerse the black puddings in boiling water, without, however, boiling them, but let them remain in it till they become somewhat firm to the touch, when they must be taken out and hung in the larder to cool.

When required, cut them into lengths, score them well with a sharp knife, or prick them all round with a trussing-needle, so as to prevent them bursting. Broil them on a moderate fire for about ten minutes, taking care to turn them round as required; when done, dish them up with mashed potatoes and serve very hot.

367. PIG'S FEET À LA STE. MENEHOULD.

Procure four large pig's feet, pickle them for eight days in common salt brine, then wash and boil them in a quart of ordinary stock for about three hours and a half, properly seasoned with a "bouquet garni," one carrot, two onions, and half a head of celery, all shred fine. When done, drain and cut them in two, lengthways; remove all the large bones, press them into shape with the hands, and let them get cold; after which, sprinkle them with salt and pepper, rub them over with a brush or feather dipped in clarified butter, then roll them in bread-crumbs and broil them over a clear fire (taking care to frequently turn them) till of a nice golden colour; then dish them up, and serve with a sharp sauce (No. 205) apart.

368. PIG'S FEET À LA GENOISE.

Prepare and cook four pig's feet as in the previous number, bone and fill them up with a salpicon à la monglas (No. 315); after which, join the two halves, tie them around with some pig's caul, prepared for the purpose, give them their original form, pass them through bread-crumbs, and broil them over a clear fire, taking care, as in No. 367, to turn them round; and when nicely done, dish them up in halves and serve with Italian sauce (No. 204) apart.

369. PIG'S EARS À LA VENITIENNE.

Take four pig's ears, singe them well over a clear flame, and clean the insides properly with a cloth after having scraped them nicely, then blanch in boiling salt water for five minutes, drain, and put them in a stewpan with a quart of broth and boil them till cooked, then let them get cold in the liquor. Cut in halves six small onions, of which the two extremities, as well as the hearts in the centre, must be removed; then cut these onions in half-circles and fry them in a stewpan with two ounces of butter without browning; add a gill of Espagnole sauce, half a pint of veal broth or beef gravy, and simmer for about ten minutes. Meantime cut the ears in small strips, and when the onions are nicely cooked skim off the fat, add the strips of ears to it, with a little salt, a dessert-spoonful of finely chopped parsley, a few drops of vinegar, and a little mustard. Toss up the lot and mix it well together, and when it is properly heated serve.

370. PIG'S EARS WITH A PURÉE OF LENTILS.

Prepare and blanch in a similar manner as the foregoing four pig's ears; drain and put them into a stewpan with enough broth to cover them; add one carrot and two onions shred fine, as well as a "bouquet garni" and a bay-leaf; boil them; and when cooked take them out, dish up with a purée of lentils or any other purée of vegetable, and serve.

371. PIG'S LIVER, BRAIZED.

Take a pig's liver, wash and wipe it well with a cloth, then lard it in the same way as the ox-tongue (No. 360). Put into a stewpan a few slices of fat bacon, one carrot, and two onions shred, and a "bouquet garni;" lay the liver at the top of these with enough broth to moisten half of the liver; set the stewpan (with the lid on) to boil, and simmer very gently for an hour; taking care meanwhile to often baste the liver with its liquor. Remove the lid, skim the liquor very carefully, and put the stewpan into the oven to give a nice tint to the lard. Meanwhile boil a gill of Espagnole sauce; dish up some purée of potatoes;

put the liver on the purée, strain the gravy in which the liver was cooked; skim off all the grease, mix it well with the Espagnole sauce, pour it over the liver, and serve.

372. PIG'S LIVER, POUNDED.

Clean a pig's liver, cut it in small pieces, and put it in a mortar with the half of its weight of fat; add to it half a pound of trimmed and cut mushrooms, one tablespoonful of fine herbs (No. 195), a tablespoonful of salt, two pinches of pepper, a little grated nutmeg, and the yolks of four eggs; pound these well together in the mortar, then add a gill of sherry, mix it well and rub the lot through a wire sieve with a wooden spoon; butter the inside of a bain-marie pan, put the mixture in it and place it in a pan two-thirds full of boiling water; boil thus for about an hour, then pour the contents into a hot dish, sprinkle it with some essence of mushrooms (No. 171), and serve.

373. CALF'S LIVER, BRAIZED À LA GENOISE.

Wash and wipe dry a calf's liver, then lard it through with strips of fat bacon and raw ham alternately, let it soak in a gill of oil seasoned with salt, pepper, and chopped parsley for about an hour, turning it over at least twice during that time. After which, pour the lot into a sauté-pan, add one carrot, two onions, one head of celery all shred fine, a "bouquet garni," and a bay-leaf; moisten the lot with one pint and a half of good broth, cover the pan and boil; then draw the pan away from the fire, and let the liver simmer gently for about an hour and a half, frequently basting it with its own liquor, then remove the liver into a stewpan with a little of its liquor and put it in the oven to glaze properly. Meantime push the sauté-pan on the fire and continue reducing the half-glaze by sharp boiling, and skim off the fat. Then dress the liver in the centre of a dish, make a border of macaroni cheese (No. 88), strain the sauce through a pointed strainer over the liver and macaroni, and serve.

Calf's liver cooked as above can also be served with any garnish or purée of vegetables instead of macaroni.

874. CALF'S LIVER, CITIZEN STYLE.

Clean and dry a calf's liver as in No. 373, then lard it through with strips of fat bacon, season on both sides with salt and pepper, put it in a sauté-pan with a quarter of a pound of butter and fry it nicely for about five minutes, taking care to give it an even colour all round. Then remove the liver from the sauté-pan and put it on a dish apart. Sprinkle three spoonfuls of flour with the butter and stir with a wooden spoon over the fire for five minutes. Add a pint of water, a pint of French white wine, one onion with two cloves stuck in it, and a " bouquet garni," season with salt and pepper, stir these with a wooden spoon till it boils, then put the liver in with about two dozen new carrots, as near of the same size as possible (scraped and cleaned), and let it simmer with the stewpan three-parts covered for two hours; then add one dozen button onions previously fried in butter, and simmer again for about half an hour; dish the liver up, skim the fat from the sauce, and garnish the liver with the carrots and onions; take the " bouquet garni " and onion with the cloves out, and if there be too much sauce reduce it on a sharp fire for five minutes; then pass it through a pointed strainer over the liver and vegetables, and serve.

375. CALF'S LIVER À LA VENITIENNE.

Cut in small slices a calf's liver and put these in a frying-pan in which a quarter of a pound of butter has already been melted with three spoonfuls of salad-oil, two onions shred fine, a little chopped parsley, salt and pepper to taste, fry these on a brisk fire, and stir constantly with a wooden spoon, until the liver is cooked and has assumed a nice bronzed colour, then squeeze the juice of a lemon over it, and serve.

---

376. REMARKS ON SAUSAGES AND HOW TO MAKE THEM.

Sausages are generally considered to be mysteries of the pork butcher, and this prejudice is not wholly without foundation, as the material used for their composition is often of a very doubtful character. On that account, and that only, I advise the making of sausages at home.

Take one pound each of lean and fat pork, both free from gristle and rind, chop them in dice and put them into a sausage-machine, the turning of which will give you the sausage meat; season with salt, pepper, a little pounded thyme and spice. Mix well together, and fill a well-cleansed skin with this forcemeat, and separate it into sausages of from three or four inches in length, by tying them with small string, as for black puddings. When these sausages are made they can be cooked either by broiling or frying. In either case they must be pricked on both sides with a trussing-needle, to prevent their bursting. If broiled, a moderate fire is required, and six minutes will be found sufficient to cook them properly, turning them over after three minutes. If fried, put a little butter or fat into a frying-pan, and when hot put the

PRACTICAL HOUSEHOLD COOKERY.   175

sausages in; the same number of minutes will cook them, provided they are also properly turned round.

Sausages must always be served very hot, on a hot dish, and are eaten either plain or with a garnish of purée of potatoes, or any other purée, as well as with rice boiled in broth (with the stewpan closely covered) for twenty minutes.

377. SAUSAGES, CITIZEN STYLE.

Put eight sausages into a sauté-pan with half a pint of French white wine and a good pinch of pepper; cover the sauté-pan and boil for eight minutes; take the sausages out and keep them hot in the corner of the stove on a dish; add one gill of Poulette sauce to the sauté-pan with the wine; stir and reduce for four minutes; then add an ounce of butter, a little chopped parsley, and stir till the butter is melted by the side of the fire, and then pour it over the sausages, and serve.

378. CREPINETTES WITH TOMATO SAUCE.

Crepinettes are made with the same forcemeat as the sausages, but in this case no skin is used. Make one pound of sausage meat as described, then flatten it on a board to the thickness of an inch and four inches wide, divide this in eight equal portions, and wrap them in pig's caul to a flat oval shape. When ready, broil them on a moderate fire for six minutes each side, then serve very hot with half a pint of Tomato sauce (No. 217) apart.

These crepinettes can also be served with rice or mashed potatoes.

CHAPTER VIII.

379. FRESH BOILED MEAT.

MEAT that has been boiled for the purpose of making broth should not be disregarded on account of its loss of savour and uninviting aspect. When the broth is made, the different sorts of meat should be taken out of the stockpot, placed on a dish, and sent to the table garnished with some of the vegetables that were cooked with it; or in other cases, special vegetables may be simply and carefully prepared (according to season and taste) as I have indicated in the chapter on Garnishes. Meat served thus will be found both profitable and useful, and ought to hold its own in the domestic cookery of this country, as well as it does in that of France and Italy; but it can also be prepared under various palatable and tasty dishes, for which see the following.

380. BEEF MIRONTON.

Cut three pounds of cold boiled beef into slices of about a quarter of an inch thick, trim off the fat and dry parts, and place the slices of beef on a dish. Peel, shred fine, and fry in two ounces of butter four onions to a nice light-brown colour; then sprinkle three tablespoonfuls of flour over them with salt and pepper to taste, and let them simmer for five minutes longer; after which, add a pint of broth and stir well on the fire for fifteen minutes; then add a teaspoonful of mixed mustard, stir, and drop the slices of beef into it; toss the sauté-pan nicely, warm the beef without boiling for a few minutes; season with more salt and pepper, if required; and then dish it up and serve.

381. BOILED BEEF WITH SHARP SAUCE.

Slice the same quantity of beef as in No. 380, lay the slices in a gratin-pan, season them with salt and pepper, moisten with a gill of good broth, and put them in the oven for about fifteen minutes; after which, pour one pint of sharp sauce (No. 205) over the beef, and serve.

In the same way the beef can be warmed up, and an Italian or Tomato sauce poured over it.

382. BOILED BEEF AU GRATIN.

Slice the boiled beef as previously directed, and put it in a gratin-dish; place about half a pound of fresh mushroom cuttings in a stewpan with a pint of broth, season with salt and pepper; boil for five minutes, and then pour this over the beef. Cover the top with bread-crumbs, set the dish in the oven for ten minutes, and serve.

383. BOILED BEEF, COUNTRYMAN'S STYLE.

Cut two pounds of beef in two-inch dice. Cut in the same style a quarter of a pound of streaky bacon, remove the rind, and fry the bacon only, with one ounce of butter in a stewpan, to a brown colour; then add a quart of common stock or water, a "bouquet garni," one onion shred, and a pound of potatoes cut in squares like the beef; boil these for fifteen minutes; after which, add the pieces of beef; warm them up, without boiling, for ten minutes; then take out the "bouquet," add some salt if necessary, dish up and serve.

M

384. MINCED BOILED BEEF.

Brown for three minutes in a stewpan three tablespoonfuls of flour with an ounce of butter; take this off the fire, add one pint of broth, salt and pepper to taste, mix for two minutes and push the stewpan on the fire, stir for ten minutes, then add three pounds of beef, previously trimmed and mixed fine, together with a tablespoonful of chopped parsley, and stir again for three or four minutes on the fire. Should the mixture be too thick, add a little more broth, stir, and serve.

This mince can be made with Italian or Tomato sauce instead of broth, and in either case the process is the same.

385. BOILED BEEF CROQUETS.

Chop fine about two pounds of boiled beef. Make a pint of Poulette sauce (No. 179), and reduce it on a sharp fire to half that quantity. Thicken it with the yolks of three eggs well beaten. Mix the chopped beef with this sauce; add one tablespoonful of chopped parsley, and season with salt and pepper; when well mixed with a wooden spoon, spread it out on a dish to a thickness of an inch and a half, let it get cold, when it will be firm and divide it into twenty equal parts. Strew on a board some bread-crumbs, and put the twenty parts of minced meat thereon, each separated by about two inches, cover these with a sprinkling of bread-crumbs, roll each into the shape of a cork, then beat the whites of the three eggs for one minute, without frothing, add to this a dessert-spoonful of salt, two of oil, and same quantity of water, mix well together, dip the croquets in the mixture, roll them again in bread-crumbs, and place them on a dish. Twenty minutes before serving, have the frying-kettle ready with hot fat, place the croquets in the frying-basket and put this in the fat to fry; when nearly done move them gently with a slice to ensure their even colouring and becoming crisp; then draw the basket out of the frying fat, drain the croquets on a clean cloth, sprinkle with salt, dish them up on a napkin, garnish with fried parsley, and serve.

386. BOILED BEEF SALAD.

Cut up the same quantity of cold boiled beef in small thin slices, properly trimmed and free from gristle, and put these on a dish.

Prepare in a bowl a similar sauce as for the sheep's feet (No. 354), pour it over the beef well mixed, and serve. This will be found very appetising in warm weather.

387. BOILED VEAL MINCED, AND POACHED EGGS.

Pare off the outside part of two pounds of boiled veal, cut it in shreds and chop very fine. Melt in a stewpan an ounce of butter, and brown two tablespoonfuls of flour in it, by stirring on the fire with a wooden spoon for three minutes; then gradually mix it with a pint of broth, stirring the while, and reduce it on a brisk fire to the consistency of sauce; then add the minced veal, a little grated nutmeg, and salt and pepper to taste; stir and mix this on the fire for three minutes, and dish it up; after which, place eight poached eggs on it, decorate with croûtons fried in butter, and serve.

Note.—Any pieces of cooked ham, bacon, or pickled tongue, properly minced, as well as mushrooms, can be added to the minced veal.

388. BOILED VEAL, MINCED À LA NAPOLITAINE.

Trim two pounds of boiled veal, and cut it in dice of a quarter of an inch thick. Put half a pint of white wine into a stewpan with two chopped shalots, a little grated nutmeg, salt and pepper, and the juice of a lemon; set these ingredients on to boil, and then pour in the minced veal, stir, and let it simmer for ten minutes. Meantime prepare a plain macaroni cheese (No. 88), dish it up, put the minced veal over it, sprinkle the lot with a little hot glaze, and serve.

Minced veal can also be prepared in croquettes (see No. 385), or au gratin, as in No. 382.

389. BOILED MUTTON.

Boiled mutton should always be eaten with plain vegetables, and served with Caper or Tomato sauce apart.

CHAPTER VIII.

REMARKS ON FISH.

THE fisheries of Great Britain have assumed such vast proportions and importance, that it makes one almost wonder how such a quantity of fish (in London some 400 tons) daily sent to the principal markets of this country can be so easily disposed of.

The flesh of the different species of British fish (there are many) is fully recognised by all to be a most delicate and nutritious food, as well as brain feeding.

Nature having thus provided an unbounded supply of fish for man's food, to him remains the duty of knowing how to use it to the best advantage, and cook, dress, and serve it in different ways, in order to relieve and improve by such means the monotony of its taste and colour.

The multiplicity of modes in preparing fish as a food, is however, so great and perplexing that I only give a few of the most useful and economical recipes for each fish, ignoring as much as possible the use of other species and crustaceans as a garnish to the numerous forms of cooking and dressing it.

There are two ways of boiling fish. The first consists in putting the whole of the fish in cold water with plenty of salt and a little vinegar; the second, in immersing in boiling salted water the fish cut in slices. The advantage of the former is, that the fish boiled whole loses none of its quality; but the cooking of the latter is quicker. However, as it is not always convenient to cook a whole fish, especially when it is a large one, and when the question of time is also to be considered, I think it is only right that the advantage derived from one should be equalised by the consideration of the other. In either case, as soon as the fish is cooked it must be taken out of the water and drained, otherwise it will lose some of its flavour and firmness. Should you have to keep the fish hot for a few minutes before serving, cover it with two or three folds of clean cloth or flannel on the strainer across the kettle, but do not on any account let it soak in hot water.

REMARKS ON SALMON.

Salmon is certainly and without prejudice the king of fish; he is highly intellectual and possesses a strongly developed instinct; in fact, is an aristocrat and a gentleman. His shape, build, and movements are most graceful and elegant, and is considered the finest specimen of the species, and can jump over obstacles and difficulties like a hunter on *terra firma*. He strongly objects to unclean or polluted rivers, and, like a hound following the fox by scent, he can detect impure water (which means danger for him) for a long distance down the river. He is more of a sea than a fresh-water fish, and must be as free as the red-deer or the eagle, and will not thrive in captivity. The season is from March to August.

390. BOILED SALMON, LOBSTER SAUCE.

The middle cut of a salmon is the most delicate part of the fish, but it is rather oily, and consequently more indigestible than the rest. Of the two halves, the one with the head is to be preferred.

Take a slice of about three pounds of salmon, in preference the cut near the head, put this on the drainer in a small fish-kettle with three quarts of boiling water and a handful of salt; boil it, and then simmer for about twenty minutes or till the fish is done, which can easily be ascertained by it separating from the bones. Then at once take the drainer out of the water, place the piece of salmon carefully on a folded napkin on the dish, decorate with a few sprigs of green parsley, and serve with Lobster sauce (No. 212) in a sauce-boat apart.

Salmon boiled in this way can also be served with shrimp, melted butter, or Hollandaise sauce.

391. SALMON À LA VENITIENNE.

Boil as in the foregoing two or three pounds of salmon cut in slices of one inch thick for twelve minutes; then strain, remove the skin, and put the slices of salmon in a sauté-pan with a pint of fish gravy (No. 20) and a spoonful of lobster butter (No. 169); let them simmer with the sauté-pan covered for ten minutes; after which, take each slice out with a flat skimmer without breaking, dish them up, by overlaying each other in a circle, pour a Venitian sauce (No. 206) over them, and serve.

392. SALMON À LA GENOISE.

Prepare a liquor called "Court Bouillon" in the following manner:—

Put a gill of salad-oil or three ounces of butter in a stewpan, with two onions and one carrot sliced, add a few trimmings of bacon or ham, a dozen pepper-corns, four cloves, a "bouquet garni," and a handful of salt; fry these ingredients over the fire for eight minutes, stirring the while; then pour in a bottle of white dry wine and two quarts of water or fish broth; let it simmer for half an hour, skim, and strain through a sieve into a small fish-kettle; then put in three pounds of salmon, cut in slices as in No. 391, boil these gently for twenty-five minutes, strain in the usual way, and dish them up with Genoise sauce (No. 207) poured over, and serve.

Note.—This "Court Bouillon" will keep a long time if boiled every four days, adding half a pint of water or fish broth and a similar quantity of wine each time. This liquor is generally used for boiling fresh-water fish.

393. BROILED SALMON. TARTARE SAUCE.

Steep two pounds of salmon, cut in slices of about one inch thick, in a dish with half a gill of salad-oil; salt and pepper. Broil these on a good and clear fire for twelve minutes each side, then dish up and serve with Tartare sauce (No. 221) apart.

394. SALMON CUTLETS À L'INDIENNE.

Slice a piece of salmon as previously described, cut these in halves, lengthwise, then rub them slightly over with oil, sprinkle each slice with salt and pepper, broil them over a clear fire for twelve minutes each side; after which, dish them up in a circle on a napkin on a dish, and serve with Indian curry sauce (No. 185) apart.

395. SALMON CROQUETS.

Pieces of cooked salmon should be used for croquets. Proceed to make a salpicon of salmon in the same way as the salpicon of lobster (see No. 314), then turn this into croquets (No. 326), fry in the same way, and serve.

396. SALMON WITH MAYONNAISE SAUCE.

Trim, wash, and shred two lettuces; season with oil, vinegar, salt, and pepper; lay these at the bottom of a dish.

Cut in small fillets the boiled salmon left from the previous day's dinner; pile these over the lettuces in the centre of the dish. Cover the lot with Mayonnaise sauce (No. 219), decorate the border of the dish with two hard-boiled eggs cut in quarters and two cleansed and boned anchovies, each cut in fillets of four, twisted round the finger and placed alternately with the eggs, and serve.

397. PICKLED SALMON.

Clean, wash, and wipe a whole salmon weighing about twelve pounds, tie the head with a string and simmer very gently in the fish-kettle on the drainer for fifty minutes in plenty of salt water and a glass of vinegar, or better still with "Court Bouillon" (No. 392). After which, if the fish is cooked in a "Court Bouillon," remove the fish-kettle to a cool place, leaving the salmon in it until it is cold. If boiled in water, drain the fish when cooked, and slide it very carefully from the strainer into a deep oval dish; and then in either case pour over it a well-beaten mixture composed of a bottle of vinegar, half a pint of oil properly seasoned with salt, a tablespoonful of pepper-corns, six cloves, two bay-leaves, and the peel of two lemons. Let the fish steep in this liquor for at least four hours, taking care to baste it often with the liquor during that time; then dish up on a large oval dish with part of its liquor strained over it; remove the string from around the head, decorate the fish and the dish with a border of peeled cucumber-slices partly immersed in the liquor, a few thin slices of lemon cut in fancy shapes and placed about on the dish, and, last but not least, a few sprigs of fennel nicely arranged about the head, tail, and centre of the fish, and then send to the table.

Remarks on Turbot.

Turbot is a very thick flat-fish, and (halibut excepted) is the largest of that class.

The greater portion of turbots supplied to the various English markets is caught on or near the numerous sandbanks between England and Holland, but the finest comes from the Flemish coasts.

The flesh of the turbot is almost as white as snow, firm, delicate, savoury, and very nourishing, and may without prejudice, on account of its superior taste and flavour, combined with its plump and fleshy shape, be compared to the Surrey chicken, and called the sea-capon.

398. BOILED TURBOT. HOLLANDAISE SAUCE.

Choose a thick and plump turbot; see that the fins or backbone are free from colour; if it has any reddish appearance about it the turbot (although it may be quite fresh) will boil a bad colour. Clean the inside thoroughly and rub with a handful of salt; trim the fins close; wash, and wipe dry; rub over with the juice of a lemon, score it with a pointed knife a quarter of an inch deep across the back two or three times; put two handfuls of salt over it and place in a turbot-kettle on the drainer with sufficient boiling water to cover the fish. Boil, and as soon as the water begins to simmer, skim it well; then let it simmer for about half an hour, more or less, according to the size of the fish. When the fish is done lift it out of the water with the drainer, put this across the kettle for a few minutes to dry, and then slip it very carefully on to a dish and serve with Hollandaise sauce (No. 184) apart.

PRACTICAL HOUSEHOLD COOKERY. 187

399. FILLETS OF TURBOT À L'INDIENNE.

After having cleaned and trimmed a small turbot, or part of one, as in No. 398, cut it in scollops, place them in a sauté-pan with three ounces of butter, a gill of fish broth or boiling water, and two tablespoonfuls of curry paste or powder nicely sprinkled and mixed with the broth; let this simmer, with the lid on the sauté-pan, for twenty minutes; after which, add to it a gill of Velouté sauce (No. 153). Let the whole boil together for three minutes longer, then dish up the fillets, by laying one over the other in a circle, pass the sauce through a tammy sieve, make it hot again, mix with it an ounce of butter, stir to melt the butter well, then pour the sauce over the fillets, and serve.

400. FILLETS OF TURBOT À L'ITALIENNE.

Prepare the fillets of turbot as in No. 399, boil them with the same quantity of butter and fish broth for twenty minutes with the pan covered; then add half a pint of Italian sauce; let the contents simmer for four or five minutes longer; dish up the fillets in the same manner as the Indienne, and pass the sauce through a tammy into the pan to be made hot again; add an ounce of anchovy butter, together with a dessert-spoonful of chopped capers. Mix these well together, pour over the fillets, and serve.

401. TURBOT CREAM AU GRATIN.

Take the remnants of a cooked turbot; bone, and trim properly; cut or separate this in small flakes or fillets and put them into a stewpan with enough Béchamel sauce (No. 155) to moisten the bottom of the pan; season this with salt, pepper, grated nutmeg, and the juice of a lemon; set the stewpan on the fire to warm the contents; after which, pile them up nicely on a gratin-dish, shake some grated cheese on the surface, pour a gill of cream over this, and set the dish in a moderately heated oven for eight or ten minutes in order to gratinate the top; then form a border around the fish, on the edge of the dish, with a purée of potatoes, hold a red-hot salamander over the whole surface to give it a light-brown colour, and serve.

402. TURBOT CROQUETS, &c.

Turbot can also be served in croquets, coquilles, mayonnaise, &c. &c. (see each heading).

403. BRILL.

This fish, bearing in shape and taste a great resemblance to turbot, is prepared in the same way and served with the same sauces, but requires scraping before cooking, in order to free it from scales.

404. JOHN DORY.

This fish, although a favourite with a great many, is but seldom sent to the table, otherwise than as a plain boiled fish, with either Lobster, Shrimp, Hollandaise, or Italienne sauce.

REMARKS ON COD-FISH.

The common cod is a fish almost universally known in cold and temperate climates. It is found in almost every sea but the Mediterranean, and as a proof of the commercial importance and value of cod, the right of its fisheries has even been, from time to time, the cause of ill-feeling between the fishermen of friendly nations.

Cod-liver-oil is a great source of income to the fishermen of the North, as well as a boon and relief to weak and consumptive persons.

405. COD WITH OYSTER SAUCE.

Crimp a piece of cod; place it on the drainer in a fish-kettle with a handful of salt; pour over it sufficient boiling water to cover it entirely. Boil it, and let it simmer for a quarter of an hour, then drain and place it on a napkin on a dish, and serve with Oyster sauce (No. 186) in a sauce-boat apart.

Cod boiled as above can also be served with Egg, Hollandaise, Melted Butter, or Tomato sauce.

406. COD STUFFED AND BAKED.

Clean, trim, and stuff the inside of a cod with some well-seasoned veal stuffing, which secure by sewing up; make several deep incisions on either side of the fish, and place it in a deep baking-dish, previously spread with plenty of butter; season with salt, pepper, two shalots, a few mushrooms and some parsley chopped fine; moisten with half a bottle of white wine and a gill of broth. Set the fish in the oven to bake, and every ten minutes, or oftener, baste with its liquor. When the fish is nearly done sprinkle it over with some fine raspings, and put again in the oven for ten minutes. When the cod is baked draw the string out without tearing the flesh of the fish; put this on a hot dish with a little broth to detach the glaze from the bottom of and around the pan, pass the lot through a tammy sieve into a small stewpan, add a little brown sauce; reduce the whole to a proper consistency; add half an ounce of anchovy butter, a little cayenne, and the juice of a lemon; stir this well together on the fire, pour it over and round the cod in the dish, and serve.

407. COD À L'INDIENNE.

Trim some pieces of cod in the shape of thick fillets, place these in a sauté-pan well buttered; moisten with some Indian curry sauce (No. 185) prepared for the purpose; cover the sauté-pan with its lid and set on a sharp fire to boil for about twenty minutes; then dish up the fillets in the form of a circle, overlaying each other, pass the sauce through a tammy, pour it over the fish, and serve.

408. COD À LA GENOISE.

Prepare some slices of cod as in the previous number, put these in a nicely oiled sauté-pan and moisten with a pint of Genoise sauce (No. 207); cover the pan and simmer on a brisk fire for twenty minutes; after which, dish up the fish as described in the foregoing, pour the sauce over, and serve.

409. COD À LA CRÊME, AU GRATIN.

Prepare the pieces of cod left from the previous day's dinner, in a manner similar to the turbot au gratin (No. 401).

410. COD IN COQUILLES.

Cod can also be served in coquilles, croquets, and mayonnaise (for which see Nos. 324, 326, and 396 respectively).

411. SALT COD. EGG SAUCE.

Salt cod should be soaked in running water, for at least twelve hours previous to being cooked. If this cannot be obtained, cover the piece of salt fish intended for cooking with warm water, and let it soak for six hours; after which, soak it for another six hours in cold water, taking care to change the water at least three times; then put it in a saucepan with plenty of cold water, boil for six or seven minutes; drain well; dish up, and garnish with plain boiled potatoes, and send to the table with some Egg sauce (No. 182) in a sauce-boat apart.

Note.—Salt cod steeped and boiled, as in the preceding

number, can also be served with melted butter, maître d'hôtel, or black butter.

Remarks on Sturgeon.

The sturgeon is generally found at the mouths of large rivers in the different seas of Europe, and used to be very highly appreciated by our ancestors; in fact, by an Act passed in the reign of Edward II. (which, I am informed, has never been repealed) that fish was called "Royal," and only allowed to be served on the table of that monarch, and forbidden to appear on any other.

Amongst the Romans, at their feasts, the sturgeon was decorated with garlands and wreaths, and used to be carried to the tables of Consuls and Emperors by the chiefs and nobles of their Court, to the sound of music.

The flesh of the sturgeon differs much in colour and taste, but a good cook can almost turn it at will into fish, meat, or poultry.

Caviare, composed of the roe of sturgeon, is very much relished, especially by the Russians, as a hors-d'œuvre, or side dish, and by them it is preserved, and exported, on a large scale to all parts of Europe.

412. STURGEON À LA VENITIENNE.

Take the half of a small sturgeon, the head-part in preference, and boil it in "Court Bouillon" (No. 392) for about two hours, with the fish-kettle covered; then drain and skim it, put the fish in a deep-baking dish with a pint of Genoise sauce (No. 207), let it simmer for ten minutes, taking care to often baste the fish with the sauce during that time; after which, dish it up, add to the sauce about a dozen small onions and a handful of mushrooms previously blanched and glazed in broth, together with an ounce of anchovy butter; mix this well on the fire, pour it over the fish, and serve.

413. STURGEON À L'ANGLAISE.

Procure a prime cut of sturgeon; remove the skin with a thin-bladed knife, by inserting the point between the flesh and skin close to the back fin, and drawing it to and fro so as to sever the skin from the flesh on both sides. When this is completed replace the skin over the sturgeon, and fasten on with a string, in order to preserve the colour of the fish. Put the fish on the drainer in the fish-kettle, with sufficient "Court Bouillon" to cover it well. Cover the fish-kettle and let it boil gently for two hours and a half; after which, draw the fish away from the fire, take it out and place on a dish in a hot closet, well covered with a folded clean cloth. Meantime take a pint of "Court Bouillon" out of the kettle in which the fish has just been cooked; strain into a small stewpan; add half a pint of port wine, and reduce the whole to a half-glaze; after which, mix with it a gill of Espagnole or any other brown sauce, a dozen button mushrooms, an ounce of anchovy butter, a little cayenne and grated nutmeg, and the juice of a lemon. Stir the lot well on the fire, and let it boil three minutes; then bring the fish out, remove the cloth, string, and skin, pour the sauce over the sturgeon, and serve.

414. STURGEON, LARDED AND ROASTED.

Remove the skin of a piece of sturgeon in the same manner as in No. 413, sprinkle the fish with salt and pepper, and if time will allow, lard with small strips of bacon on each side, or simply tie some thin slices of bacon on it; then butter a sheet of stiff kitchen paper large enough to enclose the sturgeon, put some sliced onions and carrots on the paper, as well as a few sprigs each of thyme and parsley, two bay-leaves and a laurel-leaf, place the fish on these and wrap it well in the paper, tie two more sheets of buttered paper around it, fix it on the spit to be roasted before an even fire, or in a baking-sheet to be baked in the oven, which will, in either case, take about one hour and a half or two hours, according to the size of the fish.

When the sturgeon is cooked, untie the strings and remove the paper, dish up and glaze it, then serve with Oyster, Lobster, or Indian sauce apart.

415. STURGEON AU GRATIN.

This method of dressing sturgeon should only be resorted to (as in the foregoing gratins) when it happens that a sufficient remnant is left from the previous day's meal.

Cut the sturgeon into small scollops; put into a sauté-pan enough Allemande sauce to moisten the quantity of fish left; add some fine herbs, lemon-juice, a little grated nutmeg, and half an ounce of anchovy butter; mix these ingredients well together on the fire; add the scollops of sturgeon, and when nicely hot, dish them up in a gratin dish, pour the sauce over, cover the whole with bread-crumbs and a handful of grated cheese, place the dish in the oven to gratinate, and when nicely browned, serve.

Sturgeon, in addition to the preceding modes of preparation, can also be dressed similarly to salmon, in all its varieties.

416. SKATE WITH BLACK BUTTER.

There are many varieties of skate, but amongst these the blue or grey skate are considered the best for the table, and when properly dressed are not unworthy of the epicure's notice. This fish is generally bought ready dressed and cleaned, but in case this should not be done, the following is the proper method of doing it:—

Skin the skate on both sides, cut off the tail, wash the fish thoroughly and lay it flat on the table; take a sharp knife and with it separate the fleshy parts from the backbone on both sides; after which, cut these pieces into long strips by cutting through the cartilaginous or finny parts; place these strips in a pan with plenty of fresh water in order to crimp them. In like manner separate the other side of the fish and place the pieces also in the cold water; keep the liver apart, and change the water in which the fish is placed very often and until the crimping be effected.

Put these pieces into a saucepan with sufficient water to cover the fish; add a glass of vinegar, a handful of salt, and a faggot of parsley. Set the saucepan to boil and simmer for a quarter of an hour, draw the pan away from the fire, drain the fish, and keep it hot. Meantime put the liver of the skate into a small stewpan, with enough of the liquor in which the skate was cooked to moisten it; then boil for five minutes and drain; dish up the fish and liver, pour half a pint of black butter (No. 164) over it, garnish with a handful of fried parsley, and serve.

417. SKATE À LA GENOISE.

Prepare and cook the crimped pieces of skate in the same way as in the previous number; dish these up, and pour over some Genoise sauce (No. 207), and serve.

418. SKATE, HOLLANDAISE SAUCE.

Boil in plenty of salt water with two glasses of vinegar, for about a quarter of an hour, the whole of a skate. When cooked strain, and peel off the skin from both sides, put the skate on a dish, cover it with Hollandaise sauce (No. 184), in which you have previously mixed a tablespoonful of capers, and serve.

REMARKS ON MACKEREL.

It has been proved beyond a doubt that the gills of mackerel undergo fermentation and become poisonous forty-eight hours after the fish has been caught; therefore no part of the head should be eaten, and I strongly advise the cutting-off both head and gills of every mackerel (however fresh they may be) before cooking.

419. BOILED MACKEREL.

Remove the gills as aforesaid, and cleanse the inside of one or more good-sized mackerel, cut off the end of the tail and fins, boil the fish in salt water with a little vinegar, dish up, and serve with Fennel (194) or Parsley sauce, in a sauce-boat apart.

420. BROILED MACKEREL À LA MAÎTRE D'HÔTEL.

Prepare the mackerel as in the foregoing, split the fish down the back lengthwise, to the bone. Put these halves on a dish in which you have already placed two tablespoonfuls of olive-oil properly seasoned, with salt and pepper; soak the fish well with this; then place the halves on a gridiron, over a brisk fire, for six minutes each side; dish them up, put some cold maître d'hôtel butter (No. 226) over each half, and serve on a very hot dish.

421. MACKEREL À LA GENOISE.

Cut off the heads of three mackerel; clean and wash the fish properly, place them in a fish-kettle with a pint of white wine, a few sprigs of chopped parsley, three boned and chopped anchovies, a clove of garlic and half an onion shred fine; add to it a little oil, salt and pepper to taste, and set to simmer for about half an hour; after which, take the fish out, add to the liquor a gill of Espagnole sauce and the juice of a lemon; stir the lot well together on the fire, dish up the fish, strain, and pour the sauce over it, and serve.

422. FILLETS OF MACKEREL À LA VENITIENNE.

Fillet three mackerel as follows :—Place the fish on the slab with its back toward you, then run the knife in, just below the gills, turn the edge of the blade under, press with the fingers of the left hand full on the upper end of the fish, and bearing with the blade of the knife upon the side of the backbone, draw the knife gently down to the tail, then turn the mackerel over and take the fillet off the other side. When this is done cut each fillet in two, trim the ends nicely, and put them in a buttered sauté-pan; season with salt and pepper, and add two ounces of clarified butter; cover the fillets with a round of buttered paper; set the pan over a moderate fire to simmer for about a quarter of an hour; after which, dress the fillets up in a dish in a circle, pour over some Venitian sauce (No. 206), and serve.

423. STEWED FILLETED MACKEREL.

Fillet three mackerel as in the foregoing, and take the skin off; put these in a frying or baking pan with three ounces of melted butter, salt and pepper-corns to taste, a little chopped parsley and an onion shred fine. Set these on a moderate fire to stew nicely, taking care to turn the fillets without breaking them. When cooked, dish these up in a circle, pour in the pan half a pint of Tomato or Italian sauce; stir the contents well on the fire till nicely hot, then pour the sauce over the fish and serve.

REMARKS ON SOLE.

To the public in general soles are the most important of sea-fish, as they are required by all classes of society, the upper class getting the largest and best quality, the poorer the smaller and inferior fish.

The supply of soles to the London market is very fluctuating on account of their migratory habits; retiring to great depths in the ocean, during the winter and in stormy weather.

The flesh of the sole is white, and possesses a delicacy and flavour superior to that of all other fish. It is generally recommended to invalids and convalescents as a most nourishing and digestive food.

424. BOILED SOLES.

Remove the gills, cut off the heads transversely, cleanse the insides, strip or pull off the brown skins, scrape the other sides, then with a pair of large scissors trim away the fins close up to the fillets of two large soles. After which, wash and wipe them thoroughly, then immerse in boiling salt water, and let them boil for twelve or fifteen minutes, according to their size. When the soles are cooked dish up and serve with Butter sauce (No. 157) in a boat apart.

425. FRIED SOLES.

Trim and clean four soles of moderate size, as in the foregoing. Flour these well on both sides, then pass them through breadings (No. 269) and bread-raspings (No. 268). After which, dip them in warm frying fat, and gradually increase the heat till the soles are of a nice pale-brown colour, when they must be taken out. Drain them on a cloth, sprinkle each with salt, dish up on a napkin, garnish with a few sprigs of fried parsley and a lemon cut in quarters, and serve with or without some Shrimp, Lobster, Melted Butter, or Hollandaise sauce.

Note.—Moderate-sized soles only should be used for frying, as when large they must necessarily take a considerable time in the frying, on account of their thickness, and imbibe a greater portion of the fat, and therefore contract a strong flavour. They are also less likely to appear crisp, although this is so essential a requisite in all fried fish.

426. SOLES À LA COLBERT.

Clean and trim two large soles as described in No. 425; make an incision on each side of the bone down the whole fish, break the bone in pieces with the handle of the knife, so as to facilitate removing it when cooked, pass these through breadings and bread-raspings (Nos. 268 and 269), and fry them in hot fat for about ten or twelve minutes. When the soles are properly cooked, drain on a cloth, put them on a dish, remove the pieces of bone, fill the inside with some cold maître d'hôtel (No. 226), garnish with a little fried parsley, put the dish for two minutes in the oven, and serve with a lemon cut in four.

427. SOLES WITH FINE HERBS.

Clean and trim two large soles as in the foregoing; put them on a buttered sauté-pan, sprinkle over them some chopped mushrooms, parsley, and one shalot; season with salt, pepper, and a little nutmeg; moisten with two glasses of white wine; cover the soles with a buttered paper and set them in the oven to cook. When done, drain the liquor into a small stewpan containing half a pint of Allemande sauce; add to it a spoonful of blanched and chopped parsley, a pat of fresh butter, and the juice of a lemon;

stir the whole well together on the fire; dish up the soles, pour the sauce over, and serve.

428. SOLES AU GRATIN.

After having cleaned and trimmed, in the usual way, two large soles, spread them in a well-buttered gratin-dish or gratin-pan; season with salt and pepper, moisten with half a pint of white wine, and sprinkle with a little finely chopped parsley; put these in the oven to bake for about twenty minutes; after which, pour over them half a pint of Italian sauce (No. 204.). Strew the top thickly with bread-raspings, push the dish back in the oven for a few minutes to gratinate, and just before serving pass the red-hot salamander over them.

429. SOLES À LA PROVENÇALE.

Take two large soles, trim and clean as in the foregoing, place them in a sauté-pan properly seasoned with salt, pepper, nutmeg, and chopped parsley; add to these a gill of white wine and the same quantity of salad-oil; cover the fish with a well-oiled sheet of paper, and set the pan in the oven to bake. Meanwhile shred four large onions and fry them in a gill of good oil to a nice brown colour. When the soles are done dish up, drain the onions and mix them with the liquor of the fish, pour it over the soles, and serve after having squeezed the juice of half a lemon over them.

430. FILLETS OF SOLE À LA LIVOURNAISE.

Trim and clean two soles in the usual way; place them in a sauté-pan with a gill each of white wine, good vinegar, and broth. Season properly with salt, pepper, nutmeg, chopped parsley, mace, and majoram. Cook on a good fire for ten minutes, and let them get cold; after which, fillet with a pointed knife and put back in the sauté-pan with the bones. Lay on each fillet, with a knife, a tablespoonful of raw fish forcemeat (No. 275); add a little anchovy butter, the juice of half a lemon, a few slices of cooked mushrooms and truffles on each fillet. Cover these with a buttered sheet of paper, boil, and place the sauté-pan in a very hot oven for a quarter of an hour. Meanwhile prepare as many slices of buttered toast, cut of the same shape as the fillets of soles, and dish up the fillets on them, and pour the sauce over the lot before serving.

431. SOLES WITH FRIED PARSLEY.

After having cleaned and trimmed two soles, throw them into two quarts of boiling salt water. Meanwhile boil the frying fat, and when the soles are nearly cooked strain and dry them well, then dip them in the frying fat with some parsley, and serve with a lemon cut in four, garnished with the fried parsley.

This simple mode of cooking suits any kind of salt-water fish, and can be recommended.

432. FILLETED SOLES. VENITIAN SAUCE.

Prepare eight fillets of sole and place them in a buttered sauté-pan; season with salt, pepper, and a little mace, moisten with a pint of broth, cover with a buttered paper, cook on a quick fire, dish them in a circle, pour over some Venitian sauce (No. 206), and serve.

433. SOLES À LA NORMANDE.

Trim and strip off the black skin of two soles, make a good incision along each side of the bone on the skinned part of each sole, and clean well; then butter a sauté-pan large enough to hold the two soles, strew it with some very finely chopped onions, previously blanched, lay the soles on these, season with salt and pepper, moisten with half a pint of white wine, and cook them in the oven. Meanwhile have half a pint of fish broth (No. 25) ready made, which must be boiled with a gill of white wine. Blanch separately twelve oysters, twelve mussels, and twelve mushroom buttons; fry also twelve smelts and some croûtons ready for garnish. When the soles are cooked put them on a silver dish and keep hot; add the liquor of the soles, as well as that in which the mussels were cooked, to the fish broth, and strain it through a fine cloth into a saucepan. Melt two ounces of butter in another saucepan, add to it two ounces of flour, stir this well over the fire with a wooden spoon, moisten with the liquor, and reduce it by boiling for fifteen minutes; then strain through a tammy cloth and thicken it with the yolks of two eggs. Place the oysters, mussels, and mushrooms decoratively on the soles and round them, pour the sauce over, and put the dish in the oven for five minutes, taking care not to colour the sauce; after which, garnish the border of the dish, with the fried smelts and croûtons, then serve.

Crayfish or prawns as well as truffles can also be added with advantage to the above garnish.

434. SOLE WITH WHITE WINE SAUCE.

Prepare two soles as in No. 433, put them in a buttered sauté-pan, season with salt and pepper, moisten with a pint of dry white wine, and set them into the oven to bake for twenty-five minutes. Meantime melt and mix in a stewpan two ounces of very fresh butter with the same quantity of flour, by stirring it over the fire with a wooden spoon for two or three minutes; season the same with salt, pepper, and a little grated nutmeg; moisten with half a pint of white broth, stirring the while. When the soles are cooked pour their liquor into the stewpan, stir, and boil gently for one minute; add an ounce of fresh butter; stir the sauce off the fire till the butter is well melted; dish up the soles, pour the sauce over, and serve.

REMARKS ON MULLET, RED AND GREY.

There are two distinct species of red mullet, one plain red, and the other striped red. There is also another species called grey mullet, but these are very common, and do not possess the same delicacy and flavour as the former.

Red mullet should never be drawn; the gills only should be taken out, as it is considered that the liver and trail are the best part of this fish.

435. RED MULLET, MAÎTRE D'HÔTEL.

Remove the gills of six red mullet; cut off the fins, scrape, and dip them quickly in water; wipe, and if large, score them gently across two or three times; then lay them on a dish and pour over each a tablespoonful of salad-oil; strew an onion cut in small slices, a few sprigs of parsley, salt and pepper, say three pinches of each, and let them steep so for at least half an hour; then take them out of the dish, one by one, shaking and freeing them from the oil, onions, and parsley, put them on a gridiron over a clear fire for five or six minutes each side, when they must be dressed on a hot dish, taking care not to break them, and serve with a quarter of a pound of maître d'hôtel butter (No. 226) under and over.

436. RED MULLET, ITALIENNE.

Trim the mullet as in the foregoing, and lay them in a buttered sauté-pan; season with salt and pepper;

moisten with half a pint of white wine and a little essence of mushrooms; bake in a not too hot oven, taking care to baste often. When cooked dish up, have some Italian sauce (No. 204) ready, to which add the liquor in which the mullet have been cooked, after having previously reduced it a little by a sharp boiling; add a little essence of anchovy (No. 174) and the juice of half a lemon; stir the contents well, then pour it over the fish, and serve.

437. RED MULLET À LA GENOISE.

Prepare the red mullet in a sauté-pan as in the foregoing; moisten with half a pint of red wine and some essence of mushrooms; bake, baste, and dish up in the same way; then reduce the liquor in which the fish were cooked, and mix it with some Genoise sauce (No. 207), a little anchovy butter (No. 161), the juice of half a lemon, and pour it over the fish before serving.

438. RED MULLET IN CASES.

Spread the mullet in a well-buttered sauté-pan as before, season with salt and pepper, moisten with three glasses of sherry and a little essence of fish (No. 175). Bake in the oven, not forgetting the basting. When properly done put them separately in oblong paper cases, made for the purpose and saturated with olive-oil, put these on a dish and keep hot at the door of the oven. Meanwhile add another glass of sherry to the liquor remaining in the sauté-pan, stir it in order to detach any glaze that may have formed on the sides, add a little essence of anchovy (No. 161), the juice of half a lemon, and a spoonful of blanched and chopped parsley; stir these well together; sauce the mullets in their cases with it, spread a little finely bruised lobster coral over each, and serve.

439. GREY MULLET, HOLLANDAISE SAUCE.

Remove the gills, cut the fins, cleanse the inside, scale, wash, and wipe three grey mullet; boil for about twenty minutes in salted water, strain, and serve with half a pint of Hollandaise sauce (No. 184) apart.

Grey mullet can also be prepared in the same way as red mullet, viz., Maître d'Hôtel, à l'Italienne, Genoise, and Tomato sauce.

REMARKS ON WHITING.

This fish may be considered to be thoroughly English, as it is caught in great abundance almost all round the coast, but it should be eaten as soon as possible after being caught, as it is quickly spoilt by packing and travelling.

440. FRIED WHITING.

Whiting before being fried should be skinned, and the following is the proper way of doing it :—With a cloth in your left hand, take a firm hold of the whiting at the back part of the head just below the gills, then with a pointed knife in your right hand loosen the skin on each side of the fish (just over the upper dorsal fin) by inserting the point and pulling the skin off sharp, one side after the other. When the fish is skinned and trimmed, turn the tail round into its mouth and hook it to its teeth; then dip each fish into some beaten eggs, cover it with fine breadcrumbs and fry them in the frying fat, heated beforehand for that purpose, sprinkle with salt before dishing them on a dish, paper, or napkin, with fried parsley, and serve with a lemon cut in four, or either of the following sauces, Anchovy, Plain Butter, Shrimp, or Hollandaise.

441. WHITING BOILED.

Trim only the number of whiting required, boil in some salt water for about seven minutes; after which, dish them up on a napkin on a dish and serve with either a Tomato, Shrimp, Anchovy, Plain Butter, or Hollandaise sauce.

442. BROILED WHITING.

Trim the whiting and slightly score them on both sides, rub some oil over each and broil on a gridiron which has been previously rubbed with chalk. When done on both sides dish up on a napkin and serve with maître d'hôtel butter (No. 226) or ravigote (No. 162).

443. FILLETS OF WHITING, ITALIAN.

Fillet four whiting, after having removed the skin as described in No. 438. Cut each fillet in two and place them side by side in a buttered sauté-pan; strew each with a little finely chopped parsley, season with salt and pepper, pour two ounces of melted butter, and squeeze the juice of a lemon over them, cover with a buttered sheet of paper, put the lid over the sauté-pan and boil for six or seven minutes; after which, remove the lid and paper, dress the fish carefully on a dish, pour some Italian sauce (No. 204), prepared for that purpose, over them, and serve.

444. FILLETED WHITING, VENITIAN.

Fillet four whiting as in No. 443, place these in a deep dish, season with salt, pepper, a few sprigs of thyme, two bay-leaves, three shalots cut in slices, and a few blades of parsley; add one tablespoonful of good vinegar and two of olive-oil. After having let them steep thus for at least two hours, drain on a cloth, dip each fillet separately into light-made frying batter, and throw one after another into some frying fat, properly heated for that purpose. As soon as they have acquired a light-brown colour take them out of the fat, lay on a clean cloth in order that the grease may be absorbed; dish them in a circle on a hot dish, pour some Venitian sauce over, and serve.

445. FILLETS OF WHITING, CITIZEN STYLE.

Skin and fillet four whiting as in No. 444; place these side by side in a large well-buttered gratin-dish; lay a border of plain boiled potatoes, chopped fine, round them; season the lot with salt, pepper, and a little nutmeg; moisten with two ounces of melted butter; squeeze the juice of a lemon over the fillets and sprinkle these lightly with some fine bread-crumbs; cover the lot with a buttered sheet of paper and set in the oven to bake gently for about twenty or twenty-five minutes, before serving.

446. GURNARD À LA GENOISE.

Cut off the head and fins of two gurnards. Boil the fish in water with a little salt and a glass of vinegar; when done strain and skin, dish up, and pour some Genoise sauce (No. 207) over. Then garnish them round with some quenelles of whiting (No. 275) previously made and cooked in the water in which the gurnards were boiled, and serve.

Note.—Gurnards cooked or baked as above may be served with Tomato, Sharp, Ravigote, or Italienne sauce, according to taste.

447. GURNARD À L'INDIENNE.

In the same way as the foregoing, cut off the heads and fins of the gurnards; cleanse and wipe the fish well and then stuff them with some veal stuffing, well seasoned; sew up and score slightly on both sides. Place these fish in a buttered baking-dish or sauté-pan; season with salt and pepper, sprinkle over some finely chopped parsley, moisten with a little broth, some essence of mushrooms and two glasses of sherry; and set these in the oven to bake, taking care to baste them at least every five minutes until they are done, which will take about half an hour. Then dress the fish on a dish, cut and pull away the thread with which they were sewn, place the dish in the open oven, add a little broth to detach the glaze from the bottom and sides of the vessel in which the fish were cooked, reduce it to a half-glaze and mix it with some Indian sauce (No. 185). Add a little essence of anchovies, stir it well before pouring over, and serve.

Remarks on Bream.

Bream are taken in large quantities in the Broads and rivers of Norfolk during the spring months, and sent from there to the great inland towns, where during Lent and the Hebrew Passover they are in constant demand, and command a good price.

448. SEA BREAM, MAÎTRE D'HÔTEL.

Bream is prepared similarly to red mullet (No. 435), and can also be cooked and dressed with any other fish sauce, according to taste.

Remarks on Lampreys.

Lampreys are in season from March to July, and are still considered great delicacies in the London market, although they do not possess such a high repute as in bygone days. Their average size is from one and a half to three pounds. They principally come from the Severn and the Thames, but none are in the market during the winter.

449. LAMPREY. MATELOTTE.

Put two lampreys into an earthen or tin vessel with plenty of freezing salt, with which they must be scoured well, and afterwards thoroughly washed in several waters. By this means only can they be freed from the slimy mucus which adheres to them. Then trim and cut into pieces of about three inches long; place these in a stewpan with a sliced carrot and onion, a little ground mace, a dozen pepper-corns, a few sprigs each of thyme and parsley, three bay-leaves, a few button mushrooms, and salt. Moisten this with a pint of port wine and let it stew gently on a moderate fire till done; then take half the liquor in which the fish have been stewed, reduce it in a small saucepan with a little brown sauce, add a glass of port wine, and as soon as this sauce is reduced to its proper consistency add a little butter, a little essence of anchovies, and the juice of a lemon. Pass it through a tammy into a bain-marie containing the mushrooms at first put with the fish; add two dozen small stewed onions (287) and a few quenelles of fish, previously cooked in fish broth. Keep these hot, and meantime drain the pieces of lamprey; dish them up; pour the sauce over; garnish round with the tails of either prawns, shrimps, or crayfish, and serve.

450. LAMPREY. BORDELAISE.

Cleanse two fine lampreys as in the foregoing; form them into a circular shape by fastening with a string; stew in a pint of claret with the addition of vegetables and dried herbs as in the Matelotte, to which two mashed cloves of garlic must be added, and as soon as they are properly cooked reduce their liquor in a stewpan with a similar quantity of brown sauce and a little essence of mushrooms to its proper consistency; then add a little essence of anchovies, a little grated nutmeg, a small quantity of cayenne, and the juice of a lemon; stir this well together and pass it through a tammy into a bain-marie containing two dozen button mushrooms and the tail of a small lobster, properly prepared and cut into small dice for that purpose. Dish up the lampreys after having drained them; sauce them over; garnish with a border of croûtons fried in butter, and serve.

451. LAMPREY, CITIZEN STYLE.

Clean two lampreys as in No. 450, rub them over gently with some mixed white spices, place them in an earthenware pan in a cool place, and let them be for twenty-four hours; after which, stew gently with the moisture that has run from them, add an ounce of butter and half a pint of beef gravy, or enough to cover the fish. When nearly done add a glass of port wine, then complete the cooking by sprinkling a tablespoonful of chopped parsley over the fish, and dish up, when properly cooked with their liquor, and serve.

Note.—Lampreys cut in pieces and properly seasoned are also made into pies. They are exceedingly good and appreciated in Gloucestershire, where they are prepared and baked in that style, and eaten cold as well as hot.

Remarks on Haddock.

The weight of this fish varies from two to four pounds. They are generally cured in London by smoking in sawdust or burning fir-branches, but the far-famed Scotch "haddies" come principally from Findhorn, near Aberdeen.

452. FRESH HADDOCK WITH EGG SAUCE.

Clean and wipe two haddocks, boil in salt water for about ten minutes, drain, and dish up on a napkin, and serve with a sauce-boat full of Egg sauce (No. 182) apart.

Haddock, when plain boiled, can be served with any kind of fish sauce.

453. HADDOCK BROILED. MUSTARD SAUCE.

Take two haddocks and clean them; score them four or five times with a sharp knife on both sides, and steep in a little olive-oil, salt, and pepper, for about an hour; after which, place them on a gridiron previously rubbed with chalk, and broil gently on a clear fire, taking care not to break them in turning over. When done on both sides dish up, and serve with Mustard sauce (No. 223) in a boat apart.

454. FILLETS OF HADDOCK À L'ITALIENNE.

Fillet two haddocks, remove the skin by passing a pointed knife under the fillet so as to detach the tail end of the skin from the flesh of the fish, then by taking a firm hold of this detached piece of skin and inserting the knife with the edge of the blade turned from you, draw the skin towards you and keep moving the knife to and fro, at the same time pressing the blade firmly on the skin. Having thus removed the skin, cut each fillet in two or more, trim, and lay them neatly in a sauté-pan with two ounces of clarified butter; season with salt and pepper, squeeze the half of a lemon over them, sprinkle half a tablespoonful of chopped parsley, cover the lot with a well-buttered paper, and cook for about ten minutes on a moderate fire or in the oven; after which, remove the paper, drain the fillets, dish up, and pour some Italian sauce (No. 204) over and serve.

Haddock filleted and cooked as above can be served with any other sauce, such as Hollandaise, Genoise, Venitienne, &c., &c.

455. HADDOCK AU GRATIN.

Skin, clean, and wipe two haddocks; place them in a gratin-pan or dish previously buttered for that purpose, season with salt and pepper, moisten with a gill of white wine and the liquor of a pint of tinned champignons; lay a dozen of the mushrooms on the haddocks; put an ounce of butter, divided into eight parts, on the fish; sprinkle a tablespoonful of chopped parsley and four of raspings over the fish, and put the gratin-pan in a well-heated oven for fifteen or twenty minutes. Serve on the same dish.

456. HADDOCK FRIED. BUTTER SAUCE.

Prepare this in the same manner as fried whiting (No. 240), and serve with plain Butter sauce.

457. FILLETED HADDOCK, CITIZEN STYLE, WITH MAÎTRE D'HÔTEL SAUCE.

Prepare this in the same way as fillets of whiting (No. 445), and serve with Maître d'Hôtel sauce apart.

Smoked haddocks should not be broiled but boiled, as any impurity that may be attached to the fish when bought is thereby at once removed.

458. SMOKED HADDOCK.

Trim one or more haddocks and place them in a pan covered with lukewarm water. Boil; and after one minute of ebullition drain the fish well, dish up, lay a little fresh butter on it, and serve very hot.

459. SMOKED HADDOCK, CITIZEN STYLE.

Trim and boil two haddocks as in No. 458, and then skin and bone them carefully; then chop them into small dice, and mix these well with a pound and a half of boiled potatoes, previously cooked and rubbed through a wire sieve; season with pepper, a little cayenne, and nutmeg; lay the mixture on a gratin-dish, nicely shaped; melt two ounces of fresh butter, mix with it the yolks of two eggs properly beaten, and pour it over the fish, with a few pieces of butter in addition; then set the dish in a moderately heated oven for about ten or twelve minutes, or till it is of a nice golden-brown colour, and serve.

Remarks on Herrings.

Fresh herrings are very nutritious, but ought to be eaten only when full of roe, as they lose much of their quality when otherwise.

460. FRESH HERRINGS. MUSTARD SAUCE.

Cut off the heads and fins of four herrings; clean, scrape, and wash them well; score them in the same way as broiled grey mullets or whiting; then place on a dish, season with salt, pepper, and two tablespoonfuls of salad-oil, and after having let them steep for half an hour put them on a gridiron to broil for four or five minutes on each side; then dress them on a dish and serve with Mustard sauce (No. 223) apart.

461. FRESH HERRINGS FRIED WITH PLAIN BUTTER SAUCE.

Prepare some herrings as in No. 460; steep in milk; flour and bread-crumb them; fry in boiling fat; and serve with plain Butter sauce apart.

Remarks on Halibut.

Halibut is only to be found on the northern coasts, and grows to an enormous size, 200 lbs. being their ordinary weight. Their season is March, April, and May.

462. HALIBUT. OYSTER SAUCE.

This fish is prepared and cooked in every way as cod, oyster sauce (No. 405).

It can also be fried (this being the mode the Jews eat it the most), baked, broiled, and served with any fish sauce (see Cod).

REMARKS ON PLAICE, FLOUNDERS, &c.

Plaice, flounders, and dabs are flatfishes, like soles, turbot, and halibut. They are generally plentiful in the market during their proper season, which is spring; they are caught in great quantities in the Thames.

463. PLAICE, FLOUNDERS, AND DABS, FRIED.

These fish are prepared in every respect as halibut or haddock.

REMARKS ON CONGER EELS.

Conger eels are found principally on the sea-coasts of the south of England and Ireland; they are sometimes of an enormous size, weighing as much as a hundred pounds. The flesh of the big fish is rather tough and coarse, but the smaller fish can be prepared in the same way as freshwater eels, although they are not so delicate and nutritious.

Conger is in season from March to October.

464. CONGER EEL. MAÎTRE D'HÔTEL SAUCE.

Take a piece of conger eel weighing about two pounds; cleanse it most carefully; wash and tie it round with string, and blanch in boiling salt water for ten minutes; drain, and put it in a stewpan; cover it with water, add two sliced onions, a handful of parsley, two bay-leaves, a glass of vinegar, one clove of garlic, and season with salt and pepper; let it simmer for half an hour; after which, drain and dress on a dish, and serve with Maître d'Hôtel sauce (No 159) apart.

465. CONGER EEL, ROASTED.

Cleanse, skin, and wash a piece of conger eel weighing about three pounds; place this in a dish, with salt, pepper, nutmeg, a gill of salad-oil, the juice of a lemon, a bay-leaf, two sprigs of thyme, a sliced onion, and small carrot, to steep for about two hours. After this, put the fish in a buttered baking-pan; cover with a buttered or oiled paper and bake it in a hot oven for half an hour or till well coloured; then put it on a very hot dish, remove the grease or fat from the pan in which it was baked; put in the pan a tablespoonful of chopped parsley, a gill of Spanish sauce (No 151), and the juice of a lemon; stir this well on the fire, and after boiling for a few minutes pour over the fish and serve.

REMARKS ON FRESH-WATER EELS.

There are three or four distinct species of fresh-water eels found in this country. The most common of these are the sharp-nosed and the broad-nosed eels, inhabiting and abounding in all fresh-waters throughout Europe, and in short in almost every part of the world except the Arctic regions. The eel will live a long time out of water, and migrate from place to place by crawling overland; but the strangest part of all in the construction of this fish is, that it possesses a heart located in its tail.

Eels vary in size, some weighing over ten pounds, but usually from one to three.

466. STEWED EELS, ENGLISH STYLE.

Eels are generally alive when brought into the kitchen; it is therefore necessary, on account of their tenacity of life, to know an easy way of killing them; this is done by merely inserting the point of a sharp instrument into the spine at the back of the head to the depth of an inch, when the eel will become perfectly motionless. Then scour the fish well with freezing salt, in order to remove the slimy mucus attached to the skin; after which, with a cloth in your left hand take a firm hold of the eel's head, and with the right hand proceed to detach the skin just below the gills with the point of a small knife. When this is done take hold of the loosened skin with your right hand and force it to slide off the fish; cut off the head, lay the fish flat on the table, and with the same pointed knife open it from one extremity to the other by pressing the point of the blade against the backbone on both sides; remove the gut, &c., trim away the fins, clean and wipe thoroughly both halves of the fish after having taken the bone out, then cut the eel into pieces of about three inches long, place them in a stewpan with a sliced carrot and onion, a few sprigs of parsley and thyme, a few pepper-corns, four cloves, a blade of mace, and a little salt. Moisten the lot with half a bottle of port wine, cover with a buttered paper and replace the lid on the stewpan; set this on the stove-fire to stew gently for about twenty minutes; after which drain, and trim the pieces, keeping their liquor to make the sauce, by melting two ounces of butter into a small stewpan. When this is done add two tablespoonfuls of flour and stir it over the fire with a wooden spoon until it becomes slightly coloured, then moisten gradually with the liquor in which the eels were stewed; add to it a gill or two of good stock and two glasses of port wine; stir this sauce over the fire till it boils, when it must be drawn to the corner of the stove, in order to let it throw up gently the scum, which must be skimmed off; then, if necessary, reduce the sauce to its proper consistency, pass it through a tammy into the stewpan containing the pieces of eel, add a few prepared mushroom buttons, a pat of fresh butter, a little blanched and chopped parsley, the juice of a lemon, and a teaspoonful of essence of anchovy; toss the whole well together over the fire till well mixed and boiling, then dish the eel up, pour the remainder of the sauce over it, garnish round with croûtons fried in butter, and serve.

467. EEL MATELOTTE.

Prepare a nice-sized eel as in No. 466, cut it into pieces of three inches long, and place them in a sauté-pan with two ounces of butter, the half of an onion chopped fine, and half a tablespoonful of chopped parsley. Season with salt, pepper, a little nutmeg, one clove of garlic, and two bay-leaves; set these on the fire to brown a little; after which, sprinkle a tablespoonful of flour; fry for two minutes longer, stirring the while with a wooden spoon; then moisten with half a bottle of red wine (claret, Burgundy, or Italian) and half a pint of stock; let it simmer for twenty-five minutes, and put the pieces of eel on a dish in a circular order, so that each piece rests on the other, viz., a slice of croûton and a piece of eel, and so on. Then pass the sauce through a tammy into a stewpan, add a little anchovy butter, together with the juice of a lemon; stir this on the fire till it boils, fill up the centre of the dish with two dozen button onions (No. 287), previously stewed and glazed for that purpose, pour the sauce over the lot, and serve.

468. EEL MILANAISE.

Skin, bone, and cleanse two eels as previously described; cut them in pieces about two inches long and brown them nicely in butter, properly seasoned with salt and pepper, for eight minutes; after which, take them out, squeeze the juice of two lemons over them, sprinkle each with some fine herbs and mace, egg and bread-crumb them, and fry them in clarified butter. When properly done dish up the pieces on a napkin and serve very hot, with a sharp sauce to taste, apart.

469. FILLET OF EEL, FRIED. TARTARE SAUCE.

Fillet two eels of about one and a half pound each in the usual way. Steep these in boiling water for four minutes, then rub the outside of the fillets well with a cloth, in order to remove the second oily skin; cut them in pieces three inches long, put them in a stewpan with enough water to cover the lot, add a glass of vinegar, a sliced onion and carrot, a "bouquet garni," salt, and a dozen pepper-corns. Simmer for twenty minutes; after which, let the eels cool for half an hour in the liquor; then drain, and place them on a cold dish. Mix in a basin two eggs with a tablespoonful each of oil and water, beat this with a fork as for an omelet, then dip each piece of eel in it; bread-crumb them afterwards, and fry in hot fat, previously heated for that purpose, till of a nice brown colour; then dish them up on a napkin garnished with fried parsley, and serve with Tartare sauce (No. 221) in a sauce-boat apart.

470. COLLARED EEL (COLD).

Skin, bone, and cleanse as described two eels of about two pounds each; lay each half flat on the table, the inside up; sprinkle these with salt, pepper, nutmeg, fine herbs, and ground mace. Roll them up tightly, fold each roll in white kitchen paper, and tie them round with string; place in a saucepan with a quart of ordinary stock, a sliced onion and carrot, one stick of celery, a "bouquet garni," salt and pepper to taste, two glasses of sherry, and a quarter of a pound of calf's gelatine. Boil this for half an hour, then strain the liquor through a tammy into a basin; take the packets of eel out and let them cool, as well as the liquor, which will turn into a jelly. When cold untie and remove the paper from each eel; lay on a dish, and decorate with the jelly aforesaid and a few sprigs of parsley well washed and dried. This is a delicious and not expensive mode of preparing eels; they will keep several days in cold water.

Remarks on Smelts.

Smelts are great favourites in dinner *menus*, and are also often used by cooks as a garnish to other fish, although I do not advocate their employment as such. Smelts are in season from September to May.

471. SMELTS, FRIED.

Take the smelts, pull out the gills carefully, trim the fins, and wipe the fish with a cloth. Then steep them in milk and flour them, or else flour them first and pass through beaten eggs, and afterwards put them in fine bread-crumbs. Fry in some properly heated lard or fat till of a nice colour and crisp; dish up on a napkin; garnish with fried parsley, and serve with a lemon cut in four.

Note.—The above mode is generally the one used to serve smelts, but they can also be dressed au gratin, in which case the larger ones are preferable. Proceed as for sole au gratin (No. 428).

Remarks on Whitebait.

It is said that whitebait is the rich man's fish, beginning when Parliament meets, and finishing when Parliament adjourns. The fact is, that its season proper is from February to August. There are many controversies on the subject of whitebait, as to whether it is the fry of other fish or a distinct species of fish.

Mr. Frank Buckland tells us that whitebait is nothing else but the fry of sprats, herrings, gobies, weevers, sand-eels, smelts, pipe-fish, sticklebacks, and gore-bills. Be this so or not, whitebait has now become a valuable article of food, but owing to its extreme delicacy, it cannot be conveyed any great distance without injury; neither can it be kept fresh many hours after it has been caught.

472. WHITEBAIT.

The following is the only mode of properly cooking whitebait:—Drain it on a clean cloth so that all the water is thoroughly absorbed, but abstain as much as possible from handling so delicate a fish. Then roll them in flour and place them on a coarse sieve to remove any excess of flour, by gently shaking them. Then drop them into well-heated frying fat (lard preferred) of about 400° Fahrenheit temperature, and as soon as they become crisp (which will be in about one minute, and is shown by the whity-brown colour) drain on a sieve for a minute or so. Sprinkle on a little salt; dish up on a napkin on a hot dish, and serve with quarters of lemon, cayenne pepper, and cut brown bread and butter on plates apart.

REMARKS ON SPRATS.

These small fish might be employed to better advantage and be a source of great income to fishermen were their monetary value better understood; in fact, sprats ought to be placed among the most beneficial and profitable fish caught, for by proper care and management they could be turned into food, sauce, and paste, as well as manure. The latter form of using them, however, would very soon be discarded if their different modes and preparation as an accessory to food were known.

Sprats can be preserved in the same manner as anchovies and made into paste sauce and butter (see Anchovy Butter). They can also be preserved in oil, in the same way as sardines in tins (and this should be an industry in itself), but very often are sold, I am sorry to say, with the brand of the latter name. Therefore if sprats are offered and sold to the public under different forms and names, their quality is appreciated, and should be so recognised and dealt with under their proper name, when they would, as a matter of course, very soon assume their real commercial value.

473. SPRATS, BROILED.

Clean and wipe the sprats (which must be fresh) in a coarse cloth, in order to remove the scales by gently rubbing the fish; place them afterwards on a gridiron and broil over a brisk fire for two minutes on each side; sprinkle with salt, and serve on a very hot dish with a little melted butter poured over.

474. SPRATS, FRIED.

Clean and wipe the sprats as in the foregoing, and follow the directions given for smelts fried (No. 471).

475. SPRATS AU GRATIN.

After having cleaned and rubbed the largest sprats as described, proceed as for haddock au gratin (No. 455).

476. SPRATS, CITIZEN STYLE.

Prepare the sprats in the usual way; butter a baking-dish; mix well in a basin a teaspoonful of fine herbs, a little nutmeg, salt, pepper, and a quarter of a pound of bread-crumbs; strew the bottom of the baking-dish with this mixture, then arrange a layer of sprats, sprinkle on these some of the bread-crumb mixture, and so on, for three layers of sprats; moisten with half a pint of good stock, sprinkle the remainder of the bread-crumbs over, put on the top a few pats of butter the size of a nut, and place the dish in a well-heated oven to bake for about half an hour; and before serving squeeze the juice of a lemon over them.

REMARKS ON LOBSTERS, CRABS, AND CRAWFISH.

Norwegian and Scotch lobsters are the best that come into the London market. They are known by the texture of their shells and are dark in colour.

Those coming from the Channel Islands and south coast are light in colour and thin of shell, and seldom stand the journey, most of them dying on the way. These southern lobsters are, however, very sweet and delicate in flavour, if cooked immediately after being caught.

In buying lobsters the heaviest should be selected, and the medium-sized ones are generally the best.

Lobsters should be boiled while alive by dropping them into boiling water with a little salt. The time to cook the same varies according to size; small lobster will take twenty minutes and a large one three-quarters of an hour.

Crabs make nice dishes when properly cooked and decorated; the best are caught on the south coast of Devonshire, and often run very large in size, some having weighed twelve and three-quarter pounds. Those from the north, especially from Scotland, are much smaller, and at times very sweet.

Crabs should be killed before being boiled or they are likely to shoot off their claws; you kill them by stabbing them through under the tail with either a trussing-needle or ice-prick.

Crawfish are treated in the same way as lobsters; those from the Scilly Isles, Cornwall, and Channel Islands are the best.

477. PLAIN BOILED LOBSTERS, CRABS, AND CRAWFISH.

Lobsters, crabs, and crawfish can always be obtained ready cooked, and are generally eaten with oil, vinegar, salt, and pepper, or with a Mayonnaise sauce.

478. LOBSTER À L'AMERICAINE.

Select a couple of live hen lobsters; take a firm hold of them by the back with the left hand; spread the tails over the kitchen-table and cut them across in scollops about an inch and a half thick; cut the body in half, lengthwise; save the residue liquid and the black part forming the eggs or coral by putting them into a basin; break off the claws from the shell; cut the large ones in two; then with the back of a large kitchen-knife or chopper break the shells, without, however, separating them, so as to facilitate removing the flesh when cooked; trim the other small ones and cut the body-shells again in two; put the lot in a sauté-pan with half a gill of olive-oil previously made hot and a few sprigs of thyme; toss these over a brisk fire for about five minutes. When the pieces of lobsters will have assumed a red colour, sprinkle one onion and two shalots chopped fine; stir the contents over the fire for another five minutes; then add half a gill of brandy and set fire to it; stir for a few seconds to feed the flames; after which, moisten with half a pint of white dry wine and two fresh tomatoes, peeled and chopped; season with salt and pepper, and simmer for ten minutes longer, taking care to turn the pieces over. Meanwhile melt two ounces of fresh butter in a small stewpan; add the residue mixture, with a few sprigs of chervil, tarragon, and a pounded bay-leaf; stir this gently by the side of the fire till it boils; sprinkle a small pinch of cayenne pepper; stir and add the same to the lobster; mix the lot well together over the fire, and when ready dish up the pieces of lobsters, pour the sauce over, and serve.

Note.—The above recipe, together with a few good and practical hints on cookery, was given to me by my old friend Mr. T. Garnier, for the last twelve years *chef* at the Café Royal, Regent Steet, to whom I herewith convey my most humble and grateful thanks.

Remarks on Trout.

There are several species of trout. Some are called salmon-trout and migrate to the sea; their flesh is of a pink rosy colour, and in taste differ but slightly from young salmon. Their weight varies from three to sixteen pounds. Others are non-migratory, live in lakes, rivers, and streams, and the colder and more rapid the water the better the fish. The flesh is almost white and very delicate;

the usual weight seldom exceeds three pounds, although there have been instances of common trout having been caught in lakes and rivers weighing fifteen pounds.

The season for trout is from March to September.

479. TROUT À L'ITALIENNE.

Remove the inside of two trout, through the gills, without cutting the fish; cut off the fins, wash and wipe the trout, and boil in salt water and a glass of vinegar for six minutes or more, according to the size of the fish; drain and divest of the skin, and lay them on a dish and keep hot. Meanwhile add to half a pint of Italian sauce (No. 205), previously made for that purpose, a pat of anchovy butter, a little nutmeg, and lemon-juice; work this well together, and pour over the fish before serving.

480. TROUT À LA MEUNIÈRE.

Cleanse, trim, wash, and wipe two or more trout. Score these three times on each side and pass them through the flour, taking care to shake them well, before putting in a frying-pan with three ounces of clarified butter; add a teaspoonful of blanched and chopped parsley, as well as the juice of two lemons, and when the fish is nicely coloured on both sides, serve on a hot dish with the remainder of clarified butter poured over it.

481. TROUT À L'AURORE.

Boil, skin, and trim the trout; then place on a silver or gratin-dish, mask each fish with reduced Allemande sauce (No. 156), lay a fine wire sieve across the dish, without touching the fish; then rub with a wooden spoon the yolks of two hard-boiled eggs over each fish through the sieve, taking care that the curling shreds cover the surface of each trout equally. About half an hour before serving, put them in the oven to get a fine amber hue; after which, pour round the trout some sauce made as follows:—Put half a pint of Béchamel sauce (No. 154) into a bain-marie, add to it a pat of lobster-butter, the yolks of three eggs properly beaten, a tablespoonful of tarragon vinegar, and a little cayenne; mix these well together with a small whisk or wooden spoon into the bain-marie before pouring out, and finish by making a border with two dozen mussels fried in batter.

482. BROILED TROUT. HOLLANDAISE SAUCE.

Clean and split a trout at the back, oil it over, season with nutmeg, salt, and pepper; then half an hour after, broil it over a moderately hot fire, and when done serve with some Hollandaise sauce (No. 184) in a sauce-boat apart.

Note.—Trout can be prepared in every variety of form and style in which salmon is dressed and served.

REMARKS ON PIKE OR JACK.

This fish, which might be called the water-wolf or fresh-water shark on account of its voraciousness and cannibalism, can in that respect be compared to the conger eel.

Pike will feed on ducklings, and any sort of fish, as well as on its own species, and is not at all particular as to size of its victim, as there are examples of two pike weighing some nineteen pounds having been caught alive, fastened firmly together, the head of one within the mouth and jaws of the other.

Pike are the largest of fresh-water fish, some having been caught weighing as much as sixty pounds and measuring nearly four feet in length. Of course, fish of that size are scarce, but the general weight varies from five to nine pounds, and the latter are the best for culinary purposes. The flesh is white, firm, and rather pleasing to the palate when properly prepared; but the roe causes a disagreeable, nauseous feeling, and should never be eaten.

483. PIKE À LA LYONNAISE AU BLEU.

The larger the pike the better for this dish, and it will improve if kept two days in a cool place after being caught. Scale,* draw the gills, cut off the fins, and thoroughly cleanse and wipe the pike; then with a string tie the head, and truss the fish into the shape of the letter S. Afterwards put the fish in the kettle covered with "Court Bouillon" (No. 392), and simmer for three-quarters of an hour; then take the fish-kettle to a cool place, let the pike remain in the liquor for at least twelve hours; if twenty-four all the better, as there is no comparison in the taste and quality of a pike that has soaked for twenty-four hours and one that has only been in the "Court Bouillon" for a couple of hours. When wanted, take up the fish very carefully from the strainer and lay it on a dish with the same care, remove the string, decorate with a few sprigs of fresh parsley, and moisten with a pint of sauce made with oil, vinegar, salt, pepper, and a teaspoonful of finely chopped parsley, well mixed together, in quantity of two-thirds oil to one of vinegar.

Note.—Pike cooked in the same way may also be served with Mayonnaise or Tartare sauce (Nos. 218 or 221).

---

* The easiest way to remove the scales of pike is by placing the fish in a sink and pour some boiling water over it, when the scraping will be effectually done.

484. BOILED PIKE. ITALIAN SHARP SAUCE.

After having scaled, cleansed, and wiped a nice pike, tie it up in the same way as in the foregoing, and boil it in a "Court Bouillon" (No. 392) for about fifty minutes, more or less, according to the size of the fish; after which, let it rest and cool in the liquor for twenty-four hours.

When the time comes for warming the fish, drain it, pour the "Court Bouillon" into another vessel, clean the kettle, and replace the liquor with the pike in it, to warm for about twenty minutes, without, however, letting it boil; then drain, and dish up on a napkin, remove the string, and send to table with some Italian sharp sauce (No. 205) in a sauce-boat apart.

Note.—Pike cooked in the above manner may be served with any fish sauce, according to taste.

485. PIKE BAKED, CITIZEN STYLE.

Prepare a large pike in the same manner as described above; fill the paunch with some well-seasoned veal stuffing, sew it up with a trussing-needle and fine string, truss as before specified in the form of the letter S, make several deep incisions on both sides of the fish, and place in a baking-dish seasoned with two chopped shalots, one tablespoonful of parsley, and two of mushrooms, salt, pepper, and half a dozen cloves; add between six and eight ounces of fresh butter, half a bottle of cooking sherry, and half a pint of good stock. Cover the lot with a well-buttered paper, and put the fish thus prepared in a well-heated oven to bake for about an hour, taking care to frequently baste it with its liquor. When done dish up, pour two glasses more of sherry, in order to detach all the glaze and herbs from the bottom and sides of the baking-dish in which the fish has been baked; pass this through a tammy into a small stewpan in which half a pint of good brown sauce has previously been warmed, mix and reduce the whole to a proper consistency; add one ounce of fresh butter, a teaspoonful of anchovy essence, the juice of a lemon, and a little cayenne; mix this well together on the stove, and pour over the fish before serving, having previously removed the string.

486. PIKE IN QUENELLES.

Prepare two or three pounds of pike in quenelles (see Fish Forcemeat, No. 275) in the following manner:—When cold, lay the forcemeat in large spoonfuls separately on the table, roll these with your hands into the shape of sausages, and cook them by poaching in ordinary boiling stock for five or six minutes. Meanwhile have a pint of good reduced Velouté sauce (No. 153) ready and hot; when the quenelles are properly poached, strain and put them in a bowl or deep dish; pour the sauce over, and serve.

Note.—Pike, previous to being made into forcemeat, should be filleted, and the following is the proper mode of operation. The smaller fish should be used for this purpose:—Lay the fish on the table with its back towards you, insert the knife below the gill with your left hand, press lightly on the upper part of the fish, then draw the knife down close to the backbone till the fillet is removed; repeat the same thing on the other side, and lay the fillets on the table with the skin downward; insert the edge of the knife close to the skin at the extreme end, draw it to and fro, in keeping the blade closely pressed to the skin, when it will detach itself from the fillet.

REMARKS ON PERCH.

The perch is one of the most beautiful fish. Its colour is golden bronze, transversed with bars of dark green, the whole shaded with a lovely iridescence, and fins of a splendid red tinge as seen sometimes in old-stained glass.

Its flesh is much appreciated by epicures, as witness "water souchet" as served at ministerial dinners and large banquets. It seldom weighs more than two pounds, although some have been caught in the Norfolk Broads weighing as much as four and a half pounds.

487. PERCH, FRIED.

Remove the gills, scale, and thoroughly cleanse the perch; prick them slightly on both sides, and place in a dish with a little salad-oil, salt, pepper, the juice of two lemons, an onion shred fine, and half a spoonful of chopped parsley; let the fish pickle for an hour, then wipe and flour them in the usual way, fry in a properly heated fat to a nice colour, and serve very hot with quarters of lemon.

488. PERCH, GARDENER STYLE.

Cleanse the perch as in the foregoing; clean also a handful of parsley-roots, and boil for half an hour in a quart of salted water; after which, throw the perch in and boil for five or six minutes longer; then dress in a dish with some of the liquor; spread the roots on the fish, and serve with melted butter and boiled potatoes apart.

489. PERCH AU GRATIN.

After having cleansed and scaled three or four perch in the usual way, put them in a sauté-pan properly buttered, and a little salt sprinkled over. Moisten with two glasses of sherry, and cover with a buttered sheet of paper. Boil on the stove, and afterwards put them into a moderately heated oven to bake for ten minutes, taking care to baste them meanwhile two or three times; transfer carefully to a buttered gratin-dish, sprinkle over them some fine herbs; mix the remainder of the liquor in which the fish was baked with a gill of Spanish sauce (No. 151), and pour it over; sprinkle with bread-crumbs, set on the oven to gratin for ten or twelve minutes, and serve.

490. PERCH À LA VENITIENNE.

When the number of perch required have been thoroughly cleansed, as described in the previous numbers, boil them in "Court Bouillon" (No. 392) for seven or eight minutes; dish up in a row, moisten with some Venitienne sauce (No. 206), and serve.

491. FILLETS OF PERCH À L'ITALIENNE.

The filleting of perch is done in the same way as that of pike. Lay the fillets in a sauté-pan with some clarified butter; season with salt, pepper, a little nutmeg, and lemon-juice. Set the fillets to simmer on the fire for about ten minutes, and when thoroughly done drain on a cloth, dish up in the form of a circle, pour some Italian sauce (No. 204) over, and send to table.

Fillets of perch thus prepared can also be served with any other fish sauce, from which the dish will take its name, viz., à la Hollandaise, à la Ravigotte, &c., &c.

492. FILLETS OF PERCH À LA ROMAINE.

Prepare a dozen fillets of perch in the usual manner; pickle these for an hour as for perch fried, wipe and flour in the same way, then pass them through some yolks of eggs well beaten and salted; fry in olive-oil till of a nice colour; drain, and dish up in a circle, pour some Tomato sauce (No. 217) over them, after having mixed with it a pat of anchovy butter, and serve.

493. PERCH, ANGLER'S STYLE.

Take the perch as caught by the river-side, not drawn or otherwise cleaned. Procure some stiff clay, and with it give the fish a thin coating of about the sixteenth of an inch thick. Having previously lighted a fire of wood, so as to produce a quantity of hot-fire-holding embers and cinders, bury the fish in it for about twenty minutes or more, according to the size, when it will be baked and found to eat to perfection.

Nota.—Any other kind of fresh-water fish can be cooked in this style. Anglers, when out for the day, will find it worth trying. For their particular benefit the recipe is included, and to them it is dedicated.

REMARKS ON CARP.

Carp caught in rapid waters are held in high estimation, especially on the Continent; but those found in stagnant waters and feeding on muddy food have a very muddy flavour. To prevent this taste from being so pronounced, carp should, after being taken out of a pond, be placed in running water in a box (with plenty of perforated holes) before being cooked. No doubt the monks had in olden times some excellent recipes for cooking carp, but these must have been lost with the destruction of their orders and monasteries.

Carp live to a very great age, some say for centuries,

and reach the weight of twenty-five pounds; at least some were caught of that weight. The flesh of the carp is of a white-rosy colour, rather indigestible, and it requires to be cooked in well-seasoned sauces.

It is absolutely necessary when cleaning the fish to extract an angular substance called the gall-stone, which is located at the back of the head. If not removed it will impart a bitter taste and render the best fish almost unfit for table.

494. CARP À LA BOURGIGNONE.

Take two carp of three or four pounds each; scald them to enable the scales to be removed more efficiently; draw through the gills, and clean thoroughly. Place them in a sauté-pan with half a bottle of Burgundy, a gill of brown sauce, the same quantity of good stock, four shalots, two cloves, a blade of mace, a little thyme, one bay-leaf, a few trimmings of mushrooms, and salt and pepper to taste. Set this to stew gently on the fire for about twenty minutes; then take the fish out carefully and dish them up; pass the liquor through a fine-pointed strainer into a small saucepan; boil it; draw it on the side of the stove; if not of its proper consistency as a sauce, skim it and reduce it by boiling again; then pour it over the carp and serve.

495. CARP À LA PERIGUEUX.

Prepare two or more carp as in No. 494; stew them in white wine with salt and pepper for twenty minutes, and then drain and dish up. Meanwhile prepare some perigueux butter (No 167); add to it a gill of good stock or brown sauce, a pat of anchovy butter, and the juice of a lemon. Stir this well together on the fire, and pour it over the fish before sending to the table.

496. FRIED CARP.

For this mode small fish should be used. Clean, scale, draw, and wipe six carp; split down the back and open flat; season with salt and pepper, dip them in flour, and fry to a nice colour; dish them up, garnish round with fried parsley, and serve with quarters of lemon.

497. CARP STEWED, ENGLISH FASHION.

For dressing carp in this way, see the directions for stewing eel, English style (No. 466).

498. CARP À LA SICILIENNE.

Prepare two or three nice carp in the usual way; put them in a kettle with enough "Court Bouillon" (No. 392) to boil for ten or twelve minutes; put the kettle aside in a cool place, and when the liquor is quite cold draw out the fish; remove the liquor in order to enable the kettle to be cleaned; after which, replace the fish in it with the "Court Bouillon;" set this to warm gently, without boiling, for twenty minutes; then drain and dish up the fish; pour some Sicilian sauce (No. 211) over, and serve.

499. TENCH.

This fish, being somewhat similar to the carp, may be dressed in the various modes in which that fish is prepared. Both kinds make excellent matelotte, and it is not unusual to prepare such a dish with carp, tench, and eel, all mixed and stewed together.

REMARKS ON BARBEL.

The barbel may be considered to be a water-pig, as its habits and mode of living in the water are very much like those of a pig on land. It cannot be classed as good food, as its eggs are said to be poisonous and to produce the same symptoms as bella-donna.

500. BARBEL BROILED. MAÎTRE D'HÔTEL BUTTER.

Cleanse, scale, and wipe the inside of two barbel very carefully; score them three or four times on each side; steep for half an hour in four tablespoonfuls of olive-oil; season with salt and pepper; and twenty minutes before serving broil them on a moderate fire for eight or ten minutes each side; dish up on a hot dish, and serve with some maître d'hôtel butter (No. 226) in the usual way.

Barbel can also be fried as well as baked, and served with either Sharp or Ravigote sauce.

CHAPTER IX.

REMARKS ON BEEF.

THERE is a prevailing idea in England that beef should be eaten either grilled or roasted; this is a great mistake, as there are many cuts and different parts, as described at the beginning of this work, which could not with credit to the cook be prepared in those ways. I will therefore give the different modes I consider best suited for each part.

501. ROUND OF BEEF BOILED ENGLISH FASHION.

Procure a piece of pickled round or silver-side of beef, weighing about eight pounds. Put this, after having washed it, into a pot with enough cold water to cover it well. Boil it; skim the scum as it rises to the surface; then drop in three or four whole carrots, two large onions with two cloves stuck in each, and, if handy, two heads of celery; let the pot simmer by the side of the stove for two hours, and add four whole turnips. Let the simmering be continued for another hour, then add the quarters of a small cabbage; boil gently again for an hour—making in all four hours' boiling; after which, strain the beef, and dress it on a large hot dish, with the cooked vegetables as a garnish, alternately placed with half a dozen small suet dumplings, and serve.

502. BRISKET OF BEEF-ECARLATE.

Briskets, like rounds of beef, are generally obtained from the butcher, all ready pickled, but that is not the proper way of salting or curing them: this must be effected in the following manner:—Mix well together in a pan a brine composed of six pounds of common salt, a quarter of a pound of saltpetre, half a pound of moist sugar, two bruised bay-leaves, half a teaspoonful of thyme, and same quantity of winter-savory and sweet marjoram, also three blades of mace and twelve cloves. Take a brisket of beef well covered with fat, bone it; use the bones for the stock. Rub the brisket well with the mixture for three or four minutes each day for five days in succession, taking care, in laying it on the brine in a cool place, that it should rest on the opposite side each day; then simply turn it over once a day for the succeeding five days, making altogether ten days for salting the piece of brisket—if to be eaten hot; but if intended to be pressed and eaten cold (which is the usual manner), it should remain in the mixture at least five days longer, in order that the flavour of the herbs and spices should be sufficiently absorbed. This mode of salting is equally applicable to every other kind of meat. The brisket of beef being thus ready for cooking, place it in a pan with plenty of cold water and the same quantity of vegetables as in the foregoing instructions. Boil, and skim, with the same care, for about four or five hours, according to the size of the brisket. When cooked, drain, and dress in the same manner as the round of beef, with the vegetables as a garnish, if to be eaten hot; or place in a perforated zinc box, made for that purpose, in a cool place. Lay on the meat a piece of board made to fit in the box, and put on this all the weights and stones you can get, in order to press the brisket well; leave it thus for at least twelve hours, when the weights can be removed, the piece of meat trimmed and glazed (No. 362); then dress it in a cold dish with a few sprigs of parsley and serve.

Note.—All the vegetables should be put in at the same time when the brisket is meant for pressing.

503. BRAIZED BEEF, CITIZEN STYLE.

Take a piece of top-side of beef, trim it nicely, cut some fat bacon into eight shreds of about four inches long by a quarter of an inch square, interlard the piece of beef with these by inserting each slice into a large larding-needle, then fasten the beef round with a piece of string so as to secure its shape. Put the pieces of trimmings into a braizing-pan with a few broken bones, if any; lay the piece of beef on these and garnish with two onions each stuck with two cloves, two heads of celery, two carrots, a "bouquet garni," and one blade of mace. Moisten with two quarts of good stock and one gill of brandy. Set the beef to simmer very gently for about four hours, taking care to often baste and turn it over in its gravy, in order to glaze it. Meanwhile glaze separately twenty-four small onions (No. 280) and two cabbages (No. 295). When the beef is done, drain it, remove the string, dish it up, make a border with the glazed onions and cabbages, or any other glazed vegetables that may be preferred; as well as mashed potatoes, croquettes, or mushrooms stewed in the glaze, and stuffed tomatoes, &c. &c. Skim the fat off the glaze, strain it over the lot, and serve.

This way of braizing meat can be applied to any cut or part of the animal, viz., ribs, rump, brisket, round or thick flank, as well as fillet of beef. The process of larding can also be omitted, not only as a matter of economy, but of taste as well.

504. BRAIZED BEEF MILANAISE.

Procure about ten pounds of thick flank, or a nice cut of round of beef of a similar weight; trim, interlard, and bind it with string, as described in No. 503; boil it in the stockpot for a couple of hours; after which, transfer the beef into a braizing-pan on a drainer. Moisten with half a bottle of white wine and one quart of good broth; add the same quantity of vegetables and "bouquet garni" as in the previous number. Set this to simmer very slowly for two hours, basting occasionally with its liquor in order to glaze the meat. When the beef is cooked take it out of the pan, drain it, remove the string, and keep it hot; strain the gravy through a fine strainer into a stewpan, skim off the fat, add half a pint of Espagnole sauce; set it to the boil, skim and reduce it a little. Meanwhile have one pound of macaroni cooked in the usual way, and drained, in a stewpan; season with mignonette pepper and grated nutmeg; put in a gill of the reduced sauce together with two ounces of grated parmesan cheese and an ounce of butter; toss the macaroni up, so as to mix it well with the sauce and cheese; then dress the meat on a dish, form a border round it with the macaroni, pour the remainder of the glaze sauce over, and serve.

505. BRAIZED BEEF NAPOLITAINE.

Prepare a top-side piece of beef weighing about ten pounds in the same way as for beef, citizen style. Put it in a braizing-pan, with the same kinds and quantity of vegetables and "bouquet garni," moisten with a quart of good stock and half a bottle of red wine (not port); let this simmer on a slow fire for three and a half hours, frequently basting the meat with its liquor; then put the meat on a dish, strain the liquor through a fine strainer, skim the fat, put the gravy back again in the braizing-pan with the meat, add half a pound of well washed and picked currants, and simmer for another half-hour. See that the meat is nicely glazed; after which, dress it on a dish, skim the fat from the glaze again, before pouring it over the meat, and serve.

506. BEEF À LA MODE.

À la mode beef is a popular and favourite dish in domestic cookery. Although it differs but slightly from braized beef, its success depends entirely (as the latter) on its proper cooking, which must be very slow. If too quickly cooked it will produce an insipid and white gravy, instead of the proper savoury and nourishing substance. In colour it should be of a dark red. Take about eight pounds of nicely trimmed thick flank of beef, lard this, in the direction of the grain, with half a pound of fat bacon, cut into strips half an inch thick, which must have been previously sprinkled with pepper; then fasten it round with a string, put it in a stewpan with three-quarters of a bottle of French white wine, one gill of brandy, two quarts of stock, four calf's feet, previously blanched and boned, and about two ounces of bacon-rind; season with salt and pepper, boil it, and skim; then add four large carrots, two onions, six cloves, a "bouquet garni," and two heads of celery; put it to simmer, very gently, by the side of the stove for at least five hours, with the stewpan well covered. When the beef is done take it out, as well as the calf's feet and carrots. Keep these hot by the side of the stove. Meanwhile strain the gravy through a pointed strainer into a small saucepan, remove the fat carefully, reduce the gravy one-fourth by quick boiling, untie the string, dish the beef up with the calf's feet, each cut into six pieces, around it, garnish with the carrots, shaped into corks, and a dozen glazed onions (No. 280). Pour the gravy over the lot; if too much, save it for another time.

Note.—A clove of garlic is very often inserted into the meat and gives it a nice flavour, although this is a matter of taste and not essential. Meat can be braized without the help of wine, but of course the savoury taste will not be the same.

À la mode beef is also often served as a cold dish for luncheons; in that case it would have to be cooked the day before it is wanted, and the whole of it turned into a basin, which will set to a firm jelly. When ready to serve, simply turn it out of the basin on to a dish.

507. PORTER-HOUSE STEAK.

Cut two slices, one and a half inches thick, off the thickest part of a sirloin of beef, with the fillet or undercut attached to the bone in the same manner as loin-mutton-chops. Flatten these a little with the cutlet-bat, oil, and pepper them slightly; then grill them on a clear fire for about fifteen to eighteen minutes, taking care to turn them, often as necessary, to prevent burning. Meantime put two ounces of butter in a sauté-pan, cut crossways six nice ripe tomatoes, lay these in the sauté-pan with the skin downwards, and fry them thus for five minutes without turning. When the steaks are cooked, sprinkle each side with salt, dish them up, and garnish with the tomato halves in the same way as they were cooked. Sprinkle each with a little salt and pepper before serving. Tomatoes cut in two are also grilled, but must always be kept with the skin under, otherwise they will lose part of their seed and liquor.

Porter-House steaks are also served with grilled mushrooms; in that case take a dozen large and fresh mushrooms, clean and peel them well, broil them over a not too fierce fire for four minutes, sprinkle salt and pepper over them, and dress with the steaks.

Remarks on Roast Beef and Roasting in General.

I have purposely abstained from mentioning the rump, sirloin, and ribs of beef in my braizing-recipes, because I think the former should only be used as steaks, and the two latter for roasting, as "the roast beef of Old England" is not likely to die out for a while, notwithstanding all the new recipes that may be introduced. I therefore contend that the best cuts of the animal should be reserved for that purpose, and not employed in any other way.

The roasting of meat is done, according to the kitchen arrangements, in three different ways, either by putting the meat on a baking-dish in the oven with a little suet over it, or by hanging the meat on a hook in a gas roasting-closet; but the best mode is by fixing the joint on a spit, if there is an open fire-range. This, however, requires care and attention, as the fire must be constantly replenished with fuel (wood being the best for roasting) and never allowed to get low; it is also necessary to avoid draughts between the screen and fire, as in that case a joint will take much longer to cook. The fire should also be thoroughly bright before putting the meat to roast.

When roasting before a fire, half a pint of broth should be put in the dripping-pan for basting the joint with, at least five times during the process of cooking. This applies also to game as well as poultry.

The time required for cooking joints will be modified by circumstances, as there are different qualities and natures of meat which cook more or less rapidly. Always test the joint by pressing the thickest parts with the finger before removing it from the fire; if these give way to the pressure the cooking will be perfect, but if there is a certain amount of resistance the meat is not yet cooked.

The following is the approximate time required for roasting the different joints, poultry, and game:—

For a joint of beef weighing ten pounds, two hours and a quarter.
,, a leg of mutton weighing nine pounds, one hour and three-quarters.
,, a loin or neck of veal weighing five pounds, one hour and twenty minutes.
,, a leg of pork weighing ten pounds, three hours.
,, a loin of pork weighing six pounds, one hour and forty minutes.
,, a goose weighing seven pounds, one hour and forty minutes.
,, a turkey weighing ten pounds, two hours.
,, a fowl weighing about three pounds, thirty-five minutes.
,, a pigeon, a quarter of an hour.
,, a duck, twenty minutes.
,, larks, eight minutes.
,, partridges or woodcocks, twenty minutes.
,, a pheasant, thirty-five minutes.
,, a wild-duck, a quarter of an hour.
,, a leveret, half an hour.
,, a rabbit, twenty minutes.
,, a hare's back, thirty-five minutes.

Meat for roasting requires no flavouring—the main point is to cook it when neither too fresh nor too high.

508. FILLET OF BEEF, INDIAN STYLE.

Get a fillet of beef weighing about eight pounds; trim and cut off the sinewy skin which covers it with a thinly bladed knife; lard in the usual way with thin strips of fat bacon. Put the trimmings from the fillet in an oblong or braizing-pan on the drainer; lay the fillet on them; add two onions with two cloves stuck in each, a shred carrot, one head of celery, and a "bouquet garni;" moisten with half a bottle of sherry and one pint of good stock; season with a tablespoonful of salt. Cover the pan and set it to simmer very slowly for about two hours, basting the meat frequently with its liquor while simmering. Meanwhile prepare a pint of Indian sauce (No. 185) in a stewpan apart; have also ready, and cold, half a pound of risotto (No. 108) which place on a slab or board, and make a hole in the centre; fill this hole with about a quarter of a pound of Italian salpicon (No. 307), to which a pinch of cayenne has been added. Mix these well together with a tablespoon, then form the risotto into croquets, or the shape of corks; pass them through the yolks of three eggs well beaten, and roll in bread-crumbs; then fry in the fat in the usual way to a nice colour.

When the fillet is cooked dress it on a hot dish, garnish with the croquets, strain and skim off the fat from the remainder of the liquor in which the fillet was cooked, pour it over the fillet, and serve with the Indian sauce apart.

509. FILLET OF BEEF À LA JARDINIÈRE.

Prepare and cook a fillet of beef in the same manner as the foregoing. Meanwhile prepare and cook in broth, with a good pinch of salt and a piece of sugar, all the vegetables in season that may be had, such as carrots and turnips turned in small fancy shapes, French beans cut in diamonds, asparagus-points, buds of cauliflower, small Brussels sprouts, and peas. When the fillet is cooked and well braized dish it up, garnish with the aforesaid hot vegetables all nicely, but separately, intermixed round the meat; strain the liquor in which the beef was cooked, and skim off the fat; add a gill of brown sauce to the liquor, stir, and warm up; then pour it over the fillet and serve.

510. FILLET OF BEEF WITH OLIVES.

Cook a fillet of beef in the same way as the fillet of beef, Indian style. Meanwhile bone with a pointed knife a pint of nice French or Italian olives, blanch these for five minutes in plain boiling water, and keep them hot by soaking in a gill of brown sauce or good gravy. When the fillet is cooked and nicely braized dish it up, strain, and skim off the fat from the liquor; add this to the olives, stir and mix well on the fire, and when hot pour it round the fillet before serving.

511. FILLET OF BEEF WITH MASHED POTATOES.

Procure a nice thick fillet of beef, trim and lard as for "Indian style." Put it in a deep earthenware dish, pour over it a gill of salad-oil, lay on the beef the shreds of an onion, with a few sprigs of parsley, a bay-leaf, and two good pinches of pepper; let it steep thus for at least three hours, turning over occasionally, so that the flavour of the different ingredients may be absorbed by the fillet. When properly steeped, shake off all the particles from the meat, run lengthwise a small iron skewer through it, fold the fillet with a well-oiled sheet of paper tied with string, and fix it to the roasting-spit with strong string. Put this in front of a moderate fire to roast for about two hours, taking care to baste it often with the oil in which the fillet was steeped. Half an hour before serving—that is to say, an hour and a half after the fillet was first put before the fire—remove the paper, so that the fillet may take a nice brown colour in roasting. Do not forget the basting.

When the fillet is properly cooked and nicely coloured,

make a good layer of mashed potatoes (No. 231) on a hot dish; place the fillet on it; pour a little half-glaze or good gravy over, and serve.

Note.—In roasting larded meat care should be taken that the fire be not too fierce, otherwise the lard will be scorched, and spoil the flavour of the joint. Fillet of beef roasted as above can also be served with a purée of celery (No. 236), purée of green peas (No. 232), purée of Jerusalem artichokes (No. 239), or any other purée that may be fancied.

512. FILLET OF STEAK À LA CHÂTEAUBRIAND.

Cut two fillets of beef crosswise, at its thickest part, one and three-quarter inches thick, remove the sinewy part and trim them; oil them slightly and sprinkle them with salt and pepper; put them on the gridiron to broil for about seven minutes each side. When cooked dish them up, garnish with potatoes cut filbert-shape and fried in clarified butter. Place on each steak a piece of maître d'hôtel butter (No. 226) as big as a walnut, and serve.

513. FILLETS OF BEEF MIGNONS WITH CHAMPIGNONS.

Take three pounds from the middle of a whole fillet of beef; skin and trim it; cut this in slices three-quarters of an inch thick, flatten them slightly with the cutlet-bat; steep for three hours in a marinade composed of half a pint of French white wine, a gill of oil, a bay-leaf, a sliced onion, a few sprigs of parsley, and salt and pepper. Twenty minutes before serving melt two ounces of clarified butter in a sauté-pan; shake off all the particles of marinade from the fillets, and put them in the sauté-pan to cook for about ten minutes, taking care to turn them over and colour on both sides. Meanwhile prepare a Mushroom sauce (No. 197) in a saucepan apart. When the fillets are cooked, drain, and dish them up in a circle, pour the Mushroom sauce in the centre, and serve.

Note.—Fillet of beef cut and cooked in the above style can also be served with Truffle sauce (No. 198), Financière (No. 187), Tomato purée (No. 217), or any other Sharp sauce.

514. SCOLLOPS, FILLET OF BEEF WITH CHESNUT PURÉE.

Cut three pounds of fillet of beef in scollops, three inches wide and three-quarters of an inch thick, flatten them as in No. 313, and trim them to a nice shape, either round, triangular, or square, but of an equal size; season these with salt and pepper, and cook them in a sauté-pan with a quarter of a pound of clarified butter, taking care to brown them on both sides as in the foregoing. Meanwhile prepare a purée of chesnuts (No. 237). When the scollops of beef are properly cooked dish them up in a circle, after having glazed them, fill the centre with the purée, strain some good beef gravy over, and serve.

Note.—Any purée of vegetables can be served with scollops cooked in the above fashion.

515. RUMP-STEAK À LA CHASSEUR.

Procure a slice of rump-steak weighing about three pounds, and cut one inch and a quarter thick. Place the steak flat on the table, lay your left hand slightly over it, whilst with the right you insert a sharp-pointed knife in the centre of the outside fat, as if to slice the steak in two; but the insertion must only be made within an inch all round from the three outside parts of the steak, so as to form it into the shape of a pocket. Steep the steak, thus trimmed, for two hours in a similar marinade to the foregoing. Meanwhile prepare a salpicon à la chasseur (No. 312), to which add about six ounces of sausage meat and a couple of truffles cut in small dice, making in all about a pound of salpicon; wipe the steak, put the mixture in the pocket with a spoon, sew the open part with a fine string; flatten it gently with the hands, and place it on the gridiron on a good fire for about eight minutes on each side. When cooked remove the string without tearing the meat, dish it up and serve, with a little Espagnole or half-glaze sauce apart.

Note.—Steaks cut as above can be filled and cooked with other salpicons or oysters, simply blanched in boiling water for two minutes, drained, and freed from any particle of shell.

This mode of cooking steaks has been appropriated lately by several cooks and amateurs, as of their own invention. I may, however, say that it was introduced by me at the St. James's Hall Restaurant either in 1875 or 1876.

516. RUMP-STEAK. OYSTER SAUCE.

Take a rump-steak weighing about two pounds and cut one inch thick; pour a tablespoonful of oil on a plate; pass both sides of the steak over the oil, and broil it over a moderate fire for about seven minutes each side. When cooked sprinkle both sides with salt, dress it on a dish, and serve with some Oyster sauce (No. 186) in a sauce-boat apart.

Note.—Rump-steak broiled as above can also be served plain, or with Sharp, Italian, or Tomato sauce, as well as with grilled or stewed mushrooms.

517. RUMP-STEAK. ANCHOVY BUTTER.

Prepare and cook a rump-steak as in the foregoing. Meanwhile make some anchovy butter (No. 161), lay it on a hot dish; put the steak on the butter, and serve with either chipped or fried potatoes.

CHAPTER X.

REMARKS ON VEAL.

VEAL is one of the most nutritious, palatable, and wholesome meats that can be cooked, besides playing a great part in the different culinary preparations of soups, sauces, and jellies; but veal, like lamb, should never be eaten when over two months old, for the flesh gets coarse and loses flavour and delicacy, as well as whiteness. The veal from Pontoise (France) possesses a world-wide repute for its quality, savour, and whiteness of flesh; but calves are never killed over eight weeks old in that country.

518. VEAL, HOUSEWIFE STYLE.

Procure a loin. Bone it; cut out the kidney; trim off some of the encircling fat and put the kidney back in its place; flatten the flap and fold it under so as to cover the kidney, and fillet and tie the piece of meat with string in order to keep it in shape. Or take a round cut from off a leg of veal, weighing five or six pounds; bone it, and fasten it round with string. Put either in a well-buttered braizing-pan over the fire to brown; when of a nice golden colour all round moisten with a quart of broth, add three whole carrots, two onions with two cloves stuck in each, a "bouquet garni," salt and pepper to taste, and set to simmer very gently for about two hours and a half, with the pan partly covered, not forgetting to baste often and turn the meat during that time. Then cover the pan; put a good shovel of live-coal and embers on the lid, and let it simmer for half an hour, taking care meanwhile to baste the meat at least five times with its own gravy. When the meat is cooked, which can be ascertained by pricking it with a trussing-needle, drain it, and keep hot on a dish; remove the carrots carefully by themselves—and keep them hot too—strain the gravy through a pointed strainer, skim off the fat, and reduce the gravy by quick boiling to a half-glaze; add a little caramel if not sufficiently coloured. In the meantime cut the braized carrots into shape, dish them up with the beef together with a dozen small onions, previously glazed for that purpose; sprinkle over the reduced gravy, and serve.

Note.—This mode of preparing veal is also served cold. In that case cook it the day before, and put in a basin with the strained gravy, which will set to a firm jelly; and it will only have to be turned out of the basin on to a dish to serve.

519. BRAIZED VEAL, ITALIAN STYLE.

Take a round cut of the leg or a shoulder of veal, weighing about six pounds, bone it with a sharp-pointed knife, and lard it in the usual way with well-seasoned strips of bacon, and fasten it round with string. Lay flat in a well-buttered stewpan half a dozen thin slices of fat bacon with an ounce of butter. Cut in quarters an onion, a carrot, and one head of celery; spread these on the slices of bacon; add a bay-leaf and a few sprigs of thyme, place on these the piece of larded veal seasoned with salt and pepper, and set it on the fire to brown all round. After having properly turned the meat and secured a nice even colouring, add a pint and a half of stock with half a pint of French white wine, then simmer it very gently, with the lid partly on, for about three hours, taking care, as is usual in all braizing, to carefully baste the meat, so as to glaze it well. When the meat is properly cooked, drain and put it on a dish to keep hot, strain the gravy in the usual way, and put it in a small saucepan to be reduced to a half-glaze, after having skimmed off the fat. Meanwhile prepare a dish either of macaroni, spaghetti, or ravioli, Italian style, garnish the veal with it, pour the reduced gravy over, and serve.

520. STEWED VEAL, COUNTRY STYLE.

In order to study economy, this stew should be made with the neck, breast, and trimmings of veal cutlets, the two former cut two inches wide by three long.

Melt two ounces of butter in a stewpan over the fire; put the pieces of veal in with two bay-leaves and a few sprigs of thyme; brown the veal nicely by stirring almost constantly; then sprinkle two or three tablespoonfuls of flour over the meat; continue stirring for three or four minutes longer, or till the flour is well browned; moisten with half a pint of stock and a gill of white wine; season with salt and pepper; simmer by the side of the fire for about an hour with the lid on, stirring the meat five or six times; after which, add one pint of stock with three fresh tomatoes, skinned and cut in four. Boil fast on a brisk fire for fifteen minutes; take the bay-leaves and thyme out; add some potatoes and peas, cooked separately in broth, as well as a quarter of a pound of fresh mushrooms, properly trimmed, cleaned, and blanched, also in broth. Mix these well together on the stove till it boils, then dress it up in a large dish, and serve.

521. STEWED VEAL, COUNTRY STYLE (ANOTHER).

Prepare and stew the veal trimmings as indicated in the foregoing, but half an hour before the completion of stewing add to it two shred onions, half a pound of fresh mushrooms, a tablespoonful of chopped parsley, and the juice of a lemon. Stir well, simmer for half an hour; add the quantity of broth required; boil sharp for fifteen minutes; remove the aromatic herbs, and serve separately with a purée of potatoes.

522. STEWED VEAL WITH RICE.

Proceed for this stew as in the former, and when the meat is well glazed and cooked, add a quarter of a pound of fresh mushrooms and simmer for five or six minutes longer. Have a risotto (No. 109) ready; dish it up; dress also the stewed veal in another dish, and serve.

523. SCOLLOPS OF VEAL FRIED.

Cut about two pounds of cushion* of veal into scollops or slices two inches wide by three long and half an inch thick, flatten these slightly with the cutlet-bat dipped in water, and roll each separately in flour. Melt four ounces of butter in a sauté-pan, fry the scollops in it over a brisk fire, taking care to give them a nice golden colour on both sides. When this has been obtained, sprinkle a little flour on each slice. Moisten with half a pint of good broth, let it boil for ten minutes, then add a gill of half-glaze or good gravy, one teaspoonful of fine herbs (No. 195), a quarter of a pound of cooked fresh mushrooms, and salt to taste. Toss the sauté-pan over the fire in order to warm up the contents and mix them well; dress the scollops in the form of a circle; add about an ounce of butter to the sauce; squeeze the juice of a lemon, and stir by the side of the fire. Meanwhile garnish the centre of

---

* Cushion of veal is a cut from the most fleshy part of the leg of veal, and very often called "fillet."

the dish with any purée or garnish of vegetables that may be preferred, or any paste, or rice. Pour the sauce over the scollops, and serve.

524. BLANQUETTE OF VEAL.

The breast is generally the part of veal used for blanquette. Cut three pounds of breast of veal into pieces between two and three inches square; put these in a stewpan with enough water to cover the meat well; add two-thirds of a tablespoonful of salt and half a teaspoonful of pepper. Boil and skim in the usual way; after which, add two onions with two cloves stuck in each, and a double "bouquet garni;" simmer gently for an hour, then drain in a colander, but save the broth; return the pieces of veal in the stewpan and keep hot by the side of the fire. In the meantime mix in another stewpan one ounce of butter, with the same quantity of flour, by stirring over the fire for four or five minutes, then draw it by the side of the stove. Moisten with all the liquor drained from the veal, reduce this for twenty minutes, stirring all the time to prevent burning; after which, thicken with the yolks of three eggs, strain the sauce through a pointed strainer into the stewpan containing the veal, to which half a pint of tinned, blanched, and sliced button champignons have already been added. Boil it for one minute, sprinkle in half a tablespoonful of chopped parsley; mix well; dish the blanquette, and serve.

525. CUSHION OF VEAL WITH SPINACH (FRENCH FRICANDEAU).

Trim a cushion of veal weighing about three pounds to a nice oval form and smooth surface; lard this side rather closely with thin strips of fat bacon. Strew the bottom of a braizing-pan with the trimmings of the veal, a small sliced carrot and onion, a small "bouquet garni," salt and pepper to taste, and then place the cushion on the top. Moisten with about a pint of broth; place a buttered sheet of paper over the larded part of the meat; then set it to simmer very slowly for one or two hours, with the lid on, and frequently baste it with its own liquor. When nearly done the lid and paper must be removed, so as to enable the larding to dry, although it should still be frequently basted with its own glaze, in order to give it a shiny appearance; care, however, must be taken to prevent the meat from acquiring too much colour during the process. Meanwhile dress a purée of spinach (No. 236) in the centre of a hot dish, and with a flat strainer take the piece of veal out of the pan and lay it carefully on the spinach; strain the half-glaze through a pointed strainer; skim off the fat, pour it over the meat, and serve.

Note.—Cushion of veal braized thus can be served with either jardinière, macédoine, stewed peas, à la Toulouse, stuffed tomatoes, white haricot beans, glazed onions, new carrots, or any purée of vegetables, and also with stewed mushrooms.

526. SCOLLOPS OF VEAL WITH STEWED MUSHROOMS.

Cut a cushion of veal into scollops as for scollops fried; put them in a sauté-pan with sufficient broth to cover them entirely; season with salt and pepper, and simmer them gently till the scollops are done, which will be in about an hour. Meanwhile brown in a stewpan three spoonfuls of flour with an ounce of butter, by stirring for four or five minutes; then moisten with half a pint of broth and a gill of sherry; stir and dilute this well; season with a little salt and pepper; then add to the sauce one pound of well-cleaned fresh mushrooms; simmer for six or eight minutes, and then draw by the side of the fire. When the scollops are cooked dish them up in the form of a circle and keep hot; skim off the fat from the liquor in which the scollops were cooked; reduce it a little over a brisk fire, then add the mushrooms, with a teaspoonful of finely chopped parsley and the juice of half a lemon; stir on the fire till it boils; pour it in the centre of the dish with the scollops, and serve.

Note.—Scollops cooked as above may be dressed with any purée or garnish of vegetables, as well as with macaroni, tagliatelli, spaghetti, or ravioli.

527. VEAL CUTLETS WITH SORREL PURÉE.

Saw off the chine-bone and upper end ribs of the half of the best-end neck of veal, leaving the cutlet bones about four inches long; divide these into cutlets of an even thickness; trim them nicely without showing the bone; lard the fillet of each cutlet with thin strips of fat bacon, put them in a sauté-pan with three ounces of clarified butter and fry them for four minutes only; then add a pint of veal broth, half a pint of French white wine, a small shred carrot and onion, and salt and pepper to taste; simmer very gently till the cutlets are well glazed, and meanwhile prepare a purée of sorrel (No. 238). When the cutlets are done dress them up on a dish in the form of a circle, fill the centre with the sorrel, skim off the fat, strain the gravy over the cutlets, and serve.

528. VEAL CUTLETS WITH HAM.

Cut and trim six veal cutlets as described in the previous number; put them in a sauté-pan with two or three ounces of clarified butter to colour them; after which, pour off the butter, and add one pint of veal stock with half a pint of

Espagnole sauce, and simmer till the cutlets are done. Meanwhile cut six lean slices of ham, a quarter of an inch thick and trim them to the shape of the cutlets; fry for five minutes in the clarified butter which was saved from the cutlet-pan. When the cutlets are done drain and dish up in a circle with a slice of ham between each. Skim the fat off the gravy, strain it through a small tammy over the cutlets, and serve.

529. VEAL CUTLETS MILANAISE.

Cut and pare away six veal cutlets as in No. 528, flatten slightly with the cutlet-bat dipped in water, and pass them through the yolks of three eggs well beaten and seasoned with salt; then put them into bread-crumbs and fry in a sauté-pan with four ounces of clarified butter to a nice golden colour on both sides. Meanwhile prepare some macaroni Milanaise (No. 94). When the cutlets are ready lay the half of the macaroni over the dish, dress the cutlets on it in the usual form, pour the remainder of the macaroni in the centre, sprinkle over the cutlets the butter left in the pan, and serve.

530. VEAL CUTLETS À L'ITALIENNE.

Prepare half a dozen veal cutlets as in the previous number, flatten gently with the cutlet-bat dipped in water, and with a sharp knife slice the fillets in two, without separating them at the bone. Spread on each a tablespoonful of salpicon à la financière (No. 310), to which two tablespoonfuls of D'Uxelles has previously been added, and well mixed with the salpicon; turn the slices down and flatten gently with the hands, so as to give the cutlets their natural shape; after which, rub them through breadings and raspings, and fry to a nice golden colour with four ounces of clarified butter. When cooked dress them carefully over a hot dish, and serve with a sauce-boat of Italian sauce (No. 204) or any other sauce that may be preferred.

531. VEAL CUTLETS EN PAPILLOTES.

Cut, trim, and flatten the veal cutlets as in cutlets Milanaise, put these in a sauté-pan with two ounces of butter, and fry to a nice even colour for about six minutes on each side; when done, drain, and put by on a plate. Sprinkle an ounce of flour in the sauté-pan; stir it over the fire for three minutes; add one pint of broth, stir and boil for five minutes, and strain through a pointed gravy-strainer. Clean the sauté-pan, put the sauce back and boil to reduce it to half the quantity, add three tablespoonfuls of D'Uxelles (No. 195), and reduce five minutes longer; then cut for each cutlet a sheet of stiff white paper in the shape of a heart and large enough to leave a good margin round the cutlet, oil the sheets of paper, and lay on each side a slice of fat bacon, cut in the shape of the lean part of the cutlet; spread on the bacon a tablespoonful of the sauce, then the cutlet, then another spoonful of the sauce, and lastly a slice of bacon similar to the first; fold the paper over and twist the edges tightly under into very close folds. About fifteen minutes before serving, put the folded cutlets on a girdiron to broil on a moderate fire for six or seven minutes on each side.

532. VEAL CUTLETS BROILED PLAIN.

Cut and trim the cutlets as in the foregoing; sprinkle some pepper on both sides, pour one tablespoonful of oil on a plate, pass the cutlets lightly over it, and broil them for ten minutes on a moderate fire. When done sprinkle a pinch of salt on each side, dish up the cutlets, and serve with any vegetables that may be preferred.

533. VEAL CUTLETS. TOMATO SAUCE.

Cut and pare the cutlets; dip in melted butter; pass them through bread-crumbs; broil on a moderate fire for about twelve minutes, and serve with some Tomato sauce (No. 217) apart.

Note.—Veal cutlets, plain or bread-crumbed, and broiled as above, can be served with any Sharp sauce or maître d'hôtel butter, allowing generally three-parts of a gill of sauce and an ounce of maître d'hôtel butter to each person.

534. ROAST VEAL.

The chump-end of the loin, the neck, and the loin of veal are generally the pieces used for roasting. Take about four pounds of the neck, saw off the chine-bone, chop between each bone, and shorten the rib-bones, roll the flap underneath and tie round with string; roast this before the fire, which must be moderate, for about an hour and three-quarters, basting the meat with its own gravy in the usual way, and five minutes before removing the joint from the fire sprinkle it well with salt. Strain, and skim the fat off the gravy, pour it over the meat and serve.

For roast loin of veal, take about five pounds of the part including the kidney, saw off the chine-bone, roll the flap underneath so as to enclose the kidney, and fasten it with string. Put it on a spit to roast for at least two hours before a moderate fire, basting about every fifteen minutes; sprinkle some salt five minutes before taking the joint away from the fire; strain, and skim off the fat from the gravy; dish up the meat, pour the gravy over it, and serve with water-cress sprinkled with salt, pepper, and vinegar.

R

For roast chump of loin, bone entirely, tie with string to keep it in shape, and proceed in the same manner as previous number.

535. ROAST BREAST OF VEAL WITH STUFFING.

Bone completely the breast of veal; mix one pound of well-seasoned veal stuffing (Nos. 270 or 270a) and a tablespoonful of finely chopped sage; place this along in the centre of the meat, roll up tightly, fasten round with string, tie a well-buttered sheet of paper round, and roast before a moderate fire for about an hour and three-quarters, taking care to baste as often as possible. Twenty minutes before taking away from the fire remove the paper, and when done untie the string. Dish it up and serve with some good gravy, properly strained and skimmed.

536. ROAST OR BAKED BREAST OF VEAL, CITIZEN STYLE.

Bone, trim, and roll a breast of veal (without stuffing) as in No. 535, tie round, and put in a stewpan with three ounces of butter, to fry till it is well coloured all over; then add a "bouquet garni" and a quart of stock; put in the oven to bake gently. Half an hour afterwards add two dozen new carrots nicely turned, and in another half hour the same number of button onions, a tablespoonful of sugar, and the same quantity of salt. Baste the meat frequently. When done take it up, unfold the string, and put the veal on a baking-sheet in the oven again for a few minutes to glaze. Meanwhile continue the glazing of the carrots and onions on the fire. Dish up the meat, garnish round with the glazed vegetables, remove the "bouquet garni," skim off the fat from the surface of the liquor, reduce to the consistency of a half-glaze, pour it over the veal and vegetables, and serve.

CHAPTER XI.

REMARKS ON MUTTON, LAMB, AND GOAT.

The flesh of mutton and lamb is of great benefit as a supply of food to mankind, in every part of the world the meat of the former being used on a larger scale than any other kind by all classes. It can be served to great advantage roasted, boiled, or made into numerous dishes very similar to those made of veal.

The flesh of lamb, when not too old and of good quality, is perfectly white. For taste, delicacy, and tenderness it is superior to all other butcher's meat; but it should not be more than two months old, as its flesh then begins to get coarse and loses much of its delicate flavour and whiteness.

The meat of the goat is coarse and tough, and possesses rather a strong flavour; while that of the kid five or six weeks old is delicious when properly cooked.

537. MUTTON CUTLETS À L'ITALIENNE.

Select a neck of mutton that has been killed at least four days, and cut off the neck or scrag-end with the chopper; or simply procure the best-end of a neck of mutton from the butcher, saw off the breast-part so as to leave the cutlet-bones between three and a half and four inches long; saw off also the chine or spine bone, and then with a sharp knife cut in as many cutlets as there are bones from the neck of mutton thus prepared.

Trim the cutlets by removing all the sinewy part and superfluous fat without damaging the fillet, and detach the meat about an inch from the end of each bone. Marinade the cutlets for a couple of hours, wipe and pass them over the yolks of three eggs well beaten, and bread them. Ten minutes before serving, fry them in a sauté-pan with clarified butter, taking care to give them a nice golden colour on both sides; after which, dish them up in a circle and serve with Sharp sauce (No. 205) apart.

Note.—Cutlets cooked in the above style are also served with a garnish in the centre, composed either of French beans (No. 290), asparagus-points (No. 287), stewed peas (No. 286), cucumber (No. 285), macédoine (No. 281), purée of chesnuts (No. 237), or any vegetable purée that may be fancied, as well as mushrooms or truffles.

Lamb cutlets are also cooked and served in the same manner.

538. MUTTON CUTLETS MILANAISE.

Prepare the cutlets and trim, bread-crumb, and cook in the same style as the foregoing. When cooked dish up in a circle, fill the centre with macaroni cheese (No. 88), to which two tablespoonfuls of Béchamel sauce should have been added and well mixed before serving.

539. MUTTON CUTLETS À LA SOUBISE.

Mutton cutlets for this style should be cut thick; and the proper way is to cut two bones for each cutlet and remove one rib-bone from it; after which, trim and pare carefully; then lard through the lean part of each cutlet with eight narrow strips one inch and a quarter long of bacon and tongue, well seasoned. Put the cutlets in a large stewpan with a sliced carrot, an onion stuck with two cloves, a "bouquet garni," a bay-leaf, six pepper-corns, and a blade of mace; moisten with sufficient good broth to cover it; put the lid on the pan, and set the cutlets to braize on a slow fire for about an hour and a quarter. When the cutlets are done, drain, and place them on a large dish to get cold; lay another dish over the cutlets to slightly press and give them an even surface. Meanwhile skim the fat off the gravy in which the cutlets were cooked, pass it through a tammy, and reduce it to a halfglaze by boiling. Twenty minutes before serving return the cutlets into the reduced liquor, warm them up very gently so as to give them time to glaze nicely by rolling the pan carefully. When the cutlets are properly warmed and glazed, dish them up in the usual way, fill in the centre with a purée à la Soubise (No. 229), pour the remainder of the liquor over the cutlets, and serve.

Note.—Braized cutlets as above can be served with any garnish or purée of vegetables, for making which see those articles.

540. MUTTON CUTLETS À LA POMPADOUR.

Prepare, lard, and cook the number of cutlets required as in the foregoing, and let them get cold in their liquor. Make a purée of fresh mushrooms (No. 301), to which add two or three tablespoonfuls of the liquor in which the cutlets were braized, and dilute the purée with it. When the cutlets are quite cold, take them out and place on a dish, after being drained; lay flat on each a teaspoonful of the purée (keeping the remainder hot in a bain-marie). Let this set firm on the cutlets, and about twenty minutes before serving pass them twice through the yolks of eggs, properly beaten for that purpose, and fine bread-crumbs; that is to say, to rub lightly the eggs and bread-crumbs over the cutlets first, and to repeat the same thing over again; after which, put them in a sauté-pan with enough melted clarified butter to fry over a good brisk fire, taking care to give each a nice colour. When cooked dress them in the usual form; place the remainder of the mushroom purée in the centre; sprinkle the cutlets with a little of their liquor, skimmed and reduced for the purpose, as in No. 539, and serve with Tomato sauce apart.

541. MUTTON CUTLETS À LA JARDINIÈRE.

Cut, trim, and braize the cutlets as in the foregoing, but without larding them. Meanwhile prepare a jardinière of vegetables as for fillet of beef jardinière (No. 509). Mix all the vegetables together in a stewpan with a few tablespoonfuls of Béchamel sauce. When the cutlets are cooked dish them in a circle, pour the hot jardinière in it, sprinkle a little half-glaze over the cutlets, and serve.

542. MUTTON CUTLETS À LA MAINTENON.

Cut and trim the mutton cutlets as for jardinière; slightly flatten them with the bat, and with a sharp knife slice the fillets in two without separating them at the bone; spread inside a teaspoonful of D'Uxelles (No. 195), refold the cutlets in their natural form, broil them thus four or five minutes on each side; put a thin layer of D'Uxelles on a dish; lay the cutlets on it when cooked. Pour over some D'Uxelles sauce (No. 195), place the dish in a hot oven for five minutes, and serve.

543. MUTTON CUTLETS, MAÎTRE D'HÔTEL.

Cut and trim the cutlets as for cutlets à l'Italienne; flatten them gently with the bat, oil and sprinkle with a little pepper, and broil over a brisk fire about four minutes on each side. When done to a nicety dish up, and put some maître d'hôtel butter between and on each cutlet, serve with either fried or chipped potatoes.

544. MUTTON CUTLETS BREAD-CRUMBED.

Prepare the cutlets as for maître d'hôtel. Melt about one ounce of butter in a frying-pan, dip each cutlet in it, and pass them through the bread-crumbs. After which, broil on a grill, in the same way as before; dish up, and serve with Tomato sauce apart.

Note.—Cutlets either of mutton or lamb, grilled as above, can be served with any garnish or purée of vegetables, as well as with stewed or grilled mushrooms.

545. LAMB-CHOPS.

Lamb as well as mutton chops are plainly grilled, and served with grilled tomatoes or mushrooms.

546. BREAST OF MUTTON BROILED.

The breast or upper ribs sawn off the neck of mutton when cut in cutlets can either be boiled, broiled, or used in stews.

Put the mutton in a saucepan with enough water to cover it; add any trimmings and bones that may be handy, together with a small carrot cut lengthwise in four, an onion with two cloves stuck in it, a "bouquet garni," and season with salt and pepper. Boil and skim in the usual way, and simmer till the bones can easily be taken out; drain the meat on a dish; pull out all the bones; sprinkle the meat with salt; press it under another dish with a weight at the top, and let it get cold. The broth in which the mutton was boiled must be strained and the fat skimmed off, when it can be used as a soup, by adding to it either boiled pearl barley or rice and a little chopped parsley.

When the meat is cold cut it in six equal parts. Melt an ounce of butter in a sauté-pan; dip the pieces of mutton in it; strew them with bread-crumbs and broil on a gridiron to a nice brown colour on both sides, and serve with either Tomato or Sharp sauce apart, and garnish with any purée of vegetables.

Note.—Lamb is also cooked and served in this way.

547. BREAST OF MUTTON, HOUSEWIFE STYLE.

Cut into as many pieces as there are bones the breast of mutton, cut off from the neck; put these in a sauté-pan and fry to a nice brown; then drain off the fat, and sprinkle over them three tablespoonfuls of flour. Moisten with half a pint of broth, add a "bouquet garni," a bay-leaf, and two small onions stuck with two cloves; season with salt and pepper, and let simmer gently for three-quarters of an hour, taking care to often stir the contents with a wooden spoon. Meanwhile cut in small quarters four turnips; blanch in the usual way and brown in butter till cooked; skim off the fat from the mutton, remove the "bouquet-garni," bay-leaf, and onions, add the turnips, continue simmering for a few minutes longer, and serve.

Note.—The neck-end and breast of lamb is also prepared and served in the same style.

548. MINCED MUTTON.

This mince is generally made with the remnants of cold mutton. Cut off all fat, skin, and gristle from the meat; mince it fine, and warm it well together with some Italian sauce, without, however, letting it boil; after which, dress it on a dish with poached eggs and large croûtons as a garnish.

549. HARICOT MUTTON.

Cut the end part of the neck as well as the breast of mutton between each bone; pare away all superfluous fat, put the pieces of mutton into a stewpan; fry them over a brisk fire to a nice brown; then pour off the grease, sprinkle three spoonfuls of flour over the mutton, and stir the contents for about five minutes over the fire; then moisten it with one quart of broth, and continue stirring almost constantly till it boils. Prepare about half a pound each of carrots and turnips cut in fancy shapes, such as half-moons, small pears, and big olives; add them to the mutton, as well as a dozen small onions, a "bouquet garni," two bay-leaves, and two pinches of mignonette pepper. Let the haricot mutton simmer gently by the side of the fire, with the lid on the pan, for about an hour and a half, taking care to frequently stir it; then carefully skim off the fat and grease; remove the "bouquet garni" and leaves; dish it up with the vegetables; reduce the sauce (if necessary) by sharp boiling, pour it over the mutton, and serve.

Note.—The above may be varied by substituting new potatoes, young carrots, turnips, and green peas for the aforesaid vegetables.

550. BRAIZED LEG OF MUTTON À LA BRETONNE.

Take a nice fat leg of mutton weighing about eight pounds, saw off the shank-bone, and lard it with a dozen strips of fat bacon, cut a quarter of an inch square by six inches long. Place the leg in a braizing-pan with two onions each stuck with two cloves, a head of celery split in half, two shred carrots, a spoonful of chopped parsley, a bay-leaf, and season with salt, pepper, a little nutmeg, and two blades of mace. Moisten with a quart of good stock, cover the meat with a buttered paper, and put the lid on the pan; lay on it some embers; set the pan on the fire to simmer very gently for about four hours, taking care to frequently baste the mutton with its liquor and feed the lid with live embers. Meanwhile cook a pint of white haricot beans (No. 294), strain, and put in a stewpan in which the following sauce has already been prepared: —Shred fine two onions; fry them of a light colour in a sauté-pan with a little butter; add a pint of brown sauce; season with salt and pepper; let it boil gently for fifteen minutes, then rub it through a sieve, as a purée. Having thus put the beans with the sauce, let the whole simmer about five minutes. When the mutton is properly braized take it from the braizing-pan and keep it hot; strain the liquor into a small saucepan; skim off all the fat and reduce it to a half-glaze; lay the haricot beans on a hot dish; dress the leg of mutton on it; pour over the meat the half-glaze, and serve.

Note.—To simplify the cooking, legs of mutton may be braized without larding, and garnished with plain boiled haricot beans, moistened with gravy instead of sauce.

Braized legs of mutton as above can be served à la Jardinière, à la Soubise, and à la Macédoine; for which see the respective garnishes.

Loins and saddles of mutton may also be braized and served in the same style as legs of mutton.

551. BOILED LEG OF MUTTON.

Choose a nice leg of mutton; put it in a stock-pot with a spoonful of salt and plenty of cold water; boil it; remove the scum by skimming in the same way as broth; then add a couple of carrots sliced in four, and six or eight turnips; let it simmer gently by the side of the stove for not less than two hours, and if the leg is a big one, three hours. When the mutton is done take it out of the broth and keep it hot; strain the broth into an earthenware pan, that it may be used again for boiling mutton and served as a mutton broth. Keep the carrots hot; mash the turnips with an ounce of butter, and season with salt and pepper; dish up the leg of mutton, garnish it with tablespoonfuls of purée laid egg-shape round it, intermixed with carrots nicely shaped; pour a little gravy over the mutton, and serve with Caper sauce (No. 193) in a sauce-boat apart.

552. ROAST LEG OF MUTTON.

Legs and saddles of mutton, to eat tender, should be hung in cool and draughty places at least four or five days in summer, and ten or twelve days in winter, before being cooked. Saw off the shank-bone a little below the knuckle, fix the meat on the spit to roast before a good fire for an hour and three-quarters; pour half a pint of broth in the dripping-pan, and baste in the same way as for roast beef. Five minutes before taking the meat off the spit sprinkle it with salt and pepper. When done dish it up; skim the fat from the gravy in the dripping-pan, and strain it through a pointed strainer over the meat, and serve.

Note.—Two or three cloves of garlic stuck in the leg of mutton a day or two previous to cooking it, is according to taste, a great improvement.

Shoulders, saddles, and loins of mutton, when not cut in chops and grilled, should also be roasted as above.

553. EPIGRAMMES OF LAMB WITH GREEN PEAS.

Saw off the breast of a neck of lamb in the same manner as for mutton cutlets; remove the tendon of the breast and boil in some stock with an onion and a small "bouquet garni." When the lamb is done drain it, and take out all the bones; keep these, as they will be required later on. Sprinkle some salt and a little pepper over the meat; lay it flat on a dish; press, with another dish and a weight at the top of it, till cold. Then cut the breast of lamb in pieces the size and shape of cutlets, pass these through some melted butter and bread-crumbs, and through two or three beaten eggs and bread-crumbs again. Cut the bones kept for that purpose with a large knife or chopper to a point at one end, stick one in each cutlet, and fry them in hot fat to a nice golden colour. Meanwhile have ready a pint of green peas, plainly boiled in salt water, drained, and mixed with a gill of Béchamel sauce in a stewpan, and as soon as the epigrammes are properly fried, dish them up in a circle, pour the peas in the centre, and serve.

Note.—Epigrammes of lamb prepared and cooked as above can be served with asparagus-points, macédoine, cucumbers, French beans, or any purée of vegetables.

554. EPIGRAMMES OF LAMB, ITALIAN STYLE.

Prepare and cook the epigrammes as in the foregoing. Meanwhile cook a pound of macaroni (No. 89), Italian style; lay the half of it on a dish; dress the epigrammes on it in the form of a circle; fill up the centre with the remainder of the macaroni, and serve with some Tomato sauce apart.

555. EPIGRAMMES OF LAMB À LA PROVENÇALE.

Cut, trim, and boil the epigrammes as in the foregoing, then pass them lightly through some oil, instead of melted butter, before breading them; and fry them in two gills of oil, instead of fat. Meanwhile trim, clean, and fry, also one pound of fresh mushrooms in two gills of oil, to which add a clove of garlic chopped to a paste and a tablespoonful of blanched and chopped parsley. When the epigrammes are of a nice colour and well drained, dish them up in the usual way, put the mushrooms in the centre, and serve.

REMARKS ON ROAST LAMB.

Lamb is generally cut in half lengthwise, through the spine, and divided afterwards in quarters, viz., two hind-quarters, each comprising a leg and loin attached to it, and two fore-quarters, which include the cutlets, breast, shoulder, and scrag, or neck-end of the carcass.

Each quarter may be roasted with as much advantage. Many even prefer the fore-quarter, or target, as it is called in Hampshire, to the hind-quarter; but should either of these joints be too large for a small family, each can be cut off and cooked separately, and differently, as shown in the foregoing. The shoulder can be roasted by itself, as well as the leg, and the loin likewise will make a small joint when roasted, as will also the best-end of the neck, or the whole neck and breast. It is however essential, before roasting either loin or neck and breast, to cut with a chopper between each chine-bone, as well as across the rib-bones, between the cutlet and breast part, so as to facilitate the carving of those joints when cooked. This is very often neglected, and gives no end of trouble to the carver when the joint is on the table, causing, at the same time, the splashing of gravy over the cloth.

556. ROAST LAMB.

Whatever joint may be roasted, the process is the same. Fold it with some of the lamb's caul which the butcher generally rolls with it; put the joint to roast before an even fire, and baste it two or three times with some of its gravy. When cooked dish it up, and serve with the gravy free from fat, properly strained, and poured over, together with some Mint sauce (No. 225) in a sauce-boat apart.

557. BRAIZED KID.

Take a whole kid about five weeks old, which when skinned and cleansed looks very much like a skinned rabbit. Cut it across the spine-bone just over the kidneys, so as to leave these attached to the hind-part of the kid; put both halves in a well-buttered braizing-pan; season with salt, pepper, and a piece of cinnamon about three inches long; add a few slices of gammon, a "bouquet garni," and two bay-leaves; moisten with a pint of broth, and let it simmer very gently about two hours and a half, with plenty of live embers on the lid, taking care, meanwhile, to turn over the pieces of kid and to often baste them. When cooked dish it up, strain the liquor, remove all grease, pour it over the meat, and serve.

CHAPTER XII.

REMARKS ON PORK.

THE meat of the pig is rather indigestible. Nevertheless it occupies a very high position as a food in this as well as in other countries. Hippocrates, that famous anatomist, even considered pork to be the most nutritious of all flesh. Be that as it may, what should we do without pork? Neither Italian nor French cooking could exist without it, at least, not as it ought to be.

In Ireland, the pig is recognised as the "gentleman" who pays the rent. I do not think the fellow could hold such a financial position if he did not possess in himself a superior source of income to other four-footed animals.

I do not know if his social position is as high in England; but what I do know is, that he appears, under different forms, on the best spread tables in the kingdom, as well as on the poorest. He is therefore a necessity; consequently I will now proceed to introduce his gastronomic qualities under the best possible forms.

558. PORK CUTLETS. GHERKIN SAUCE.

Cut and trim the pork cutlets in the same way as veal or mutton cutlets; marinade them for about an hour with a little oil, salt, nutmeg, and pepper, and the juice of a lemon all well mixed together; grill them over a clear fire about seven minutes on each side; see that they are well done without being scorched; dish them up in the usual way, pour some Gherkin sauce (No. 192) in the centre of the dish, and serve.

Note.—Pork cutlets plainly grilled as above can be served with any sharp sauce.

559. PORK CUTLETS À LA MILANAISE.

Proceed as in No. 558. When the cutlets have been properly marinaded, dry, and pass them over some beaten eggs and bread-crumbs; fry them in a sauté-pan with clarified butter, and serve with a garnish of either fresh mushrooms, spinach or beans, and Tomato sauce.

Note.—Cutlets cooked as above can be served with any purée of vegetables or fried onions and a sharp sauce apart.

560. PORK CUTLETS WITH STUFFING.

Prepare and cook the pork cutlets in the same manner as veal cutlets à l'Italienne (see No. 530).

561. PORK CUTLETS WITH PURÉE OF CHESNUTS.

Cut and trim the cutlets as described; put them in a buttered sauté-pan with a shred onion, some chopped parsley, and a few sprigs of thyme; fry them on a brisk fire for a few minutes till the cutlets are nicely coloured on both sides; moisten with a little stock; season with salt, pepper, and nutmeg, and simmer gently for about an hour. When properly glazed, drain, and dish up with a purée of chesnuts (No. 237) previously prepared for that purpose; skim off carefully all the fat from the liquor, strain the gravy through a pointed strainer over the cutlets, and serve.

562. PORK CUTLETS À L'INDIENNE.

Trim and fry the cutlets as in the foregoing; drain off all the fat; add half a pint of Espagnole sauce (No. 151), and a spoonful of curry-paste or one and a half spoonfuls of curry powder. Cover the sauté-pan and simmer gently for about fifteen minutes, taking care to turn the cutlets over during that time; dish them up, fill the centre with plain boiled rice, strain the sauce over the cutlets, and serve.

563. ROAST NECK OF PORK.

Saw off the chine-bone, and separate between the bones of a neck of pork with a small chopper or meat-saw. Prepare a stuffing for the pork, by chopping half a dozen sage-leaves and four onions of medium size; boil the mixture four minutes in plain water, then drain well, and put it in a stewpan with a large pinch of pepper, two of salt, and an ounce of butter; fry this on a slow fire for about ten minutes. Meanwhile score the outside part of the neck with a pointed knife; make an incision to place the stuffing; fasten the neck with string and roast it before a good fire for an hour and a quarter. When well done remove the string, dish the meat up, pour some good gravy on the dish, and serve with Apple sauce (No. 181) apart.

564. ROAST LOIN OF PORK.

Trim, score, and separate the bones of a loin of pork, as previously described for the neck; make an incision in the upper part of the loin, to receive some pork stuffing, made as in the foregoing; tie the part round with string, and roast the meat before a brisk fire, for about an hour and a half. When well done remove the string, dish up the joint with some nice brown gravy, and serve with Apple sauce apart.

565. ROAST LEG OF PORK.

Saw off the shank-bone of a fresh leg of pork; make a large incision below the knuckle, between the rind and meat, for the purpose of receiving the stuffing of sage and onions, previously made as for roast neck of pork. Secure this by sewing it up with small twine; score with a pointed knife the skin in parallel lines a quarter of an inch apart, by holding the leg firmly with the left hand. Then roast it before a good fire for about two hours and a half. When done remove the twine, dish the leg up with some rich gravy, and serve with Apple sauce apart.

566. BOILED LEG OF PORK.

Saw off the shank-bone of a salted leg of pork, put it in a large saucepan with four carrots, as many parsnips, and an onion stuck with three cloves. Fill the pan nearly full of cold water, and boil it gently for about three hours, more or less, according to the size of the leg. When the pork is done, drain, and dish it up with the parsnips and carrots alternately placed, as a garnish. Pour some plain gravy under, and serve with peas-pudding made as follows:—Drain a pint of yellow split-peas soaked overnight in cold water; tie them loosely in a pudding-cloth and boil with the pork for about three hours; turn them out of the cloth; pound in a mortar and rub the compound through a fine wire sieve, moistening at times with a little of the pork liquor, to help the purée passing; then put it in a stewpan with the yolks of three eggs, an ounce of butter, salt, pepper, and nutmeg to taste; mix well together with a wooden spoon, on the fire; spread a well-buttered pudding-cloth; place the purée in the centre of it; with the left hand draw the corners up, and with the right tie round the pudding with string; put it again with the pork liquor to boil for an hour; then carefully turn it out on a dish without breaking, and serve.

567. ROAST SUCKING PIG.

A sucking pig for roasting should not be more than three weeks old, for after that the meat loses delicacy. Have the pig properly scalded, drawn, cleansed, and the pettitoes cut off before leaving the pork-butcher's. Fill the paunch with a stuffing similar to the one for roast neck of pork; to which add, after the sage and onions have been fried, two or three handfuls of stale bread-crumbs, an ounce of butter, and the yolks of two eggs; stir well and mix together over the fire for five minutes. When the sucking pig is well stuffed saw the paunch with twine; give it its usual shape, and carefully fasten it at each end on the spit with small iron skewers run through the shoulders and hips; put the spit with the meat to roast before a bright fire for about two hours, taking care to often baste it with a paste-brush dipped in olive-oil, as this style of basting gives more crispness to the skin and an even and good colour to the pig.

When the meat is done remove from the fire and the spit. Cut off the head and split in two; put the brains in a small stewpan; trim off the snout and jaws, leaving only the cheeks and ears, and keep these hot; divide the meat of the pig straight down the back to the spine with a sharp knife, and finish it with a meat-saw; place the two sides on a hot dish, without disturbing the stuffing, take the twine or thread away, place the cheeks and ears at each end of the dish, pour some good brown gravy under, and serve with the following sauce:—Add to the brains set apart a spoonful of blanched chopped parsley, half a pint of Espagnole sauce or some good gravy, two ounces of butter, salt and pepper to taste, and the juice of a lemon; stir this well together over the fire, and when nearly boiling pour it in a sauce-boat.

Note.—Tomato, Robert, Ravigote, or Italian sharp sauce can be substituted for this sauce.

568. ROAST SUCKING PIG À LA PROVENÇALE.

Roast a quart of large chesnuts; remove their skins while hot, and pound them in a mortar with three ounces of butter; rub this through a wire sieve and put the purée into a stewpan with a few chives, sweet-basil, parsley, thyme, and a bay-leaf well chopped, a little grated nutmeg, salt, pepper, and the yolks of three eggs. Mix these well together on the fire; fill the paunch of the sucking pig, and roast it in the same way as in the foregoing; after which, dish up in the same style and serve with Tomato sauce apart.

569. ROAST SUCKING PIG À L'ITALIENNE.

Make a polenta (No. 100) with three-quarters of a pound of polenta flour and a quart of water. When nearly cooked add four ounces of picked sultana raisins, the same quantity each of grated parmesan cheese and butter, and a good pinch of grated nutmeg. When this has been well stirred and mixed together, fill with it the paunch of a nice sucking pig prepared as in No. 567; fasten it with twine in the usual way; roast the pig in the same manner; cut it in the same style, and serve with Italian sauce (No. 205) in a sauce-boat apart.

570. BOILED HAM WITH SPINACH.

Care must be taken when about to cook a ham, after having previously sawn off the shank-bone and removed the thigh-bone, that it should have soaked in plenty of cold water, the length of time depending entirely upon the age of the curing of the ham. Properly seasoned home-cured hams should be soaked for at least twenty-four hours; foreign hams require to be soaked even longer, varying from twenty-four hours to four days and nights. Care, however, should be taken that the water is changed every morning and night. English hams easily yielding to the pressure of the hands are new, and in such cases a soaking of six hours will be quite sufficient. It is also advisable, when a ham is being soaked for several days, that its shiny surface should be scraped off every time the water is changed. When the ham has had its proper soaking, fold around it about two pounds of good hay; then put it in a large oval pot or stewpan, with plenty of cold water; cover the pan and boil and simmer very gently on a slow fire for about four hours, or till it is done, according to the size of the ham. When the ham is done take the pan to a cool place, leaving it to soak in the hay liquor for about three-quarters of an hour, by which means it will retain the whole of its moisture; if taken out of the pan to get cold, all its richness exudes from it. The ham, having thus partially cooled, must be taken out, put on a dish, and trimmed. Divest it of the rind to within four inches from the knuckle-bone, then with a sharp knife trim the part of rind left, in the shape of either leaves, palms, squares, or ovals, arranged in a fan-like form. Trim the fat of the ham smooth, without however removing more of it than is actually necessary to give a neat appearance; after which, put it on a baking-sheet in the hot oven, for ten or twelve minutes, then wipe the surface with a clean cloth, glaze with a brush, and return it to the hot oven for about five minutes. Meanwhile have some spinach ready on the fire; dish up the ham and garnish with well-dressed spinach, placed round it in tablespoonfuls, and serve with Madeira sauce made as follows:—Put half a pint of Madeira or sherry in a stewpan, with a little meat-glaze and a small pinch of mignonette pepper. Boil on a brisk fire for five minutes; add a pint of Espagnole sauce, and continue reducing it till the sauce has reached a proper consistency or coats the spoon; then strain through a pointed strainer into the sauce-boat.

Note.—I strongly advocate the use of hay when boiling hams, as the flavour thereby imparted is superior to all other ingredients or more expensive vegetables.

571. BRAIZED HAM WITH STEWED PEAS.

Follow the directions given in the foregoing as to the trimming and soaking of the ham; boil it in water without hay for an hour; strain and wash it clean, and wipe the pan; replace the ham in it with two carrots, two onions, a head of celery, a "bouquet garni," two blades of mace, and four cloves. Moisten with sufficient ordinary stock to float the ham, and simmer very gently on a slow fire for about four hours, taking care not to allow it to boil but merely simmer, in order to obtain tenderness and mellowness. When done remove the pan with the ham to a cool place, leaving it, as in the foregoing, to cool in its liquor. When nearly cold take it out of the pan and trim it as described; then put it back into the pan with its own stock, and warm it gently, without boiling, over a slow fire. When warmed through, place the ham on a baking-dish in the oven for a few minutes to dry the surface; glaze and dish it up; garnish round with stewed peas (No. 286); pour some bright Espagnole sauce over the peas, and serve.

Note.—Hams boiled or braized as in Nos. 570 and 571 can also be dressed with jardinière, French, broad, or haricot beans, green peas, new carrots, Brussels sprouts, and macédoine.

572. BAKED HAM, HOUSEWIFE STYLE.

Put a ham that has been only trimmed and soaked, as previously described, in a large oval pan with plenty of cold water; boil, and let it simmer very gently for an hour; take the pan with the ham in it, away from the fire to get cold. Meanwhile mix to rather a thick paste, one pound and a half of flour with plain water. When the ham is cold take it out of the pan; drain it; remove the whole rind and trim off the fat; then wrap up the ham closely with the paste; fold this with a buttered sheet of paper; fasten it on the spit, and roast before a moderate fire for some three hours, taking care meanwhile, to often baste the paper with any sort of fat. Then take the spit away from the fire, remove the paper carefully from the paste, without breaking the latter; cut a small round hole in the centre of the paste, into which introduce, little by little, half a bottle of Madeira or Marsala wine; stop up the hole with fresh paste; fold the ham again, with a buttered sheet of paper, and roast for half an hour longer. Then take it away from the fire, place on a dish, remove the paper and paste from around, and serve with Madeira sauce (see Boiled Ham and Spinach) apart, together with a dish either of cauliflowers, haricot or French beans, green peas, or carrots, cooked in salt water.

REMARKS ON BOAR.

The boar is a pig in a wild state, and its flesh although tough is similar to pork, except the head, which is the most delicate part. All other parts of the animal are cooked in the same manner as pork.

573. BOAR CUTLETS À LA SARDE.

Cut and trim the cutlets as described for pork cutlets, and marinade them for twenty-four hours. Half an hour before serving, drain and wipe the cutlets dry, and fry them in a sauté-pan, with butter, on a brisk fire, for eight minutes. When done drain the butter from the pan, moisten well with Mustard sauce (No. 223), and season with salt and pepper. Let the cutlets simmer in this three minutes on each side, and then dish them up, pour the sauce over them, and serve with a garnish of potato purée.

574. BOAR CUTLETS, ENGLISH STYLE.

Cut, trim, and marinade the cutlets for two or three days. Wipe them dry, pass them through clarified butter and bread-crumbs, and broil them over a clear and brisk fire for four minutes each side; sprinkle some salt over each cutlet; dish up with a garnish of fresh mushrooms, either stewed or grilled, and serve with Gooseberry sauce (No. 180) apart.

575. BOAR CUTLETS À L'ESPAGNOLE.

Cut and trim the cutlets and fry them in a sauté-pan with clarified butter over a brisk fire; season with salt and pepper to taste, and when they are of a nice amber colour dish them up nicely in a circular form, add to the gravy in which the cutlets were cooked a glass of white wine, half a pint of Espagnole sauce (No. 151), a teaspoonful each of blanched chopped parsley and fennel; reduce the sauce on a brisk fire for about five minutes; pour it over the cutlets, and serve.

Boar's legs are cooked in the same style as legs of pork, but when about to be marinaded, add a gill of vinegar to the marinade.

576. BOAR'S HEAD STUFFED.

Singe and clean the head most carefully, and bone it, beginning under the throat, taking care not to cut the skin on the top when the knife passes over the bony part of the head; remove all the fatty and sinewy parts from inside the head, and spread it out on a large dish and rub it well with a mixture of four pounds of salt, four ounces of saltpetre, and four ounces of moist sugar. When well rubbed all over, let it remain spread on the mixture; cover the meat with two bay-leaves, a few sprigs each of thyme, sweet-basil, and parsley, one dozen cloves, and the slices of two onions, and put the dish in a cool place. Two days afterwards give it a second rubbing; spread the head on the opposite side; replace the aromatic herbs on the top, and let it remain thus for five or six days longer, taking care however, to turn the head over the brine every day during that time. To dress the head, take it out of the brine and wipe it well with a cloth before laying it on the table.

Chop up two pounds of lean veal free from skin and gristle, and one pound of fat bacon; pound these together in the mortar, or pass it through the sausage-machine; season it well with salt, pepper, and nutmeg, and put it on a dish apart. Cut a cured and cooked ox-tongue, two pounds of lean pork, two pounds of fat bacon, or the same quantity of calf's udder boiled in broth, and two pounds of peeled truffles, all cut in irregular shapes, but not larger than inch dice; mix them, and then with the pounded meat make a layer on the inside of the head about an inch thick;

put a layer of the mixed dice of tongue &c. over this, with a few pistachio kernels, the skin of which must have been previously removed by scalding; cover these with a layer of meat, and proceed with the dice and pistachios alternately till the whole mixture is used. When the head is sufficiently filled, the two sides should be turned over and sewn up with a small trussing-needle and twine, so as to thoroughly secure the stuffing. The head must be wrapped in a strong and well-spread buttered cloth and bound round very tightly with tape an inch and a half wide, so as to preserve its original form. Place it in a large pan with any game carcasses or trimmings of meat there may be at hand, and four cow-heels, also a "bouquet garni," four carrots, four onions, with a clove stuck in each, a little ginger, salt, and pepper, a bottle of white wine, a gill of brandy, and as much stock as will be required to cover the head well; then boil it, and simmer gently, with the lid on, for at least five hours; after which ascertain if it is properly done by inserting a trussing-needle. If the needle does not go in easily, continue the simmering for a quarter or half an hour longer. Then remove the pan, and leave the head to cool in its own liquor. Before the broth is cold however, the head must be taken out. See if it has shrunk in the cloth; if so it must be carefully tightened so as preserve its shape, and then put back into its broth to complete the cooling. When quite cold take the head out of the pan and put it in the oven for a minute or two, after having untied and removed the cloth; wipe off the fat from the surface with a clean cloth; trim the back part of the head; see that the ears have their proper form, and if not use some small wooden skewers, and hide these with a mixture of lard and mutton suet. Glaze the head with a dark-coloured glaze made for that purpose; decorate the snout with a little piping; place modelled tusks and glass eyes to complete the dressing; then dish up, and ornament with aspic jelly.

Note.—Hog's-head is also stuffed as above; but for this purpose the head should be cut off deep in the shoulders before the pig is scalded, and then the bristles singed with lighted straw so as to have all the appearance of a wild boar's head.

CHAPTER XIII.

REMARKS ON VENISON.

THE flesh of that ruminant and light-footed mammalian animal, the roebuck or deer, is both delicate and tasty, but must be hung in a draughty place for at least a fortnight before it is fit for the table. Those living in wild and mountainous parts are the best, and the pale-brown, yellow-colour breed is superior to the red one for cooking purposes.

577. ROEBUCK CUTLETS À LA CHASSEUR.

Roebuck cutlets should be cut in the same style as mutton cutlets, and after being trimmed, should be fried with clarified butter on a brisk fire and seasoned with salt and pepper. Meanwhile have ready in a stewpan on the fire, some game essence (No. 172), to which add and warm up as many slices of cooked pickled ox-tongue as there are cutlets; dish up the cutlets alternately with the slices of tongue, pour the sauce over, and serve.

578. ROEBUCK CUTLETS À LA SURPRISE.

Prepare and trim the cutlets of a well-hung neck of roebuck; marinade them as mutton cutlets for two hours, and drain, flour, and fry them with butter on a brisk fire for two or three minutes on each side. Meanwhile have ready and cold a stuffing composed as follows:—Pound in a mortar a little cooked veal and ham free from skin and gristle, season with salt, pepper, a good pinch of aromatic herbs, and a gill of rum, mix with the brains of the roebuck cooked in good broth and cut in very small dice, after having been previously washed and soaked in water in the usual way. Cover or surround both sides of the cutlets with this forcemeat, then pass them through bread-crumbs, beaten yolks of eggs, and bread-crumbs again; fry them with clarified butter in a sauté-pan, and serve with Suprême sauce (No. 188) apart.

579. ROEBUCK CHOPS, GRILLED.

Cut and trim the chops of roebuck in the same manner as mutton chops, flatten them slightly with the cutlet-bat, broil over a moderate fire, turning them over every two or three minutes till done; then sprinkle each with salt and pepper; dish them up, taking care not to spill the gravy that may be on their surface; pour some good brown gravy under, and serve with some currant jelly apart.

580. BREAST OF ROEBUCK À LA LYONNAISE.

Cook the breast of a roebuck in good broth, to which a glass of white wine and a "bouquet garni" have been added; when the meat is well done, drain, bone, press between two dishes, and let it get cold. Meanwhile skim off the fat and strain the broth in which the breast has boiled; return it to the stewpan and reduce by one-third, over a brisk fire; then add one pound of nice chesnuts, previously peeled and blanched, so as to clean them of their second skin; continue the boiling till the chesnuts are well done and nicely glazed. When the meat is cold, cut it in pieces two inches wide; squeeze the juice of two lemons and sprinkle some pepper and grated nutmeg over them; dip each piece in some clarified butter and bread-crumbs, and broil them for a few minutes over a clear fire. When nicely browned dish them up in a circle, garnish the centre with the glazed chesnuts, and serve with the remainder of the glaze apart.

581. HARICOT OF ROEBUCK.

Cut the scrag-end of the neck and breast of venison between each bone, put them in a sauté-pan, and fry to a nice brown; drain off all the fat, and sprinkle over them two tablespoonfuls of flour. Continue frying them for three or four minutes longer; after which, moisten with half a bottle of claret and a quart of broth; add a "bouquet garni," two large carrots, and three turnips cut into fancy shapes, and a dozen small button onions; set the pan over the fire, and stir the contents with a wooden spoon till it boils, then let it simmer gently for about an hour and a half. When the meat and vegetables are cooked, take them out of the sauté-pan with a large perforated spoon, and put them into another stewpan on the fire with half a pint of its liquor, free from fat, to keep it hot. Skim off all the grease from the remainder of the liquor, reduce it on a brisk fire to a half-glaze, strain it through a pointed strainer over the meat and vegetables, season with salt and pepper, simmer for five minutes, dish up and serve.

582. ROEBUCK FRY.

Clean and cut the fry of a roebuck into small scollops, season these with salt and pepper, and roll them well over the flour; then fry them to a nice brown in a sauté-pan with some clarified butter. When done, dish up with fried parsley, and serve with sharp Italian sauce (No. 205) apart.

583. ROEBUCK'S BRAINS.

These brains are prepared, cooked, and fried in the same style as sheep's or calf's brains.

584. JUGGED VENISON.

Cut in three-inch pieces either shoulder or breast of venison; fry these to a nice brown in a stewpan with some fat bacon that has been at least four days in brine; drain off the fat; sprinkle three tablespoonfuls of flour over the venison; fry it, and toss the stewpan for three minutes longer; moisten with a bottle of claret and a quart of broth; season with salt and pepper; add a "bouquet garni," and set the pan on the fire, stirring very frequently until it boils; then simmer gently. Meanwhile fry in butter for five minutes, two dozen small button onions, and when the venison has boiled for half an hour add to it the onions and a pint of button champignons; continue the simmering till the meat is done and tender, which will take about two hours, then throw the "bouquet garni" away; skim off all scum and grease from the surface, and pour it over a dish; garnish round with fried croûtons cut triangle-shape, and serve.

585. LOIN OR SADDLE OF ROEBUCK À L'ECOSSAISE.

Trim nicely a well-hung loin or saddle of venison; cover the fillet with thin slices of fat bacon, and place it in a large sauté-pan with a carrot, two onions sliced, a small "bouquet garni," four ounces of butter, six cloves, and four ounces of streaky bacon cut in narrow strips. Fry these on a moderate fire for an hour with the lid on, taking care to turn the meat and baste it often with the butter; then add a pint of good broth, and continue simmering and basting the meat till done. Meanwhile prepare some croquets of potatoes (No. 326). When the meat is ready dish it up, garnish with croquets of potatoes; strain the liquor in which the venison was cooked into a small stewpan, add half a pint of Espagnole sauce (No. 151), with two tablespoonfuls of currant jelly, and salt and pepper to taste; stir this on the fire for a few minutes, or till the jelly is well melted, pour it in a sauce-boat, and serve.

586. HAUNCH OF ROEBUCK ROASTED.

Saw off the shank-bone; remove and pare away the sinews and dark skin of a well-seasoned haunch of venison; wrap it in a buttered sheet of paper and roast it for about an hour before a good fire, taking care to baste it twice with a little butter. A quarter of an hour before the meat is ready remove the paper; sprinkle some salt and pepper over it; continue the roasting, and baste it once more. Then take the haunch away from the fire; dish it up on a very hot dish, and serve with a sauce-boat of Venison sauce (No. 196) and a dish of plain boiled French beans apart.

Note.—Haunch of venison is generally served on a hot-water dish.

587. HAUNCH OF ROEBUCK LARDED AND ROASTED.

Trim and saw off the bone below the knuckle, of a haunch of venison; make a circular incision about six inches in diameter on the top of the leg with a pointed knife, and remove the skin, so as to leave the surface perfectly smooth and bare, in order to lard it rather thickly. Marinade it for two days in a liquor made as follows:—Fry in a stewpan with an ounce of butter for five minutes a shred carrot and two onions, a few sprigs of parsley, one of thyme, two shalots, and two blades of mace; add a quart of boiling water, a pint of good vinegar, two tablespoonfuls of salt, and half a tablespoonful of pepper. Boil and simmer very gently for about half an hour, and pour the contents into an earthenware pan or basin large enough to hold the haunch of roebuck. After having marinaded this two days, take the joint out of the liquor three hours before serving, wipe it well, and butter it with a brush dipped in melted butter; then cover the leg with a soft paste made of flour and boiling water, well beaten and mixed, so as not to leave any clotting, taking care, also, that the paste should be hot when wrapping the leg with it, in order that its layer should not be more than the sixteenth of an inch thick; after which, cover this with two well-buttered sheets of paper, and roast before a moderate fire for two hours and a half or more, according to the size of the leg; then remove the paper and paste from the meat, dish it up on a hot-water dish, and serve with a sauce made as follows:—Boil and strain through a cloth the liquor in which the haunch was marinaded; brown nicely in a stewpan one ounce of flour with one of butter; moisten it with the marinade, stirring the while, and reduce it by a quarter of its quantity over a brisk fire; add a gill of port wine, stir again over the fire, and serve.

Note.—A haunch of venison can remain in the marinade in a cool place for a week or more without fear of being spoilt. It can also be roasted without a coat of paste round it, and then one hour will be sufficient to cook it.

588. HASHED VENISON.

The remains of the leg or haunch should be cut in thin slices not more than two and a half inches square. Put about a pint of Venison sauce (No. 196) in a stewpan on the fire; when it boils add the slices of meat to it; draw the stewpan by the side of the fire and cover it. Let the meat warm up gradually, by tossing the pan frequently, without, however, letting the contents boil. When properly warmed dish up in a large hot dish, with the sauce poured over, and serve with croûtons fried in butter.

Remarks on Hare.

The flesh of this puny quadruped is always savoury, but varies in taste according to the nature of herbs it feeds on; those living on high and mountainous ground are superior in flavour and delicacy to those living on marshy land. These can be recognised by the colour of the fur; the darker the back and the whiter the under part the better the hare. Hares should only be eaten in winter.

589. JUGGED HARE.

In skinning a hare, draw the blood carefully through a fine strainer into a basin containing an ounce of melted butter, and keep it covered in a cool place till wanted. Throw away the whole of the intestines; wipe the hare with a cloth and cut it into two-and-a-half-inch pieces; put these in a jar or basin to marinade for one day if possible, with a bottle of claret and some aromatic herbs, such as bay-leaves, a few sprigs of parsley, thyme, and marjoram.

When wanted, brown in a stewpan, with two ounces of butter, four ounces of streaky bacon cut in strips, two inches long by half an inch thick, two onions, two medium-sized carrots, one head of celery, and two leeks, all nicely shred, and a "bouquet garni." When properly browned, moisten with a gill of good vinegar, stir, and let this dry in the stewpan on the fire with the vegetables. Then moisten with the wine in which the hare has soaked; add the pieces of hare and a quart of broth; salt and pepper to taste; boil, stir occasionally, and draw by the side of the stove to simmer very gently, with the lid on, and stir occasionally. Meanwhile fry in butter two dozen button onions to a nice golden colour all round; glaze them in a pint of Espagnole sauce or some good veal stock till well done. When the pieces of hare are tender pass the liquor through a fine wire sieve; put the pieces of meat and bacon into a bain-marie to keep hot; return the strained sauce into the stewpan and reduce it on a brisk fire if necessary. Draw it away from the fire; skim off the fat, and add gradually about half a pint of the sauce to the basin containing the preserved blood, taking care to stir quickly in order to mix the two well together; return this to the stewpan, stirring the while; after which, skim off the fat from the onions, and pour these with their glaze into the blood sauce. Add also two dozen forcemeat balls, made with sausage-meat and the yolks of two eggs well mixed together, rolled into small nuts and fried to a nice brown in boiling fat. Stir the whole over the fire till nearly boiling, pour it over the hare, and keep hot till wanted; dish up together, garnished with a dozen croûtons.

590. CIVET OF HARE.

Skin, preserve the blood, clean, and cut a hare in the same manner as described in No. 589. Cut half a pound of streaky bacon into one-inch dice, fry these in a stewpan to a yellow colour and put them on a plate; fry afterwards, in the same pan, the pieces of hare to a brown colour; sprinkle over them two tablespoonfuls of flour, and continue the frying for three minutes longer, tossing, meanwhile, the pieces of meat in the pan. Then add the fried bacon, a small carrot, a "bouquet garni," an onion stuck with four cloves, salt and pepper to taste; moisten with a bottle of claret and a quart of broth; stir till it boils, and remove to the side to simmer gently with the lid on. Meanwhile fry a dozen button onions in a stewpan, with an ounce of butter, for five minutes, add them, with a pint of champignons sliced in two, to the civet, after the latter has simmered for at least half an hour; then continue gently boiling till the hare is done. When the pieces of hare are tender skim off all the fat from the surface; remove the bouquet, large onion, and carrots; dish up the meat and bacon; pour half a pint of the hare sauce gradually into the basin containing the blood; stir this constantly; pour it back with the civet sauce; stir on the fire till it nearly boils; pour it over the hare, garnish with fried croûtons, and serve.

591. LEVERET À LA CHASSEUR.

Cut up the leveret into small joints as follows:—Separate the hind-legs even with the loins, remove the shoulders, divide the loin into six parts, and split the head and neck in halves. Place all these in a sauté-pan with two ounces of butter, fry them of a light-brown colour over a brisk fire, then add a tablespoonful of chopped shalots, parsley, and mushrooms, well mixed together; put the lid on and simmer for about ten minutes; after which, drain off the grease, add a pint of good broth, half a pound of nice clean mushrooms, a piece of glaze as big as a walnut, a little grated nutmeg, salt and pepper to taste. Simmer the whole with the lid on for ten minutes. Squeeze the juice of half a lemon; stir the contents; dish up the pieces of hare and mushrooms; pour the sauce over, and serve with a garnish of croûtons fried in clarified butter.

592. FILLETS OF HARE LARDED.   VENISON SAUCE.

Fillet two hares and split these into halves; lard them in the same style as fillets of beef, and place them at the bottom of a stewpan lined with thin layers of fat bacon. Moisten with half a pint of Madeira and half a pint of good veal stock. Season with two bay-leaves, salt, and pepper; put a round of buttered paper on the fillets, and set them in the oven to simmer for twenty-five minutes, taking care to often baste them with their own liquor. When they are nearly done remove the paper in order to dry and glaze the larding; drain the fillets upon a cloth; dish them up in a circle; pour in the centre some Venison sauce (No. 196), and serve.

593. HARE'S BACK WITH SHARP ITALIAN SAUCE.

Lard the back of a hare with small strips of fat bacon; fix on the spit and wrap in a buttered sheet of paper; then roast it before a clear fire for twenty-five minutes; remove the paper; continue roasting and basting for five minutes longer, when the meat will be glazed, and then dish up and serve with some Italian sauce (No. 205) in a sauce-boat apart.

594. ROAST HARE.

Skin a hare (saving the blood) and clean it as previously described. Cross the hind-legs; that is, pass one through the other; roll the flank round on each side and secure it with wooden skewers. Hold the loin and legs over the fire for a few minutes, to set the flesh and facilitate larding. Lard the thick part of the legs and fillet; put the hare on the spit; cover it with buttered paper, but see that it is doubled over the fillets; then roast it before a good fire for thirty-five minutes, making the fire more brisk on the side of the hind-quarter. Remove the paper; glaze the hare by basting it with its own gravy for two or three minutes longer; after which, dish it up with the gravy. Meanwhile have ready a pint of Venison sauce with which the blood of the hare has been diluted and thickened as described for jugged hare. Pour this into a sauce-boat and serve with the hare.

REMARKS ON RABBITS.

There are two kinds of rabbits, the wild and tame, the former being the better of the two. Rabbits, being so very fertile in their progeny, are always plentiful in the market, and can at all times be had for a trifle; therefore I should consider it a sin if we were not to prepare and serve them in the most advantageous and best possible manner known in cookery.

The flesh of young rabbits is very tender, as well as a delicate and wholesome food, and makes good and nutritious soups.

To farmers and others living in country places, where butcher's meat can only be had with difficulty, this animal is a great boon, as it affords them fresh meat, a food so essential for health and strength to mankind. The flesh of tame rabbits can be made equal in taste and flavour to that of wild, if they are given some aromatic plants to eat for a few days previous to being killed.

595. STEWED RABBIT.

Skin, draw, and wash a rabbit clean; cut it into two or three inch pieces; slice a quarter of a pound of streaky bacon into two-inch strips half an inch thick; fry them in a sauté-pan, with an ounce of butter, to a yellow colour;

remove the bacon to a plate; fry the pieces of rabbit in the same pan for ten minutes; sprinkle over them two tablespoonfuls of flour; continue to fry and stir on the fire for three minutes longer; add half a pint of good broth, half a pint of claret, a "bouquet garni," salt and pepper to taste, eighteen small button onions, previously fried in butter, and the strips of fried bacon. Simmer this with the lid on for about twenty minutes; take out the "bouquet garni," dish up the stew, and serve with fried croûtons.

596. RABBIT STEWED À LA CHASSEUR.

Skin, draw, and wash a rabbit clean; cut off each hind-leg at the joint, even with the loins; remove the shoulders in the same way; separate the neck from the head; split both in halves, and divide the loin or back into six pieces. Put these into a sauté-pan with two ounces of clarified butter, and fry them over a brisk fire to a nice brown colour; then sprinkle over them a tablespoonful each of finely-chopped shalots, parsley, and fresh mushrooms; cover the pan and set it over a slow fire for about ten minutes; after which, sprinkle in a tablespoonful of flour; toss and stir over the fire for two or three minutes longer; add a pint of broth, a small piece of meat-glaze, and half a pound of fresh mushrooms; season with salt, pepper, and a pinch of grated nutmeg. Simmer this for ten minutes, taking care to stir it occasionally, and then squeeze the juice of a lemon over the contents; stir again; dish up with a garnish of croûtons, and serve.

597. RABBIT À LA PROVENÇALE.

After having skinned and cleaned a rabbit in the usual way, cut it into two-inch pieces; put a gill of salad-oil into a sauté-pan with a clove of garlic chopped very fine; fry the pieces of rabbit with it to a nice brown colour over a brisk fire; drain off the fat; moisten with a pint of broth, half a pint of Tomato sauce, six fresh tomatoes cut in quarters, and salt and pepper to taste. Stir this over the fire and simmer gently with the lid on for twenty minutes; sprinkle a tablespoonful of finely chopped parsley a few minutes before removing the pan from the fire; then dish it up, pour the sauce over, and serve.

598. CURRIED RABBIT.

Clean and cut a rabbit as in the foregoing; cut in small dice two onions of medium size, and fry them in a sauté-pan over a moderate fire for five minutes, with two ounces of butter and an ounce of curry powder; stir the while, to prevent burning. Then add the pieces of rabbit, and brown them round slightly; after which, sprinkle over the lot three tablespoonfuls of flour. Continue the stirring three minutes longer; add a quart of good stock and salt and pepper to taste, and simmer for three-quarters of an hour with the lid on, when the rabbit will be done. Pour the contents of the sauté-pan into a colander, over a basin; clean and put the pieces of rabbit into a stewpan; strain the sauce from the basin through a tammy into the stewpan with the rabbit; all but boil it, and then dish it up; pour the sauce over, and serve with half a pound of rice, previously boiled in plain water, properly washed afterwards in cold water, to remove the starch and separate the grain, and either warmed up by steam or spread on a dish in a hot closet to dry and warm.

599. RABBIT À LA NAPOLITAINE.

Prepare a rabbit as before, and brown the pieces in a stewpan with two ounces of butter, then drain off the grease, add a quart of Neapolitan sauce (No. 208), previously made for the purpose, salt and pepper to taste, and simmer for an hour with the lid on, taking care to give it an occasional stir; then sprinkle a tablespoonful of finely chopped and blanched parsley, and squeeze the juice of a lemon over the contents; stir the lot for half a minute; dish it up; pour the sauce over, and serve.

600. RABBIT À LA POULETTE.

Clean and cut a rabbit in small joints, put these in a stewpan with a "bouquet garni," two onions each stuck with three cloves, one head of celery, one carrot, a gill of vinegar, salt and pepper to taste, and enough stock or water to cover the whole. Simmer it for about an hour with the lid on. Meanwhile prepare some Poulette sauce (No. 179). When the meat is cooked and tender, strain the broth through a colander into a basin, to be used as soup; put the pieces of rabbit in the stewpan with the Poulette sauce, toss these up over the fire for two minutes without boiling, then dish it up with the sauce poured over, and garnish with fried croûtons before serving.

601. ROAST RABBIT.

Skin, draw, and clean a rabbit; cut the fore-legs at the first joint, and the hind-legs above the knuckle-joint; then truss it by securing the head with string passed between the shoulders and the hind-legs, crossed in the same style as for roast hare. Tie with a string a slice of fat bacon on the back of the rabbit; dish it up, and serve with Hare sauce (No. 200) apart.

Note.—Rabbits, besides being prepared as in the foregoing methods, can also be dressed in almost every variety of form in which chickens cut in small quarters are prepared, and they are also made into purée, quenelles, croquets, and salpicons.

CHAPTER XIV.

REMARKS ON POULTRY.

ALTHOUGH England is rich in poultry, the supply is far from being equal to the demand, and the quality (apart from Surrey chickens) is not what it should be; hence the large importation of that most delicate and nutritious of all food from various foreign countries.

There is no country in the world where encouragements for breeding poultry are more offered and better recompensed than in England, nearly every town in each county having its poultry-show, and valuable prizes are yearly given, as well as fabulous prices paid for bird winners, £100 having been paid for a game-cock a few years ago at the Crystal Palace show; but the greatest number of exhibitors are fancy breeders, whose only aim is perfect plumage and colour, instead of quality and quantity of flesh.

If the authorities were to award prizes to the largest poultry breeders of their respective counties, the effect would be different, and the nation as well as the farmers would benefit.

Several kinds or species of birds are included in poultry, such as chickens, capons, ducks, geese, turkeys, pigeons, guinea-fowls, swans, and pea-hens, and those are of different breeds, especially the chickens, pigeons, and ducks. Dorking and game fowls are considered the best for the table; the former are recognised by their double claws, and the latter by their slate-coloured legs. Real Surrey chickens possess a well-deserved reputation for plumpness, tenderness, and delicacy of flavour.

Both knowledge and care are required to select good poultry; old and tough fowls can easily be detected by a slight tinge of violet seen through the skin of the thigh, as well as by the thin necks and feet. A young and tender chicken has always large feet and big knee-joints, which disappear with age; the flesh of the pinion and breast should be tried, and if these are found to be tender the bird can be cooked with confidence.

An old turkey has, in a similar manner, a violet tinge on the legs and back, but a young one will be recognised by the whiteness of its flesh and fat.

The fat of young ducks and geese is transparent and light-coloured. Break off the lower part of the beak; if it breaks easily the bird is young.

Pigeons when old have fillets of a dark violet colour, but when it is of a light red they are young birds.

Beware of floured poultry, as well as of broken breasts.

602. STEWED CHICKEN WITH RISOTTO.

Select a nice plump tender chicken, draw and singe it over the flame of a gas-burner, cut it up in small joints in the following manner:—Lay the chicken on the table with the head towards you, and with a sharp knife in the right hand cut off the neck, then the wings or pinions at the second joint, then the legs at the knotty bend of the first joint; then make an incision from the point of the breast-bone to the wing-joint on both sides; turn the chicken round and make two other incisions to separate the thighs from the body; take off both wings and thighs, by laying the chicken on its side; separate the breast from the back and cut across in two. Put these pieces in a sauté-pan with two ounces of butter and fry them to a nice brown; moisten with a pint and a half of good broth and a gill of Marsala; season with salt, pepper, and a pinch of grated nutmeg; simmer with the lid on till the pieces of chicken are done, which will take about half an hour. Meanwhile prepare a thick risotto (see Risotto). When the chicken is ready, remove the pieces on to a dish and keep them hot; add the gravy to the risotto; stir, and dish it up when cooked; arrange the pieces of chicken nicely on the top; place the two pieces of the back in the middle of the dish; lay across, one over the other, the two legs, the two pieces of neck, and the pinions; fill up the other two openings or squares thus formed with the thighs and wings, and cover the lot with the two pieces of breast, and serve.

603. STEWED CHICKEN À LA MARENGO.

Cut a tender chicken in small joints as in the foregoing. Melt in a sauté-pan an ounce of butter with a gill of salad-oil; add a bruised clove of garlic, a bay-leaf, two sprigs of thyme, salt and pepper to taste; fry the pieces of chicken with these, for about twenty-five minutes on a brisk fire until the pieces are done, when they must be removed from the sauté-pan, placed on a dish, and kept hot; throw away the aromatic herbs, and pour half a pint of Tomato sauce into the sauté-pan, with the half of that quantity of good broth or gravy and a dozen sliced champignons; stir this and let it boil for five minutes over a brisk fire, then draw the pan away, add the juice of half a lemon, stir the contents well together, dish up the pieces of chicken in the same way as in No. 602, garnish the dish with the champignons and croûtons fried in butter, and as many eggs fried in oil as there are persons, and serve.

604. STEWED CHICKEN WITH MUSHROOMS.

Cut up the chicken as for stewed chicken with risotto. Melt in a sauté-pan an ounce and a half of butter, put the pieces of chicken in the pan, taking care not to lay one over the other; sprinkle salt and pepper to taste, and fry for about twenty-five minutes on rather a brisk fire, turning the pieces of meat over when wanted. Meanwhile prepare a brown garnish of mushrooms (No. 301). When the chicken is done, dress the pieces on a dish, garnish with the mushrooms, pour the sauce over, and serve with a few croûtons.

605. STEWED CHICKEN, HOUSEWIFE STYLE.

Cut up a chicken; shred a middle-sized onion and carrot; fry these in a stewpan for five minutes with a quarter of a pound of butter, stirring the while with a wooden spoon; add the pieces of chicken, season with salt and pepper, and continue the frying and stirring for another five minutes. Spread four tablespoonfuls of flour; fry for three minutes longer, and moisten with a pint and a half of good stock and four ripe tomatoes cut in quarters; stir the contents till boiling to prevent burning, and simmer twenty minutes with the lid on. Add half a pound of fresh mushrooms properly cleaned and a tablespoonful of chopped parsley; simmer for another ten minutes; see that the sauce is well seasoned; dish up, and serve.

606. STEWED CHICKEN À LA CHASSEUR.

Select a nice tender chicken; draw, singe, and cut it up in the same style as the foregoing; place the pieces in a sauté-pan with two tablespoonfuls of olive-oil and one ounce of butter; fry these over a brisk fire for five minutes; sprinkle in two shalots chopped fine; stir the contents over the fire for another five minutes; moisten with half a pint of dry white wine; add a quarter of a pound of fresh mushrooms properly cleaned and finely sliced; season with salt, pepper, and two bay-leaves. Continue the stewing for fifteen minutes longer, taking care to turn the meat over as required; then add a piece of glaze the size of a nut and a similar quantity of fresh butter; stir it till properly melted, and when done dish up the pieces of chicken. Squeeze the juice of a lemon and add a teaspoonful of finely chopped parsley to the sauce; stir it over the fire for a few seconds; pour it over the chicken, and serve.

607. FRICASSEE OF CHICKEN.

Cut up a good chicken as in No. 602; drop the pieces into a basin containing two quarts of clear lukewarm water, and let them soak for fifteen minutes; drain and put into a stewpan with one quart of water, an onion with a clove stuck in it, a "bouquet garni," a sliced carrot, and the quarter of a head of celery; season well with salt and pepper, and boil it; skim carefully, then simmer for about half an hour with the pan partly covered, when the pieces of chicken will be done. Strain the broth through a colander into a basin and keep it apart; immerse the pieces of chicken in cold water and drain them on a clean cloth. Meanwhile stir for five minutes in a stewpan over the fire without browning, two ounces of flour, with the same quantity of very fresh butter; add gradually the chicken broth and the liquor in which half a pint of champignons have boiled for five minutes; stir the contents well whilst over the fire, so as to work it into a smooth sauce till it boils, when the stewpan must be drawn from the fire; let it simmer for about half an hour, in order to throw up the scum; then skim it, and thicken the sauce with the yolks of four eggs, in the usual way; stir this over the fire until it is nearly boiling, pass it through a tammy or gravy-strainer into the stewpan already containing the pieces of chicken; add to it the cooked champignons and an ounce of butter; stir this gently over the fire, and when near ebullition dish up the pieces of chicken in the usual manner; pour the sauce over; garnish with the champignons and fried croûtons, and serve.

608. STEWED CHICKEN À LA PROVENÇALE.

Slice two large onions into rings, and fry them in a sauté-pan with half a gill of olive-oil, till of a nice light-brown colour; then add the pieces of a tender chicken, cut as for stewed chicken and risotto; season with salt and pepper, a few sprigs of parsley, a bay-leaf, and a crushed clove of garlic. Fry these on a brisk fire to a nice brown colour, for about twenty minutes. Meanwhile stew for five minutes in a stewpan half a pound of fresh mushrooms and four shalots chopped fine, together with a tablespoonful of chopped parsley. Moisten the whole with a tablespoonful of salad-oil and a gill of Madeira wine; then add a gill each of either Espagnole sauce or good broth and Tomato sauce, and boil it. When the pieces of chicken have simmered for twenty minutes, take them out with a fork and put in the stewpan with the sauce. Simmer together with the lid on for seven or eight minutes; dish up the chicken in the usual way; pour the sauce over, and serve.

609. STEWED CHICKEN À L'AFRICAINE.

Cut up a chicken as for stewed chicken and risotto; cut also half a pound of raw ham or gammon in slices three inches long by about two wide; melt two ounces of clarified butter in a stewpan; add the pieces of chicken and ham, together with a small "bouquet garni" composed of parsley, thyme, bay-leaf, and a clove of garlic; season with a small pinch of cayenne, and fry it over a good fire till the pieces of chicken have acquired a nice golden colour; drain off the fat; moisten with three parts of a pint of good white stock (veal broth), a gill of French white wine, a small piece of glaze, half a teaspoonful of curry paste, and half a pound of fresh mushrooms properly cleaned and cut in small pieces; let the contents boil for about fifteen minutes with the pan partly covered; after which, draw the stewpan away from the fire; remove the "bouquet garni;" add half an ounce of butter and the juice of half a lemon; dish up the pieces of chicken alternately with the slices of ham; pour the sauce over; decorate the base of the dish with fried croûtons, and serve.

610. CURRIED CHICKEN.

Cut up a chicken as in the foregoing; shred and fry an onion in a stewpan with an ounce of butter for about three minutes; add the pieces of chicken and continue the frying till they are slightly coloured all over; sprinkle two tablespoonfuls of flour; season with salt and pepper; stir over the fire for three minutes longer, and moisten with a pint of good stock and half a tablespoonful of curry paste. Simmer it for about twenty minutes with the pan half covered; pour the contents of the stewpan into a colander over a basin; clean the stewpan; rub the sauce through a tammy or hair-sieve into the stewpan again. Take up from the colander each piece of chicken, clean and return them to the stewpan with the sauce, and warm them up without boiling. Meanwhile have some rice cooked as for curried rabbit. When the sauce is all but boiling dish up the pieces of chicken; pour the sauce over, and serve with the boiled rice apart.

611. STEWED CHICKEN AND MUSSELS.

Cut up the chicken in small joints as in the foregoing, fry these in a sauté-pan all round to a nice golden colour with two ounces of clarified butter, and season with salt, pepper, and grated nutmeg; moisten with a pint of veal stock or Espagnole sauce; simmer it for about twenty minutes; after which, skim off the fat, add two quarts of mussels (No. 306) previously cooked for the purpose; let it simmer for a few minutes; squeeze in the juice of half a lemon; toss the contents, and dish up the pieces of chicken in the usual way; pour the sauce over; garnish round with the mussels and half a dozen croûtons fried in butter, and serve.

Note.—Oysters may be substituted for mussels.

612. STEWED CHICKEN À LA SICILIENNE.

Cut a nice and tender chicken in the usual way; place the pieces in a sauté-pan with an ounce of butter, two ounces of streaky bacon cut in dice, and a shred onion; fry them to a nice brown on a brisk fire; moisten with either a pint of broth or water; season with salt, pepper, and a bay-leaf, and let it simmer for about twenty minutes. Meanwhile prepare a Sicilian sauce (No. 211) and a purée of chesnuts (No. 237). When the pieces of chicken are well done lay the purée on a dish, dress on this the pieces of chicken and bacon; pour a little Sicilian sauce over, and serve with the remainder of the sauce apart.

613. STEWED CHICKEN À LA PIÉMONTAISE.

Fry with two ounces of butter in a sauté-pan the pieces of a chicken (cut as above), with a bay-leaf, a few sprigs

U

of thyme, and season with salt, pepper, and grated nutmeg; when of a nice colour all over moisten with either a pint of Espagnole sauce or good gravy; simmer it for twenty-five minutes by the side of the fire. Meanwhile make a polenta (No. 100); and when it is well cooked and the pieces of chicken are tender, lay the polenta on a hot dish; arrange the pieces of chicken in a pyramidal form; reduce the liquor in which the chicken was cooked to a half-glaze, then strain it through a pointed gravy-strainer over the chicken, and serve.

Note.—A few truffles cut in thin slices and cooked with the chicken will greatly improve this.

614. FRITOT OF CHICKEN À L'ITALIENNE.

After having singed, drawn, and cut a chicken as for stewed chicken with risotto, marinade the pieces in a basin for three or four hours with half a gill of salad-oil, the juice of half a lemon, salt and pepper, a few sprigs of thyme and parsley, one bay-leaf, and a sliced onion. Then dry them on a cloth, flour them well all over, and fry them in properly heated fat to a nice golden colour. When done drain the pieces of chicken on a cloth; dish them up in the usual way; garnish with fried eggs and croûtons, and serve with Italian sauce in a sauce-boat apart.

615. FRITOT OF CHICKEN À LA MILANAISE.

Cut up a chicken as in No. 614; rub each piece with clarified butter, and when well set dip them into some light batter and fry them in the hot fat to a nice golden colour. Meanwhile have some macaroni Milanaise (No. 94) ready, dish it up with the pieces of chicken on the top in a pyramidal form, and serve with Tomato sauce apart.

616. CHICKEN WITH DEVILLED SAUCE.

Draw and singe a chicken carefully; then twist the legs neatly through the sides, without, however, tearing the skin, and cut it lengthwise through the breast-bone into halves, without separating it at the back; remove as many bones as possible without interfering with the shape of the chicken; sprinkle with salt and pepper, rub both sides with clarified butter, and broil them on a moderate fire for eight or ten minutes on each side. When of a nice brown colour and properly done, dish up the chicken with some Devilled sauce (No. 201) poured under, and serve.

617. BOILED CHICKEN WITH TARRAGON.

Draw, singe, and trim the feet and wings of a nice chicken; cut the under part of the thighs close up to the bend of the joint; loosen the skin all round the thighs by introducing the fingers through the vent, and push the legs inside so that the feet only are seen; lay the chicken on its breast, twist the pinions round to make them lie even with the back, turn the skin of the breast upon the back, then run a trussing-needle and string through the pinion on the left, and again through its lower joint on through the upper joint of the thigh; the needle must now be brought round and inserted through the other wing in a similar manner, and the strings drawn tight and fastened. The legs must also be secured by running the needle through the upper part, leaving the drum-sticks under, and pass the needle through the back, then draw and tie the strings, so as to give the chicken a plump appearance; rub it with half a lemon to keep it white, and place it in a stewpan with a pint and a half of water, an onion with two cloves stuck in it, a small "bouquet garni" (no garlic), salt and pepper to taste, and two or three sprigs of tarragon. Boil, and simmer very gently for about thirty-five minutes with the lid on, taking care to turn the chicken over after a quarter of an hour's ebullition. When the chicken is done, strain the gravy through a pointed gravy-strainer into a small stewpan; add a few drops of caramel to give it a rich colour, and set it on the fire to boil fast for about seven minutes, in order to reduce it to a half-glaze. Meanwhile untie the chicken, place it on a dish with two or three sprigs of tarragon blanched in boiling water for two minutes, and keep hot. When the sauce has reached its proper consistency pour it over the chicken, and serve.

Note.—The chicken will eat better if broth is substituted for water.

618. BOILED CHICKEN WITH ROCK-SALT.

Clean and truss a good chicken as in No. 617; rub it with lemon, and cook it in the same manner. When the broth has been properly reduced pour it over the chicken; place a good teaspoonful of rock-salt on the breast, and serve.

619. BOILED CHICKEN WITH RICE.

Prepare, truss, and cook a chicken in a quart of broth as in the foregoing. When the chicken is done strain the broth into another stewpan, and keep the chicken hot by the side of the fire. Meanwhile boil half a pound of properly washed rice (see Rice) with the strained broth for about eighteen minutes; then add a pinch of grated nutmeg, a tablespoonful of grated cheese, and half an ounce of butter. Mix these well together and pour it over a dish, put the chicken on it, sauce over with about a gill of Béchamel sauce, and serve.

Note.—If half a pint of the chicken broth is kept apart in a small stewpan after being strained, and then reduced

PRACTICAL HOUSEHOLD COOKERY. 309

to an essence or half-glaze, it can be substituted for Béchamel sauce.

620. ROAST CHICKEN.

It is advisable when about to roast poultry to dip the bird or birds into boiling water for two minutes, in order to open the pores of the skin, which process will make the meat eat very tender and more juicy than otherwise.

After having selected a good chicken, drawn, singed, and trussed, for roasting in a similar way as for boiling, but without pushing the legs under the thighs, butter a sheet of paper as well as the breast of the chicken; fold the sheet of paper over, tie it round with string, and set it to roast before a moderate fire for about thirty-five minutes. When the chicken is done untie the string; dish up; strain, and free the gravy from grease; pour it over the chicken; garnish round with water-cress, previously sprinkled with salt, pepper, and vinegar, and serve.

Note.—Rashers of bacon fried and Bread sauce are sometimes served with roast chicken.

621. CHICKEN WITH MAYONNAISE SAUCE.

This dish is generally made with the remnants of chicken. Cut the cold chicken in pieces; place on a dish the hearts of a few French lettuces, properly cleaned, dried, and cut in quarters; keep four of the nicest apart; dress the pieces of chicken over the salad; pour sufficient Mayonnaise sauce (No. 219) to cover and coat the chicken; decorate the dish with the four quarters of lettuce and some hard-boiled eggs also cut in quarters; add, in a similar manner, a few slices of cooked beetroot cut in fancy shapes, and the fillets of three or four anchovies, properly boned and twisted round the finger, and serve.

622. CHICKEN WITH TARTARE SAUCE.

This is prepared in the same style as the foregoing, but substitute Tartare sauce (No. 221) for Mayonnaise.

623. BOUDINS OF CHICKEN À LA RICHELIEU.

Make some chicken forcemeat (No. 272), rather stiff; add to it an onion cut in small dice, previously blanched, drained, and fried in plenty of butter for about eight minutes without colouring; then butter some strips of kitchen paper four inches long by two and a half wide; lay on these lengthwise about three inches of forcemeat one inch and a half wide, and the same measurement in thickness, and with a teaspoon make a hollow in the centre of each boudin about three inches long by half an inch deep and one inch wide; fill these up with a salpicon à la financière (No. 310), but mixed with a well-reduced Allemande sauce instead of Financière sauce, and cover the salpicon of each boudin with chicken forcemeat again, so as to hide it completely. Then poach them gently in a sauté-pan with broth for about fifteen minutes; after which, take them out carefully with a flat skimmer, lay them on a clean cloth to drain, remove the paper if still attached to them, dish up the boudins in a circle, and serve with a well-reduced Espagnole sauce poured under them.

Note.—Boudins of chicken can also be served with salpicon à l'Italienne (No. 307), à la Valenciennes (No. 316), or with either a purée of fresh mushrooms or truffles.

624. QUENELLES OF CHICKEN À LA TOULOUSE.

Prepare some chicken forcemeat (No. 271), sprinkle some flour on the slab or board, and spread the forcemeat on this, to the thickness of about an inch, with the blade of a knife dipped in boiling water; sprinkle a little flour over, and divide the layer in strips four inches long by one inch and a half wide; roll these slightly with the fingers, so as to give them an oblong shape, then place the quenelles in rows in a buttered sauté-pan about an inch apart; pour some boiling broth gently by the side, so as to cover them, and simmer for about ten minutes. When done remove them carefully with a flat skimmer, and drain them on a clean cloth; dish up the quenelles in a circle, fill up the centre with salpicon à la Toulouse (No. 311), but not chopped so fine, and well-diluted with Velouté sauce (No. 153), and serve.

Note.—Quenelles of chicken are always made and poached in the same way, but can be served in different styles, such as à l'Italienne (No. 307), à la Royale (No. 309), à la financière (310), or any other salpicon, provided these are properly diluted with their respective sauce, and the ingredients are not chopped so fine as for salpicon. These are usually known under the name of "Ragout," but in order to simplify matters as much as possible, I give them under the same heading, being prepared in the same manner, but, as already mentioned, not minced so fine.

625. CHICKEN PANCAKES.

Prepare and keep warm in a stewpan some salpicon à la financière (No. 310), mixed with a well-reduced Allemande or Béchamel sauce instead of financière.

Fry the number of pancakes required (see Pancakes); lay on each two tablespoonfuls of the chicken salpicon; turn and roll both sides of the pancake over, so as to enclose the mixture; cut these across in half; dish them up in the form of a pyramid, and serve garnished round with fried parsley.

626. CAPON À LA NAPOLITAINE.

Boil for fifteen minutes one pound of macaroni, then strain the water through a colander, cut the macaroni in three-inch lengths, and put them in a stewpan with an ounce and a half of fresh butter and one ounce of grated parmesan cheese. Toss up the contents over the fire for a few minutes and draw it away. Meanwhile have a nice capon properly singed; clip the claws; cut off the neck close to the back, but leave as much of the crop-skin as possible; draw the entrails, &c., through an incision made at the back of the neck; then with a strong-bladed knife remove the angular part of the breast-bone, without, however, tearing the breast or cutting the fillets; stuff the capon with the cooked macaroni; draw the skin of the crop at the back so as to close up the paunch, and with a small trussing-needle and twine sew it up, and fasten both ends of the twine to the back of the capon; then truss the capon for roasting, dip it in boiling water for two minutes, dry it all round, and wrap it up in a well-buttered sheet of paper; tie this round with string, and roast it before a moderate fire for about fifty minutes, taking care to baste it three or four times. When done remove the paper and string; dish up; pour some rich gravy, properly strained, over, and serve.

627. CAPON À LA PIÉMONTAISE.

Prepare a capon in a similar manner as the foregoing; roast and peel a pound and a half of nice chesnuts, put them in a basin with half a pound of sausage meat; season with salt, pepper, nutmeg, and a good pinch of allspice. Moisten with a gill of broth or Madeira wine. Mix the lot well together; fill up the capon with it; when properly stuffed and trussed dip it in boiling water for two minutes;

dry, butter, and wrap it up in the same manner as in No. 627; roast it before a moderate but even fire for about fifty minutes, and when done dish it up in the same way, and serve with some good gravy poured over.

628. CAPON À LA LUCULLUS.

Draw, singe, and prepare a capon as previously described for capon à la Napolitaine; then cut in small slices one pound of clean calf's liver and half a pound of fat bacon; fry these in a stewpan for a few minutes with an ounce of butter; moisten with a gill of Marsala. Season with salt, nutmeg, spice, and the peel of a pound of truffles; simmer for seven minutes; let it get cold and pound it in a mortar; then add the peeled truffles cut the size of small nuts; mix the whole well together and stuff the capon with it; truss it in the usual way; dip it for two minutes in boiling water; dry, and lay a slice of fat bacon over the breast; wrap up the capon with a sheet of buttered paper, and roast it before an even fire for about an hour. Meanwhile prepare a risotto à l'Italienne (No. 109). When the capon is ready dish it up, place the risotto in tablespoonfuls as a garnish round it, and serve with a rich gravy, to which a little essence of truffles has been added, in a sauce-boat apart.

Note.—It is advisable, when time permits, to stuff a capon two or three days before it is wanted, and keep it in a cool place.

629. CAPON, CITIZEN STYLE.

Mince fine half a pound of beef kidney fat; mix it with three handfuls of bread-crumbs, three tablespoonfuls of fine herbs (No. 195*a*), the yolks of two eggs properly beaten, salt, pepper, and grated nutmeg to taste; stir all well together, and with it stuff a capon, previously prepared for that purpose, as in the foregoing; truss it in the usual way; dip it in boiling water for two minutes; dry it, and lay a good slice of fat bacon over the breast; wrap it in a well-buttered sheet of paper, and roast it before an even fire for about an hour. Meanwhile cook separately, in salt water, a few potatoes cut in shape of crescents, cauliflower, beans, and peas. When the capon is properly cooked take it from the fire, remove the paper and string, dish it up and garnish it with the cooked vegetables placed separately around; pour some good gravy under, and serve with Butter sauce in a boat apart.

630. BOILED CAPON AND RICE.

This is done in the same manner as boiled chicken and rice (see No. 619).

631. BOILED CAPON AND TARRAGON.

Prepare and boil a capon in the same style as boiled chicken and tarragon, and serve it with boiled pickled ox-tongue apart.

632. BRAIZED CAPON À LA MILANAISE.

Singe, draw, and truss a capon as previously described. Cut one pound of truffles into pieces the size of a broad-bean; after having peeled them pound the trimmings with one pound of fat bacon, season with salt, pepper, grated nutmeg, a chopped bay-leaf, and thyme; mix this together with the truffles in a stewpan and simmer gently for about ten minutes, stirring occasionally with a wooden spoon. Moisten with a gill of good gravy and continue stirring and simmering for another ten minutes; let the mixture get cold; then stuff the capon with it; fasten the crop-skin, and truss the bird as for boiling; let it remain thus, if possible, in a cool place for two days, when the flavour of the truffles will have penetrated well into the flesh. When wanted, prepare four or five dozen ravioli (No. 97). Set the capon in a stewpan with enough good broth to cover the pinions, simmer very gently for about an hour and a quarter, taking care to turn it over after three-quarters of an hour's cooking. When properly done remove the string; dish up; garnish round with the ravioli; reduce the gravy to a half-glaze by sharp boiling; strain it, and serve it in a sauce-boat, with the capon and rivioli.

Poulardes are cooked and dressed in every way as capons.

633. BRAIZED DUCK WITH STEWED PEAS.

Select a young and tender duck, singe, draw, and truss it as for roasting; put it in a stewpan with an onion with two cloves stuck in it, one carrot, and a small "bouquet garni." Moisten with a pint of good broth, season with salt and pepper, and simmer it very gently with the lid on for about an hour and a quarter, taking care to turn the bird after forty minutes' cooking. Meanwhile prepare a garnish of middle-sized peas (No. 286). When the duck is well done take it out of the pan, remove the string, dish it up with the peas, strain the gravy; skim off all the grease, reduce it over a brisk fire if necessary; pour it on the duck, and serve.

634. BRAIZED DUCK WITH GREEN PEAS.

Prepare a duck as described; put it in a stewpan with an ounce of butter; fry for about ten minutes, turning it round to ensure an even colouring; take it out and place it on a dish; then fry to a light-brown colour half a pound of streaky bacon free from rind and gristle and cut one inch square; sprinkle over these an ounce of flour; continue to fry and stir the contents with a wooden spoon for three minutes longer; then moisten with a pint of good stock, add an onion with two cloves stuck in it, a "bouquet garni," salt and pepper to taste; stir till boiling. Then put in the duck, together with a quart of medium-sized green peas; simmer very gently with the pan partly covered for about an hour and a quarter, taking care to turn the duck after thirty minutes' simmering. When done remove the "bouquet garni" and onion; put the bird on a plate, skim off very carefully all the grease from the peas; dish these up with the bacon; untie the duck and place it in the centre of the dish; pour the gravy over, and serve.

635. DUCK WITH TURNIPS.

After having prepared a duck as above, fry it in a stewpan with an ounce of butter to a nice golden colour all round; then take it out and sprinkle three tablespoonfuls of flour in the same stewpan; stir this over the fire for about three minutes; moisten it with a pint and a half of good broth; boil it, stirring the while to prevent burning; put in the duck, together with a small "bouquet garni," an onion stuck with two cloves, and season with salt and pepper, and simmer gently with the pan partly covered for about fifty minutes. Meanwhile peel and cut a pound of nice tender turnips into fancy shapes, such as half-moons and olives, add these to the duck and continue the simmering till they are done; remove the "bouquet garni" and onion. Dish up the bird in the usual way; garnish round with the turnips; skim off all the grease from the sauce, pour it over the duck, and serve.

636. BRAIZED DUCK WITH STEWED OLIVES.

Prepare and braize a duck as in No. 635. Meanwhile stone a pint of nice French olives; stew these with the duck for six or seven minutes; dish up the bird, after having removed the string; garnish round with the olives; skim off very carefully all the grease from the gravy; squeeze in the juice of half a lemon, pour this over the duck, and serve.

637. BRAIZED DUCK WITH CABBAGE.

Cut, clean, and blanch in salt water for five minutes a nice savoy cabbage. Meanwhile have ready trussed in the usual way a good duck, which place in a stewpan with a pint and a half of good stock, an onion stuck with three cloves, and a carrot; cover this with the cabbage properly strained; add half a pound of Bologna sausage and the same quantity of steaky bacon; season with salt and pepper; set to simmer very gently, with the pan covered, for about an hour; after which, remove the lid, place the stewpan in the oven for fifteen minutes, to finish cooking and brown the cabbage; then take out the bird, remove the string, take the carrot and onion away, put the bacon and sausage on a plate, and strain the liquor through a colander into a small stewpan; press the cabbage well; dish it up with the duck and keep hot by the side of the oven. Meanwhile skim off the fat from the gravy, reduce it to a half-glaze on a brisk fire, pour it over the duck and cabbage, cut the sausage and bacon into slices, decorate the dish alternately with it, and serve.

638. ROAST DUCK.

Slice a pound of onions and mix them with eighteen sage-leaves, blanch in salt water for five minutes, then drain and chop them fine; fry them in a stewpan with an ounce of butter well seasoned with salt, pepper, and grated nutmeg for about ten minutes, stirring the while with a wooden spoon; then add an ounce of bread-crumbs, and stir the mixture over the fire for two or three minutes longer. When cool stuff the duck with it; truss the duck in the usual way; dip it in boiling water for two minutes; dry, and set it to roast before a brisk fire for twenty minutes. When done, untie the string; dish up, pour under some rich gravy free from fat, and serve.

639. ROAST GOOSE.

Having selected a fine fat goose, draw and singe it as previously described for capon à la Napolitaine; then stuff it with one pound and a half of onions, two dozen green sage-leaves, the goose-liver, and two ounces of bread-crumbs, the whole prepared in a similar manner to the stuffing as for roast duck. When the goose is thus properly stuffed truss it in the usual way for roasting, and then dip it in boiling water; dry it, and set it before an even fire to roast for about an hour and a half, according to size, taking care to frequently baste it. When the goose is well cooked take it away from the fire, remove the string, dish up, pour some rich brown gravy under, and serve with Apple sauce (No. 181) in a sauce-boat apart.

640. ROAST GOOSE STUFFED WITH CHESNUTS.

Prepare a goose as in the previous number; cut the liver into small dice, and chop up fine two onions and fry these with about an ounce of chopped fat bacon for seven or eight minutes. Meanwhile prepare a garnish of chesnuts (No. 278); add the stuffing to it, season it with salt, pepper, and nutmeg, mix the lot well together, and stuff the goose with it; then truss in the usual way, dip in boiling water, and set it to roast before an even fire for about an hour and a quarter, taking care to often baste it. When the goose is ready dish it up as usual, pour some good brown gravy under it, and serve.

641. GOOSE À LA NAVARRAISE.

Chop fine one pound of veal cushion, free from skin and gristle, half a pound of fat bacon, the goose-liver, an onion, a clove of garlic, and a few sprigs of parsley; fry these in a stewpan with an ounce of butter for ten minutes; season with salt, pepper, and allspice; add four ounces of cooked rice; mix the whole well together and let it cool. Meanwhile prepare a fat goose as previously described for braizing (see Capon Napolitaine), and as soon as the mixture is set, stuff the goose with it; truss it afterwards in the usual way for boiling; place it in an oval braize-pan with two ounces of butter, two bay-leaves, and a shred onion; fry till the goose is nicely coloured all round, then moisten with a quart of ordinary stock or water and a gill of vinegar, season with salt and pepper, and set it to simmer gently, with the pan partly covered, for about an hour and a half, taking care to turn the goose over once, and baste it often. Add gradually more broth if necessary. When the goose is properly braized take it out of the pan and keep it hot; strain the broth through a gravy-strainer into another stewpan containing a thick half-cooked risotto; stir this on the fire and complete its cooking; then dish it up, place the goose in the centre, and serve with a good gravy in a sauce-boat apart.

642. GOOSE À L'ALLEMANDE.

Prepare a garnish of sauerkraut (No. 297) without bacon or sausage. When this has boiled four hours add a goose properly singed, drawn, and trussed for boiling, together with half a pound of streaky bacon and the same quantity of Frankfort sausages; cover the stewpan closely and simmer for at least two hours, taking care, however, to remove the bacon and sausages when done, which will be in about forty minutes. Cut the bacon in squares two and a quarter inches thick, and cut the sausages in the same style; keep these hot in a little broth till wanted. When the goose is cooked remove it from the pan, untie the string; strain and press the sauerkraut in a colander; dish it up; put the goose in the centre; garnish round alternately with the sausage and bacon, and serve.

643. STEWED GOOSE WITH TOMATOES.

Draw, singe, and cut a goose into sixteen parts (see stewed chicken with risotto), bone these as much as possible, then place them nicely in a large well-buttered sauté-pan with two ounces of clarified butter, half a pound of chopped fat bacon, two chopped onions, and a tablespoonful of chopped parsley; season with salt and pepper; fry the lot over a brisk fire till the pieces of goose are nicely coloured all round, then moisten with a pint and a half of broth add six nice ripe tomatoes, previously peeled and cut in slices; simmer till well done; then dish up the pieces of goose in the same style as chicken marengo, pour the sauce round, and serve.

644. BRAIZED TURKEY À L'ITALIENNE.

For this dish select a fine young turkey weighing about eight pounds, trim, singe, and draw it in the same style as capon à la Napolitaine; sew up the vent-opening; cut off the feet, scald the legs in order to divest them of their black skin, and remove the angular breast-bone; then make a risotto à l'Italienne (No. 110) with one quart of rice, for which use the giblets of the turkey. When the risotto has cooled down a little, stuff the turkey with it, draw up the crop-skin and sew it carefully, as described for capon à la Napolitaine. Truss it as for braizing, then place it in an oval braizing-pan with enough stock to cover the pinions; add two onions, each stuck with two cloves, and one head of celery; season with salt and pepper; boil, and then simmer with the pan partly covered for two hours, taking care to often baste the bird, and turn it over after an hour's simmering. When done, take out the turkey and put it with half a pint of its liquor on a baking-dish in the oven for ten minutes to glaze. Meanwhile strain a pint of the broth through a tammy into a small stewpan, reduce it by sharply boiling over the fire, and when the turkey has been glazed, dish it up with its gravy free from fat, and serve with the reduced sauce apart.

645. BRAIZED TURKEY À LA JARDINIÈRE.

Prepare a nice fat turkey as in the foregoing, without stuffing; truss for braizing; cover with thin slices of fat bacon, and wrap in a well-buttered sheet of paper; place it in a stewpan with a carrot, one head of celery, two onions, each stuck with two cloves, a "bouquet garni," and enough stock to cover the paper; season with salt and pepper; boil, and then simmer very gently for two hours with the pan partly covered. In the meantime prepare separately a garnish à la jardinière, composed of a quarter of a pound of French beans (No. 290), four ounces of cauliflower-head (No. 292), four ounces of asparagus-points (No. 287), four ounces of turnips (No. 284), and four ounces of carrots (No. 283) turned into small pear-shaped pieces. Having cooked them separately, mix the lot well together by tossing in a sauté-pan, and keep hot.

When the turkey is properly cooked, remove the string, paper, and bacon; dish it up, garnish round with the vegetables and serve, with Béchamel sauce (No. 154) in a sauce-boat apart. The gravy must be strained and put by for use.

x

646. BOILED TURKEY WITH CELERY.

Prepare and draw a nice hen-turkey as in the previous number, stuff it with veal or sausage-meat stuffing, and truss it for boiling. Put it in an oval braizing-pan with enough white stock to cover it; add a carrot, an onion stuck with two cloves, one head of celery, and a "bouquet garni." Boil it, and simmer gently for two hours. Meanwhile prepare a garnish of celery (No. 282), and when the turkey is properly cooked remove the string, dish it up, garnish round with celery, pour the Celery sauce over the turkey, and serve.

647. BOILED TURKEY WITH OYSTER SAUCE.

Prepare, stuff and boil a turkey as directed for boiled turkey with celery, and when ready dish it up and garnish with Oyster sauce (No. 186) before serving.

648. ROAST TURKEY À LA PIÉMONTAISE.

Draw and singe a nice young turkey as described for turkey à l'Italienne; prepare one pound of either veal or sausage-meat, put it in a large basin with two pounds of well-roasted and peeled chesnuts; moisten with half a pint of broth; season well with salt, pepper, nutmeg, and allspice; mix well together, and stuff the turkey with it. Sew up the paunch, truss the bird for roasting; dip it in boiling water for two or three minutes; wipe it dry; lay a thin slice of fat bacon over the breast; wrap up the bird in a well-buttered sheet of paper, tie it with string, and set it to roast before a nice even fire for about two hours, according to size, taking care to baste it often. When the turkey is cooked, dish it up, after having removed the paper and string, and serve with good gravy free from fat.

649. ROAST TURKEY À LA NAPOLITAINE.

Prepare a turkey as in the previous number. Boil two pounds of macaroni in the usual way for fifteen minutes, strain the water through a colander, cut the macaroni in three-inch lengths, and put them into a stewpan with three ounces of butter, two ounces of grated parmesan cheese, two pinches of pepper, and one of nutmeg. Shake this up over the fire till the cheese is properly melted and mixed, and then with a spoon stuff the turkey with it; sew up the breast-skin; truss the bird for roasting, dip it in boiling water, dry, butter it well all round, wrap it in a buttered sheet of paper, tied on with string, and then roast it before a good even fire for about two hours, frequently basting it. When done, remove the turkey from the fire, untie the string and paper, dish up, strain and skim off the gravy, pour it over the turkey, and serve.

650. ROAST TURKEY STUFFED WITH TRUFFLES.

For this purpose a fine young turkey should be stuffed at least two days previous to being cooked, and kept in a cool place during that time, for the same reason as already stated for braized capon à la Milanaise. Peel two pounds of truffles, cut these into size of broad-beans and put them in a large basin, pound the trimmings in a mortar and add them to the truffles, together with two pounds of sausage-meat and half a pound of minced pickled cooked ox-tongue. Season with salt, nutmeg, a little pounded mace, and thyme; moisten with a gill of Madeira; mix well together, and stuff the turkey with it. Draw the crop-skin to the back and sew it up in the usual way, and truss it for roasting. When wanted, dip it in boiling water; dry it, and lay a large thin slice of fat bacon over the breast; wrap it up in a well-buttered sheet of paper; tie it round and roast it before a good even fire for two hours, taking care to baste it frequently. When done, take it from the fire, remove the paper and string, strain and skim the gravy, dish up the turkey, pour the gravy over, and serve.

651. TURKEY'S GIBLETS, HOUSEWIFE STYLE.

Clean and singe the giblets of a turkey, blanch the lot in boiling salt water for three minutes, then cut each—the gizzard and neck—in four, and the pinions in two; cut also the liver in four, and put it on a plate apart. Fry to a light-brown colour, in a stewpan with one ounce of butter, about six ounces of streaky bacon, cut in inch-dice, free from rind and gristle; then take these out, and fry the giblets for ten or twelve minutes on a brisk fire, taking care that the pieces are not laid one over the other. After which, sprinkle over a tablespoonful of flour; continue the frying for about three minutes longer; stir with a wooden spoon; moisten with a pint and a half of stock or water; season with salt and pepper; add a "bouquet garni," and boil and simmer for three-quarters of an hour, with the pan partly covered. In the meantime peel and cut into half-moons one pound of turnips, fry these in a stewpan to a nice golden colour, with an ounce of butter, and put them on a plate; peel and fry also one dozen button onions, and add them to the turnips; then peel two pounds of potatoes to an egg-shape. When the giblets have simmered three-quarters of an hour, add the bacon, turnips, onions, and potatoes, and simmer for twenty minutes longer; then add the liver, previously fried for two or three minutes; boil again gently for another ten or twelve minutes, and draw the pan away from the fire, remove the "bouquet garni," and skim off carefully all the grease and scum; dish up the giblets in the centre; pour

PRACTICAL HOUSEHOLD COOKERY.

the vegetables and sauce over, sprinkle the lot with a teaspoonful of chopped and blanched parsley, and serve.

652. STEWED PIGEONS WITH GREEN PEAS.

Select three nice house-pigeons; pick, draw, and singe them as chickens; return the liver to the inside of the birds; cut off the necks, and truss for braizing (see Boiled Chicken with Tarragon). Remove the rind of half a pound of streaky bacon, cut it in inch-dice, fry these to a nice brown colour in a stewpan with an ounce of butter, and take them out; put in the pigeons in their stead, and fry them to a golden colour all round over a brisk fire; then put them aside with the bacon; sprinkle in the same stewpan two tablespoonfuls of flour, and stir this with a wooden spoon over the fire for three or four minutes; moisten with one and a half pint of good broth, season with salt and pepper, and boil, and stir it to prevent burning. Then add the pigeons, together with the bacon, a " bouquet garni," and a quart of fresh shelled green peas; simmer gently, with the pan partly covered, for about half an hour or thirty-five minutes; then remove the string from the birds, take the " bouquet " out, skim all the scum and grease off the peas and bacon, pour these on a dish, put the pigeons in the centre, and serve.

653. STEWED PIGEONS WITH MUSHROOMS.

Prepare, truss, and cook three pigeons as above, but instead of green peas substitute two dozen button onions, previously blanched and browned in butter, together with one pint of nicely turned champignons also blanched in their liquor, and the whole added to the sauce with the bacon, pigeons, and " bouquet garni." Season the mixture in the usual way, and simmer gently for thirty-five minutes; then remove the pigeons, untie the string, and dish them up; take the "bouquet" out; skim off all fat and scum; garnish the pigeons round with the onions, mushrooms, and bacon, pour the sauce over, and serve.

654. PIGEON CUTLETS WITH MACÉDOINE.

Select three young and fat pigeons, cut these lengthwise in half, remove the wings and part of the breast-bones, tuck the leg-bones inside, season well with salt and pepper, and fry the halves or cutlets in a sauté-pan on a brisk fire, with two ounces of butter, for fifteen minutes. Take them out and press them between two dishes till cold; after which, turn each cutlet into a nice form, and dip them in melted butter and bread-crumb them; broil them over a slow fire till of a golden colour, and then dish them up in a circle, fill the centre with a garnish of macédoine (No. 281), and serve.

655. PIGEONS À LA CRAPAUDINE.

Take three nice young pigeons, properly drawn and singed, and cut them lengthwise across the breast, without separating them at the back; flatten them with the cutlet-bat and remove the bones from the legs and breasts; put these in a sauté-pan with one and a half ounce of butter, season with salt and pepper, and fry them for fifteen minutes over a brisk fire; then put them between two-baking tins and press with a four-pound weight at the top. In the meantime chop fine two shalots, and fry them in the same saucepan for a few minutes; then add half a pint of good stock, half a gill of vinegar, one teaspoonful of chopped parsley; season with salt and pepper; boil it, and reduce it by half; then squeeze the juice of a lemon in it. When the pigeons are quite cold, dip them in half an ounce of melted butter and bread-crumb them; after which, broil them over a clear fire to a nice golden colour on both sides, strain the sauce through a pointed strainer over a dish, put the pigeons on it, and serve.

656. ROAST PIGEONS.

Draw and singe three young pigeons as above and truss them for roasting; cover the breast of each bird with a thin slice of fat bacon, tie on with string, and set the birds to roast before a good fire for fifteen minutes. When done take them from the fire and remove the string; dish up the pigeons with the bacon on the breasts; pour the gravy under; garnish round with watercress, previously seasoned with salt, pepper, and vinegar, and serve.

Note.—Wild pigeons should always be roasted.

657. GUINEA-FOWL, HOUSEWIFE STYLE.

Pick, draw, singe, and cut in pieces two young guinea-fowls as for stewed chicken and risotto; put the pieces in a stewpan with three ounces of butter and fry them over a brisk fire to a nice brown all over; then moisten with a gill of sherry and simmer for five minutes; add half a pint of broth, salt and pepper to taste, and half a pound of fresh mushrooms cut in slices; then simmer till the pieces of fowl are tender, and sprinkle in a tablespoonful of finely chopped parsley and squeeze in the juice of a lemon, toss up the whole whilst over the fire, and dish it up in the same style as stewed chicken, pour the sauce over, and serve.

658. ROAST GUINEA-FOWL.

Draw, singe, and truss two guinea-fowls for roasting; cut six ounces of fat bacon in small strips of an inch and a half long, and lard the breasts with a larding-needle; wrap each fowl in a well-buttered paper, and tie this with string; then set the birds to roast before an even fire for about half an hour, and baste them twice; remove the paper, and continue roasting for eight or ten minutes, or till the strips of bacon are nicely coloured, without, however, letting them get too brown. When done take them from the fire, remove the string, dish them up with their gravy nicely strained and skimmed, and garnish with watercress, seasoned as described for roast pigeons, and serve.

Note.—Guinea-fowls are poultry, although very often served as a substitute for game, on account of their dark-coloured flesh.

659. ROAST CYGNET.

Cygnet should only be eaten in September; after that month they get tough.

Clean, draw, and singe a cygnet in the same style as a goose. Chop fine two pounds of beef-steak; season with three chopped shalots, two pinches of grated nutmeg, two of pepper, and a teaspoonful of salt, and moisten with a gill of broth. Stuff the cygnet with this in the usual way and truss it for roasting; lay on the breast two nice slices of fat bacon, and wrap it in two sheets of well-buttered paper; roast it before a clear fire for about three hours, during which time it must be frequently basted. When done, serve it with a rich gravy.

660. ROAST PEA-FOWL.

Pea-fowls are seldom cooked now, though young birds when fat and full in the flesh are very good roasted; but they should first be larded over the breast and thighs and put to marinade for a day in a pint of white wine, some aromatic herbs, salt, pepper, cloves, a blade of mace, and a slice of gammon; they should then be roasted in a similar manner to cygnet, and served with a sharp or devilled sauce mixed with the gravy of roast fowl and garnished with seasoned watercress.

CHAPTER XV.

REMARKS ON GAME.

The markets of this country are generally well supplied with game, and such birds as pheasants, partridges, grouse, snipes, and wild-fowl are always plentiful in season.

Pheasants when young have very small spurs, and the tenderness of the flesh is ascertained by pressing the pinions.

Wild-duck, widgeon, teal, and other water-fowl are selected in a similar manner.

Woodcock are also selected by trying the pinions and breast.

Partridges and grouse are tested in the same way, but their age can be ascertained by carefully examining the long feathers of the wing; those round at the tip belong to old birds, the pointed ones to young.

The high flavour and peculiar delicacy of game, when hung properly, is superior to that of all other animal food. Pheasants cooked within three days of being killed have none of their characteristic taste, and will simply eat as chicken; but if hung for twelve or fifteen days in a cool place, the pleasant and agreeable aroma so much appreciated by epicures is fully imparted to the flesh. To obtain this the colour of the lower part of the birds should be of a dark-green before cooking. Should they, however, be found too high or even putrefied, do not on that account throw them away, as the following recipe (like many others given in this work, but very little known) will remove all unpleasant taste and flavour from any game :—

Wash the birds that may be full of maggots, &c., first in vinegar, then soak them in cold milk for half an hour, and then let them be wiped and cooked in the usual way, when they will eat to perfection.

661. SALMI OF PHEASANTS.

Roast two hen-pheasants, and when cold remove the legs and cut off the drum-sticks; then cut the fillets with the pinion-bones attached to them, separate the breast from the back, trim them both and cut them crosswise into halves and put these pieces in a stewpan. Pound in a mortar the drum-sticks and trimmings, and mix this purée with some Salmis sauce (No. 199), previously prepared; stir the contents well together, pour it over the pieces of pheasant, and warm it gradually without boiling. When ready squeeze in the juice of half a lemon, stir, and dish it up as a fricassée of chicken; pour the sauce over, garnish round with fried croûtons, and serve.

Note.—A few button mushrooms and slices of truffles, previously cooked with the Salmis sauce, will greatly improve this dish.

662. PHEASANT, HOUSEWIFE STYLE.

Draw and truss for braizing two nice pheasants, fry them on a brisk fire in a stewpan with two ounces of butter, two ounces of fat bacon, a shred union, carrot, and half a head of celery, and season with salt, pepper, and a bay-leaf. When of a nice golden colour all over, moisten with a pint and a half of water, set to simmer for about thirty-five minutes, with the pan partly covered, taking care to frequently baste them with their own liquor, and to turn them over once.

In the meantime prepare a thick risotto, and when the pheasants are properly cooked place them on a hot dish, strain and skim off the fat from their liquor and add it to the risotto, stir this well together, and when ready dish it up, put the pheasants on the top, and serve with some good gravy in a sauce-boat apart.

663. PHEASANTS À LA NAPOLITAINE.

Select and draw two nice young pheasants; lard the breasts in the usual way with small strips of fat bacon; wrap them in well-buttered paper, and set them to roast before a moderate fire for twenty-five minutes, taking special care to baste them frequently with clarified butter; after which, remove the paper from the birds and roast them ten minutes longer; baste again two or three times, and see that the strips of bacon do not colour too much. Meanwhile prepare some macaroni Italienne (No. 89), and when ready, and the pheasants are properly cooked, pour the macaroni over a dish, place the pheasants in the centre, and serve with some good gravy in a sauce-boat apart.

Note.—In order to roast game to a nicety, attention and experience are required, as it is of the utmost importance that birds should be removed from the fire as soon as they are done. This is generally found to be the case when a certain amount of evaporation is emitted from the bird's flesh.

664. PHEASANTS À LA MILANAISE.

Pick, draw, and truss two pheasants for boiling, and braize them as for pheasants, housewife style. When done, put them on a dish and keep hot; add one pint of broth to the liquor in which the birds were braized, boil this and pass it through a tammy, then skim off the fat, and put it in a stewpan with some of the liquor, two savoy cabbages each cut in four, the cores taken out, and previously blanched for five minutes in boiling salt water, and half a pound each of Bologna sausage and streaky bacon; season with salt, pepper, and a "bouquet garni;" cover with a sheet of buttered paper, to prevent the cabbages colouring, simmer for three-quarters of an hour with the pan covered; then remove the paper and "bouquet;" squeeze the gravy out of the cabbage by pressing it in a colander; cut the sausage and bacon into slices a quarter of an inch thick; cut also the cabbage into small squares; untie the pheasants and dish them up; place alternately cabbage, sausage, and bacon around the pheasants, and serve with the remainder of the birds' liquor, previously reduced to a half-glaze, in a sauce-boat apart.

665. ROAST PHEASANT STUFFED WITH TRUFFLES.

Select two young and plump pheasants, and draw them in the same way as a turkey. Peel two pounds of fresh truffles, cut them into small filbert shaped-pieces, and put them in a stewpan; pound the trimmings in a mortar, with a quarter of a pound of chopped pickled cooked ox-tongue and the same quantity of fat bacon; add this to the truffles with one pound of sausage-meat; season with salt, pepper, and nutmeg; set it to simmer for about ten minutes; stir frequently; then moisten it with a gill of either rum, Madeira, or broth; mix well together, and let it cool. When properly set stuff the pheasants with it; sew up the vents and breast-skin; truss them for roasting; wrap in a sheet of paper and put them by in a small box or jar tightly shut, in a cool place for two or three days; or better still, bury them (folded in the paper) a foot deep in the ground for the same number of days, when the truffles will have imparted their aroma and flavour, to the flesh of the birds.

Three-quarters of an hour before serving, bring the birds out; remove the paper; lay on each breast a thin slice of fat bacon; tie these round with twine, and set them to roast before an even fire for thirty-five minutes, frequently basting them. When done (see note on Pheasants à la Napolitaine) remove the string, dish up the birds with good brown gravy, and serve with Bread sauce in a boat apart.

Note.—When pheasants are roasted without stuffing, serve then with seasoned watercress.

666. BOUDINS AND QUENELLES OF PHEASANT.

Follow the same directions as given for boudins of chicken à la Richelieu and quenelles à la Toulouse.

667. SALMI OF PARTRIDGES.

Roast for twenty minutes, let cool, and cut up two partridges as in salmi of pheasants. Pound the liver and trimmings of the birds in the usual way, and add them to the Salmis sauce (No. 199), together with half a pint of button champignons or fresh mushrooms nicely shred; simmer and stir till the mushrooms are done, then pour the sauce over the pieces of partridge, and warm the contents of the stewpan, gradually, by the side of the fire, without boiling; squeeze in the juice of half a lemon, and then dish up the pieces in a pyramidal form, pour the sauce over, garnish with croûtons fried in butter, and serve.

668. STEWED PARTRIDGE WITH CABBAGE.

After having picked, drawn, singed, and trussed two partridges, with the legs tucked in as for boiling, fry them to a nice colour all round in a sauté-pan with an ounce of butter. Cut a good cabbage (savoy preferred) into quarters and blanch it for five minutes; then steep it in cold water, cut off the cores, press the water out, and put it in a stewpan with the partridges nicely imbedded in it; season with a "bouquet garni," two medium carrots, two onions with two cloves stuck in each, salt and pepper to taste; moisten with enough broth to cover the cabbage, add half a pound of streaky bacon, and cover the whole with a buttered sheet of paper; close the stewpan tightly, and set it to simmer for an hour and a half. When done take out the birds and bacon, and put them in the oven to keep hot; remove the "bouquet garni" and onion; put the carrots apart; drain and press the cabbage in a colander, and lay it on a dish; untie the partridges and place them on the cabbage; cut the bacon in thin slices and the carrots in fancy shape, garnish the dish round alternately with them, and serve with some good brown gravy in a sauce-boat.

669. BRAIZED PARTRIDGES À LA PERIGUEUX.

Draw and truss two partridges as in No. 668; tie a thin slice of fat bacon on each breast; put them in a stewpan with an ounce of butter, and fry them to a nice golden colour all over; then moisten with a gill of essence of truffles (No. 170), the same quantity of Madeira, and three gills of good broth; season with salt, pepper, and a "bouquet garni;" lay a buttered sheet of paper over the partridges, cover the stewpan, and boil and simmer gently for forty-five minutes. Meanwhile prepare a Financière sauce (No. 187). When the birds are well braized, dish them up on a block of crumb of bread, previously cut six inches long by four inches wide and three inches thick, fried in butter as croûtons; pour the half of the sauce over the partridges, put the remainder in a sauce-boat, and serve.

670. ROAST PARTRIDGES.

Prepare and truss two young partridges as directed for roast pheasants (without stuffing); cover each breast with a thin slice of fat bacon, and tie these round with twine; then set the birds to roast before a good even fire for about twenty minutes; remove the string from the birds; dish them up with a good brown gravy, garnish round with seasoned watercress, and serve.

671. BOUDINS AND QUENELLES OF PARTRIDGES.

For the preparation of boudins and quenelles of partridges, see Boudins and Quenelles of Chicken.

672. ROAST GROUSE.

Pick, draw, singe, and truss a brace of grouse as for roasting pheasants; lay and tie a thin slice of fat bacon on the breast of each bird, and set them to roast before an even fire for twenty minutes. When done, dish the birds on a croûton of bread (see Braized Partridges à la Perigueux); garnish with seasoned watercress, and serve with good gravy, Bread sauce, and fried bread-crumbs, in sauce-boats.

673. ROAST BLACK-GAME.

These should be prepared and trussed in the same manner as grouse, roasted for twenty minutes with a slice of fat bacon tied on the breast of each bird, and served with the same ingredients as in No. 672.

674. ROAST SNIPE.

Pick four snipe entirely, neck and head; draw them, but reserve the trail and liver, which chop and fry in a stewpan with a little butter for five minutes, and keep hot. Twist the legs so as to bring the feet behind the thighs, and run the bill through the thighs and body. Put a noose of string round the joints, across the lower part of the breast, bring both ends round the head and tip of the bill, and fasten it on the back. Cover the snipe with thin slices of fat bacon and tie these on with twine. Cut, toast, and butter four slices of bread, four inches long by two and a half wide, and half an inch thick; set the birds to roast before a clear fire for eighteen minutes; place the buttered toast under to receive the gravy from the birds, and baste frequently. When ready, remove the string, lay the fried trail and liver on the buttered toast, which will now be soaked with gravy, dish up the birds on these pieces of toast, and serve with a garnish of seasoned watercress and a sauce-boat of good gravy.

675. SALMI OF SNIPE.

Draw four snipe, reserving the trail and liver, and roast them for eighteen minutes, without running the bill through the body. When cooked and cold, cut them in two lengthwise; remove the neck, skin, and feet; trim the halves, and put them in a sauté-pan. Pound the trimmings and bones in a mortar, and put the purée in a stewpan with two shalots, a "bouquet garni," two cloves, and half a bottle of claret; boil and reduce it to one-half; then add one and a half pint of Espagnole sauce. Simmer for half an hour, skim off the fat as it rises to the surface, strain the sauce through a tammy into a small stewpan, and reduce it again until it coats the spoon; pour this sauce over the birds to warm without boiling. Meanwhile chop the trail, &c., and fry them with a little butter in a small stewpan, seasoned with a little blanched and chopped parsley, salt, and pepper. When the salmi is properly warmed, dish up the pieces, pour the sauce over them; lay the trail mixture on eight croûtons of bread, and with these garnish round and serve.

676. ROAST WOODCOCK.

These are prepared, trussed, and roasted in the same manner as snipe. They are also very often roasted without being drawn at all, but should be given two minutes longer to cook, and then served with seasoned watercress and toast.

677. ROAST PLOVER.

Pick, draw, singe, and truss plover for roasting in the same manner as pigeons (see No. 656), and serve them in the same style.

Note.—Various kinds of big-winged game are sometimes served surrounded with small birds, such as roast pheasants, garnished with larks, quail, &c.; in that case the pheasants are put in the centre of the dish on pieces of toast.

678. ROAST QUAIL.

Pick, draw, and truss the birds required as directed for pheasants; lay on each a thin slice of fat bacon, large enough to cover it, fold a vine-leaf over each of these and tie them round the breast with twine; fasten them to a spit, and set them to roast before a clear fire for ten or twelve minutes; then remove the string, but leave the bacon; dish them on croûtons fried in butter, garnish with seasoned watercress, and serve with gravy apart.

Y

679. QUAIL À LA JARDINIÈRE.

Truss six quail as for braizing, put them in a stewpan, cover them with thin slices of fat bacon, moisten with a gill of Madeira and half a pint of good broth; add a shred carrot, onion, and a "bouquet garni." Boil them; cover the pan and simmer for eighteen or twenty minutes; and meanwhile prepare a jardinière as for fillet of beef jardinière (No. 950). When the quail are ready, pour the sauce on to a dish, garnish the centre with the birds, pour a few spoonfuls of half-glaze over the birds and jardinière, and serve with a sauce-boat of half-glaze apart.

680. ROAST LARKS.

Cut as many thin pieces of toasted bread, two inches long by one inch and a half wide, as there are larks; cut also in a similar manner twice as many thin slices of fat bacon, and lay these on each side of the toast. Take the larks, cut off the heads and legs, and draw out the gizzards with the point of a small knife. Then run the larks, side by side on a thin skewer, putting a piece of toast with the slices of bacon between each bird; tie both ends of the skewer to the spit, and set them to roast before a clear fire for eight minutes, taking care to baste them. When done, dish them up alternately with the toast and bacon, and serve with some good gravy in a sauce-boat apart.

681. LARKS, HOUSEWIFE STYLE.

Cut off the necks, legs, and pick out the gizzards of twelve larks, place them in a sauté-pan previously spread with butter, season with salt and pepper, and fry them to a nice brown colour over a brisk fire. Then add half a pint of good gravy or broth, half a pound of nicely cut fresh mushrooms, set to simmer for five minutes, add the juice of a lemon and a little finely chopped parsley, toss up the contents, dish up the larks with some fried croûtons, pour the mushrooms and sauce over, and serve.

682. ROAST WHEATEARS.

These small birds are generally plentiful along the south coasts of England, and are in season in August and September, when their condition is such as to resemble small lumps of butter. They are highly esteemed and considered a great delicacy by epicures, and should be prepared and roasted in the same manner as larks, but I strongly recommend to be served with them polenta à la Napolitaine.

683. ROAST WILD-DUCK, WIDGEON, TEAL, AND WATER-HEN.

These wild-fowls are all drawn, trussed, and roasted in the same style as roast pheasants, before a clear fire for about a quarter of an hour, and then served with quarters of lemon, cayenne pepper, and gravy separately.

684. SALMI OF WILD-DUCK.

Pick, draw and roast a wild-duck for a quarter of an hour, as described in No. 683. When cold, cut it into small joints; take off the skin; trim the pieces and put them in a stewpan; put into another stewpan the trimmings and bones with half a pint of claret, four shalots, a small "bouquet garni," an onion with three cloves stuck in it, two pinches of salt, and a small one of cayenne. Boil this down to half its quantity, then add one pint of Espagnole sauce, and reduce it to a nice consistency, after which pass it through a tammy over the pieces of wild-duck;

warm the salmis without boiling, squeeze the juice of half a lemon; toss up the contents; dish up the pieces of bird in the usual way, pour the sauce over, garnish round with croûtons fried in butter, and serve.

685. WIDGEON, HOUSEWIFE'S STYLE.

Roast two widgeon. When done, cut them in small joints and put in a stewpan with a quarter of a pound of red-currant jelly, half a pint of port, and the juice of a lemon; season with salt and cayenne pepper; simmer with the pan partly covered for seven minutes; then dish up, pour the sauce over, garnish with croûtons cut and fried in the usual way, and serve.

686. SALMI OF WIDGEON OR TEAL.

Pick, draw, and truss two of these birds for roasting; place them in an earthen dish, strew some thinly-sliced carrot and onion, parsley, thyme, and bay-leaf about them, season with salt, pepper, the juice of a lemon, and a gill of salad oil; let them thus marinade for twelve hours, taking care to frequently turn them over. Twenty minutes before serving, run them upon a skewer, place the vegetables, &c., upon their breasts, wrap in two sheets of oiled paper fastened on with twine, tie them on the spit at both ends, and set to roast before a clear fire for fifteen minutes. When cold, cut into small joints in the usual way; put the trimmings, and the gravy that has run into the pan from the birds, into a stewpan with four shalots, two cloves, a blade of mace, thyme, and bay-leaf, together with half a pint of claret and some mushroom trimmings; season with salt and pepper; boil for five minutes; then add half a pint of brown sauce or good broth; stir the sauce over the fire till it boils, then draw it by the side of the stove to clear itself; skim it; boil it again for ten minutes; then pass it through a tammy sieve over the pieces of wild-fowl into a stewpan; set them to warm without boiling. When ready, dish up in a pyramidal form, pour the sauce over, garnish round with fried croûtons, and serve.

687. SALMI OF WATER-HEN.

Draw, truss and roast before a brisk fire, for a quarter of an hour, two water-hens. Cut them in four, pound the trimmings and carcases, and put them into a stewpan with two tablespoonfuls of salad oil, an ounce of butter, half a pint of claret, salt, pepper, the peel of a lemon, and half a pint of good gravy, as well as the gravy dropped from the birds into the dish. Simmer the lot for half an hour; dish up the pieces of wild fowl in the usual way; squeeze the juice of half a lemon into the sauce, pass this through a pointed strainer over the dished fowl, garnish with fried croûtons, and serve.

CHAPTER XVI.

*HOT AND COLD MEAT PIES—PUDDINGS—
GALANTINES AND POTTED GAME.*

688. BEEFSTEAK AND KIDNEY PIE.

CUT two pounds of beefsteak (top side or thick flank) into scollops three inches long by two wide, and flatten these slightly with the cutlet bat. Cut also six sheep's kidneys, or the half of an ox-kidney, into slices a quarter of an inch thick; season the lot well with salt, pepper, and a little pounded aromatic herbs; chop fine four chalots; then make a layer with the meat and kidney at the bottom of an oval earthenware baking dish; strew over some of the chopped shalots and the yolk of an egg boiled hard and cut in quarters, then another layer of steak, kidney, shalot, and egg; and so on till the whole of it is used. Fill this up with good broth nearly to the level of the meat, and cover the whole with a thin layer of puff paste (No. 318), previously made for that purpose, taking care first to pass a brush dipped in water over the border of the dish, and press the paste on this with the thumb. Make a vent-hole in the centre, cut the paste round the border, roll these trimmings together to the eighth of an inch, and cut it with a pastry-cutter into four or five small leaves or other fancy shapes, pass the brush, dipped in water again, on one side of these, and lay them flat around the hole in the centre; gather the remainder of the paste, turn it into a rose, and place it loose over the vent; then with a pastry-brush dipped in the yolk of an egg brush the paste slightly over, and set it to bake in a moderately-heated oven for an hour and three quarters or two hours. When done, remove the pastry rose from the vent-hole and pour in through it, with the help of a funnel, one or two gills of good hot broth or gravy; replace the rose and serve the pie, or put it by to be served cold.

Note.—Mushroom or truffle trimmings intermixed with the steak will greatly improve this pie.

689. BEEFSTEAK AND OYSTER PIE.

Proceed to cut and season two pounds of beefsteak as in the previous number, and substitute two dozen oysters for the kidney, but these should first be blanched and bearded and their liquor added to the broth; then cover with puff paste as the foregoing. Bake in the same style, and serve.

690. VEAL AND HAM PIE.

Cut two pounds of cushion of veal into thin scollops, after having been freed from skin and sinew; flatten these with the cutlet bat and lay them flat on the table, and spread on each some sausage meat the size of a large walnut. Season with salt and pepper and pounded aromatic herbs, lay over each scollop a thin slice of either cooked ham, gammon, or lean bacon, free from rind and gristle; twist these round with the ham inside, and arrange nicely in an earthenware baking-dish; fill up nearly to the level of the meat with good stock, cover the dish with a puff paste, in the same manner as beefsteak and kidney pie, and set it to bake for about two hours. When ready, add some more hot broth through the vent-hole, and put by till wanted.

691. MUTTON PIE.

Remove the scrag and spine-bone from a neck of mutton; shorten the ribs to about three inches; cut the neck into neat cutlets; pare off the superfluous fat; put the whole of the trimmings into a stewpan with a pint and a half of water; season with salt, and boil for half an hour, taking care to skim the broth in the usual way. Meanwhile season the cutlets with salt and pepper, place them in a circular form in a large pie-dish, and garnish the centre with potatoes turned into small egg shapes. When the broth is ready, strain it and skim off the fat, pour it over the potatoes in the pie-dish, strew over them a teaspoonful of finely-chopped parsley; cover the pie-dish with puff paste, as in beefsteak and kidney pie; set it to bake in a moderate oven for an hour and three quarters; then add a little more broth, and serve.

Note.—This pie should be eaten hot.

692. PIGEON PIE.

Draw and singe three young pigeons; cut off the feet and put them by; cut the pigeons in four; season each piece with salt and pepper; cut also one pound of rump-steak into small scollops; beat them with the cutlet bat; season these also with salt and pepper, then with one-third make a layer at the bottom of a pie-dish. Place six quarters of pigeons over them, intermixed with as many halves of yolks of hard-boiled eggs, and the pigeons' livers, then a layer of scollops of beef, then the other half of the pigeons and eggs; finish with the remainder of the beef scollops; add the necessary quantity of hot broth or good stock; cover the dish with puff paste in the usual way (see No. 318); imbed the feet of the pigeons in the top of the paste, so as to leave the claws out in a symmetrical form, and bake for about an hour and a half. When done, add some more broth to the pie, and put it aside till wanted.

Note.—Mushroom trimmings, finely chopped with a little parsley, will improve this pie.

693. CHICKEN PIE.

Draw, singe, and cut two chickens into small joints; trim these nicely and put the backs aside, to be used for soup or essence of chicken. Cut half a pound of cushion of veal into small scollops, flatten these slightly with the cutlet bat; cut also half a pound of lean bacon into thin slices; cover the bottom of a pie-dish alternately with veal and bacon; season with salt, pepper, and a little chopped parsley; lay on these the half of the pieces of chicken with the yolks of two hard-boiled eggs cut in two and seasoned with salt, pepper, and chopped parsley; add another layer of veal and bacon; repeat the seasoning; lay on these, in a similar order, the remainder of the chicken; season again and finish with a few slices of bacon, properly trimmed and laid on the top. Moisten two-thirds full with good stock and half a gill of mushroom ketchup; cover the lot in the usual way with puff paste (see No. 318). Bake in a moderately-heated oven for about an hour and a half. When ready, replenish the gravy through the vent-hole, and serve either hot or cold.

694. GIBLET PIE.

This pie should be made with two sets of either goose or turkey giblets. Put the liver apart, blanch the giblets for about two minutes in boiling water, immerse them in cold, and drain them on a cloth; then cut them into pieces two inches long, and put in a stewpan with a carrot, an onion stuck with four cloves, a "bouquet garni," and season with salt and pepper. Moisten with a quart of stock, and simmer gently for about an hour; then remove the "bouquet garni," carrot, and onion; strain the gravy through a strainer into a small stewpan; drain the giblets upon a cloth; skim off all the fat from the gravy, and boil it over a brisk fire for about a quarter of an hour. Meanwhile, cover the bottom of a pie-dish with scollops of beefsteak, well flattened with the cutlet bat, and season with salt, pepper, a little chopped parsley, sweet basil, and two chalots. Add the giblets in neat order, together with the liver, previously set apart; sprinkle over it some fine herbs, and a small pinch of cayenne; moisten with the reduced gravy; cover the lot with puff paste (see No. 318), bake it for an hour and a half, and serve.

695. RABBIT PIE.

Skin, empty, and clean thoroughly a nice young rabbit, and cut it into small joints as for rabbit stewed à la Chasseur. Trim these pieces nicely, leaving as little bone as possible to them; put the trimmings into a stewpan with the head and neck cut in half; add a pint and a half of good stock, an onion stuck with four cloves, a "bouquet garni," a piece of rind of bacon, and any trimmings of veal that may be had. Season with salt and pepper; boil, skim, and simmer for half an hour. Meanwhile place the pieces of rabbit in a pie-dish, well intermixed with half a pound of streaky bacon free from rind and gristle, previously blanched for five minutes and cut into inch-dices. Season the lot well with four chopped shalots, parsley, fine herbs, and salt and pepper; when the stock is ready, strain it through a cloth over the rabbit. Cover the pie-dish with puff paste in the usual way (see No. 318), and bake for an hour and a half; then serve, or put it in a cool place till wanted.

696. LARK PIE.

Pick, singe, clean, and draw two dozen larks as for roast larks (No. 680). Cut off the heads, wings, and legs and put them aside; cut in small scollops one pound of cushion of veal, and half a pound of lean bacon, free from rind and gristle; lay alternately one-third of these slices at the bottom of the pie-dish; put on them twelve larks, close together, spread the half of two finely-chopped shalots, a little parsley, and thyme. Season with salt and a pinch of cayenne; make another layer with one-third of the scollops; put on these the other twelve larks, then another layer of ingredients and seasoning, then lay upon the birds the remainder of the veal and bacon; fill up the dish two-thirds full with good stock or gravy. Cover the lot with puff paste. Bake in a moderately-heated oven for about an hour and a half, replenish the gravy in the usual way, and put it by till wanted.

Note.—Two or three fresh mushrooms finely chopped, and the yolks of four hard-boiled eggs, cut in quarters and properly spread with the seasoning, will improve this pie. Any other small birds can also be made into a similar pie.

697. PARTRIDGE PIE.

Pick, draw, and singe three partridges; cut off the feet and wings; cut the partridges into small joints, cover the bottom and sides of a pie-dish with thin layers of fat bacon, place the pieces of partridges in close order on these; season well with salt, pepper, and aromatic herbs; lay upon these six small scollops of fillet of beef, well flattened and seasoned, make another layer with slices of fat bacon; soak the whole with game or ordinary broth flavoured with essence of game. Cover the dish with puff paste in the usual way (see No. 318). Dig the feet into the top of the paste in decorative style; bake it in a moderately-heated oven for one hour and a half, add a little more hot broth through the vent-hole, and serve.

Note.—Blackgame, pheasants, grouse, quail, or any other winged game can be made into a similar pie.

698. SNIPE PIE.

Pick and singe three snipe as previously described. Cut off the heads, wings, and legs; cut the birds into fours; remove the gizzards, but leave the trail; then cover the lining of a pie-dish with thin slices of fat bacon; place the pieces of snipe in close layers on these slices; season well with aromatic herbs, salt, and pepper; squeeze in the juice of a lemon, pour a sufficient quantity of melted clarified butter into the dish to cover the birds, and put another layer of fat bacon on the top. Cover the dish with puff paste (see No. 318). Bury the feet of the birds on the top of the paste in a symmetrical form. Bake the pie in a moderately-heated oven for one hour and a half, and keep it in a cool place till wanted.

Note.—Woodcock, widgeon, and teal can be made into a similar pie.

699. GAME PIE IN MOULD.

For pies in moulds a short paste (No. 790) is substituted for puff paste, and this should be made first. Skin and draw a hare; save the blood, remove the two fillets from each side of the spine, and cut these into strips half an inch thick and put them aside on a plate; bone the remainder of the hare; put the bones, head, and neck into a stewpan, after having split the two latter in halves; pare off one pound of cushion of veal from skin, gristle, and sinew; put the trimmings in the stewpan with the bones of hare; remove also the rind of one pound of fat bacon; put this aside, add the rind to the stewpan, together with a boned calf's foot cut in pieces, a "bouquet garni," one onion with four cloves stuck in it, and moisten with three pints of stock; season with salt and pepper; boil; skim the broth in the usual way and simmer for about an hour, meanwhile chop up the pieces of boned hare, veal, and half the quantity of the fat bacon, previously freed from rind; pass them through the sausage machine, taking care to add the blood of the hare whilst grinding the meat. When done lay the forcemeat on a dish and season it well with allspice; and cut the remainder of the fat bacon into strips the same size as the fillets of hare. Take an eight-inch oval pie-mould, butter the inside, and line it at the bottom and round the sides, half an inch above the top of the mould, with short paste, previously made for that purpose and rolled to an even thickness about the third of an inch; lay some of the forcemeat at the bottom of the mould, then three or four strips each of bacon and fillet of hare, nicely intermixed and laid lengthwise, then another layer of forcemeat and strips, and finish with a layer of forcemeat. When the broth has boiled its proper time, and is well reduced, strain it through a cloth and pour about three quarters of a pint of it into the pie, making at the same time a few holes in the forcemeat with a trussing needle; lay a bay-leaf on the top; cover the pie with short paste, having previously moistened the border of the mould with water, then press the two together between the thumb and finger to form the edge. Cut the superfluous paste even with the mould, and pinch round again; roll out the remaining paste, cut it of the same shape as the top of the pie, to make a second cover; moisten the first with a brush dipped in water, and lay this second cover over it; brush over the top with the yolk of a beaten egg, then with a pointed knife cut a round hole half an inch wide in the centre, and cover it with a loose piece of paste. Set it in a well-heated oven to bake for about two hours and a half, but should the oven be too fierce, cover the pie with a sheet of buttered paper to prevent the crust getting too brown.

Note.—A pound or two of truffles cut in quarters and properly mixed with the forcemeat will greatly improve the flavour of this pie. The flesh of a boned rabbit can also be substituted for veal, and any kind of boned winged game can likewise be added to the pie.

700. PORK PIE IN MOULD.

Make about two pounds of short paste (No. 790), roll it up, and put aside till wanted. Cut two pounds of griskin of pork in slices, season these with chopped onion, sage, thyme, salt and pepper, and put them on a dish; cut also two pounds of streaky bacon, free from rind and gristle (previously boiled for ten minutes) in slices, and put them with the pork; to these add three pounds of good apples, which, when peeled and the cores taken out, must be cut in thick slices and put on a plate; take a tin mould, about three inches deep, butter it and line the inside with the short paste, previously made and rolled out to an even thickness about the third of an inch; arrange the bacon, apples, and pork in this, in alternate layers, till the whole is used up. Moisten the border round the mould with water; cover the pie with the remaining paste; press the two borders together round the edges with the thumb and finger, trim it, and make a small round hole in the centre, cover it with a piece of loose paste; egg the top of the pie with a brush, and set it to bake in a moderately-heated oven for two hours and a half, and serve hot.

701. BEEFSTEAK AND OYSTER PUDDING.

Chop fine half a pound of beef suet, and mix it with a pound of sifted flour on the slab; gather this together with the hands, make a hole in the centre to receive a teaspoonful of salt and about a gill of water. Mix and work this well together to a stiffish paste, using a little more water if necessary, and a little more flour to dry it, then with it line a pudding basin previously buttered, keeping enough paste apart to cover it. Fill the basin with beefsteak and oysters similarly prepared as in No. 689, but with only half the quantity of broth. When the pudding is filled, wet the edges of the paste round the top of the basin with a paste-brush dipped in water, and cover with the remaining suet paste rolled out to the size of the top of the basin; press this down all round the edge with the thumb, and twist the edges of the paste over so as to give it a corded appearance; tie the basin in a pudding-cloth, and boil in enough water for about two hours and a half, taking care that the water always covers the pudding; then take it out, untie the cloth, turn the pudding over on a dish, lift the basin carefully without breaking the paste, pour some good gravy under, and serve.

702. BEEFSTEAK AND KIDNEY PUDDING.

Proceed with the paste as in the previous number, fill the pudding basin with scollops of beefsteak and kidneys properly seasoned as for No. 688; moisten with a gill of broth; cover the basin as in the foregoing, then boil for two hours and a half, taking care that the water always covers the basin, and serve.

703. MUTTON PUDDING.

Line a basin with paste, made as for beefsteak and oyster pudding Prepare some mutton as for mutton pie (No. 691), or if preferred, cut part of a leg of mutton into thick scollops; season with salt, pepper, chopped parsley, shalots, and thyme; make a layer of meat and one of sliced potatoes; moisten with a little mutton broth if possible; cover the basin as before, tie in a pudding-cloth, and let boil, with enough water to cover the basin, for two hours and a half or three hours; then turn the pudding over a dish, pour some good gravy under, and serve.

704. SMALL-BIRD PUDDING.

Any kind of small birds, such as larks, sparrows, wheatears, &c., &c., can be used for this pudding. Pick three dozen birds, clean, cut off the heads and feet and draw the gizzards; cut also half a pound of streaky bacon in small dice, free from rind. Line a pudding basin, previously buttered, with paste made as for beefsteak and oyster pudding; put in it a layer of birds and bacon alternately; season with pepper, chopped parsley, shalots, a little grated nutmeg, and salt; make another layer of birds, bacon, and seasoning till all are used; moisten with a gill of good broth, cover the basin with paste as previously described, tie it round with a pudding cloth, and boil two hours and a half; when ready remove the cloth, turn the basin over a dish, remove it carefully without breaking the paste, and serve with some good gravy poured under.

705. GALANTINE OF VEAL AND HAM.

Procure a breast of nice white veal; bone it, and remove all superfluous fat and skin; lay it flat on the table, inside upwards. Make nine small incisions across this, without, however, cutting through the flesh; make three pounds of sausage meat, spread this on a dish; cut into small dice one pound each of cooked ham and ox-tongue, and half a pound of fat bacon; put these into the sausage meat.

Skin two ounces of pistachio kernels, after having been scalded, and add them to the sausage meat. Season with salt, pepper, and allspice. Mix the lot well together with the hands, then spread this forcemeat on the veal and roll it tight; butter a pudding-cloth, place the veal on it, and roll up again very tight; fasten at each end with string, thus giving it the appearance of a cushion; put it in an oval stewpan, with the bones chopped up and the trimmings of veal, two calf's feet in halves, one carrot, one onion with four cloves stuck in it, and a "bouquet garni;" season with salt, two dozen peppercorns, and two blades of mace. Cover the galantine well with water, boil it, and simmer very gently for about three hours; then draw the stewpan away from the fire, and let the galantine partially cool in its liquor for three quarters of an hour; after which drain and remove the cloth, wash this clean in hot water, and tie up the galantine again as before, and put it on a baking-sheet to be pressed, with a piece of board or dish and a seven-pound weight on the top, for at least a couple of hours. Meanwhile strain the broth, skim off all the grease, reduce by a sharp boiling, clarify most carefully, and pass through a jelly-bag or fine cloth into a pan, and put it in a cool place to set firm into aspic jelly. When the galantine has been properly pressed, take it out of the cloth, put in front of the open oven for two minutes to melt the fat, which must be wiped off with a clean dry cloth; then glaze the galantine as previously described for glazing ox-tongues. Put it on a cold dish, garnish round with the aspic jelly, cut in fancy shape a few sprigs of dried parsley, and serve.

706. GALANTINE OF CHICKEN.

Pick, singe, draw, and bone completely a fine and large Surrey chicken, draw inside the skin from the legs and pinions, and spread the chicken out on the table; cut off part of the fillets to cover the thinner parts of the skin; season with salt, pepper, and allspice. Chop up fine one pound each of lean veal and fat bacon, both free from skin and gristle. Season with nutmeg, salt, pepper, and aromatic herbs, and pound it in a mortar with the yolks of two eggs and the peel of a pound and a half of truffles, and put it in a basin. Cut in half-inch dice half a pound each of cooked ox-tongue and fat bacon, add these to the forcemeat, together with the truffles, previously peeled, also cut in dice. Mix the lot well together with the hands; then spread it on the chicken; twist this round, sew it up with a trussing-needle and twine, and roll it tight in a well-buttered cloth, which must be fastened at each end with string, in a similar way as galantine of veal and ham; then place it in an oval stewpan, with the bones of the chicken and trimmings of veal, &c., as well as two calf's feet cut in two, one carrot, one onion stuck with four cloves, a "bouquet garni," two blades of mace, and twelve peppercorns. Moisten with a gill of brandy and enough white stock to cover the galantine; boil and simmer gently for two hours, and then proceed in every respect as for galantine of veal and ham.

Note.—Galantines of turkey and pheasant are made in the same way.

707. POTTED HARE.

Procure an earthenware pan, with cover, of about seven inches in diameter. Skin, empty, and bone entirely a nice hare; reserve the blood to mix with the forcemeat. Chop up two pounds of streaky bacon with half of the flesh from the legs and shoulders of the hare, all free from sinew, gristle and rind, season well with allspice, pound it in a mortar, adding the blood whilst pounding. Lard the fillets of the hare with small strips of bacon, cut these fillets across; season with allspice, and fry them with the remaining part of the hare in a sauté-pan with an ounce of butter for about ten minutes in order to dry the moisture contained in the hare; then put a layer of the forcemeat one inch thick in the earthenware pan; lay on this one half of the hare's flesh, another layer of forcemeat, the other half of the hare, and the remaining forcemeat; cover with thin slices of fat bacon, put the cover on the pan, and place it in a large stewpan with three inches of boiling water, cook in a hot oven for three hours, and when cold, cover the potted meat with melted fat or clarified butter and put by in a cool place, when it will keep fresh for months.

Note.—Pheasants, partridges, larks, and rabbits can be potted in the same way.

CHAPTER XVII.

REMARKS ON VEGETABLES.

ENGLAND is not so rich in vegetables as she is in other products and necessaries of life, as there are several kinds quite unknown in this country which are highly esteemed abroad, such as cardoons, goat's-beard or viper's grass, blite, mad-apple, &c.; whilst sorrel and artichokes are but slightly cultivated. Potatoes, as a matter of course, hold the leading position amongst vegetables. What could we do without potatoes? They were, however, quite unknown in Europe three centuries ago, having been imported from South America (according to some authorities) in 1586 by Sir Francis Drake; but their general introduction dates only from 1592. There is no vegetable—in fact, eggs and rice excepted, there is nothing in the world that can be cooked and dressed in so many different ways as potatoes. Some two hundred styles, I believe, have been attained. This reminds me of a dinner I provided at the St. James' Hall in 1876 to some forty Irish members of Parliament, which I hope may not be out of place if related here.

In taking the order from Major O'Gorman (whom I had the pleasure of knowing well), I had strongly impressed upon me the necessity of having plenty of potatoes for that dinner, as they were all Irish gentlemen, and very fond of them. I promised to comply with his wishes, and on the day and time appointed the dinner was duly served with ten different styles of cooked potatoes. These were passed round in the usual way, with the entrées, when Major O'Gorman, who was in the chair (a good strong one, as he weighed about twenty stone), summoned me to his presence and complained in very strong terms that no potatoes could be had. "Major!" said I, "there must be some mistake, as you all seem pretty well supplied with them; you have actually three sorts on your plate, and to all appearance are enjoying them!" The poor Major was quite amazed to see that they were all partaking of potatoes without knowing it. Recovering, however, from his surprise, he at once ordered plenty of boiled potatoes, but that did not prevent his being chaffed about his mistake for a long time afterwards.

708. BOILED POTATOES.

Potatoes are boiled either with the skin on or off. The former is the best. Wash off the dirt by scrubbing with a hard brush, and rinse them well; put into a saucepan with enough cold water to cover them, and a teaspoonful of salt for every quart of water; boil till the potatoes are nearly done, which can be ascertained by inserting a trussing-needle into one or two of them; then drain off the water, cover the stewpan, and place it by the side of the fire for about five minutes, when the steam and moisture will evaporate and the potatoes get floury; then peel as quickly as possible, and serve.

Note.—Potatoes will generally require boiling for a quarter of an hour, but in some instances a longer time is necessary. In all cases they should be served as soon as cooked.

709. POTATO PURÉE.

See No. 231.

710. POTATOES À LA MAÎTRE D'HÔTEL.

Boil two pounds of potatoes gently so as not to break them, then peel and cut them in slices, a quarter of an inch thick; put these in a stewpan with half a pound of maître d'hôtel butter (No. 226), half a pint of white broth, and a teaspoonful of finely-chopped parsley. Mix the lot well by tossing the pan over the fire; squeeze over them the juice of a lemon, and serve.

711. POTATOES WITH CREAM.

Boil, peel, and cut in slices two pounds of potatoes as in No. 710; put them in a stewpan with one pint of cream or milk, simmer for ten minutes; then add one ounce of butter if cream, but if milk two ounces, divided in seven or eight pieces; add a pinch of salt and a little nutmeg; toss till the butter is well melted, and serve.

712. POTATOES SAUTÉES.

These are prepared either with raw or cooked potatoes; the latter style is the most in use. Any cold boiled potatoes left from the previous day are cut in slices and browned to a nice golden colour with fresh butter, either in a sauté or frying-pan; season with salt, pepper, and a little chopped parsley, and serve.

713. POTATOES SAUTÉES À LA LYONNAISE.

Cut some potatoes in slices as above, say two pounds; melt three ounces of fresh butter in a clean frying-pan, in which fry three finely sliced onions to a brown colour; then add the potatoes and toss them now and then, till they are of a nice brown; season with salt, pepper and half a teaspoonful of chopped parsley, moisten with a little good gravy if handy, mix well together, and serve very hot.

714. POTATOES SAUTÉES À L'ITALIENNE.

Peel and cut in oval slices, the thickness of a crown piece, two pounds of nice raw Regent potatoes; fry these gently on a moderate fire in a sauté-pan with three ounces of clarified butter to a nice golden colour, then drain the butter into a saucepan containing half a pint of hot tomato sauce. Glaze the potatoes with half a pint of good gravy, and dress them in pyramid form on a dish; squeeze the juice of a lemon in the tomato sauce, pour it over the potatoes, and serve.

715. POTATOES À LA BÉCHAMEL.

Peel, cut, fry, and glaze two pounds of potatoes as in No. 714; then cover them, when dished up, with half a pint of good Béchamel sauce, and serve.

716. POTATOES AU GRATIN.

Prepare two pounds of potatoes as in No. 715, mask them in the same way with Bechamel sauce, sprinkle over them two ounces of grated cheese and a tablespoonful of raspings, then add an ounce of fresh butter divided into five parts, with a pinch of grated nutmeg; place the dish in a moderately-heated oven till it has attained a golden colour, and serve.

717. POTATOES À LA SAVOISIENNE.

Boil two pounds of potatoes for fifteen minutes; peel and cut them into thin slices; make a layer with these in a deep gratin-dish; sprinkle on it a tablespoonful of grated cheese, a few pieces of butter, and a gill of good gravy. Repeat the layer of potatoes and so on; then cover the whole with a quart of cream reduced to half, by boiling; season with a pinch of powdered cinnamon; place the dish in the oven to bake, and when of a nice brown all over, serve.

718. POTATOES À LA PROVENÇALE.

Boil in their skins two pounds of potatoes for fifteen minutes. Meanwhile chop fine an onion, a clove of garlic, a few sprigs of parsley, and a few fresh mushrooms. Fry these in a sauté-pan with a gill of salad-oil and an ounce of butter to a nice brown colour. When the potatoes are properly cooked, peel and cut them in thin slices; add three boned and chopped anchovies to the stewpan; stir the contents, then add the potatoes; toss them well together, simmer for eight or ten minutes, and squeeze the juice of half a lemon before serving.

719. POTATOES À LA BEAUFORT.

Select two pounds of nice even round potatoes; peel them, and with a round vegetable-scoop make a hole the size of a cork, two-thirds deep, in the centre of each. Fill these up with either cooked veal or beef nicely chopped, and properly seasoned with salt, pepper, and a little grated nutmeg; add a piece of butter as big as a Windsor bean on the top of each; place the potatoes with the meat up side by side on a baking-sheet; moisten with good gravy or broth. Cover the potatoes with a buttered sheet of paper, and set them to bake in a moderately heated oven till cooked, taking care to baste them two or three times during that time. When done, serve with the remainder of the gravy in a sauce-boat apart.

720. POTATO CROQUETS.

Boil two pounds of peeled potatoes in the usual way (see No. 708). When cooked, rub them through a wire sieve into a stewpan; add one ounce of butter and the yolks of two eggs properly beaten. Work this well together with a wooden spoon; then sprinkle a paste-board with flour; divide the purée in equal parts, roll these on the board to the shape of corks, dip them in egg, bread-crumb, and fry them in hot fat to a golden colour, and serve.

721. POTATOES À LA DUCHESSE.

Prepare some mashed potatoes as in the previous number. Sprinkle a paste-board with flour; shape the purée on it in oval cakes two inches long by one and a half wide and one inch thick; then fry them in clarified butter; drain them on a cloth, and serve.

722. FRIED POTATOES.

Peel one pound of potatoes, cut these in half-inch slices and then in quarter-inch strips; dry them in a cloth and fry in boiling fat over a brisk fire for about twelve minutes, giving an occasional stir with the frying-basket to secure an even cooking and prevent them adhering to one another. When of a nice golden colour, drain them on a clean cloth by twisting and shaking them over; then sprinkle with salt, dish up, and serve.

723. CHIPPED POTATOES, FRIED.

After having peeled one pound of potatoes, cut them in very thin slices, say the sixteenth of an inch, and dry in a cloth; then fry them in hot fat over a brisk fire for about ten minutes, taking care to stir occasionally with the frying-basket, to secure an even colouring; drain on a cloth, sprinkle with salt, and serve.

724. FRIED POTATOES, PAILLE.

Peel and slice one pound of potatoes as above, then cut these in shreds the size of straws, dry, and fry in hot fat for about seven minutes. When of a nice golden colour, drain, sprinkle with salt, and serve.

Note.—This style is generally served with roast game.

725. FRIED POTATOES SOUFFLÉES.

Peel one and a half pound of kidney potatoes to the shape of an egg, and slice them lengthwise to an eighth of an inch thick, taking care to have all of the same size; dry in the usual way and fry in hot fat for six minutes; then gather them in the frying-basket, and drain and cool by the side of the stove; keep the fat on the fire to increase the temperature by a few degrees, and when the potatoes are quite cold, throw them in the fat again for five minutes to complete the cooking, when the reaction of the heat will cause them to swell like eggs. This being attained, drain them quickly over a clean cloth, sprinkle with salt, and serve at once.

726. POTATO SOUFFLÉ.

Wash and bake in their skins a pound of potatoes: this will take about three-quarters of an hour if the oven is well heated. When soft, squeeze them over a wire sieve and rub through with a wooden spoon into a large basin. Put into a stewpan a gill of milk with an ounce of butter; bring this to boil, giving it an occasional stir; season slightly with salt, pepper, and a pinch of grated nutmeg; then draw the pan away from the fire, add its contents gradually to the yolks of four eggs properly beaten, stirring the while. When the liaison is made, mix it well with the mashed potatoes; whisk the whites of the four eggs to a stiff froth, add it to the mashed potatoes, and stir it into the mixture. Pour the whole into a well-buttered soufflé or pie dish; set it to bake in a well-heated oven for about twelve minutes, when it will have risen and become of a golden colour, then serve.

727. NEW POTATOES WITH BUTTER.

Wash and scrape two pounds of small new potatoes (as much as possible of the same size). Put them in a stewpan with a teaspoonful of salt and enough cold water to cover them. Set them to boil two minutes only; then drain off the water and dry them on a cloth. Melt three ounces of fresh butter in a sauté-pan, add the potatoes, and simmer on a good fire for about twenty minutes, taking care to often toss them, in order to give them an even colour all round. When properly done, sprinkle some salt and a teaspoonful of finely chopped parsley, dish up, and serve.

728. PLAIN BOILED CABBAGE.

Trim off the outer leaves of a cabbage, divide it in four, soak these in cold water for an hour with a handful of salt; when well washed, drain and squeeze the water out of them, cut off the stalks, and throw the cabbage into boiling water with a tablespoonful of salt. When properly cooked, pour them into a colander, drain the water out by pressing the cabbage with a small plate, and serve.

729. CABBAGE, COUNTRY STYLE.

Trim off, divide, clean, and blanch for five minutes a cabbage as described in No. 728; then squeeze the water out and put the cabbage in a stewpan. Moisten with good broth, season with salt and pepper, then cover with a layer of bacon cut in thin slices and a buttered sheet of paper on the top. Boil with the stewpan covered for twenty minutes, then stand in the oven for ten minutes, and serve.

730. STUFFED CABBAGE.

Pick out all the nice leaves of a big savoy cabbage; wash these well and blanch them in boiling salt water for five minutes, then drain and wipe them dry, lay them flat on the table in the form of a ten-inch square. Chop up in small dice one pound of cooked veal and a quarter of a pound of cooked ham, and mince very fine a clove of garlic; then mix these with half a pound of plain boiled rice, season with salt and pepper, and put the mixture in the centre of the cabbage-leaves; fold these up and tie them well all round with string. Boil in the stock-pot for twenty minutes, then put it on a baking-dish, moisten with a little gravy, and set it in a hot oven for ten minutes. When nicely browned remove the string and serve with some gravy in a sauce-boat.

731. BOILED CAULIFLOWER. BUTTER SAUCE.

Pare off the coarse outer leaves of two medium cauliflowers, cut the stalks and pare away the tough skin round it, throw these in a basin of cold water, adding half a gill of vinegar, in order to draw out any caterpillar or insect that may be in them, then plunge them in boiling water with a teaspoonful of salt, and boil for twelve or fifteen minutes according to size. When the cauliflowers are done, which can be ascertained by pressing a small piece between the fingers; if this should give way easily to the pressure, although still retaining a certain firmness, they must be taken off from the fire, carefully removed with a slice and drained on a sieve, then dished up and served with Butter sauce (No. 157).

732. FRIED CAULIFLOWER.

Trim, wash, and boil two cauliflowers as in No. 731, then drain and cut them into pieces. Melt two ounces of fresh butter in a frying-pan, add the pieces of cauliflower, season with salt and pepper, and fry to a nice brown all round, taking care to toss them, in order to prevent burning; then dish up, and serve.

733. FRIED CAULIFLOWER WITH PARMESAN CHEESE.

Prepare and fry the cauliflowers as above; when of a nice brown, sprinkle two tablespoonfuls of grated parmesan cheese, toss and dish up the cauliflower; warm a gill of good gravy in the same frying-pan, pour it over the cauliflower, and serve.

734. CAULIFLOWER AU GRATIN.

Boil two cauliflowers as in No. 731. Meanwhile put one ounce of butter and one ounce of flour in a stewpan, stir over the fire for three minutes, then add one pint of water or white stock; season with salt and pepper; boil for ten minutes, stirring the while, then draw by the side of the fire. When the cauliflowers are done and drained, cut them in pieces. Grate one ounce and a half each of parmesan and Gruyère cheese and mix it well together; put a layer of cauliflower at the bottom of a gratin-dish, then a layer with one-third of the grated cheese and a layer of sauce; pile up the remaining cauliflower on the top; cover with another third of cheese and the sauce, sprinkle the third part of the cheese over the sauce, and add a tablespoonful of raspings. Baste with an ounce of melted fresh butter, and set the dish to bake in a hot oven for about a quarter of an hour. Meanwhile put the salamander in the fire to be made red hot, pass this over the top of the cauliflower to give a light brown colour, and serve.

735. CAULIFLOWER À LA GENOISE.

Prepare and boil two nice cauliflowers as previously described, fry in butter; dish them up and pour half a pint of Genoise sauce over them (No. 207), to which four boned and chopped anchovies have been added, and serve.

736. CAULIFLOWER À LA BÉCHAMEL.

Trim, wash, boil, and fry in butter two cauliflowers as above; dish them up and pour over some Béchamel sauce (No. 154), and serve.

737. BOILED BRUSSELS SPROUTS.

Select one pound of light-green and hard Brussels sprouts, cut the stalks and pare off the outside leaves; wash, drain, and throw them in three quarts of boiling water with a teaspoonful of salt. Boil fast for a quarter of an hour, drain them on a clean cloth, and serve.

738. BRUSSELS SPROUTS WITH BUTTER.

Pick and boil a pound of nice Brussels sprouts as in the foregoing; drain and fry them in a frying-pan with half an ounce of butter for five minutes, taking care to toss them to prevent burning. Sprinkle with salt, pepper, and grated nutmeg, toss up, and serve.

739. TURNIPS WITH GRAVY.

Select six tender and medium-sized turnips, peel and wash them well, then blanch in boiling water with a teaspoonful of salt for five minutes; drain, and cut into four. Melt one ounce of fresh butter in a sauté-pan, add the pieces of turnips, fry them to a nice light brown, season with salt, pepper, and nutmeg, moisten with a pint of good stock or gravy, sprinkle in a teaspoonful of powdered sugar, cover the pan and simmer for about twenty minutes. When done, which can be ascertained by trying them with a trussing-needle, dish them up, pour the gravy over, and serve.

740. TURNIPS À LA SAVOISIENNE.

Choose, peel, and blanch six nice tender turnips for five minutes; then drain and let them get cold; after which cut them in slices the eighth of an inch thick and fry with an ounce of fresh butter to a nice golden colour, taking care to season them with salt and grated nutmeg. Put a layer of these at the bottom of a buttered gratin-dish, sprinkle on them a tablespoonful of grated cheese with a similar quantity of gravy or good stock, then another layer of turnips, and so on, finishing with grated cheese and raspings mixed with an ounce of melted butter. Bake this in a hot oven to a nice brown colour, then add two or three tablespoonfuls of gravy over, and serve.

741. MASHED TURNIPS.

Peel, cut in eight parts, and blanch in the usual way half a dozen turnips; then drain and fry in a stewpan with an ounce of butter for five minutes; season with salt, pepper, and nutmeg; moisten with a gill of good white stock. Simmer gently with the lid on, and when well done rub through a fine wire sieve into the stewpan again; add an ounce of fresh butter, a tablespoonful of powdered sugar, and half a pint of good white stock or milk, mix well together over the fire with a wooden spoon, and when nicely smooth and hot, serve.

742. CARROTS À L'ITALIENNE.

Young carrots only should be used for this dish. Cut off the the green part of a bunch of new carrots, blanch in boiling water for about ten minutes, drain, and when cool peel off the skin with a knife or rub it off with a cloth; put them in a stewpan with an ounce of fresh butter, a tablespoonful of powdered sugar, and a pint of good broth. Boil on a brisk fire for about twenty minutes or till they are well glazed. Season with salt, pepper, and a tablespoonful of finely chopped parsley, add half an ounce of fresh butter, toss them over the fire, and when the butter is properly melted, dish up and serve.

743. CARROTS, HOUSEWIFE STYLE.

Select a nice bunch of new carrots, and blanch them in boiling water for ten minutes; drain, and when cold rub their skin off with a cloth; slice them a quarter of an inch thick, put in a stewpan with an ounce of butter, a pint and a half of milk, a good pinch of salt, and a little grated nutmeg. Partly cover the stewpan and boil on a brisk fire for about twenty minutes, taking care to stir occasionally with a wooden spoon to prevent burning. When the milk is properly reduced, dish up and serve.

744. PURÉE OF CARROTS.

Scrape, clean, cut in slices, and blanch for ten minutes half a dozen nice long carrots; then proceed for the purée as for mashed turnips (No. 235), and serve.

745. CELERY WITH BEEF MARROW.

Select six heads of fresh celery, trim the outside leaves, cut the roots to a point and the green parts straight, leaving each head about six inches long; then cut these lengthwise, in halves, and wash well. Blanch in boiling water for ten minutes, and immerse in cold water. When properly drained, put them carefully in a stewpan with a pint and a half of good broth; season with salt and pepper; simmer gently for about an hour; when well glazed, dish up on a hot dish. Have ready about two ounces of beef marrow boiled for four minutes in salt water; add it to the glaze in the stewpan; toss it and mash it well; squeeze the juice of half a lemon; toss again; then pour it over the celery, and serve.

746. CELERY AU GRATIN.

Trim, cut in halves, and blanch six heads of celery as in the foregoing, then braize it in broth, properly seasoned, for an hour; after which, dish it up as before, but without marrow and lemon-juice; sprinkle the top with grated cheese, put the dish in the oven to get brown; then pour a gill of good gravy over, and serve.

747. CELERY WITH GRAVY.

Trim as in the foregoing and blanch for ten minutes six whole heads of celery, then immerse them in cold water, drain, and put them in a stewpan with a pint and a half of broth and an ounce of butter; season with salt and pepper; cover the stewpan and simmer for an hour and a half; when well done, dish up, pour the remainder of the gravy over, and serve.

748. VEGETABLE MARROW. BUTTER SAUCE.

Cut the vegetable marrows, according to their size, in two, four, or six, lengthwise; peel and remove all the seed, and then drop them into boiling salt water and simmer till tender. When done, drain them carefully; dish the pieces inside up, pour some Butter sauce (No. 216) over, and serve.

749. VEGETABLE MARROW, HOUSEWIFE STYLE.

Select three small vegetable marrows about four inches long, peel, cut them lengthwise in quarters, and remove the seed. Blanch for five minutes in boiling water; drain and put them in a frying-pan with an ounce of butter and half a gill of salad-oil, previously made hot; fry on a brisk fire; season with salt and pepper; and when done, sprinkle two tablespoonfuls of grated cheese, dish up, and serve.

750. VEGETABLE MARROWS À L'ITALIENNE.

Prepare and blanch three marrows as in No. 749; when drained, fry them till cooked, with two ounces of butter; when tender, dish them up, cover with Tomato sauce, and serve.

Note.—Marrows fried in butter can be served with a Sharp, Espagnole, Velouté, or Béchamel sauce.

751. JERUSALEM ARTICHOKES. BUTTER SAUCE.

Scrub and wash well in plenty of water a pound of Jerusalem artichokes; peel and boil them in salt water for about fifteen minutes. When done, drain them upon a cloth; dish up, pour some Butter sauce (No. 216) over, and serve.

752. JERUSALEM ARTICHOKES À L'ITALIENNE.

Wash and peel a pound of artichokes as in No. 751, blanch them in boiling salt water for five minutes, then drain and put them in a stewpan with an ounce of melted butter. Moisten with half a pint of broth, season with salt, pepper, and nutmeg, and simmer very gently for about twenty-five minutes, with the stewpan covered, taking care to turn them, in order to acquire a deep yellow colour. When done, dish them up, squeeze the juice of a lemon over the remainder of the glaze, pour it over the artichokes, and serve.

Note.—Pickled Jerusalem artichokes prepared in the following manner eat very well with cold meat :—

Wash and peel four pounds of artichokes as previously described, cut these in thin slices, boil for five minutes in enough vinegar to soak them, and properly seasoned with salt, a dozen cloves, and two dozen peppercorns ; pour the lot into an earthenware pickle-jar, let the contents get cool, and then cover with a cork. It will keep for months, and any quantity can be taken out as wanted.

753. GREEN ARTICHOKES. BUTTER SAUCE.

Cut half an inch off the top of six artichokes, pare off the bottoms and loose leaves, and boil them in plenty of salt water for about three-quarters of an hour; drain them upside down on a cloth, and remove the fibrous substance from the inside with the handle of a spoon, then dish up on a napkin, and serve with Butter sauce (No. 216) in a sauce-boat apart.

754. ARTICHOKES À LA BARIGOULE.

Trim six artichokes as in the foregoing, boil them in the same way, and remove the inside in a similar manner, then squeeze the water out, and season them slightly with salt and pepper. Meanwhile pour a gill of salad-oil into a frying-pan, and when hot, fry the top of the leaves in it for about three minutes, then the bottoms in a similar way, and drain the artichokes upside down on a cloth. Chop up fine half a pound of fresh and trimmed mushrooms, a handful of parsley, and four shalots, put these into a stewpan with three ounces of scraped fat bacon and an ounce of butter; season with salt, pepper, and a little chopped thyme; fry the lot for about seven minutes, stirring the while; then lay it on a plate and divide it in six parts; put each part of this mixture in each artichoke; place a thin slice of fat bacon on the top of each; tie round with string to keep them in shape; put them in a sauté-pan; moisten with half a pint of good stock; bake in the oven for fifteen minutes; remove the string, dish them up, and serve.

755. ARTICHOKES À L'ITALIENNE.

Trim, boil, and remove the inside of six artichokes as in the previous number; dish them up, pour half a pint of boiling Sharp Italian sauce (No. 205) in the centre, and serve.

756. FRIED ARTICHOKES.

Trim and pare off four nice artichokes as described for artichokes, Butter sauce. Cut them lengthwise in slices a quarter of an inch thick, remove the fibrous substance close to the bottom, and throw the pieces in cold water, with a gill of vinegar to keep them white. Prepare a batter with a gill of salad-oil, a quarter of a pound of flour, four yolks of eggs, salt and pepper to taste. When these ingredients have been well mixed together, if it is found that the batter is too thin, add a little flour; if too thick, a little cold water; then drain the pieces of artichokes, and with the hand mix them well in the batter till they are all evenly coated; after which, fry them in hot fat, previously heated to the right temperature for that purpose. When of a nice brown colour draw them out, and drain on a wire sieve; sprinkle with salt, dish them up on a napkin, and serve.

Note.—In addition to the above, artichokes either plain boiled or raw, can also be eaten à la poivrade, a mixture of oil, vinegar, salt, and pepper.

757. SEA-KALE. BUTTER SAUCE.

Trim, clean, and tie the sea-kale up in small bunches, put these in boiling salt water and boil for about twenty minutes; when tender, drain and dish up on a napkin (after having removed the string), and serve with Butter sauce (No. 216) in a sauce-boat apart.

758. ASPARAGUS WITH BUTTER SAUCE.

Scrape along the white stalks of the asparagus with a knife held in a slanting position; pare off the loose leaves from the heads; plunge in cold water; then tie them up in bundles of about twenty-five in each according to size, taking care to have all the heads turned the same way; cut the stalks even. Put the asparagus in boiling water, with half an ounce of salt for each quart of water; boil for twelve or fifteen minutes according to size; and when done, which is ascertained by pressing with the fingers, take them out by the string and immerse at once in cold water; then drain immediately, dish them up on a napkin, remove the string, and serve with Butter sauce (No. 216) in a sauce-boat apart.

Note.—Asparagus should not be done too much; in fact,

it ought to remain always firm to the touch, and should never be kept in water after being cooked, as it then gets flabby and spongy, like all other boiled vegetables, which will be spoiled in the same way if allowed to remain in water after being cooked.

759. ASPARAGUS À LA MILANAISE.

Scrape, tie, and boil the asparagus required as in No. 758; dish up on a napkin, and serve with a sauce-boat containing one ounce of grated parmesan cheese and two ounces of fresh butter, previously melted and well mixed together and seasoned with pepper.

760. ASPARAGUS WITH BROWN BUTTER.

Prepare and cook as above the asparagus; drain and dish up on a napkin, and serve with some brown butter (No. 164) previously made for that purpose in a sauce-boat apart.

761. ASPARAGUS WITH OIL AND VINEGAR.

Trim and boil the asparagus as described in the foregoing, and after having dipped it in cold water and drained, let it get quite cold (if laid on the ice with a cloth all the better). When ready dish up in the usual way, and serve with oil, vinegar, salt, and pepper, in a sauce-boat, all well mixed together to taste.

Note.—The above style of serving asparagus is the most usual on the Continent.

762. SPINACH À L'ITALIENNE.

Pick off the stalks of three pounds of spinach, wash well in two waters, drain upon a sieve or colander, and put it in about three quarts of boiling water with half an ounce of salt, and boil for six or seven minutes; then turn the spinach upon the sieve or colander and immerse in plenty of cold water till quite cold (otherwise it will assume a yellow tinge). Afterwards squeeze the water out, spread the spinach on the chopping-board, and chop slightly with a knife; then fry in a sauté-pan with two ounces of anchovy butter till done, adding meanwhile two ounces of Malaga raisins (previously washed in lukewarm water), when well mixed together over the fire, dish up, garnish with croûtons fried in butter, and serve.

763. SPINACH, HOUSEWIFE STYLE.

Pick, wash, blanch, and chop three pounds of spinach as described in No. 762; then fry in a sauté-pan, with two ounces of butter, two cloves of garlic, and four anchovies chopped fine, till done; season with salt, pepper, and nutmeg, and just before dishing up add a little fresh butter, stir the whole well together, and serve with croûtons fried in butter.

764. SPINACH À LA PROVENÇALE.

Prepare, blanch, and chop up the spinach as above; after which, fry it with a gill of salad-oil and two cloves of garlic chopped fine till cooked; season with salt and pepper, dish it up with croûtons, and serve.

765. SPINACH WITH BUTTER.

Pick and wash three pounds of spinach as described in the foregoing, then boil till it becomes quite tender and soft to the touch, drain the water, immerse it in cold, and afterwards squeeze all the water from it between two plates, chop fine and rub it through a coarse wire sieve; then put it in a stewpan with two ounces of fresh butter; season with salt, pepper, and grated nutmeg; stir the spinach over the fire with a wooden spoon until it becomes quite warm, then add gradually half a pint of good broth, still stirring the spinach. When well mixed together and made quite hot, add a little more fresh butter, and when this is melted and properly mixed with the spinach, dish it up, garnish round with croûtons fried in butter, and serve.

766. SPINACH WITH CREAM.

Prepare the spinach as above, stir it with a wooden spoon over the fire in a stewpan, with two ounces of butter and seasoned with salt and nutmeg till warm; then add gradually half a pint of cream, a little butter and a dessert-spoonful of pounded sugar; continue the stirring over the fire till the lot is well mixed together and hot, and dish up as in the foregoing.

767. BOILED PEAS À L'ANGLAISE.

Put a quart of fresh shelled peas in two quarts of boiling water, with a few sprigs of mint and seasoned with a small teaspoonful of salt. Boil quickly till done, which will take between fifteen and twenty minutes; then drain and put them in a sauté-pan with two ounces of fresh butter, sprinkle a little salt and pepper, toss them till the butter is melted, and serve.

768. STEWED PEAS WITH BACON.

Remove the rind of a quarter of a pound of streaky bacon and cut it in dice half an inch thick; fry these in a stewpan with one ounce of butter for five minutes, then sprinkle two tablespoonfuls of flour and stir over the fire for four minutes longer; after which, add a pint of water, one quart of peas, and a few green onions, stew for about half an hour with the stewpan covered, then season according to taste, remove the onions, skim off the fat, and serve.

769. PEAS À LA FRANÇAISE.

Put a quart of fresh shelled peas in a stewpan with a gill of water, a few green onions and the heart of a cabbage-lettuce cut in four, three ounces of butter, a teaspoonful of salt, and the same quantity of lump-sugar. Set the stewpan on a slow fire to stew gently for about half an hour with the lid on. Meanwhile knead together a tablespoonful of flour with two ounces of butter, and when the peas are done add this paste to them. Toss the stewpan over the fire till the butter is melted and the peas properly thickened, then taste if well seasoned, and serve.

Note.—If tinned peas are used, throw them in boiling water, drain, season and finish as with fresh peas.

770. FRENCH BEANS.

Pick and remove the strings of one pound of French beans, and if large and old, shred them lengthwise; then throw them in plenty of boiling water with a good pinch of salt, and boil on a brisk fire till tender, which must be ascertained by trying them; after which, drain them in a colander, dish up with an ounce of fresh butter in a lump, sprinkle a little salt over, and serve.

771. FRENCH BEANS SAUTÉS.

Pick the stalks and strings of a pound of French beans, and boil them as in the previous number; then drain them well and put in a frying-pan with two ounces of melted butter; fry these over a brisk fire for about ten minutes; season with a little salt and chopped parsley, toss the contents well, squeeze the juice of a lemon over, toss again, and serve.

772. FRENCH BEANS À LA MAÎTRE D'HÔTEL.

Remove the corners and strings of a pound of French beans; boil and drain them as previously described. Meanwhile have ready in a stewpan a gill of either Bechamel or Suprême sauce, with two ounces of fresh butter, a teaspoonful of blanched and chopped parsley, seasoned with salt, pepper, and grated nutmeg, well mixed together over the fire; then add the beans, toss the whole well together, and when quite hot squeeze the juice of half a lemon over, toss again, and serve.

773. DRIED WHITE HARICOT BEANS.

Soak one pound of dried haricot beans, in plenty of cold water, for about twelve hours previous to cooking, then pick out all the imperfect ones and throw the best into a stewpan with three quarts of cold water and a tablespoonful of salt. Boil with the stewpan covered till tender, drain the water through a colander and return the beans in the pan, with three ounces of fresh butter and a teaspoonful of chopped parsley; season with salt and pepper, and moisten with a little broth or the liquor of the beans; toss the beans till the butter is melted, and serve.

774. HARICOT BEANS, HOUSEWIFE STYLE.

Soak a pound of haricot beans as in No. 773, cook them in salt water for a quarter of an hour, and drain in the usual way. In the meantime have ready hot in a stewpan a pint of mutton gravy, seasoned with salt, pepper, and nutmeg; put the beans in it, and continue the cooking till tender, add an ounce of fresh butter, and serve.

Note.—Plain boiled haricot beans are also served as a salad; in that case they should be cold, and seasoned with oil, vinegar, salt, pepper, and a teaspoonful of either chopped parsley, tarragon, or chevril.

775. BROAD BEANS À LA POULETTE.

Boil in plenty of water till tender, with a good pinch of salt in it, two pounds of freshly shelled broad beans. Drain, and remove their skin; then stir in the same stewpan for three minutes over the fire, half an ounce of butter, with a similar quantity of flour, and make a liaison with the yolks of two eggs, half a gill of cream, and another half ounce of butter. When properly thickened, add the beans to the sauce, with a small teaspoonful of pounded sugar; toss the stewpan to mix well, and serve.

Note.—Broad beans can also be prepared à la maître d'hôtel, and in the same manner as haricot beans, for which see above.

776. PURÉE OF BROAD BEANS.

Boil till tender two pounds of broad beans, and drain them as described, then rub them with a wooden spoon over a fine wire sieve, and return the purée to the stewpan, with either a gill of cream, Béchamel sauce, or a good gravy, and two ounces of butter; stir the contents over the fire till hot, and serve.

777. LENTILS À LA MAÎTRE D'HÔTEL.

Soak for about four hours and wash one pound of lentils, and boil them in about two quarts of water and a dessertspoonful of salt till done, then drain them in the usual way. Meanwhile prepare a quarter of a pound of maître d'hôtel butter, to which mix a tablespoonful or two of the liquor in which the lentils were boiled; add these to the sauce, toss them up till hot and well-mixed, and serve.

778. LENTILS, HOUSEWIFE STYLE.

Wash, cook, and drain a pound of lentils, as in No. 777. Meanwhile cut about two ounces of streaky bacon (free from rind) in very small dice, and fry them with half an ounce of butter for three minutes. When the lentils have been properly drained, return them to the stewpan with either a gill of Espagnole sauce or good gravy; add the bacon to it, stir, and serve.

779. STUFFED TOMATOES À LA PROVENÇALE.

Select six firm tomatoes of equal size and ripeness. Put them in boiling water for two minutes, in order to help the removal of the skin; when peeled, cut them across in halves, remove the seeds, and place them in a sauté-pan, well spread with salad oil, by the side of the fire. Meanwhile chop very finely an onion, half a handful of parsley, six large fresh mushrooms, and two anchovies; fry these for five minutes in a stewpan with about an ounce of scraped fat bacon, season with salt, pepper and chopped thyme, and moisten with either good gravy or Espagnole sauce; then put this stuffing over the twelve halves of tomatoes. Sprinkle some fine raspings over, set the sauté-pan over a brisk fire for about five minutes, then in a hot oven for seven or eight minutes or till they are properly baked, after which dish carefully without breaking, and serve.

780. GRILLED TOMATOES.

Remove the stalks of six ripe tomatoes, cut them across in halves, and set them (skin downward) on a clear fire to grill seven or eight minutes, according to size. Move them gently over the bars of the grill, without however, turning them. When cooked, season each half with salt and pepper, dish them on buttered toast, previously made for that purpose, and serve.

Note.—Tomatoes are also made into salad.

Remarks on Mushrooms.

Mushrooms should be soaked in water with a little salt and vinegar, then washed in plain water and wiped dry before cooking, and as a safeguard against poisoning, should be cooked with a peeled onion. If the onion remains white, the mushrooms are good; but if the onion becomes black or even slightly coloured, they are poisonous, and should at once be destroyed. A piece of silver thrown with the mushrooms when being cooked will also answer the same purpose, and be distinguished by the same process.

781. MUSHROOMS AU GRATIN.

Select a dozen large mushrooms; cut the stalks and remove the skin; place the mushrooms (the hollow part upwards) in a well buttered sauté-pan; fill them with a similar preparation to that for stuffed tomatoes, but substitute the cut stalks chopped fine for mushrooms; strew some fine raspings over them, and put the sauté-pan in the hot oven to gratinate for about a quarter of an hour, then dish them up in a pyramidal form, and serve with some good gravy apart.

782. MUSHROOMS À LA BORDELAISE.

Clean and trim the mushrooms as in the foregoing, put them in a frying-pan with some salad oil and a clove or two of garlic chopped very fine; fry over a moderate fire for ten or twelve minutes, and season with salt, pepper, and a little chopped parsley. When done, squeeze the juice of half a lemon, dish up the mushrooms, and serve.

783. MUSHROOMS À LA MILANAISE.

Select, clean, and trim some nice mushrooms, marinade them for an hour in a little oil, vinegar, salt, and pepper; after which wipe and flour them; then pass them in the yolks of eggs well beaten and mixed with some grated Parmesan cheese, seasoned with salt, pepper, and allspice, and fry in butter and oil, previously made hot in a frying-pan for that purpose. When of a nice brown colour and crisp, dish up and serve.

REMARKS ON ONIONS.

The qualities and virtue of the onion are great, and they will never be too much known or appreciated.

The onion is the most wholesome of all vegetables, and is at the same time a safeguard against many ailments.

Whenever and wherever a person is suffering from any infectious fever, let a peeled onion be kept on a plate in the room of the patient. No one will ever catch the disease, provided the said onion be replaced every day by one freshly peeled, as then it will have absorbed the whole of the poisonous atmosphere of the room, and become black.

Onions are good for a cold, cooked as well as raw; they can be served as a vegetable, and are constantly in request for culinary purposes.

Garlic is also a safeguard against cholera, by keeping a clove in the mouth as you would a lozenge for cough.

784. STEWED ONIONS.

Peel four Spanish onions of equal size, and boil them for a quarter of an hour in plain water; drain and put them in a sauté-pan, previously spread with fresh butter; moisten with a good pint of broth, and season with salt, pepper, and a dessert-spoonful of pounded sugar. Put them in a hot oven to bake for about twenty minutes, taking care to baste them often when nearly done, set the pan over a brisk fire, roll the onions in their liquor, and when well glazed, dish up, pour the remainder of the glaze over, and serve.

Note.—Onions can also be served stewed in milk. Proceed as above, but substitute a quart of milk for the broth.

785. REMARKS ON SALADS AND SALAD DRESSING.

Man eats nearly everything, either cooked or uncooked, and foremost among the latter are herbs and roots, prepared for food with special condiments and ingredients, and called salad.

The raw materials used in France and Italy for salads are numerous and varied: for instance, celeriac, radishes, rampion, beetroot-bulb, and the potent onion; the stems and leaf-stalks of asparagus, celery, purslane and arti-. chokes; the leaves of lettuce, endive, cress, dandelion, and chicory; the flowers of the bitter pungent nasturtium, and the fruits and seed-pods of cucumbers, capsicums, tomatoes, beans, peas, and the like; as a matter of fact, there are more things in earth and field capable of salad treatment than the somewhat prejudiced English gastronomic philosophy ever dreamt of.

There is an art in dressing a salad really well, as no ingredient should be more prominent in its taste than the other. There must be neither too much of it nor too much in it, but just enough of each.

Although many men of high social positions have won

honour and distinction in salad making, the gift of preparing such tasty delicacies is essentially womanly. To her delicate fingers must be left the care of washing the leaves separately and drying them by affectionate pressure in a white cloth; let her reach the acme of perfection by rubbing the mystic "chapon" or crust of bread with the fragrant clove of garlic. Let her dry the salad-bowl, and put the pepper in with moderation and the salt to taste; then, like one of the five wise virgins, she will have her olive oil to hand, to pour in two and a half tablespoonfuls to each one of French vinegar, together with a touch of mustard; and if to these are added half a teaspoonful of chopped tarragon or chevril, and the whole be properly stirred and blended with a wooden spoon and fork, she will have concocted the best salad dressing desirable, and will only have to add, when required, the carefully-wiped leaves and "chapon" and toss them about, to bid them absorb the magic mixture.

In addition to the above-mentioned herbs, plain boiled potatoes, carrots, cauliflower, beetroot, haricot beans, truffles, and any kind of cold cooked fish, lobster, crab, and eggs, are also made into salads. Let the potatoes, carrots, beetroot, truffles, and eggs be thinly sliced, and the cauliflowers cut into small heads; substitute chopped onion for garlic, or omit it altogether if not agreeable, and spread a teaspoonful of finely-chopped parsley.

786. REMARKS ON SANDWICHES AND CANAPES.

Sandwiches are made with ham, beef, chicken, pickled tongue, smoked salmon and herrings, tinned sardines and anchovies (fish as well as paste), caviare, hard-boiled eggs, salad, watercress, or mustard cress. With respect to meat sandwiches, the process is always the same. Select a tin loaf, which should be a day stale, cut as many slices one eighth of an inch thick as there are sandwiches required; then blend with a knife a little mustard with fresh butter, spread this on the slices of bread, cover evenly one half of these with the meat, previously cut very thin for that purpose, then reverse the other half slices of buttered bread over the meat. Press the sandwiches slightly with the hand, and pile four of them together; then trim them with a sharp knife, by cutting off all the crust, and cut them through either in square or triangular form and dish them up on a napkin.

Note.—When beef or chicken sandwiches are made, salt should be sprinkled over the meat before being covered, and with chicken the mustard must be omitted.

787. SARDINES ON TOAST.

Fish sandwiches are made differently to those of meat or poultry. The slices of bread are toasted and buttered whilst hot, then sardines, split in halves, boned, and scaled, are laid on the toast and served with the fish uppermost.

Note.—Smoked salmon, as well as anchovies and caviare, are served in the same way; but with respect to salmon the slices must be cut very thin, and they can be served either raw or broiled on oiled paper on a gridiron over a slow fire for one minute each side and served when cold.

788. ANCHOVY CANAPES.

Cut as many slices of crumb of bread, two and a half inches long, by one and a half wide and a quarter of an inch thick, as there will be canapés required; fry these in clarified butter to a nice golden colour; and when cold, spread a little anchovy butter on each. Steep some anchovies in cold water; dry them with a cloth; split, bone and trim them; then place four halves lengthwise on each piece of bread, leaving three small spaces between each fillet; fill the first with chopped hard-boiled yolk of egg, the middle with chopped parsley, and the third with chopped hard-boiled white of egg; dish on a napkin and serve.

Note.—Anchovy paste can be substituted for the fillets; in that case, after having spread the paste over the bread, add a slice of hard-boiled egg in the centre.

789. SMOKED HERRING CANAPES.

Cut and fry the bread as described in 788; spread these pieces with anchovy butter, and cover them with smoked herrings, previously trimmed, skinned, boned, and cut into fillets lengthwise, and steeped in olive oil for some four hours, then wiped and moistened again with fresh oil; and serve, properly dressed, on a napkin.

CHAPTER XVIII.

REMARKS ON PASTE AND SWEET DISHES.

I HAVE already given the recipes for ordinary paste (No. 95) to make tagliatelli with, and puff paste (Nos. 318 and 319) for patties, bouchées, pies, &c. ;—I will now proceed with a proper description of paste for raised pies, short paste for tarts, brioche paste, almond paste, &c., &c., to make cakes and pastry with.*

790. SHORT PASTE FOR RAISED PIES.

Put one pound of sifted flour on the slab, spread it out in the centre, then add a teaspoonful of salt, a quarter of a pound of butter, and a gill and a half of cold water. Proceed to work the whole together with the hands into a very firm paste in the following manner: When the ingredients have been worked into a paste, bring it to the edge of the slab, then use the palms of both hands alternately with great force to spread and divide the paste into small parts. Sprinkle a few drops of water over the paste and knead it together, this is called "breaking and kneading" and must be repeated four times. The paste must then be gathered

---

* With respect to pastry and sweet dishes, their names and styles are legion, and are so complicated in their shapes, colours, and tastes, that they furnish enough materials for a large work of their own. I will limit myself to simply giving what I consider the most useful and practical recipes, and at the same time recommend Mr. Jules Gouffé's most valuable "Royal Book of Pastry and Confectionery" to those who wish to know more on this subject.

up, placed in a clean cloth, pressed together, and is ready for use.

791. SHORT PASTE FOR TARTS.

Spread a pound of sifted flour on the slab with a hollow in the centre, then add half a pound of butter, two ounces of pounded sugar, a pinch of salt, two whole eggs, and rather more than a gill of water. Work these together with the hands to a firm paste, and use it to cover fruit tarts, and lining tartlets, &c.

792. BRIOCHE PASTE.

Spread a quarter of a pound of sifted flour on the slab, with a small well in the centre; then put half an ounce of German yeast in it, and dissolve with a little tepid water; when this is done add sufficient water to mix the whole into a rather soft paste. Knead this into the form of a round ball, put it into a stewpan capable of containing three times its quantity, score it with a knife round the sides. Put the lid on, and set to rise in a rather warm place. In summer the fermentation will proceed satisfactorily if it is merely placed on the kitchen table, or in some such place of moderate warmth. This is termed setting the sponge. Meanwhile put three-quarters of a pound of flour on the slab, spread as before with a well in the centre, put a teaspoonful each of salt and pounded sugar, together with two tablespoonfuls of water to dissolve them, after which add ten ounces of butter and six whole eggs. Work the whole together with the hands, until well mixed, first by rubbing it with both fists held flat on the slab, and moving them to and fro, so as to thoroughly reduce any remaining lumps in the paste. By the time the paste is mixed, the sponge will probably have risen sufficiently. To be perfect, it must rise to three times the original size. When spread out on the paste prepared to receive it, it should have the appearance of a sponge, from which it takes its name.

Both the above should then be thoroughly mixed together, and placed in a napkin spread in a basin, with a little flour shaken over; shake again a little flour over the paste, fold the ends of the napkin over all, and set the basin in a cool place free from any current of air.

This kind of paste should be made the evening previous to the day it is required. The first thing the following morning, the brioche paste must be turned off the napkin on to the slab; shake some flour under and over it; fold the paste over half a dozen times, pressing it down with the knuckles each time; put the paste back into the napkin in the same way as before; and about three hours afterwards knead again in a similar manner, previously to its being baked.

If this paste when finished, appears to be full of small globules of air, and is perfectly elastic to the touch, it is certain to be well made.

After that, spread slightly with butter a baking-sheet, and form the paste into buns or rolls; egg these well with the paste-brush, make a little round incision on the top, and bake in a brisk oven for about twenty-five minutes.

Note.—Parmesan or Gruyère cheese is sometimes introduced in brioches, in which case a quarter of a pound of the former should be grated, or the same quantity of the latter cut up in dice and well mixed with the paste.

793. ALMOND PASTE.

Blanch in boiling water for three minutes half a pound of Jordan almonds; cool, peel, wash, drain, and wipe them in a cloth; then pound them to a paste in a mortar; moisten with a few drops of lemon juice while they are being pounded, to prevent them from turning oily; when this is done, add to the mortar half a pound of butter, half a pound of pounded sugar, one tablespoonful of orange-flower water, and a pinch of salt; pound all these well together, adding three eggs, broken one after the other; when well mixed, put in a basin. Make one pound of puff paste as described in No. 319, give it five turns, cut it into two equal pieces, and roll with the rolling-pin each separately to half an inch thick, then put one half on a buttered baking-sheet, spread the almond paste on it, leaving a margin of about one inch and a half all round; wet the edge of the paste and lay the other piece over, press with the thumb all round to stick the two together, egg the top, and bake in the oven for fifty minutes. Let the cake cool, then sprinkle some pounded sugar over, and serve.

794. VICTORIA CAKE.

The following ingredients are required to make the above cake: One pound of sifted flour, ten ounces of fresh butter, six eggs, three ounces of pounded sugar, three ounces of pounded almonds, four ounces of dried cherries, two ounces of green citron shred fine, one teaspoonful of cinnamon powder, a gill of whipped cream, half an ounce of German yeast, half a gill of brandy, and one teaspoonful of salt.

Place the butter in a good-sized white kitchen pan, and work it with a clean wooden spoon for about ten minutes, by which time the butter should present the appearance of thick cream; then add three eggs, the cinnamon, pounded sugar and almonds, the cherries, citron, brandy, and about one-fourth part of the flour; work the whole quickly together for a few minutes with the spoon, then add gradually the remainder of the flour and eggs, still working the paste with the wooden spoon. When the lot has been used up, spread the paste out in the centre of the pan, and add to it the yeast and salt dissolved in a spoonful of tepid water, and the cream, whipped first before being added. When the paste is properly mixed, take a tin hoop measuring about six inches in diameter by three deep, line the inside of this hoop with buttered paper cut three and a half inches wide, lay this on a baking-sheet lined also with a sheet of buttered paper, put the paste in the mould and let it rise by fermentation, to twice its original quantity, by keeping it in a moderately warm place, then put in an oven, not too hot, to be baked till of a light colour.

Note.—It is impossible to determine on the exact length of time that this or any other cake should remain in the oven before it is done. This depends mainly upon the construction of the oven, but the way to ascertain whether a cake is properly baked is by running a small wooden skewer down its centre; if this should be found dry and free from paste when withdrawn, the cake may be safely turned out of the hoop, when it will be found of a light colour, and have a smooth surface.

795. PARISIAN CAKE.

Have the following ingredients ready to make the paste required for Parisian cake : One pound of sifted flour, ten ounces of fresh butter, three ounces of pounded sugar, four whole eggs and four yolks, half a pint of cream, four ounces of Jordan almonds and one of bitter ditto, two ounces of candied orange peel, half an ounce of yeast, and a teaspoonful of salt.

Shred in small narrow strips the orange peel. Blanch and remove the hulls from the almonds, then wash and pound them to a very soft paste, adding a few drops of water to prevent them becoming oily, and mix with the cream; let them steep thus for half an hour in a cool place.

For mixing this paste, follow in all respects the directions given for Victoria paste, adding the orange peel after having put the paste in the mould, and mixing it with the yeast dissolved in a little tepid water; after which let it ferment, and bake as described in the foregoing.

Note.—It is advisable to put these cakes back in the oven for two or three minutes after they are turned out of the mould, to prevent their becoming shrivelled on the surface, or shrinking and falling in.

796. SAVOY CAKE.

Ingredients: Four ounces and a half each of potato flour and finest Vienna flour, fourteen eggs, and one pound of pounded sugar. Separate the yolks from the whites of the eggs, put the former in a basin and the whites into an egg-bowl, in a cool place, add the sugar to the yolks, with a pinch of salt and a few drops of either orange, lemon, orange-flower, vanilla, or bitter almond essence.

Work these together with a wooden spoon until the whole presents the appearance of a thick creamy batter, then the whites must be whisked into a firm snowy froth. Meanwhile let both flours be well mixed in with the batter, and as soon as the whites are satisfactorily whisked, mix them also with the paste by adding them in small quantities at first, until it has become smoothly diluted, then add the remainder of the ingredients, and mix thoroughly well together.

Chop very fine one pound of either beef or veal suet, then melt it in a stewpan and strain through a cloth, pour this into the mould, turn it round in all directions, so that the fat may touch all the angles and recesses, afterwards pour it out, and turn the mould on a plate and let it stand in a warm place for a few minutes, that the fat may be entirely drained off; then shake about three-quarters of a pound of finely-pounded sugar into the mould, in order that it may effectually cover the whole of its inside with a perfectly smooth surface. When this is done, pour the mixture in the mould, put this on a baking-sheet in the oven, which must be heated moderately, and particular care taken to keep it closed as much as possible while the cake is baking, and do not increase its temperature. When the cake is of a light colour, it must be turned out of the mould, reversed on the baking-sheet, and returned to the oven for two or three minutes longer.

797. PLUM CAKE.

Ingredients required: One pound and a half each of flour, currants, and butter; one pound each of pounded sugar and dried cherries slightly chopped, and one pound of candied citron, orange and lemon peel in equal quantities all shred small; half a pound of ground almonds, eight whole eggs, half an ounce of ground spice, consisting of cloves, cinnamon, and nutmeg mixed in equal proportions, a teaspoonful of salt, and a pint of brandy.

Put the butter in a large white earthen pan, and work with a wooden spoon until it presents the appearance of a creamy substance; then add gradually the flour, sugar, and eggs, still working the paste with the wooden spoon. When thoroughly mixed, add gradually also the remaining ingredients and work it well together, then pour into a convenient-sized tin hoop (previously lined with double bands of buttered paper) and place it on a baking-sheet with two sheets of buttered paper under the cake, and put it in a moderately-heated oven to bake to a light colour, taking care not to increase the heat during the operation.

798. PLAIN SEED-CAKE.

Ingredients: Six eggs, half a pound each of pounded sugar and butter, a teaspoonful of salt, half an ounce of carraway-seeds, and one quartern of common dough. Spread the dough on the slab, add the whole of the above-named ingredients to it, and work well together with the hands so as to mix the lot well with the dough. The eggs should be added only two at a time. When the paste is ready, put it into a plain mould, previously spread with butter, and put it to rise in a warm place; and as soon as the fermentation has taken place in a satisfactory manner, put the cake in the oven to bake till of a light colour.

799. POUND-CAKE.

Ingredients: One pound each of flour, butter, and pounded sugar; eight eggs, half a gill of brandy, a pinch of salt, and a few drops of orange or lemon essence. Put the butter in a large basin, work with a wooden spoon until it assumes the appearance of a thick cream, then add gradually the flour, sugar and eggs, and when the whole is properly made into a paste, add the brandy, salt, and essence. Mix well together with the spoon, and pour it in any kind of mould, previously spread with butter, or in a tin hoop lined with buttered paper.

800. SAVARIN CAKE.

Ingredients: One pound of flour, two ounces of sugar, ten ounces of fresh butter, eight eggs, two ounces of shred almonds, half an ounce of German yeast, and a teaspoonful of salt.

Put one-fourth of the flour on the slab with the yeast, and proceed to dissolve it as described for making brioche paste, then place in a similar manner in a stewpan in a warm place to ensure its gradual rising. In the meantime dissolve the salt with a teaspoonful of tepid water in a large white pan or basin, put the remainder of the flour with the butter, sugar, and four eggs; mix the whole together with the right hand, beating up the paste until it easily leaves the sides of the pan, then break in the other four eggs, and work it for five minutes longer; when the sponge has risen to twice its original quantity, add it and mix it well with the paste. Butter a cylinder mould, strew this with the shred almonds, half fill the mould with the paste, let it stand in a moderate temperature, and when it has risen to the top of the mould, put the savarin to bake in a moderate oven for about an hour. When done turn the cake out of the mould, let it cool for about fifteen minutes, then pour over some hot syrup flavoured with curaçao or other liqueur, and serve warm.

801. BABA.

Ingredients: One pound of flour, ten ounces of butter, two ounces of pounded sugar, three ounces of Muscatel raisins, two ounces of currants, one ounce of candied citron, a small pinch of saffron (infused in half a gill of boiling water), half a gill of either brandy or rum, a teaspoonful of salt, eight eggs, and half an ounce of German yeast.

Dissolve the yeast with one-fourth of flour as in No. 800, and let it rise in the same manner; meanwhile spread out the remainder of the flour so as to form a well in the centre, dissolve in this the salt with a few drops of tepid water, then with it put the butter, sugar, and broken eggs; mix the lot thoroughly with the hands on the slab, and work it well by gathering the paste up closely with the hands, and jerk it down on the other part of the paste for about five minutes, and as soon as the sponge is sufficiently risen, spread it over the paste and mix both lightly together; add the stoned raisins and some well-washed currants, candied citron chopped fine, the rum, and the infusion of saffron; work the whole well together, spread a large mould with butter; half fill it with the paste, and put it in a warm place until it rises to the top of the mould, bake it in a moderately-heated oven to a golden colour, when done turn the baba out of the mould on to a dish, and serve.

Note.—The rum or brandy may be omitted, and the baba served with a sauce composed of apricot jam warmed up in a stewpan with half a pint of syrup and a gill of rum, and poured over the baba.

802. GENOESE CAKE.

Ingredients: Half a pound each of flour, pounded sugar, and butter, four eggs, half a gill of brandy, and a good pinch of salt.

Mix the flour, sugar, eggs, brandy, and salt well together in a basin with a wooden spoon; then add the butter (merely melted by the side of the fire); work this well with the paste; pour it afterwards on a baking-sheet, previously spread with butter, to the thickness of about an eighth of an inch, and bake in a moderately-heated oven to a light colour; when done, turn it on a sheet of paper, and cut or stamp it out either in circular, oblong, oval, angular, leaf-like, or any other fancy shapes; these should then be decorated with white of egg and sugar prepared as for meringues (No. 867), and ornamented with currants, &c.

803. GINGER CAKE.

Ingredients: One pound of flour, twelve ounces each of fresh butter and pounded sugar, two ounces of ground Jamaica ginger, and eight yolks of eggs.

Work the whole of the above-named ingredients into a paste on the slab, then gather this into a compact mass and separate into four parts, roll these to the thickness of the sixth of an inch, and with a tin cutter stamp out as many cakes as the paste will produce; place them on a slightly buttered baking-sheet, pass a paste-brush over when they are about half done, shake some sugar over, and set them back in the oven to finish baking of a very light colour.

804. SPANISH CAKE.

Ingredients required: Half a pint of water, a quarter of a pound of butter, two ounces of pounded sugar, five ounces of flour, three eggs, a few drops of orange essence, two ounces of chopped almonds, and a pinch of salt.

Put the water, butter, salt, and sugar into a stewpan on the fire, and as soon as these begin to boil withdraw the stewpan; add the flour, stir the whole well together with a wooden spoon for about three minutes, when the paste should be of a soft and compact appearance, then add the essence and one egg; mix these well with the paste, then mix in the other two eggs, and if the paste should be stiff, add another egg, or the yolk only may be added; this paste, when properly made, should be laid out on a baking-sheet in small round balls the size of a pigeon's egg, and egged over with a paste-brush, then the chopped almonds must be mixed with a tablespoonful of pounded sugar and a very small quantity of white of egg, and strewn over the balls with a little sifted sugar shaken over, and baked of a very light colour, then served either plain or garnished with cream or any kind of preserve.

805. MADELEINES.

These are made with the same kind of paste as for Genoese cakes, to which currants, dried cherries, candied peel, or angelica may be added. When the paste is ready, pour it into a sufficient number of small fluted or plain madeleine moulds previously buttered inside, then place them on a baking-sheet, and bake in an oven of moderate heat. When properly baked turn out of the moulds, and let them get cold before serving.

806. RICE CAKE.

Put one pound of pounded sugar in a whipping-bowl with sixteen eggs; whip both together over a very slow fire for fifteen minutes; then add half a pound of ground rice, three-quarters of a pound of fresh butter slightly melted in half a gill of Maraschino. Mix the whole lightly together; then butter and flour a cylinder mould three inches high, put the paste in it, and bake it in a moderate oven. When done, turn the cake out of the mould, glaze it by pouring over a coating of apricot jam reduced with syrup, and sprinkle over the hot jam an ounce of chopped almonds, and let the cake cool before serving.

807. PASTE FOR SPONGE CAKE AND BISCUITS.

Ingredients: Eight eggs, one pound of pounded sugar, one ounce of vanilla sugar, and a quarter of a pound each of wheaten and potato flour.

Separate the yolks from the whites of eggs; put the latter in the egg-bowl and the former in a basin, which mix with both sugars, and work with a wooden spoon. Whisk the whites, add them lightly to the yolks, then sprinkle both flours, and mix well together to a smooth paste. Meanwhile have ready spread with butter two moulds kept hot at the mouth of the oven, and strewn with fine dried sifted sugar inside; fill the moulds, within an inch from the border, with the paste, and put in a well-heated oven to bake. When done, which will be when a trussing needle thrust into the centre of the cake comes out dry and free from dampness, turn them out of the moulds; and when cold, trim off the paste that comes above the moulds.

808. ITALIAN BISCUITS.

Ingredients required: Six eggs, half a pound of sugar, five ounces of flour, a few drops of essence of either lemon or orange, six ounces of chopped almonds, and a pinch of salt.

Break the eggs, and divide the whites from the yolks by putting the latter into a basin and the former in a whipping-bowl; add the pounded sugar, essence, and salt to the yolks, work these well with a wooden spoon till they present the appearance of a thick creamy batter. Then add half the flour, and mix it well in, after which whip the whites of the six eggs to a firm froth, and mix them lightly with the paste with the remainder of the flour, taking care to keep the mixture as firm and light as possible. Butter and flour a baking-sheet, fill a biscuit forcer with some of the paste, and force it out gently on the baking-sheet in round or oval shapes twice the size of a five-shilling piece. When the whole of the paste is used up in this manner, strew the chopped almonds equally over the biscuits; then shake over the surface some pounded sugar, and bake them of a very light colour in rather a slack oven.

Note.—These biscuits are most appropriate for dessert.

809. CHAMPAGNE BISCUITS.

Ingredients: Half a pound each of pounded sugar, fresh butter, and flour; eight eggs, a quarter of an ounce of carraway seeds, and a pinch of salt.

Put the butter in a basin, and work it with a wooden spoon until of a thick creamy appearance; then add gradually the sugar, flour, yolks of eggs, the carraway seeds, and salt. Work those well together with the spoon, then mix the eight whites of eggs, previously whisked firm for the purpose; lay a sheet of paper on a baking-sheet, fill a biscuit-forcer with some of the paste, and proceed to force out the paste on the sheet of paper in the shape of a finger three inches long by one wide, leaving an inch space between each biscuit; shake over some sifted sugar; when all the paste has been used, bake in a moderate oven for about ten minutes, then let them cool before removing them from the paper.

Note.—These biscuits are only served for dessert.

810. APPLE TART.

Make a puff paste (No. 319) at six turns, and roll it to a quarter of an inch thick. Butter an open tart mould, line it on a baking-sheet with the paste, and trim it on a level with the top of the mould; fill this with apples, previously peeled, the cores removed and cut in quarters, or slices about a quarter of an inch thick; add a sufficient quantity of pounded sugar to sweeten the apples, and strew over the rind of a lemon rubbed on sugar and then scraped off. Cover the tart with puff paste, egg it over with a paste-brush, make some fanciful, but slight incisions on the top with the point of a knife, and let it bake of a light golden colour; when done, turn it carefully out of the mould, shake some sifted sugar upon, and serve when cold.

811. FRUIT TARTS IN GENERAL.

When apricots, peaches, or any kind of large plums, are used for making tarts, the stones must be removed. In other respects they are invariably made and baked as the foregoing. Cherry, damson, raspberry, and currant tarts are made with the same directions, except that the stones of the two former need not be removed.

812. APPLE FRITTERS.

Peel and cut the apples in rather thick slices, remove the cores with a tin cutter, and put the slices in a basin with about half a gill of brandy and a tablespoonful of pounded sugar, as well as some grated peel of either lemon or orange; toss the slices gently in the liquor, and let them steep thus for several hours if possible. Meanwhile make a batter paste (No. 317). Warm up to the right temperature a proper quantity of fat in the frying-kettle, and a quarter of an hour before serving drain well on a cloth the slices of apples; dip each of these separately in the batter, and drop them quickly in the frying fat; accelerate the fire when all the slices are in, stir with the skimmer, and when the fritters are crisp and of a nice golden colour, drain them on a cloth, shake some sifted sugar on both sides, and dish up on a napkin on a hot dish, and serve.

813. PINE-APPLE FRITTERS.

Trim the pine-apple without waste, cut it into small pieces the size of a finger, steep them in a basin with a little Maraschino and a spoonful of pounded sugar; then proceed to dip each piece in the batter, as described in the preceding number, and fry them in every respect as apple fritters.

814. ORANGE FRITTERS.

Peel the number of oranges required for fritters, divide them into quarters, remove the pips, and steep them in a basin with half a gill of brandy and a spoonful of pounded sugar; toss these quarters well, so as to enable the brandy to be absorbed. Meanwhile prepare some light-made batter

(No. 317), and proceed (when about to send to the table) in the same way as for apple fritters.

815. BEIGNETS FRITTERS.

Put a pint of water into a stewpan, with a quarter of a pound of fresh butter, one ounce of pounded sugar, and a small pinch of salt; boil it; then draw the pan away from the fire, add gradually while stirring with a wooden spoon, half a pound of flour and the grated peel of a lemon; stir this over the fire four minutes longer, then take it away from the fire and break in one egg, mix it thoroughly before adding another, and continue in the same way until five eggs have been used, if the paste is rather stiff, use one more, as this must be of such consistency as not to spread when dropped from the spoon. Warm some frying-fat in the frying kettle; when hot, draw it to the side of the fire, spread the paste one inch and a half thick on a stewpan cover, hold the cover in the left hand over the frying kettle, dip the hooked handle of a kitchen ladle in the hot fat, and with it detach portions of the paste, the size of a walnut, and let them drop in the hot fat. When the paste has been all used, push the kettle on the fire, and stir the fritters with the skimmer till done, which can be ascertained by trying them with the finger; if found of an even yellow colour, and firm to the touch, they are ready; then drain them on a wire sieve, sprinkle with pounded sugar, dish on a hot napkin, and serve.

Note.—The fat for frying sweet fritters must be quite fresh, and only used for frying similar sweet dishes, and on no account should fat be used in which fish has been fried.

816. BROWN-BREAD PUDDING.

Ingredients required: Three quarters of a pound of brown-bread crumbs, six ounces of pounded sugar, six eggs, half a pint of whipped cream, a little grated lemon rind, a pinch of cinnamon powder, one pound of morella cherries, and a good pinch of salt.

Mix the bread crumbs, sugar, the yolks of eggs, lemon, cinnamon, salt, and whipped cream, well together in a basin, then add the whisked whites of six eggs, and set it aside. Spread a plain mould with butter, strew it with brown-bread crumbs, and put a large spoonful of the mixture at the bottom of the mould; then arrange a layer of cherries upon it, cover these with some of the mixture, then another layer of cherries, and so on till all has been put in the mould. This must now be placed in a moderately-heated oven to bake for about an hour. When done turn it out of the mould on a dish, pour some cherry sauce around, and serve.

817. SEMOLINA PUDDING.

Ingredients: Twelve ounces of semolina flour, six ounces of pounded sugar, a quarter of a pound of butter, six eggs, a pint of good milk, a tablespoonful of orange-flower water, and a pinch of salt.

Mix the semolina with the sugar, orange-flower water, the half of the butter, two eggs, milk, and salt, in a stewpan over the fire until it boils; continue stirring till the paste is perfectly smooth and ceases to adhere to the sides of the pan, when it must be withdrawn from the fire, and the remainder of the eggs and butter added gradually and well mixed with the paste; then spread the inside of a mould with butter, fill it with the paste, put the bottom of the mould in a deep sauté-pan half filled with boiling water, place in the oven to bake for about an hour and a quarter. When done, turn the pudding out of the mould on a hot dish, pour either a custard or fruit sauce over, and serve.

818. CABINET PUDDING.

This pudding is made with sponge cake. Spread the inside of a plain mould with butter, stone two ounces of raisins, pick, wash, and dry the same quantity of currants, cut in small dice about an ounce of candied citron and two ounces of dried cherries; lay at the bottom of the mould some of the mixed fruit, on these lay some slices of sponge cake, and continue alternate layers till the mould is two-thirds full. Then beat the yolks of six eggs for about a minute, and add while stirring a pint of boiled milk, half a gill of brandy, and a quarter of a pound of pounded sugar. When the lot is well mixed together, pass slowly through a tammy into the mould; let it thus stand for a few minutes, after which cook the pudding in a bain-marie for half an hour, then turn it out of the mould on to a hot dish, and serve with a custard sauce or a sauce made as follows:—Put the yolks of six eggs into a stewpan with half a pint of syrup, stir this over the fire until the sauce coats the spoon, then add a gill of brandy, or some other liqueur, pass the sauce through a tammy, and pour it over the pudding before serving.

819. CHESTNUT PUDDING.

Peel and boil two pounds of fine chestnuts, remove the second skin, and rub the pulp through a fine wire sieve; place the purée in a stewpan with a pint of milk or cream, two ounces of butter, a quarter of a pound of sugar, a teaspoonful of vanilla essence, and a pinch of salt; stir the lot over the fire until the mixture thickens, then quicken the stirring so as to prevent the contents from adhering to the bottom of the pan, and as soon as it detaches itself from the sides of the said pan remove it from the fire, add the yolks of six eggs, properly beaten, and the whites of four, whipped firm. When these have been well mixed together with the spoon, pour it into a plain mould well spread with butter, and boil in a bain-marie for about an hour. When done, turn the pudding carefully out of the mould into a hot dish, and serve with a little apricot jam, previously warmed and diluted for the purpose.

820. GINGER PUDDING.

Put a pint of good milk into a stewpan on the fire, with a quarter of a pound each of sugar and butter, and a pinch of salt. As soon as it boils, draw the stewpan from the fire; sprinkle six ounces of flour. Stir the whole together, put it back on the fire, stirring the while for five minutes longer, then remove the pan from the fire; add gradually, one by one while stirring, six eggs and six ounces of preserved ginger cut into small pieces. Mix the lot well together, spread a mould with butter, pour the mixture in it, and cook in a bain-marie for about an hour and a half; then turn the pudding out of the mould into a hot dish, and serve with custard sauce, made with syrup from the ginger, poured over it.

821. LEMON PUDDING.

Rub on sugar the peel of four lemons, put this with the juice of two in a basin with a pint of good milk, the yolks of eight eggs, and the whites of three whisked, a quarter of a nutmeg grated, a good pinch of cinnamon powder, a small pinch of salt, and six ounces of pounded sugar. Mix the lot well together with a wooden spoon, after which put a border of puff paste round the edge of a pie-dish, spread the inside with butter, pour the mixture into it, and put in a moderately-heated oven to bake for about half an hour. When done, shake over some sifted sugar, and serve.

822. BREAD AND BUTTER PUDDING.

Cut about a pound of thin slices of bread and butter, and put them in a pie-dish, which must only be half full, together with a quarter of a pound of well-washed and dried currants, and two ounces of chopped candied citron between the slices. Boil one pint of milk with the peel of a lemon, a pinch of salt, and six ounces of sugar; break four eggs into a basin beat them up with a fork, then add the milk gradually to them. Strain the lot through a tammy into the pie dish; let it soak thus for ten minutes, and bake in a well-heated oven for half an hour. When done, shake over the top some sifted sugar, and serve.

823. COLLEGE PUDDING.

Chop up three-quarters of a pound of beef marrow, and put it in a basin with one ounce each of candied lemon, orange peel, and candied citron, all chopped coarse, also half a pound of well-washed and dried currants, half a pound of bread crumbs, and a quarter of a pound of pounded sugar; mix these well together with the hands, then add three eggs, half a gill of brandy and one of sherry; work the lot well together with a wooden spoon; butter two moulds slightly, put the mixture in them, and bake the puddings in a moderately-heated oven for half an hour. When done, turn the puddings out of the moulds on to a hot dish, and serve with a sauce made as follows:—Put the yolks of three eggs into a stewpan with one ounce of pounded sugar and a gill of sherry; whisk the eggs over the fire without boiling; when the sauce thickens, pour it over the puddings, and serve.

824. TAPIOCA PUDDING.

Put a pint of milk into a stewpan with six ounces of tapioca, three ounces of sugar, one ounce of butter, a pinch of salt, and the grated rind of half a lemon; stir the lot over the fire till it boils, then cover the stewpan and let it simmer for a quarter of an hour, after which draw the stewpan from the fire, add the yolks of three eggs, and the whites of two whipped; mix the lot well together, and pour it into a pie-dish previously spread with butter, put the pudding in a moderately-heated oven to bake for about half an hour, and serve.

Note.—Sago, semolina, rice, vermicelli, macaroni, and tagliatelli can be prepared and baked in the same manner, and vanilla or orange-flower water essence substituted for lemon rind.

825. RICE PUDDING.

Wash half a pound of Italian rice, and boil it for fifteen minutes in a stewpan with a pint and a half of good milk, a quarter of a pound of pounded sugar, a pinch of salt, and a small stick of vanilla or any other flavouring, after which draw the stewpan from the fire, add the yolks of three eggs well beaten, mix the lot well together, and pour it into a pie-dish previously buttered; bake in a well-heated oven for twenty minutes, and serve.

826. PLUM PUDDING.

Put in a large basin three-quarters of a pound each of picked and finely-chopped beef suet, stoned raisins, well-washed and picked currants, moist sugar, bread crumbs, peeled russet apples, with the cores removed and cut in small dice, and a quarter of a pound each of candied citron, orange, and lemon, all cut in small dice. Mix these thoroughly with three pounded cloves, a good pinch each of cinnamon, nutmeg, and salt, a gill of sherry, half a gill of brandy, and four eggs, one at a time. When the lot has been well worked together with the hands, it should remain in a cool place for at least six hours before setting the pudding to boil. I advise the mixture to be made the day before the pudding is required. Then a pudding basin must be buttered and filled with the mixture. Fasten a strong cloth over the top (previously spread with butter or flour) by bringing the four ends round the bottom of the basin, where they must be tied securely. Meanwhile have a stock-pot, with about six quarts or more of boiling water, ready on the stove; place a strong stick or iron bar across the pot, hang the pudding to it with strings to prevent the basin touching the bottom of the pot, and let it boil for at least six hours, (if more all the better), taking care to replenish the pot with boiling water when wanted.

When done, turn the pudding out of the mould on to a hot dish, sprinkle it with pounded sugar, pour half a pint of warm brandy or rum over it before serving, and light with a match when the pudding is on the table.

Note.—The following sauce is a very good substitute for rum or brandy:—Put the yolks of four eggs into a stewpan with two ounces of pounded sugar, a gill of sherry or any other white wine, the peel of half a lemon rubbed on sugar, and a small pinch of salt. Whisk this sharply over a slow fire until it assumes a frothy appearance, then pour it over the pudding.

827. ROLEY-POLEY PUDDING.

Pick and chop very fine one pound of beef suet, put it in a basin with one pound of flour and a good pinch of salt, mix these to a stiffish paste with about three gills of cold water, then roll it out to a quarter of an inch thick and of an oblong shape; spread any kind of jam on the paste, and roll this round to the form of a long roll. Roll the pudding afterwards in a buttered cloth, tie both ends up tightly with string, and tie it with string lengthways, to keep it in shape; then drop it in plenty of boiling water, and let it boil for about an hour and a half. When done, turn the pudding carefully out of the cloth, put it on a hot dish, and serve.

828. GOOSEBERRY PUDDING.

Make half a pound of suet paste as described in the previous number, line a pudding-basin with it, and fill it up with picked gooseberries; spread a layer of moist or brown sugar over the fruit, cover this with a round of paste, and tie a cloth tightly over the top, then set it in a stewpan full of boiling water to boil for an hour and a quarter; when done, remove the cloth, turn the pudding out of the basin on to a hot dish, spread some brown sugar over, and serve.

Note.—Currant and raspberry pudding, cherry, apricot, greengage, damson, and black currant puddings, are all made in the same way.

829. APPLE PUDDING.

Line a pudding basin with half a pound of suet paste made as in the foregoing, then cut some cooking apples in quarters, peel, core, and fill the basin with them, add two or three cloves and a little chopped lemon peel, spread a layer of moist sugar. Cover the apples with paste, then tie the top with a cloth. Boil and serve the pudding as directed above.

830. PANCAKES.

Mix half a pound of flour in a basin with a tablespoonful of pounded sugar, a small pinch of salt, a gill of milk, and three eggs. Melt two ounces of butter in a stewpan with three gills of milk on the fire, and add it gradually to the paste in the basin, so as to make a smooth batter; if found to be too thick, a little more milk must be added; melt a quarter of a pound of fresh butter in a small stewpan, and keep it by the side of the fire. Warm a pancake-pan, butter it with a brush dipped in the melted butter, then pour in some of the batter so as to cover the bottom of the pan when spread. Fry the pancake until it is coloured on one side, then toss it over to colour it on the other side; when done, slip on to a hot dish, shake over some sifted sugar, and roll it up. Repeat the same thing till all the batter is used up; lay the pancakes in close circular order in double or treble rows, and serve them very hot, with some cut lemons on a plate.

Note.—The batter can be flavoured with a dessert-spoonful of orange-flower water.

831. PANCAKES WITH JAM.

Prepare a batter as in the foregoing, and as each pancake is fried spread any kind of jam upon it, roll it up, and place on a dish in the oven; when all the pancakes are fried, sprinkle some pounded sugar over them, glaze them with a red-hot salamander, dish up on a napkin as before described, and serve.

832. OMELET SOUFFLÉ.

Separate the whites of six eggs from the yolks, put the whites in the egg-bowl, and the yolks in a basin with a quarter of a pound of pounded sugar and a teaspoonful of orange-flower water or any other essence, or the grated peel of a lemon; mix these well with a wooden spoon for five minutes, then whip the white of the eggs to a firm froth and mix them lightly with the yolks, after which butter a silver or baking-dish, pour the egg mixture over as lightly as possible, smooth over in the form of a dome with a knife, and put it in a moderately-heated oven to bake for ten or twelve minutes; when ready shake over the omelet some pounded sugar, and send it immediately to the table.

Note.—All soufflés should, as soon as taken out of the oven, be at once sent to the table, and in order that this should be done with success, the servant must wait in the kitchen for it, otherwise if the soufflé is left too long, even in the oven, it will collapse and get spoiled.

833. CHOCOLATE SOUFFLÉ.

Break a quarter of a pound of chocolate into pieces, put it in a stewpan over the fire with a gill of milk, and work with a wooden spoon to a smooth paste, then add a quarter of a pound of flour, two ounces of pounded sugar, a small pinch of salt, and three gills of milk. Stir this to a nice batter, then add the yolks of six eggs, two at a time, and mix well, after which whisk the whites of six eggs into a firm froth, and add them lightly with the paste; butter a dish as in the previous number, pour the batter into it, and arrange it as described in the foregoing; then put it in the oven to bake for about twenty minutes, sprinkle over some sifted sugar, and serve the soufflé at once.

834. VANILLA SOUFFLÉ.

Boil a pint of milk and let it get cold, then mix with it a quarter of a pound of flour, three ounces of sugar, two ounces of vanilla sugar, and a small pinch of salt. Stir this over the fire until it boils; then withdraw the stewpan from the fire, add the yolks of six eggs, mixing in only two at a time, and when properly mixed add the whites of the eggs previously whisked firm, and proceed to bake the soufflé as described for chocolate soufflé, and serve quickly.

835. COFFEE SOUFFLÉ.

Put a quarter of a pound of roasted coffee beans into a stewpan with a pint and a half of boiling milk, let it boil for two minutes; cover the stewpan closely, and let it thus stand for an hour, after which strain the milk through a pointed strainer, and with it proceed to make a batter as described for vanilla soufflé with similar ingredients, but omit the vanilla sugar; bake and serve the soufflé in the same way.

836. CHEESE SOUFFLÉ.

Grate a quarter of a pound of Parmesan cheese, and half that quantity of Gruyère cheese; mix a quarter of a pound of flour in a stewpan over the fire with a pint of milk, a teaspoonful of salt, and two pinches of pepper until it boils, then withdraw the stewpan; mix in the grated cheese and the yolks of six eggs, added two at a time. Whip the whites of the six eggs very fine, mix them lightly to the paste, and pour into a buttered dish to bake in a moderately-heated oven for about twenty minutes, and serve immediately as previously described.

837. RICE SOUFFLÉ.

Wash a quarter of a pound of Italian rice, then drain and put it in a stewpan, with a pint and a half of milk, a quarter of a pound of sugar, two ounces of vanilla sugar, and a pinch of salt. Simmer the lot very gently for an hour, afterwards let the rice cool a little, and mix in the yolks of six eggs, one at a time. Whip firm the whites of the six eggs, and mix them lightly in the rice; then pour the lot into a buttered dish, and put it in a moderately-heated oven to bake for twenty minutes. Shake some sifted sugar over the soufflé, and serve at once.

838. OMELET WITH RUM.

Break six eggs in a basin, add a teaspoonful of pounded sugar, and a small pinch of salt, beat these with a fork, and fry the omelet as described in No. 253. When cooked, fold on a dish. Sprinkle some sugar over the omelet, glaze with a red-hot iron poker, pour a gill of hot rum over, set fire to it, and serve alight.

839. OMELET WITH APRICOT JAM.

Break six eggs as in No. 838, add a good pinch of pounded sugar and a small one of salt, beat, and fry the omelet with two ounces of good butter, as described; before folding lay three spoonfuls of apricot jam in the centre, then fold the sides of the omelet over the jam, turn it on a hot dish, sprinkle over with sugar, pass a red-hot iron or poker over it, and serve.

Note.—Any kind of jam or preserve may be substituted for apricot jam, and sweet omelets should be served rather moist in the centre.

840. SNOW EGGS.

Boil a quart of milk in a stewpan, with two ounces of sugar and the grated peel of a lemon. Meanwhile break six eggs, put the yolks in a basin and the whites in the egg-bowl, whip to a firm froth, then mix in a quarter of a pound of sifted sugar, and with a spoon drop some of this mixture, about the size of an egg, into the boiling milk. When six spoonfuls have thus been dropped, put the stewpan by the side of the fire, and let the contents simmer for four minutes, turning the whites over when they are set, on one side, and when quite firm, on both sides, drain them on a sieve; repeat the process till all the white mixture is used; let the milk cool a little to make a plain custard with, then add the six yolks of beaten eggs and two ounces of sugar, stir over the fire till the same begins to thicken and forming a coating on the spoon. Withdraw the stewpan from the stove, stir for three minutes longer, then strain the sauce through a pointed strainer, and when quite cold, dish up the eggs in a pyramidal form, pour the custard sauce over, and serve.

841. STEWED APPLES.

Peel eight cooking apples, core and cut them in halves; place them in a stewpan with a quart of water, half a pound of loaf sugar, four cloves, and the peel of a lemon. Set them to simmer very gently till the apples are done, taking care to turn them over when half cooked, then take them out with the skimmer and dish up nicely. Meanwhile reduce the syrup by quick boiling, strain it over the apples, and serve.

Note.—Stewed fruit can be served both hot and cold, but the latter is the best. In that case the syrup should only be poured over the fruit when cold, and just before serving.

842. STEWED PEARS.

Peel very smooth eight stewing pears, and put them whole with their stalks, in a stewpan with a quart of water, half a pound of loaf sugar, a little prepared cochineal, and a small piece of stick of vanilla. Simmer very gently for about an hour (more or less according to the quality and size of the pears), let them cool in their syrup, then dish up; reduce the syrup quickly by half, and when cold, and just before serving, pour it over the pears and serve.

843. STEWED PLUMS.

Select a pound of nice plums; wash and put them in a stewpan with enough water to cover them well, add two ounces of loaf sugar and a piece of cinnamon, simmer for about forty minutes; when done, dish them up, add two ounces of loaf sugar to the syrup, and reduce it by half over a brisk fire; then strain it, and when cold, and just before sending to the table, pour the syrup over the plums and serve.

844. STEWED GREENGAGES.

Select two dozen fine greengages, and put them in a copper sugar-boiler, with half a pound of loaf sugar and three-quarters of a pint of water; when boiling, cover the pan, and let it simmer for ten minutes; then take the greengages out and dish them up, reduce the syrup by half, and when cold, pour it over the fruit, and serve.

845. STEWED MIRABELLE PLUMS.

Select three dozen Mirabelle plums, put them in a copper sugar-boiler, with six ounces of lump sugar and three-quarters of a pint of water. Boil and finish as in the foregoing.

846. STEWED APRICOTS.

Pick a dozen not over-ripe apricots; cut them in halves, remove the stones, break them, take the almonds out, and blanch and peel them. Put half a pint of water, with six ounces of lump sugar, in a copper sugar-boiler; boil it, put in the apricots, and simmer for five minutes, then dish them up; reduce the syrup by half, and when cold pour it over the apricots, place half an almond taken from the stones on each piece of apricot, and serve.

847. STEWED CHERRIES.

Pick a pound of cherries; put a quarter of a pound of lump sugar in a copper sugar-boiler with one quart of water, boil this, and put the cherries in. Cover the pan, and simmer for five minutes; after which dish the cherries, reduce the syrup by half, let it cool, pour it over the cherries, and serve.

848. STEWED FRUIT WITH RICE.

Any kind of stewed fruit can be served with rice; this is a great improvement to the fruit, and makes it, at the same time, a more substantial sweet dish. Blanch half a pound of rice in boiling water for three or four minutes, cool it in cold water, drain, and put into a stewpan with a quart of milk and one ounce of sugar; boil gently until the rice is done, then lay it at the bottom of a dish, dress the stewed fruit on it in a circle, pour over the lot the syrup in which the fruit was cooked, and serve.

Note.—The process of cooking the rice for stewed fruit is always the same, and can be served with as much taste and style hot as well as cold.

849. STEWED DRIED FRENCH PLUMS.

Soak two pounds of dried French plums for a couple of hours in plenty of cold water, then strain and put them in a stewpan with enough cold water to cover them, add the peel of a lemon, a piece of cinnamon, and half a pound of broken lump sugar to it; set the stewpan on the fire to simmer gently for about two hours, or till the plums are soft to the touch; when they are done enough, add half a pint of claret; give this a slight stir over the fire, and as soon as a white scum begins to form on the top, draw the stewpan from the fire, pour the contents in a basin to get cold, and serve properly dished up with its syrup.

Note.—Rice boiled as in No. 848 is also a great improvement when served with stewed plums.

850. APPLE CHARLOTTE.

Peel and core twelve or fifteen nice cooking apples, cut them in thin slices, put them in a sauté-pan with two or three ounces of pounded sugar, and a quarter of a pound of fresh butter, previously melted; toss the apples over the fire till they are soft to the touch, but not cooked. Take a plain round mould, cut some thin slices of crumb of bread, one of about one inch and a half round, some heart-shape pieces, and some narrow strips the height of the mould. Melt some fresh butter in a stewpan, dip the round and heart-shape pieces in it; place the round one in the centre at the bottom of the mould, and the heart-pieces round it overlapping each other, and the points resting on the round piece; dip the strips of bread in butter, and stand them round the sides of the mould, also overlaying one another. Fill the lined mould with the apple, and put it in a hot oven to bake until the bread is crisp and of an even yellow colour; then turn the charlotte out of the mould on to a napkin on a dish, and serve hot.

851. PEAR CHARLOTTE.

Proceed for this as in the foregoing, but substitute pears for apples, and add a little vanilla sugar to the sauté-pan when cooking the pears, then fill up the mould. Bake it in the oven, and serve as above.

852. COFFEE CUSTARDS.

For six custard-cups, boil three cupfuls of milk with one ounce and a quarter of pounded sugar, and when a little cool, mix the yolks of five eggs, a small pinch of salt, and one cup of strong black coffee; when these have been well mixed together, strain it through a silk sieve; have some boiling water in a shallow stewpan. Fill the six custard cups with the custard, place them in the stewpan with boiling water, set this over a slow fire for the water to simmer only very gently; put the cover on the stewpan and some live coals on the cover.

When the custards are set, take off the cover, let them cool in the water; then wipe the cups, put them on a dish, and serve.

853. CHOCOLATE CUSTARDS.

Proceed with the number of custards as directed in the foregoing, mixing the milk with three ounces of melted chocolate instead of coffee, and finish in every way the same.

Note.—Custards flavoured either with vanilla, orange-flower water, or lemon-peel are made and set in the same way as the above.

854. MINCE-MEAT.

Pick, wash, and dry three pounds of currants; stone three pounds of raisins; cut one pound of russet apples in quarters, peel and core them; finely chop half a pound each of candied orange peel, lemon-peel, and candied citron cut in thin slices; chop up the raisins and apples and mix well the lot together in a basin.

Pick and chop very finely one pound of beef suet and one pound of roast lean beef; add both to the basin with the fruit, together with one pound of pounded sugar, one ounce of ground cinnamon, half an ounce of lemon-peel chopped very fine, half an ounce each of pounded cloves and allspice, and a quarter of an ounce of grated nutmeg; mix the whole well together, moistening with half a pint of sherry and a pint of brandy. Put the mince-meat into jars and tie closely down with brown paper.

Note.—Mince-meat should be made at least a fortnight before using it; and if a month, all the better.

855. MINCE PIES.

Make a puff paste of six turns (No. 318), roll it out thin, and with it line some small tartlet-moulds; fill them with mince-meat, cover them with a similar rolled paste, press and cut them round, then egg them over with a paste-brush dipped in yolks; cut a small pattern on the top, and bake in a well-heated oven for about a quarter of an hour. When done take out of the moulds, dish up, and serve.

856. CLARIFIED SYRUP FOR JELLIES.

Whatever quantity of syrup may be required, put three gills of cold water to one pound of finest loaf-sugar into a copper sugar-boiler, and half the white of an egg, whipped with a little water; whisk the lot together on the fire until it boils, then pour a few drops of cold water to enable the scum to rise, which must at once be removed with a silver spoon; let the syrup simmer gently, until the whole of the scum has been thrown up and removed, adding a little more cold water if necessary; then strain the syrup through a napkin or jelly-bag into a basin and put by in a cool place for use.

857. LEMON JELLY.

Calf's-foot, isinglass, and gelatine are the foundations or basis of all kinds of jellies, bavarois creams, and blanc-mange.

I have already described the manner of making a plain calf's-foot jelly (No. 227), which is the most wholesome stiffening to use. Isinglass is the best, being prepared from the bladder of sturgeons. It is perhaps the purest and cleanest, but it is also the dearest; consequently gelatine is generally the stiffening used, on account of its lower cost.

Put two ounces of gelatine in a stewpan with three-quarters of a pound of loaf-sugar and the juice of two lemons. Whisk the whites of two eggs in a basin, mix them with a quart of water, and pour the whole into the stewpan with the gelatine; stir the liquid over the fire with the whisk until it boils; then take the stewpan off the fire, let it cool for a few minutes; after which, pour the contents into the jelly-bag over the yellow peel of four lemons to strain, pour it back again, and again, until it is quite clear.

Should there be no jelly-bag and frame handy, a kitchen stool upside down, with a fine diaper broth-napkin, previously rinsed in hot water, tied to the four legs, and a bain-marie put underneath to receive the strained jelly, will make a very good substitute for a jelly-bag and stand, but the proper jelly-bag is to be preferred.

Press out or squeeze the juice of six lemons; strain through a silk sieve and filter with some filtering or white blotting paper into a water-bottle or decanter. Meanwhile have a three-pint jelly-mould in about three inches of broken rough ice, mix the filtered juice with the jelly, pour it in the mould, and let it set for some two hours. When the jelly is set firm, ten minutes before sending to the table, dip the mould in warm water, wipe with a cloth, shake it gently, so as to free the jelly from the mould without breaking, and turn it out carefully on a dish.

Note.—As there are several kinds of gelatine with more or less stiffening power, it is advisable, after having clarified the jelly, to try a little in the ice first, to see if it be too stiff, in which case a little more syrup may be added.

858. STRAWBERRY JELLY.

Pick the stalks off one pound and a half of nice ripe strawberries, and put them into a basin; boil three pints of clarified syrup and let it cool five minutes; then pour it over the strawberries; cover the basin closely and let them steep thus for an hour; after which, filter the syrup through a jelly-bag. Meanwhile melt two ounces of gelatine on the fire with a little water, strain in the usual way, and when cool mix it with the strawberry syrup. Set a three-pint jelly-mould in plenty of rough ice, pour in a quarter-inch layer of syrup and let it set slightly; then arrange a few fine picked strawberries on it, pour in one or two spoonfuls of syrup to keep the strawberries in position, and let it set; then pour some more syrup in the mould, and when this layer is set, arrange another row of strawberries, and continue the process till the mould is full; place a baking-sheet on the mould with some ice on the top, and let it stand thus, for a couple of hours; when perfectly firm, turn the jelly out of the mould on to a dish, after having dipped it in warm water, as previously described, and serve.

859. ORANGE JELLY.

Prepare this jelly as directed for lemon jelly, substituting orange juice and peel for the lemon, and put a quarter of a pound less of loaf-sugar.

860. MADEIRA JELLY.

Mix one pint of clarified calf's-foot jelly with three gills of clarified syrup in a sugar-boiler on the fire, and when boiling draw the pan away and let it cool; after which, add half a pint of Madeira with a few drops of prepared cochineal and a tablespoonful of filtered lemon-juice; mix the lot thoroughly well, and pour into a mould properly imbedded in the ice; put a baking-sheet with some ice on the top and let it set for two hours; after which, turn the jelly out of the mould on a dish, as described in the foregoing, and serve.

Note.—All liqueur and wine jellies are prepared as directed above; but in cases of sweet liqueurs such as curaçao, Maraschino, crême de noyeau, parfait amour, &c., &c., the proportions of syrup should be decreased by half a gill, and the liqueur increased by the same quantity.

861. BLANC-MANGER FLAVOURED WITH ALMONDS.

Blanch ten ounces of Jordan and one ounce of bitter almonds for two minutes; drain and remove the skins, then pound them in a mortar; moisten with a few drops of water; put the paste in a basin with a pint of water, cover the basin closely with a sheet of kitchen paper, twisted round the border of the basin, and let it stand thus in a cool place for about an hour; after which, strain the milk from off the almonds through a napkin with pressure by wringing it at both ends over a basin.

Melt two and a half ounces of gelatine with half a pound of sugar and one pint and three-quarters of water in a stewpan; stir over the fire till the gelatine is melted, then strain it through a silk sieve, and when cold add it to the strained almond milk with a teaspoonful of orange-flour water; mix the lot well together and pour into a three-pint mould, properly imbedded in ice, as described for lemon jelly; let it remain in the ice for a couple of hours, after which, turn the blanc-manger out of the mould in the same style as a jelly, and serve.

862. COFFEE BAVAROIS CREAM.

Put a quarter of a pound of freshly roasted coffee-beans into a stewpan with a pint and a half of boiling milk, cover the pan and put it aside for two hours, to allow the milk to infuse and draw all the flavour of the coffee. Break the yolks of eight eggs into a stewpan, add ten ounces of pounded sugar; mix these well together with a wooden spoon, and when the milk infusion is ready, strain and add it to the yolks of eggs; stir the lot over the fire with a wooden spoon till the cream or custard begins to thicken, but avoid boiling it, and when it coats the spoon take it off the fire and stir for two minutes longer. Meanwhile have ready one ounce and a half of gelatine, previously steeped in cold water for a quarter of an hour; drain and mix it with the hot cream, the heat of which will be sufficient to melt it. When this is done, strain the whole through a pointed strainer into a basin; put this on about six pounds of broken rough ice, and stir all the time till the contents begin to set; then whip a pint of double cream, remove the basin from the ice, and mix in the whipped cream lightly. Pour the mixture into a three-pint mould and return it to the broken ice; cover the mould with a stewpan-cover, with ice on the top, and let it remain thus in a cool place for about an hour and a half; then when wanted, dip the mould entirely into a basin of water as hot as the hand can bear, take it out quickly and wipe the top of the cream with a clean cloth, then put a dish over the mould; reverse and remove it, and serve.

863. VANILLA BAVAROIS CREAM.

Put half a stick of vanilla in a stewpan with one pint of boiling cream; cover the pan and let it steep for a couple of hours. Break eight yolks of eggs in a stewpan, mix in half a pound of pounded sugar and the vanilla cream when ready; stir these over the fire until the custard coats the spoon, without boiling; then add one ounce and three-quarters of drained gelatine, previously steeped in cold water for fifteen minutes; stir till melted, and strain the lot through a pointed strainer into a basin; put this on broken ice and stir the contents until it begins to set, then mix in lightly one pint and a half of whipped double cream. Fill a mould with the mixture, put it in the ice, cover the mould with the lid of a stewpan with ice on the top, and after two hours the cream will be set, and can be turned out of the mould in the same manner as the foregoing, and serve.

864. CHOCOLATE BAVAROIS CREAM.

This cream is made in the same way as the above, merely substituting a quarter of a pound of chocolate instead of vanilla to the boiling cream.

865. STRAWBERRY CREAM.

Pick the stalks off one pound of strawberries and rub the fruit through a silk sieve or tammy into a basin; mix in half a pound of pounded sugar and the juice of a lemon; steep one ounce and a half of gelatine for fifteen minutes in cold water, dissolve it in a small stewpan on the fire with a little water, and strain it through a pointed strainer into the strawberry pulp. Whisk a pint and a half of double cream, and proceed to finish it as for vanilla cream.

Note.—Raspberries and red currants are prepared in the same manner as the above.

A copper sugar-boiler should always be used to prepare red fruit, as tinned stewpans will destroy their colour.

866. CREAM À LA ROMAINE.

Blanch four ounces of Jordan with one ounce of bitter almonds; remove the skins, wipe them dry, and chop them rather fine; put these in a sugar-boiler, and stir them over the fire with a wooden spoon until they have acquired a light-brown colour; then throw them into a pint of milk, kept boiling for that purpose; add to it six ounces of sugar and eight yolks of eggs; stir the whole quickly until the yolks are set. Remove the boiler from the fire, and continue stirring for a few minutes longer; then add one ounce and a half of melted gelatine (see Strawberry Cream); after which, rub the lot through a tammy, like a purée, into a basin; mix in lightly a pint of whipped cream; pour the mixture into a mould, and put it in the ice to set, as previously described.

867. MERINGUES.

Meringues, if put in a dry place, can be kept a long time, and may often be served with advantage as a sweet, if filled with either whipped cream or preserve; therefore, whenever whites of eggs are to be had, they should be employed for the purpose.

Whisk the whites of twelve eggs to a firm white froth; then with a table-spoon mix very lightly one pound of sifted sugar, taking care not to work the froth too much, for fear of softening it. Cut some stiff white kitchen paper into strips two inches wide, and with a table-spoon gather the froth nearly full, by shaping it up at the side of the bowl in the form of an egg, and drop it upon one of the bands of paper, at the same time drawing the edge of the spoon sharply round the outer base of the meringue, so as to give it a smooth and oval appearance, in order that it may resemble an egg; proceed in this manner until the froth is all used up, keeping the meringues about two inches apart from each other. As each band is filled, place them close to each other on boards of about an inch thick, made for that purpose with well-seasoned wood, and cut, of course, to the size of the oven; sprinkle some sifted sugar over the meringues, and put them in a very moderately heated oven to bake of a light fawn-colour. When done, each meringue must be carefully removed from the paper. Scoop out the white part of the inside with a dessert-spoon, place them in neat order on a baking-sheet, and return them to a very slack oven to dry, taking care not to let them acquire any more colour.

When cold, they can be stored away in a box in a dry place; and when wanted, whip some double cream, season it with a little pounded sugar and either a few drops of orange-flower water or a little pounded vanilla; garnish each meringue with a tablespoonful of this cream; join two together, dish them up in a pyramidal form on a napkin upon a dish, and serve.

Note.—Currant jelly or any kind of marmalade can be substituted for whipped cream, but a teaspoonful of either will be found sufficient.

868. HOW TO FREEZE ICES.

In order to be able to freeze ices, creams, &c., it is necessary to have at hand an ice-tub with a hole and peg to it, an ice-pot or freezer, and an ice-spaddle. A freezer with two or three partitions is the best adapted for family use, as by that means two or three sorts of ices can be made at the same time, without extra tubs and rough ice.

The freezer, properly cleaned, must be put in the centre of the tub, in a cool place, surrounded with roughly pounded ice, mixed with three or four handfuls of common or bay salt, within two inches of the top of the freezer. Pour in the mixture intended for freezing, lay a piece of white paper across the top, and put the lid on; then begin to turn the freezer by the handle of the lid from right to left for about twenty minutes, when the lid must be taken off to see if the mixture begins to freeze at the sides; work this with the spaddle by pushing it in the centre, and continue turning the pot every two seconds; put the lid on and repeat the turning until the mixture is firmly set; then draw the water off by taking out the peg; replenish it with fresh ice and a handful of salt, place a damp piece of flannel over the top, and keep it in a very cool place until wanted.

869. LEMON-WATER ICES.

Rub off the rind of two lemons on some lumps of sugar; add the juice of ten lemons, a pint and a half of clarified syrup (No. 856), and half a pint of plain water. Mix thoroughly and strain through a hair sieve, and freeze as previously described.

870. CHERRY-WATER ICE.

Pick off the stalks of two pounds of cherries, pound them in a mortar with their stones; rub them through a tammy; then add the strained juice of three lemons, one pint and a half of clarified syrup, and half a pint of water. Mix and freeze as in No. 868.

871. ICED VANILLA CREAM.

Boil in a stewpan one quart of cream; put in it two sticks of vanilla, split lengthwise in four; when boiling, cover the stewpan and let the cream infuse for an hour.

Break eight yolks of eggs in a stewpan, add ten ounces of pounded sugar, and stir them together with a wooden spoon; after which, mix in the vanilla cream and stir over the fire without boiling until the cream coats the spoon, then strain it through a tammy into a basin and let it get cold, giving it an occasional stir to prevent a skin forming on the top. When cold pour it in the freezer previously set in the ice (see No. 868), work it in the usual way, and when it is set, mix in half a pint of whipped double cream, close the freezer, continue turning it, as described in "How to Freeze," then cover the freezer and put it by till wanted.

To dish ices, particular care must be taken, after having removed the flannel from the tub, to wipe around the top of the freezer with a cloth, before taking off the lid; then dish up the ice with a spaddle on a napkin upon a dish in an irregular pile, and serve.

Should however, the ice be preferred to be served moulded, proceed as follows:—When the cream has been worked as described and properly set, fill the ice-mould with it. Cut a sheet of white paper to fit the mould, leaving about an inch all round; put the cover on this, and if not well closed, spread some butter over the opening, then imbed the mould in the pounded ice and salt, place a piece of folded wet flannel on the top, and let it thus remain in a cool place till the ice is wanted; after which, wipe the top carefully, turn the ice out of the mould in the same manner as a jelly, on to a napkin on a dish, and serve.

Note.—Chocolate, orange, and lemon ice cream are prepared in the same way, simply substituting the selected flavouring for vanilla.

872. ICED COFFEE CREAM.

Put a quarter of a pound of freshly roasted coffee-berries into a quart of boiling cream, cover the stewpan, and let it infuse for an hour.

Mix eight yolks of eggs in a stewpan with ten ounces of pounded sugar, stir the lot with a wooden spoon; add the coffee cream, stir over the fire without boiling until the eggs thicken and coat the spoon; then strain the cream, and finish the freezing as directed in No. 871.

873. ICED STRAWBERRY CREAM.

Pick two pounds of ripe strawberries and rub them through a tammy or silk sieve into a basin; add to this purée ten ounces of pounded sugar, a quart of cream, and the strained juice of a lemon; mix the lot well together with a wooden spoon, strain it through a silk sieve into the freezer, properly set in ice (see No. 868); add a few drops of prepared cochineal to give the cream a pink tinge; work the contents with the spaddle, and when partly set, mix in half a pint of whipped double cream, and finish the freezing as directed in the foregoing.

Note.—Raspberry and currant ice creams are prepared in the same way.

874. ICED FRUIT PUDDING.

Stone a quarter of a pound of raisins and cut them in halves; wash and dry two ounces of currants; cut one ounce of candied orange-peel or citron, and a similar quantity of angelica in small dice; put these in a sugar-boiler with half a gill of Maraschino and simmer until the liqueur is reduced, when the sugar-boiler must be removed from the fire. Boil one quart of cream, put in it a stick of vanilla split lengthwise in four, and let it steep for an hour with the lid on. Break eight yolks of eggs into a stewpan, mix in half a pound of pounded sugar, add the vanilla cream, and stir the contents over the fire without boiling, until the cream thickens and coats the spoon; then strain in the usual way into a basin, giving it an occasional stir, to prevent a skin forming on the surface, and when cold pour it into the freezer ready set in the ice (see No. 868), and proceed to freeze in the usual way till the cream begins to set; then mix in gradually the chopped fruit, stir these in the ice with the spaddle, continue and finish the freezing as in vanilla ice cream, and serve either moulded or roughly set on a napkin on a dish.

Note.—Any kind of preserved fruit, such as greengages,

plums, pine-apple, apricots, &c., cut in small dice, can be substituted for the above fruit.

875. NESSELRODE PUDDING.

Peel two pounds of fine chesnuts; blanch them in boiling water to remove the second skin, and put them in a stewpan over the fire, with a quart of clarified sugar syrup and half a stick of vanilla, to simmer gently until the chesnuts are well done; then drain and rub them through a hair sieve into a basin.

Mix in a stewpan eight yolks of eggs with half a pound of pounded sugar; add one quart of cool boiled cream, stir the contents over the fire without boiling, until the eggs begin to thicken; then mix in the chesnut purée and half a gill of Maraschino; strain the lot through a tammy into a basin to get cold. Meanwhile wash and dry two ounces of currants; stone two ounces of raisins and cut them in halves, and two ounces of either candied citron or mirabel plums cut in small dice; put these mixed fruit into a sugar-boiler over the fire, with half a pint of clarified syrup and boil them for ten minutes, then strain in the usual way. When the chesnut cream is cold, pour it in the freezer ready set in the ice (see No. 868), work it with the spaddle until it is partly frozen, then add gradually the chopped fruit; mix them well with the ice cream, continue and finish the freezing as in No. 874, and serve in the same style.

876. APPLE JELLY.

Select some good Colville or Wellington apples; peel, core, slice, and put them in the preserving-pan with enough water to cover them well. Boil the apples till they are melted, then drain them on a hair sieve over a basin previously weighed; now weigh the juice, and for every pound of it add ten ounces of lump-sugar. Put the juice and sugar in the pan, again properly cleaned, over the fire till the sugar is dissolved, then pass the jelly through a napkin and boil it in small quantities, say six pounds at a time, till the jelly marks 28° on the syrup-gauge, when it will be done. Pour this into pots, and when cold, lay on each top of the jelly a round of paper (cut of the right size) dipped in brandy, then another round of paper tied around the top of the pots with string, and keep the preserve in a dry cool place.

Note.—The apple marmalade which remained on the sieve may be used for charlotte or open tarts.

877. APRICOT JAM.

Cut eight pounds of apricots into slices; put them in a basin with five pounds of pounded sugar; stir with a wooden spoon till the sugar is melted; then put the whole into the preserving-pan to boil for ten minutes, stirring the while with the skimmer; take this out of the jam, let what is on it cool, and if it feels greasy under the finger the jam is done. The same thing can also be ascertained by pouring a little into a cold plate; if it shows little tendency to spread, it is done. Pour the jam into pots, and cover them with paper when cold, as described in the previous number.

878. QUINCE JELLY.

Cut the quinces in quarters; peel, core, slice, and weigh them, and allow for every pound of fruit put in the preserving-pan a quart of water; then boil till the quinces are reduced to a pulp; drain them on a sieve over a basin, and to each pound of juice add ten ounces of lump-sugar; after which, finish as for apple jelly.

879. CURRANT JELLY.

For this jelly it is advisable to have half red and half white currants, say four pounds of each, and two pounds of raspberries; put the lot into the preserving-pan with a quart of water, and boil it on a sharp fire for about eight minutes, stirring the whole with a skimmer, to prevent the fruit adhering to the bottom of the pan; then pour the fruit into a hair sieve, over a basin; rub and press it well to squeeze all the liquor out of it; after which, weigh the juice, put it back in the pan, and for every pound ten ounces of lump-sugar must be added; stir the contents over the fire until the sugar is well melted; strain the syrup through a tammy; boil it in two parts on a brisk fire, and when marking 28° on the syrup-gauge it is done; then finish as the apple jelly.

List of Utensils Required for a Family of Six Persons.

I herewith give the list of kitchen utensils required for a family of from six to twenty-four persons. Of course, this list can to a great extent be modified, according to the number and circumstances of the family; but it must be borne in mind that there are but few households where there is not, now and then, an extra number of guests during the year, and that nothing tends to upset the temper of a cook more than the want of certain indispensable utensils at the time when everybody is busy, and which cannot then be obtained. I therefore strongly recommend the furnishing of every necessary implement in a kitchen, if good cooking is to be expected:—

PRACTICAL HOUSEHOLD COOKERY.

Two iron gridirons of eight and ten inches respectively, for meat and fish.

One fish-kettle with drainer, two feet long by about nine inches wide.

One turbot-kettle with drainer, about eighteen inches long.

Two oval braizing-pans with their covers and drainers, twelve and fifteen inches long by eight and ten inches wide, and seven inches deep, respectively.

Two untinned copper sugar-boilers, six and ten inches in diameter respectively, for stewed fruit, syrup, &c.

One bain-marie, with a set of five or six pans all in tinned copper.

One four-gallon tinned copper stock-pot and cover, for making ordinary stock and broth.

One two-gallon stock-pot and cover, for broth.

Twelve tinned copper stewpans and covers, varying in size from four to twelve inches in diameter.

Three sauté-pans with covers, eight, ten, and twelve inches in diameter.

Two ordinary tinned iron pans, for blanching vegetables, &c.

One copper preserving-pan, fourteen inches in diameter.

One tinned copper slice, for boiled meat, &c.

One broth-skimmer.

One copper skimmer for preserves.

Three tinned iron gravy-spoons.

Three tinned iron soup-ladles of different sizes.

One cutlet-bat.

One chopper.

One meat-cleaver.

One meat-saw.

Four kitchen-knives, assorted.

One steel.

Two colanders, of six and nine inches in diameter respectively, for draining, &c.

Three baking-sheets, with two-inch return pieces, from eight to twelve inches in diameter, for baking meat, &c.

Three plain baking-sheets, to fit in the oven for baking pastry, &c.

Two tin colanders, four and five inches in diameter, to strain sauces, &c. These should have very fine holes and may be in many instances substituted for a tammy sieve.

Two oval tinned copper dishes for gratin, ten and fifteen inches respectively.

One round tinned copper dish for gratin, nine inches diameter.

One salamander to glaze and brown gratin.

Two tinned iron frying-kettles, ten by seven inches, and fourteen by ten, and six inches deep, respectively. These are made in one piece without any soldering.

Two wire frying-baskets.

Three iron frying-pans, seven, eight, and nine inches diameter respectively, the former to be kept specially for omelets.

Two wire sieves, one very fine.

One silk sieve.

Two tammy sieves.

Six diaper cloths for straining broth and jellies.

One jelly-bag and stand.

Two pointed strainers.

Six wooden spoons of different sizes.

One hard-wood forcemeat-presser.

One marble mortar, nine inches diameter, with one hard-wood pestle.

One wood block to chop meat on.

Two chopping-boards, fifteen by ten, and two inches thick.

One set of measures, from half a gill to a quart.
One set of scales and weights, from a quarter of an ounce up to twenty-eight pounds.
One copper egg-boiler and two whisks, one large and one small.
Six common dishes.
Three pie-dishes.
Six earthenware pans, of three different sizes.
Twelve basins of different sizes.
One sausage-machine.
One filter.
One pair of large scissors to cut the fins of fish.
Two tin funnels.
One clock.
One meat-safe.
One ice-bucket with a hole, and a peg by the side at the bottom.
One freezer with three divisions.
One spaddle.
One large daubing-needle, for larding large braizing joints.
One medium ditto, ditto, ditto.
One box of twelve larding-needles for venison, sweetbread, fillet of beef, and cushion of veal.
One tin sugar-dredger for pounded sugar.
One seasoning-box with half a dozen compartments.
One glazing-brush.
Two pastry-brushes.
One oval copper pie-mould.
Two moulds for creams, jellies, and ices.
Two cylinder ditto.
Two open tart-moulds.
One plain mould for savarin.
One ditto, ditto, for charlotte.

Twelve small moulds for madeleines.

Two boxes of paste-cutters, one plain and the other fluted.

On box of long cutters for vegetables.

One syrup-gauge, and a tall testing-glass to ascertain the quantity of sugar in syrup and preserves. This gauge, to be correct, must register zero when plunged in cold water.

Six iron skewers of different sizes.

One ice-prick.

Three trussing-needles of different sizes.

One eight-cup French coffee percolator.

INDEX

OF BROTH, SOUPS, MACARONI, RICE, AND RISOTTO.

—⊷—

	No.		No.
BROTH, or Consommé	2	Gnochetti with Butter	99
Chicken	7	Soup, Goose Giblet	130
For Children or Convalescents	137	Gravy	5
		Gravy, Chicken	18
Condensed or Glaze	16	Game	19
Crayfish	29	Fish	20
Fish	25	Vegetables	21
Another	26		
Frog	27	**SOUP,** Hare, English Style	63
Game à la Chasseur	10	Hare, Susinoise	67
Another	11	Jelly, Simple	150
How to Make, in a few Minutes	13	Julienne	14
		Leek	38
Mutton or Scotch	136	Lettuce	42
Partridge	9	Lettuce, Stuffed	43
Rabbit à la Provençale	8	Lombardo	58
Refreshing	12		
Snail, for Obstinate Cough	149	**MACARONI** Cardinale	86
Veal	6	Cheese	88
Vegetables	30	Citizen Style	90
Another	31	Country Style	93
		Dominicaine	87
SOUP, Artois	62	Gratin	92
Asparagus, Clear	33	Italian Style	89
Beef-tea	148	Milanaise	94
Beer and Wine	128	Monglas	85
Bread and Raspings	140	Napolitaine	91
Brunoise	17	Palermo	83
Cabbage	34	Plain	81
Milanaise	35	Reine	84
Calf's Tail, Indian	133	**REMARKS** on, and Paste of all Descriptions, and how to Cook it, page 49	
Chantilly	49		
Clermont	47		
Cock a Leekie	135	Sarde	82
Condé	23		
Dawn	77	Soup, Manor-House	39
Egg	60	Minestrone	106
Poached Styrienne	131	Mock-Turtle	65
Another	132	Modena	54
Endive	46	Navarin	63

INDEX.

	No.		No.
Soup, New Carrot	41	Soup, Rice, and Chesnuts	124
Onion Lyonnaise	78	Flour	146
Onion Maigre	79	à la Française	117
Ox-tail	66	au Gratin	120
Oyster	127	Rice and Milk	122
Pap à la Reine	139	and Pheasant	119
Simple	138	with Plain Broth	102
Paste with Broth or Milk	147	with Potatoes	104
Soup, Green Pea	40	Remarks on, page 61	
Pearl-Barley	126	and Vegetables	105
Polenta Napolitaine	101	Risotto à la Chasseur	111
Piémontaise	100	à la Genoise	125
Soup, Polish	22	à l'Italienne	109
Polonaise	134	Another	110
Potato Flour	144	Housewife Style	121
Potato, Swiss	76	Milanaise	108
Purée of Crayfish, or Bisque of Crayfish	123	Piémontaise	107
		Poniastowsky	115
Purée of Chicken	64	Portugaise	113
Crecy	24	Spanish Style	112
Frog	28	à la Turque	114
Game	64	Soup à la Romaine	56
Green Peas	50	à la Rossini	59
Lentils	52	Sago	142
Potatoes and Chervil	55	Semolina	145
à la Reine	61	Sheep's Head	80
Turnips	37	Sorrel, Clear	44
White Haricot Beans	53	Sorrel, Thick	45
Quenelles of Chicken	72	Spring	15
of Game	72	Stock, Family	3
German	74	for Gravy and Sauces	4
Potatoes	71	Ordinary	1
à la Reine	75	Soup, Sturgeon	129
of Rice	69	Tagliatelli à la Chasseur	96
of Vegetables	70	à la Genoise	96a
Venitienne	73	Housewife Style	95
Ravioli à l'Italienne	97	Soup, Tapioca	143
à la Romaine	98	Tripe Milanaise	55
Rice, Boiled for Stewed Fruit	848	Turnips	36
Soup, Rice, and Cabbage	103	Velouté	141
and Cream Chasseur	118	Venitienne	57
and Cream Reale	116		

INDEX

OF SAUCES, BUTTER, AND ESSENCES.

	No.		No.
SAUCE, Allemande	156	Sauce, Hollandaise or Dutch	184
Apple	181	Horse-radish	191
Béchamel	154	Cold	224
Another	155	Indian	185
Blanquette	178	Italian	204
Butter	157	Sharp	205
for Asparagus	216	Maître d'Hôtel	159
Anchovy	161	Mayonnaise	218
Cayenne and Curry	168	Another	219
Clarified	160	Ravigote	220
Crayfish or Lobster	169	Mint	225
Horse-radish	165	Mushrooms	197
Maître d'Hôtel	226	Mustard	223
Melted	176	Napolitaine	208
Montpellier	163	Onion	202
Noir or Brown	164	Oyster	186
Perigord	167	Poulette	179
Ravigote	162	Ravigote	189
Truffle	166	Red Currant Jelly	215
and Ketchup	177	Remarks on Different Sauces, Essences, and Melted Butter, page 80	
Bread	183		
Caper	193		
Cucumber	203	Remoulade	222
Devilled	201	Robert	190
Egg	182	Romaine	209
Espagnole	151	Salmis	199
Another	152	Shrimp	213
Essence of Anchovies	174	Sicilian	211
Chicken	173	Suprême	188
Fish	175	Tartare	221
Game	172	Tomato	217
Mushrooms	171	Truffle	198
Truffles	170	Uxelles, D'	195
Sauce, Fennel	194	Stuffing	195
Financière	187	Velouté	153
Genoise	207	Venison	196
Gherkin	192	Venitienne	206
Gooseberry	180	Victoria	214
Hare	200	White	158

GENERAL INDEX.

	No.		No.
ALLEMANDE Sauce	156	Baked Pike, Citizen Style	485
Almond Paste	793	Barbel Broiled Maître d'Hôtel	500
Blanc-manger	861	Remarks on, page 234	
Anchovy Butter	161	Batter Paste, for Frying	317
Canopés	788	Bavarois Cream Chocolate	864
Essence	174	Coffee	862
Fried	336	Romaine	865
on Toast	787	Strawberry	865
Apple Charlotte	850	Vanilla	863
Fritters	812	Beans, French	770
Jelly	876	For Garnish	290
Pudding	829	Maître d'Hôtel	772
Sauce	181	Purée of	236
Stewed	841	Sautés	771
Tart	810	Broad, for Garnish	289
Apricot Jam	877	Poulette	775
Stewed	846	Purée of	776
Artichokes Barigoule	754	Haricot, Dried	773
Butter Sauce	753	for Garnish	294
Fried	756	Housewife Style	774
Italienne	755	Béchamel Sauce	154
Poivrade	756	Another	155
Jerusalem, Butter Sauce	751	Beef Boiled Countryman Style	383
for Garnish	293	Croquets of	385
Italienne	752	Gratin	382
Pickled	752	Mince of	384
Artois Soup	62	Mironton	380
Asparagus with Brown Butter	760	Salad of	386
Butter Sauce	758	Sharp Sauce	381
Soup, Clear	33	Braized à la Mode	506
Milanaise	759	Citizen Style	503
Points, for Garnish	287	Milanaise	504
Oil and Vinegar	761	Napolitaine	505
Aurore, Eggs à l'	252	Brisket of, Ecarlate	502
Trout à l'	481	Fillets of, Green Peas	511
		Indienne	508
BABA Cake	881	Jardinière	509
Back of Hare, Italian Sharp		Jerusalem Artichokes	511
Sauce	593	Mashed Potatoes	511
Baked Cod Stuffed	406	Mignons with Cham-	
Ham, Housewife Style	572	pignons	513
Perch, Angler Style	493	with Olives	510

INDEX.

	No.		No.
Beef, Fillets of, Purée of Celery	511	Boiled Mackerel	419
Fillet of Steak Châteaubriand	512	Mutton	389
		Leg of	551
Kidney Piémontaise	350	Pike, Italian Sharpe Sauce	484
à la Milanaise	504	Plaice	463
Napolitaine	505	Pork, Leg of	566
Porter-House Steak	517	Salmon, Lobster Sauce	390
Remarks on, and Roasting in general, page 241		Turbot, Hollandaise Sauce	398
		Turkey, Celery Sauce	646
Round of, Boiled English Style	501	Oyster Sauce	647
		Minced, Poached Eggs	387
Rump Steak, Anchovy Butter	517	Napolitaine	388
		Whiting	441
Chasseur	515	Bouchées à la Chasseur	322
Oyster Sauce	516	of Crabs	322
Scollops of, with Chesnut Purée	514	Financière	322
		Italienne	319
Steak and Kidney Pie	688	of Lobster	322
Oyster Pie	689	Monglas	322
Kidney Pudding	702	Oysters	322
Oyster Pudding	701	Palermo	320
Tea	148	Royale	321
Beer and Wine Soup	128	Toulouse	322
Beignet Fritters	815	Valenciennes	322
Birds, Pudding of Small	704	Boudins of Chicken, Richelieu	623
Biscuits, Champagne	809	Partridge	671
Italian	808	Pheasant	666
Bisque of Crayfish with Rice	123	"Bouquet Garni," or a Bunch of Aromatic Herbs, page 11	
Black Game Pie	697		
Game, Roast	673	Brains, Calf's, Fried	330
Pudding, Broiled	366	Omelet	264
Blanc-manger, Almond	861	Ox, Montpellier Butter	365
Blanquette Sauce	178	Napolitaine	364
Veal	524	Roebuck	583
Boar Cutlets, English Style	574	Braized Beef, à la Mode	506
Espagnole	575	Citizen Style	503
Sarde	573	Milanaise	504
Head, Stuffed	576	Napolitaine	503
Remarks on Wild, page 279		Cabbage for Garnish	295
Boiled Beef, Countryman Style	383	Calf's Liver Genoise	373
Brisket of, Ecarlate	502	Capon Milanaise	632
Round of, English Style	501	Duck with Cabbage	637
Brill	403	Green Peas	634
Capon with Rice	630	Olives	636
Capon with Tarragon	631	Ham with Stewed Peas	571
Chicken with Rice	619	Kid	557
with Rock-salt	618	Mutton Cutlets Jardinière	541
with Tarragon	617	Pompadour	540
Cod, Oyster Sauce	405	Soubise	539
Crabs	477	Leg of, Bretone	550
Crawfish	477	Partridges Perigueux	669
Eggs	240	Pig's Liver	371
Haddock, Smoked	458	Turkey Italienne	644
Ham with Spinach	570	Jardinière	645
Lobsters	477	Veal, Cushion of	525

INDEX.

	No.		No.
Braized Veal, Housewife Style	518	Broiled Salmon Cutlets, Indienne	394
Italienne	519	Tartare Sauce	393
Macédoine	525	Sausages	376
with New Carrots	525	Sheep's Kidney	345
Onions glazed	525	Sprats	473
Spinach	525	Tomatoes	780
Stewed Mushrooms	525	Trout, Hollandaise Sauce	482
Stewed Peas	525	Veal Cutlets, Plain	532
Stuffed Tomatoes	525	Tomato Sauce	532
Toulouse	525	Whiting	422
White Haricot Beans	525	Broth or Consommé	2
Bread and Butter Pudding	822	Chicken	7
Breadings	269	Condensed, or Glaze	16
Bread Raspings Soup	140	for Convalescents and Children	137
Raspings	268	Crayfish	29
Sauce	183	Fish	25
Panada	265	Another	26
Bream, Maître d'Hôtel	448	Frog	27
Remarks on, page 207		Game Chasseur	10
Breast of Mutton, Broiled	546	Game	11
Housewife Style	547	How to Make, in a few Minutes	13
Roebuck, Lyonnaise	580	Mutton or Scotch	136
Veal, Roast	536	Partridge	9
with Stuffing	535	Rabbit Provençale	8
Brill	403	Refreshing	12
Brioche Paste	792	Snail, for Obstinate Cough	149
Brisket of Beef Ecarlate	502	Veal	6
Broad Beans for Garnish	289	Vegetables	30
Poulette	775	Another	31
Purée of	776	Brown Bread and Butter Pudding	822
Broiled Black Pudding	366	Brunoise Soup	17
Boar Cutlets, English Style	574	Brussels Sprouts, Boiled	737
Chops of Lamb	545	Boiled with Butter	738
Mutton	545	for Garnish	291
Roebuck	579	Bunch or "Bouquet Garni," page 11	
Epigrammes of Lamb with Asparagus-points	553	Butter, Anchovy	161
Cucumber	553	Cayenne and Curry	168
French Beans	553	Clarified	160
Green Peas	553	Crayfish or Lobster	169
Italienne	554	Horse-radish	165
Macédoine	553	and Ketchup Sauce	177
Provençale	553	Maître d'Hôtel	226
Haddock, Maître d'Hôtel	453	Melted	176
Kidney Veal, Indienne	349	Montpellier	163
Mackerel, Maître d'Hôtel	420	Noir or Brown	164
Mullet, Grey, Maître d'Hôtel	439	Périgord	167
Mullet, Red, Maître d'Hôtel	435	Ravigote	162
Mutton Cutlets	543	Sauce	157
Bread-crumbed	544	for Asparagus	216
Maintenon	542	Truffle	166
Pig's Feet Genoise	368		
St. Menehould	367		
Pigeons, Crapandine	655		
Pork Cutlets, Gherkin Sauce	558		

INDEX. 443

	No.
CABBAGE, Boiled	728
Braized for Garnish	295
Country Style	729
Soup	34
Milanaise	35
and Rice Soup	103
Red, Stewed	296
Stuffed	730
Cabinet Pudding	818
Cake, Baba	801
Genoese	802
Ginger	803
Madeleines	805
Parisian	795
Plain Seed	798
Plum	797
Pound	799
Rice	806
Savarin	800
Savoy	796
Spanish	804
Victoria	794
Calf's Brains, Fried Citizen Style	330
and Liver	329
Italienne	328
Milanaise	331
Head, Devilled Sauce	355
Italian Sauce	355
Oil and Vinegar	355
Ravigote Sauce	355
Sharp Sauce	355
Tomato Sauce	355
Liver, Braized, Genoise	373
Citizen Style	374
Forcemeat	274
Fried Milanaise	331
Palermo	333
Venitienne	375
Feet, Italian Sauce	356
Foot Jelly, Plain	227
Tail Soup, Indienne	133
Canapés, Anchovy	788
Smoked Herring	789
Capon Boiled with Rice	630
with Tarragon	631
Braized Milanaise	632
Citizen Style	629
Lucullus	628
Napolitaine	626
Piémontaise	627
Caper Sauce	193
Caramel, or Burnt Sugar, page 12	
Carp Bourgignone	494

	No.
Carp, Fried	496
Perigueux	495
Remarks on, page 231	
Sicilienne	498
Stewed, English Style	497
Carrots, Housewife Style	743
Italienne	742
New, for Garnish	283
Soup	41
Purée of	236, 744
Cases, Red Mullet in	438
Cauliflowers, Béchamel	730
Boiled, Butter Sauce	731
Fried	732
for Garnish	272
Genoise	735
au Gratin	734
Parmesan Cheese	733
Purée of	236
Caviare, see Remarks on Hors-d'œuvres, page 145	
Celery, with Beef-Marrow	745
Gratin	746
Gravy	747
for Garnish	282
Purée of	236
Champagne Biscuits	809
Chautilly Soup	49
Charlotte, Apple	850
Pears	851
Chateaubriand Steak	512
Cheek, Ox, Italienne	359
Ox, with Purée of Vegetables	358
Cheese, Omelet	260
Another	261
Soufflé	837
Cherries, Stewed	847
Cherry Water, Iced	876
Chesnuts for Garnish	278
Pudding	819
Purée	237
and Rice Soup	124
Chicken Boiled with Rice	619
Rock-salt	618
Tarragon	617
Boudins Richelieu	623
Broth or Consommé	7
Curry of	610
Devilled Sauce	616
Essence of	173
Forcemeat for Garnish	271
Another	272
Fritot Italienne	614
Milanaise	615

INDEX.

	No.		No.
Chicken, Galantine of	706	Conger Eels, Roast	465
Gravy	18	Consommé or Broth	2
Liver	301	of Chicken	7
Mayonnaise Sauce	621	for Children or Convalescents	137
Pancakes of	625		
Pie	693	with Poached Eggs Styrienne	131
Purée Soup	64		
Quenelles Toulouse	624	Another	132
Soup	72	Coquilles à la Chasseur	324
Rissoles of	325	Cod	410
Roast	620	Turbot	402
Stewed Africaine	609	Court Bouillon for Fish	392
Chasseur	606	Crabs Boiled	477
Housewife Style	605	Crayfish, Bisque of	123
Marengo	603	Broth	29
Mushrooms	604	Butter	169
Mussels	611	Crawfish, Boiled	477
Piémontaise	613	Cream Chocolate Bavarois	864
Provençale	608	Coffee Bavarois	862
with Risotto	602	Romaine Bavarois	866
Sicilienne	612	Strawberry Bavarois	865
Sandwiches	786	Vanilla Bavarois	863
Tartare Sauce	622	Ice, Chocolate	871
Chocolate Bavarois Cream	864	Coffee	872
Cream Ice	871	Currants	873
Custard	853	Lemon	871
Soufflé	833	Raspberry	873
Civet of Hare	590	Strawberry	873
Clarified Butter	160	Vanilla	871
Syrup for Jellies and Ices	856	Crepinettes with Mashed Potatoes	378
Clarifying Broth	2		
Clermont Soup	47	Rice	378
Cocks-Combs for Garnish	303	Tomato Sauce	378
Cock a Leekie Soup	135	Crecy Soup	24
Cod à la Crême Gratin	409	Cromeskis à la Russe	327
Coquilles of	410	Croquets of Cod	410
Croquets	410	Lobster	326
Genoise	408	Potatoes	720
Indienne	407	Salmon	395
Mayonnaise	410	Turbot	402
Oyster Sauce	405	Croustade à la Toulouse	323
Remarks on, page 128		Croûtons for Soup and Garnish	24
Stuffed and Baked	406	Cucumber for Garnish	285
Salt, Black Butter	411	Sauce	203
Egg Sauce	411	Currant Iced Cream	873
Maître d'Hôtel	411	Jelly	879
Melted Butter	411	Sauce	215
Coffee, Bavarois Cream	862	Curry or Cayenne Butter	168
Cream, Iced	872	Curry of Chicken	610
Custard	852	Rabbit	598
Soufflé	835	Prawns for Garnish	305
Collared Eels	470	Custards, Chocolate	853
Condé Soup	23	Coffee	852
Conger Eels, Maître d'Hôtel	464	Plain	840
Remarks on, page 213		Cutlets, Boar, English Style	574

INDEX.

	No.
Cutlets, Espagnole	575
Sarde	573
Lamb	537
Mutton, Asparagus-points	537
Bread-crumbs	544
with Cucumber	537
French Beans	537
Italienne	537
Jardinière	541
Macédoine	537
Maintenon	542
Maître d'Hôtel	543
Milanaise	538
Pompadour	540
Purée of Chesnuts	537
Soubise	539
Stewed Mushrooms	537
Peas	537
Pigeons Macédoine	654
Pork, Gherkin Sauce	558
Indienne	562
Milanaise	559
with Purée of Chesnuts	561
Stuffing	560
Roebuck Chasseur	577
Surprise	578
Salmon Indienne	394
Veal Broiled Plain	531
Tomato Sauce	532
and Ham	528
Italienne	530
Milanaise	529
Papillote	531
Purée of Sorrel	527
Cygnet, Roast	559
DABS, Fried	463
Dawn Soup	77
Devilled Sauce	201
Duck Braized with Cabbage	637
Green Peas	634
Olives	636
Roast	638
Stewed, Green Peas	633
Turnips	635
Wild, Roast	683
Salmis of	684
EELS, Collared	470
Fillets of Fried, Tartare Sauce	469
Matelotte	467
Maître d'Hôtel	464
Milanaise	468

	No.
Eels, Conger, Remarks on, page 213	
Fresh-water, Remarks on, page 214	
Roast	465
Stewed, English Style	466
Eggs à l'Aurore	252
Boiled	240
Brouillés with Asparagus-points	248
with Brown Butter	241
Cream and Butter	243
Dauphine	251
Fried	242
Gratin	250
au Plat	244
with Tomatoes	246
Poached	245
Remarks on, page 112	
with Sauce	249
Sauce	182
Snow with Custard	840
Soup	60
Poached, Styrienne	131
Another	132
Endive Purée for Garnish	236
Salad	785
Soup	46
Epigrammes of Lamb with Asparagus-points	553
Cucumber	553
French Beans	553
Green Peas	553
Italian Style	554
Macédoine	553
Provençale	555
Espagnole Sauce	151
Another	152
Essence of Anchovies	174
Chicken	173
Fish	175
Game	172
Mushrooms	171
Truffles	170
FAMILY Stock	3
Feet, Calf's, with Italian Sauce	356
Pig's, à la Genoise	368
à la Ste. Menehould	367
Sheep's, with Oil and Vinegar	354
Fennel Sauce	194
Fillets of Beef Champignons	513
Green Peas	511
Indian Style	508

INDEX.

	No.		No.
Fillets of Beef Jardinière	509	Fresh Meat, Boiled	379
Jerusalem Artichokes	511	Fricassée of Chicken	607
Mashed Potatoes	511	Fritters, Apple	812
Mignons with Champignons	513	Beignets	815
Olives	510	Orange	814
Purée of Celery	511	Fritters, Pine-apple	813
Châteaubriand	512	Frittot of Chicken Italienne	614
Eels, Fried, Tartare Sauce	469	Milanaise	615
Haddock, Citizen Style	457	Frog Broth	27
Hare Larded, Venison Sauce	592	Purée of	28
Mackerel Venitienne	422	Fruit, Stewed Apples	841
Perch Italienne	491	Apricots	846
Romaine	492	Cherries	847
Venitienne	490	French Dried Plums	849
Soles Livournaise	430	and Rice	848
Venitienne	432	Greengages	844
Turbot Indienne	399	Mirabelle Plums	845
Italienne	400	Pears	842
Veal, or Cushion of	525	Pudding, Iced	874
Whiting, Citizen Style	445	Frying, Remarks on, page 142	
Italienne	443		
Venitienne	444	**GALANTINE** of Chicken	706
Financière Sauce	187	Turkey	706
Fine Herbs	195	Veal and Ham	705
Fish Broth	25	Game Broth Chasseur	10
Another	26	Another	11
Essence of	175	Essence	172
Forcemeat of Raw	275	Forcemeat of	273
Another	276	Gravy	19
Gravy	20	Pie in Mould	699
Omelet	257	Purée Soup	64
Remarks on, page 181		Quenelles of	72
Flounders	463	Remarks on, page 329	
Foot, Calf's, Jelly, Plain	227	Garnishes—	
Forcemeat, Calf's Liver	274	Asparagus-points	287
Chicken	271	Broad Beans	289
Another	272	Brussels Sprouts	291
Fish, Raw	275	Cabbage Braized	295
Another	276	Red Stewed	296
Game	273	Carrots, New	283
Lobster	277	Cauliflowers	292
Veal	270	Celery	282
Another	270a	Chesnuts	278
Fowl, Guinea, Housewife Style	657	Chicken Liver	304
Roast	658	Cocks-combs	303
Pea, Roast	660	Cucumber	285
Freeze Ices, How to	868	French Beans	290
French Beans	770	Haricot Beans, White	294
for Garnish	290	Jerusalem Artichokes	293
Maître d'Hotel	772	Lettuces	279
Santés	771	Macédoine Béchamel	281
Fresh Dried Plums, Stewed	849	Mushrooms	301
		with Wine	302
		Mussels	306

INDEX.

	No.
Garnishes—	
Onions, Button, Glazed	
for Matelotte	288
Glazed	280
Peas, Stewed	286
Prawns with Curry	305
Remarks on, in general, and on Truffles and Mushrooms in particular, page 128	
Sauerkraut	297
French	298
Truffles in Champagne	300
in Glaze	299
in Madeira	300
in Sherry	300
Turnips	284
Genoese Cake	802
Genoise Sauce	207
German Quenelles Soup	74
Gherkin Sauce	192
Giblet Omelet	264
Pie	694
Soup	130
Turkey, Housewife Style	651
Ginger Cake	803
Glaze, How to Prepare	362
How to Glaze Meat	362
Gnochetti with Butter	99
Goose Allemande	642
Navarin	641
Roast	639
Stewed with Chesnuts	640
Tomatoes	643
Gooseberry Sauce	180
Gratin Boiled Beef	382
Cauliflowers	734
Celery	746
Cod à la Crème	409
Eggs	250
Haddock	455
Macaroni	92
Mushrooms	781
Perch	489
Potatoes	716
Rice	120
Smelts	471
Soles	428
Sprats	475
Sturgeon	415
Turbot Cream	401
Gravy, Chicken	18
Fish	20
Game	19
Soup	5

	No.
Gravy, Vegetable	21
Greengages, Stewed	844
Green Peas Anglaise	767
Française	769
Stewed with Ham	768
Pea Purée	232
Purée Soup	50
Soup	40
Grouse, Roast	672
Guinea-Fowl, Housewife Style	657
Roast	658
Gurnard Genoise	446
Indienne	447
HADDOCK, Fresh, Broiled	
Maître d'Hôtel	453
Egg Sauce	452
Fillets of, Citizen Style	457
Fried, Butter Sauce	457
à l'Italienne	454
au Gratin	455
Remarks on, page 209	
Smoked	458
Citizen Style	459
Halibut, Oyster Sauce	462
Halibut, Remarks on, page 212	
Ham, Baked, Housewife Style	572
Boiled with Spinach	570
Braized with Stewed Peas	571
Sandwiches	786
Hare, Back of, with Sharp Italian Sauce	593
Civet of	590
Fillets of, Larded, Venison Sauce	592
Jugged	589
Potted	707
Remarks on, page 290	
Roast	594
Sauce	200
Soup, English Style	68
à la Susinoise	67
Haricot Beans, Garnish of White	294
Haricot of Mutton	540
Purée Soup of	53
Dried	773
Dried, Housewife Style	774
Hashed Venison	588
Herrings, Fresh, Mustard Sauce	460
Fried with Plain Butter	461
Remarks on, page 212	
Smoked	789
Hollandaise Sauce	184

INDEX.

	No.
Hors d'Œuvres, or Side Dishes, Remarks on, page 145	
Horse-radish Butter	165
Sauce	191
Cold	224
How to Glaze Meat	362
How to Make Sausages	376
How to Prepare Glaze	362
ICED Chocolate Cream	871
Coffee Cream	872
Currant Cream	873
Fruit Pudding	874
Lemon Cream	871
Water	869
Nesselrode Pudding	875
Raspberry Cream	873
Strawberry Cream	873
Vanilla	871
Ices, Cherry Water	870
Indian Sauce	185
Italian Sauce	204
Sharp Sauce	205
JAM, Apricot	877
Jellies, Lemon	857
Madeira	860
Orange	859
Strawberry	858
Jelly, Preserved Apple	876
Currant	879
Quince	878
Calf's Foot, Plain	227
Simple	150
Jerusalem Artichokes, Butter Sauce	751
Artichokes, Garnish of	293
Italian	752
Pickled	752
Purée of	239
John Dory	404
Jugged Hare	589
Venison	584
Julienne Soup	14
KETCHUP and Butter Sauce	177
Kid, Braized	557
Kidney, Beef, Milanaise	504
Napolitaine	505
Piémontaise	350
Sheep's, Chasseur	347
Grilled	345
Stewed with Fine Herbs	346

	No.
Kidneys, Veal, Broiled à l'Indienne	349
Stewed à la Romaine	348
Kitchen Utensils, List of, page 432	
LAMB Chops	545
Cutlets	537
Epigrammes of, with Asparagus-points	553
with Cucumber	553
French Beans	553
Green Peas	553
Italian Style	454
Macédoine	553
à la Provençale	555
Quarter of, Roast	556
Remarks on Roast, page 269	
Lamprey Bordelaise	450
Citizen Style	451
Matelotte of	449
Remarks on, page 207	
Larks, Housewife Style	681
Pie	696
Potted	707
Roast	681
Leek Soup	38
Lemon Cream Ice	871
Jelly	857
Water	869
Lentils, Housewife Style	778
Maître d'Hôtel	779
Purée of	234
Purée Soup of	52
Lettuce, Garnish of	279
Soup of	42
Stuffed Soup of	43
Leveret à la Chasseur	591
List of Utensils required for a Family of Six Persons, page 432	
Lombardo Soup	58
Lobster Boiled	477
à l'Americaine	478
Forcemeat of	277
Remarks on, page 221	
Sauce	212
Loin of Mutton, Roast	552
Pork, Roast	565
MACARONI Cardinale	86
Cheese with	88
Citizen Style	90
Country Style	93
Dominicaine à la	87

INDEX.

	No.
Macaroni, Gratin au	92
How to Cook, see Remarks on, page 49	
Italian Style	89
Milanaise à la	94
Monglas à la	85
Napolitaine à la	91
Palermo à la	83
Plain	81
Reine à la	84
Remarks on, and Paste of all Descriptions, and How to Cook it, page 49	
Sarde à la	82
Macédoine Béchamel, Garnish of	281
Mackerel Boiled	419
Broiled Maître d'Hôtel	420
Fillets of, Venitienne	422
Genoise	421
Remarks on, page 195	
Stewed	423
Madeira Jelly	860
Madeleine Cake	805
Maître d'Hôtel Butter	226
Sauce	159
Manor-House Soup	39
Marrow, Vegetable, Butter Sauce	748
Housewife Style	749
Italienne	750
Mashed Potatoes	709
Mayonnaise Sauce	218, 219
Ravigote Sauce	220
Meat, Fresh, Boiled	379
Boiled, Remarks on, page 9	
Melted Butter Sauce	176
Meringues	867
with Jelly	867
Whipped Cream	867
Mince-Meat	854
Pies	855
Minced Beef	384
Mutton	548
Veal with Poached Eggs	387
Minestrone	106
Mint Sauce	225
Mirabelle Plums, Stewed	845
Mock Turtle Soup	65
Mode of Preparing Sweet-Bread, Brains, Liver, and Scollops of Veal, page 150	
Modena Soup	54
Montpellier Butter	163
Mullets, Grey, Genoise Sauce	439
Hollandaise Sauce	439

	No.
Mullets, Italienne	439
Maître d'Hôtel	439
Tomato Sauce	439
Red, à la Genoise	437
in Cases	438
Italienne	436
Maître d'Hôtel	435
Remarks on Red and Grey, page 202	
Mushrooms Bordelaise	782
Essence of	171
Gratin	781
Milanaise	783
Remarks on, page 381	
Sauce	197
Garnish of	301
with Wine, Garnish of	302
Mussels, Garnish of	306
Mustard Sauce	223
Mutton, Boiled	389
Breast Broiled	546
Housewife Style	547
Chops	545
Cutlets, with Asparagus-points	537
with Bread-crumbs	544
Cucumber	537
French Beans	537
Italienne	537
Jardinière	541
Macédoine	537
Maintenon	542
Maître d'Hôtel	543
Milanaise	538
Pompadour	540
with Purée of Chesnuts	537
Soubise	539
with Stewed Mushrooms	537
with Stewed Peas	537
Haricot of	549
Leg of, Boiled	551
Braized Bretonne	550
Roast	552
Loin of Roast	552
Minced	548
Pie	691
Remarks on, page 259	
Saddle of, Roast	552
Shoulder of	552
NAPOLITAINE Sauce	208
Navarin Soup	63
New Carrots Soup	41

2 F

INDEX.

	No.
New Carrots, Garnish of	283
Noir or Brown Butter	164
OBSERVATION with respect to French Words in Bills of Fare, page 141	
Omelet with Artichokes	259
Asparagus-points	264
Brains	264
Cheese	260
Another	261
Fish	257
Giblets	264
Ham or Bacon	254
Jam	839
Kidneys	258
Mushrooms	264
Onion	255
Oysters	262
Parsley	253
Peas	264
Piémontaise	263
with Rum	838
Sorrel	264
Spinach	264
Soufflée	832
with Tomatoes	256
Truffles	264
Onions, Butter, Glazed for Matelotte	288
Glazed	280
Remarks on, page 382	
Sauce	202
Soup à la Lyonnaise	78
Maigre	79
Stewed	784
Orange Fritters	814
Jelly	859
Ox-Brain, Montpellier Butter	365
Napolitaine	364
Ox-Cheek Italienne	359
with Purée of Vegetables	358
Ox-Palate, Fried	357
Ox-Tail Soup	66
Ox-Tongue, Fresh, with Gherkin Sauce	366
Pickled, Madeira Sauce	361
Sandwiches	786
Oysters, Bouchées of	322
Fried	335
Salpicon of	313
Oyster Sauce	186
Soup	127
PANADA, Bread	265

	No.
Panada, Rice	266
Semolina	267
Pancakes	830
Chicken	625
with Jam	831
Pap Soup à la Reine	139
Simple	138
Parisian Cake	795
Partridges, Boudins of	671
Braized à la Perigueux	669
Pie	697
Quenelles of	671
Roast	670
Salmis of	667
Stewed with Cabbage	668
Paste, Almond	793
Batter for Frying	317
for Brioche	792
Italian with Broth or Milk	147
Short, for Raised Pies	790
Short, for Tarts	791
for Sponge and Biscuits	807
Ordinary, for Tagliatelli	95
and Sweet Dishes, Remarks on, page 387	
of all Description, Remarks on, and How to Cook it, page 49	
Patties, Hot	318
Pea-Fowl, Roast	660
Pea, Green, Soup	40
Pearl-Barley	126
Pears, Charlotte of	851
Stewed	842
Peas, Dry, Purée of	233
Green, Purée of	232
à l'Anglaise	767
à la Française	769
Stewed, for Garnishes	286
Stewed with Ham	768
Perch, Baked, Angler Style	493
Fillets of, à l'Italienne	491
à la Romaine	492
à la Venitienne	490
Fried	487
Gardener Style	488
au Gratin	489
Remarks on, page 229	
Perigord Butter	167
Pheasant, Boudins of	666
Housewife Style	662
à la Milanaise	664
à la Napolitaine	663
Quenelles of	666
Roast, Stuffed with Truffles	665

INDEX.

	No.		No.
Pheasant, Salmi of	661	Pork, Leg of Boiled	566
Pickled Jerusalem Artichokes	752	Roast	565
Salmon	397	Loin of Roast	564
Ox-Tongue, Madeira Sauce	361	Neck of Roast	563
Pie, Beef-Steak and Kidney	688	Pie in Mould	700
and Oyster	689	Remarks on, page 271	
Black Game	697	Porter-House Steak	517
Chicken	693	Potatoes à la Beaufort	719
Game, in Mould	699	à là Béchamel	715
Giblet	694	Chipped, Fried	723
Lark	696	with Cream	711
Mutton	691	Croquets	720
Partridge	697	à la Duchesse	721
Pigeon	692	Fried	722
Pork, in Mould	700	Soufflées	725
Rabbit	695	au Gratin	716
Snipe	698	à l'Italienne	714
Veal and Ham	690	à la Lyonnaise	713
Pigeon's Cutlets Macédoine	654	à la Maître d'Hôtel	710
à la Crapaudine	655	Mashed	709
Pie	692	New, with Butter	727
Roast	656	Paille	724
Stewed, with Green Peas	652	Provençale	718
Mushrooms	653	Sautées	712
Wild	677	Savoisienne	717
Pig's Ears with Purée of Lentils	370	Soufflé of	726
à la Venitienne	369	Potato Flour Soup	144
Liver, Braized	371	Potato Swiss Soup	76
Pounded	372	Potted Hare	707
Feet à la Genoise	368	Larks	707
Ste. Menehould	367	Rabbit	707
Sucking, à l'Italienne	569	Poularde	632
à la Provençale	568	Poulette Sauce	179
Roast	567	Poultry, Remarks on, page 298	
Pike, Baked, Citizen Style	485	Pound Cake	799
Boiled, Italian Sharp Sauce	484	Prawns with Curry, for Garnish	305
à la Lyonnaise	483	Preserved Jelly	876
Quenelles of	486	Pudding (Meat), Beef-steak and	
Remarks on, page 225		Kidney	702
Pine-apple Fritters	813	Beef-steak and Oyster	701
Plaice and Flounders	463	Bird, Small	704
Remarks on, page 213		Black	366
Plain Seedcake	798	Mutton	703
Plovers, Roast	677	(Sweet) Apple	829
Plum Cake	797	Bread and Butter	822
Stewed	843	Brown Bread and Butter	816
Polenta Piémontaise	100	Cabinet	818
Napolitaine	101	Chesnut	819
Polish Soup	22	College	823
Polonaise Soup	134	Iced Fruit	874
Pork, Cutlets of, Gherkin Sauce	558	Ginger	820
à l'Indienne	562	Gooseberry	828
à la Milanaise	559	Lemon	821
with Purée of Chesnuts	561	Nesselrode	875
Stuffing	560	Plum	826

	No.		No.
Pudding, Rice	825	**RABBIT** à la Chasseur	596
Roly-Poly	827	Curry of	598
Semolina	817	Napolitaine à la	599
Tapioca	824	Pie	695
Purée of Carrots	236	Potted	707
Cauliflower	336	Poulette à la	600
Celery	236	Provençale à la	597
Chesnuts	237	Remarks on, page 294	
Endive	236	Roast	601
French Beans	236	Stewed	595
Jerusalem Artichokes	239	Broth à la Provençale	8
Lentils	234	Raspberry Cream Ice	873
Peas, Dry	233	Ravigote Butter	162
Green	232	Sauce	189
Potatoes	231	Mayonnaise Sauce	220
Sorrel	238	Ravioli à l'Italienne	97
Soubise	229	à la Romaine	98
Spinach	236	Red Currant Jelly Sauce	215
Tomatoes	228	Red Mullets à la Génoise	437
Turnips	235	in Cases	438
Vegetables	230	à l'Italienne	436
Crayfish Soup, or Bisque of	123	à la Maître d'Hôtel	435
Chicken Soup	64	Refreshing Broth	12
Crecy Soup	24	Remarks on Barbel, page 234	
Frog Soup	28	Beef and Roasting in General, page 241	
Game Soup	64	Boar, page 279	
Green Peas Soup	50	Boiled Meat, page 9	
Lentils Soup	52	Bream, page 207	
Potatoes and Chervil Soup	48	Carp, page 231	
à la Reine Soup	61	Cod, page 188	
Turnips Soup	37	Different Sauces, Essences, Melted Butter and Jellies, page 80	
White Haricot Beans Soup	53	Eels, Conger, page 213	
		Fresh-Water, page 214	
QUAILS à la Jardinière	679	Eggs, page 112	
Roast	678	Fish, page 181	
Quarter of Lamb, Roast	556	Frying, page 142	
Quenelles of Chicken à la Toulouse	624	Game, page 329	
Partridges	671	Garnishes in General, and on Truffles and Mushrooms in particular, page 128	
Pheasants	666		
Pikes	486	Haddock, page, 209	
Rabbit	624	Halibut, page 212	
Chicken Soup	72	Hare, page 290	
Game Soup	72	Herrings, page 212	
German Soup	74	Hors d'Œuvres or Side Dishes, page 145	
Potato Soup	71		
à la Reine Soup	75	Lamb, page 259	
Rice Soup	69	Lamprey, page 207	
Vegetable Soup	70	Lobsters, Crabs and Crawfish, and How to Boil them, page 221	
Venitienne	73		
Quince Jelly	878		

INDEX. 453

	No.
Remarks on Mackerel, page 195	
Mullets, Red and Grey, page 202	
Mushrooms, page 381	
Mutton, Lamb, and Goat, page 207	
New Zealand Mutton and American Beef, page 8	
Onions, page 382	
Paste and Sweet Dishes, page 387	
Perch, page 229	
Pike or Jack, page 225	
Plaice, Flounders, &c., page 213	
Pork, page 271	
Poultry, page 296	
Rabbit, page 294	
Rice, page 61	
Roasting, page 241	
Salad, page 383	
Salmon, page 182	
Sandwiches, page 384	
Sausages, page 174	
Smelts, page 218	
Soles, page 197	
Sprats, page 220	
Sturgeon, page 191	
Tripe, page 156	
Trout, page 223	
Turbot, page 186	
Veal, page 248	
Vegetables, page 356	
Venison, page 284	
Whitebait, page 219	
Whiting, page 204	
Remoulade Sauce	222
Rice, Boiled, for Stewed Fruit	848
and Cabbage Soup	103
Cake	808
Cream Soup à la Chasseur	118
à la Reale Soup	116
and Chesnut Soup	124
Flour Soup	146
à la Française Soup	117
au Gratin Soup	120
with Milk Soup	122
Panada	266
Pheasant Soup	119
Plain Broth	102
Potatoe Soup	104
Pudding	825
Remarks on, page 61	
Soufflés of	837

	No.
Rice, Vegetable Soup	105
Risotto à la Chasseur	111
Genoa Style	125
Italian Style	109
Another	110
Housewife Style	121
Milanaise	108
à la Piémontaise	107
à la Poniastowsky	115
à la Portugaise	113
Spanish Style	112
à la Turque	114
Rissoles of Chicken	325
Roast Chicken	620
Cygnet	659
Duck	638
Wild	683
Eels, Conger	465
Goose	639
Grouse	672
Guinea-Fowl	658
Hare	594
Lamb, Quarter of	556
Larks	681
Mutton, Leg of	552
Loin of	552
Saddle of	552
Shoulder of	552
Partridges	670
Pheasants	665
Pigeons	656
Wild	677
Plovers	677
Pork, Leg of	565
Loin of	564
Neck of	563
Quails	678
Rabbit	601
Roebuck	586
Snipe	674
Sturgeon	414
Sucking Pig	567
Teal	683
Turkey Napolitaine	649
Piémontaise	648
Stuffed, with Truffles	650
Veal	534
Water-Hen	683
Wheatears	682
Widgeons	683
Woodcocks	676
Robert Sauce	190
Roebuck, Brain of	583
Breast of, Lyonnaise	580
Cutlets of, Chasseur	577

INDEX.

	No.		No.
Roebuck, Cutlets of, Surprise	578	Salt Cod Maître d'Hôtel	411
Chops of, Grilled	579	Melted Butter	411
Fry of	582	Sandwiches, Beef	786
Haricot of	581	Chicken	786
Haunch of, Larded	587	Ham	786
Roast	586	Ox-Tongue	786
Loin of, or Saddle à l'Ecossaise	585	Remarks on, page 384	
		Sardines on Toast	787
Roly-Poly Pudding	827	Sauce, Allemande	156
Romaine Sauce	209	Apple	181
Soup à la	56	Béchamel	154
Rossini, Soup à la	59	Another	155
Rump-Steak à la Chasseur	515	Blanquette	178
Anchovy Butter	517	Butter	157
with Oyster Sauce	516	Butter and Ketchup	177
		Butter, for Asparagus	216
SADDLE of Mutton, Roast	552	Bread	183
Sago Soup	142	Caper	193
Salad, Beef	386	Cucumber	203
Dressing of all Description	785	Devilled	201
		Egg	182
of tomatoes	785	Espagnole	151
Remarks on, page 383		Another	152
Salmi of Partridges	667	Fenuel	194
Pheasants	661	Financière	187
Teal	686	Genoise	207
Water-Hen	682	Gherkin	192
Widgeon	686	Gooseberry	180
Wild Duck	684	Hare	200
Salmis Sauce	199	Hollandaise	184
Salmon, Broiled, Tartare Sauce	393	Horse-Radish	191
Croquets	395	Cold	224
Cutlets à l'Indienne	394	Indian	185
Genoise Sauce	392	Italian	204
Hollandaise Sauce	390	Sharp	205
Lobster Sauce	390	Maître d'Hôtel	159
Mayonnaise Sauce	396	Mayonnaise	218
Melted Butter	390	Another	219
Pickled	397	Ravigote	220
Remarks on, page 182		Mint	225
Shrimp Sauce	390	Mushroom	197
Smoked, on Toast	787	Mustard	223
à la Venitienne	391	Naphlitaine	208
Salpicon à la Chasseur	312	Onion	202
à la Financière	310	Oyster	186
à l'Italienne	307	Poulette	179
of Lobster or Crab	314	Ravigote	189
à la Monglas	315	Red Currant Jelly	215
of Oysters	313	Remoulade	222
à la Palerme	308	Robert	190
à la Royale	309	Romaine	209
à la Toulouse	311	Salmi	199
à la Valencienne	316	Shrimp	213
Salt Cod with Brown Butter	411	Sicilian	211
with Egg Sauce	411	Suprême	188

INDEX.

	No.		No.
Sauce, Tartare	221	Snipe, Roast	674
Tomato	217	Salmi of	675
Truffle	198	Soles, Boiled	424
Uxelles, D'	195	à la Colbert	426
Velouté	153	au Gratin	428
Venison	196	Fried	425
Venitienne	206	Fine Herbs	427
Victoria	214	Fillets of, à la Livournaise	430
White	158	à la Venitienne	432
Sauerkraut	297	à la Normande	438
French	298	with Parsley	431
Sausages, Citizen Style	377	à la Provençale	420
How to Make	376	Remarks on, page 197	
Remarks on, page 174		with White Wine	434
Savarin Cake	800	Sorrel, Purée of	238
Savoy Cake	796	Soup, Clear	44
Scollops of Beef with Chesnut		Thick	45
Purée	514	Soubise Purée	229
Veal, Fried	523	Soufflé, Cheese	836
à la Genoise	334	Chocolate	833
with Mushrooms	526	Coffee	835
Sea Kale, Butter Sauce	757	Omelet	832
Semolina Panada	267	Rice	837
Pudding	817	Vanilla	834
Soup	145	Soup Artois	62
Sheep's Feet with Oil and Vinegar	354	Asparagus, Clear	33
		Beef-Tea	148
Head Broth	80	Beer and Wine	128
Kidneys à la Chasseur	347	Bread and Raspings	140
Grilled	345	Brunoise	17
Stewed with Fine Herbs	346	Cabbage	34
		Milanaise	55
Tongue, Gherkin Sauce	320	and Rice	103
à la Napolitaine	353	Calf's Tail, Indian	133
with Spinach	351	Chantilly	49
Short Paste for Raised Pies	790	Clermont	47
Sponge and Biscuits	807	Cock a Leekie	135
Tagliatelli	95	Condé	23
Tarts	791	Dawn	77
Shoulder of Mutton, Roast	552	Egg	60
Shrimp Sauce	188	Poached Styrienne 131,	132
Sicilian Sauce	211	Endive	46
Skate with Brown Butter	416	Gnochetti with Butter	99
à la Genoise	417	Goose Giblet	130
à la Hollandaise	418	Gravy	5
Small Birds, Pudding of	704	Hare, English Style	68
Smelts, Fried	471	Hare, Susinoise	67
au Gratin	471	Jelly, Simple	150
Remarks on, page 218		Julienne	14
Smoked Haddock	458	Leek	38
Citizen Style	459	Lettuce	42
Herring	789	Stuffed	43
Salmon, on Toast	787	Lombardo	58
Snail Broth, for Obstinate Cough	149	Macaroni, *see* Macaroni.	
Snipe, Pie of	698	Manor-House	39

INDEX.

	No.
Soup, Minestrone	106
Mock-Turtle	65
Modena	54
Navarin	63
New Carrots	41
Onion Lyonnaise	78
Maigre	79
Ox-Tail	66
Oyster	127
Pap à la Reine	139
Simple	138
Paste	147
Pea, Green	40
Pearl Barley	126
Polish	22
Polonaise	134
Potato Flour	144
Swiss	76
Purée of Crayfish, or Bisque of	123
Purée of Chicken	64
Crecy	28
Frog	24
Game	64
Green Peas	50
Lentils	52
Patatoes and Chervil	48
à la Reine	61
Turnips	37
White Beans	53
Quenelles of Chicken	72
of Game	72
German	74
of Potatoes	71
à la Reine	75
of Rice	69
of Vegetables	70
à la Venitienne	73
Rice, see Rice and Risotto	
à la Romaine	56
à la Rossini	59
Sago	142
Semolina	145
Sheep's Head	80
Sorrel, Clear	44
Thick	45
Spring	15
Stock, Family	3
Sturgeon	129
Tapioca	143
Tripe Milanaise	55
Turnips	36
Velouté	141
Venitienne	57
Spanish Cake	804

	No.
Spinach with Butter	765
Cream	766
Housewife Style	763
à l'Italienne	762
à la Provençale	764
Purée of	236
Sprats, Broiled	473
Citizen Style	476
Fried	474
au Gratin	475
Remarks on, page 220	
Spring Soup	15
Stewed Carp, English Style	497
Chickens à la Africaine	609
à la Chasseur	606
Housewife Style	605
à la Marengo	603
with Mushrooms	604
Mussels	911
à la Piémontaise	613
à la Provençale	608
with Risotto	602
à la Sicilienne	612
Duck with Green Peas	633
Duck with Turnips	635
Eels, English Style	466
Fruit, Apples	841
Apricots	846
Cherries	847
French, Dried Plums	849
with Rice	848
Mirabel Plums	845
Pears	842
Plums	843
Goose with Chesnuts	640
Tomatoes	643
Mackerel	423
Mutton Cutlets with Mushrooms	537
Mutton Cutlets with Peas	537
Onions	784
Partridges with Cabbage	668
Peas with Ham	768
Pigeons with Green Peas	652
Mushrooms	653
Rabbit	595
Sheep's Kidneys with Fine Herbs	346
Veal, Country Style	520
Another	521
Kidneys à la Romaine	348
with Rice	522
Stock, Family	3
for Gravy and Sauces	4
Ordinary	1

INDEX.

	No.
Strawberry Cream, Bavarois	865
Cream Ice	873
Jelly	858
Sturgeon à l'Anglaise	413
au Gratin	415
Remarks on, page 191	
Roast, Larded	414
à la Venitienne	412
Soup	129
Sucking Pig, Italienne	569
à la Provençale	568
Roast	567
Suprême Sauce	188
Sweetbread, Mode of Preparing, page 150	
Syrup, Clarified, for Jellies and Ices	856

TAGLIATELLI à la Chasseur . . . 96
    à la Genoise . . . 96a
    Housewife Style . . 95
    Paste, Ordinary . . 95
Tapioca Pudding . . 824
    Soup . . . 143
Tartare Sauce . . . 221
Tarts, Apple . . . 810
    of Fruit in General . 811
Teal, Roast . . . 683
    Salmi of . . . 686
Tench 499
Tomatoes, Grilled . . 780
    Purée . . . 228
    Salad 785
    Sauce . . . 217
    Stuffed, Provençale . 779
Tongue, Fresh Ox, Gherkin Sauce . . . 366
    Pickled Ox, Madeira Sauce 361
        Sandwiches . 786
    Sheep's, Gherkin Sauce . 352
    à la Napolitaine . . 353
    with Spinach . . 351
Tripe, Citizen Style . . 340
    Fried 344
    à l'Italienne . . 339
    à la Lyonnaise . . 341
    à la Milanaise . . 337
    and Onion . . 342
        Another . . 343
    Remarks on, page 156
    à la Romaine . . 338
    Soup à la Milanaise . 55
Trout à l'Aurore . . 481
    Broiled, Hollandaise Sauce 482

	No.
Trout à l'Italienne	479
à la Meunière	480
Remarks on, page 223	
Truffles, Butter	166
in Champagne	300
Essence of	170
Glaze	299
Madeira	300
Sherry	300
Sauce	198
Turbot, Coquilles of,	402
au Gratin	401
Croquets	402
Fillets of, à l'Indienne	399
à l'Italienne	400
Hollandaise Sauce	398
Mayonnaise of,	402
Remarks on, page 186	
Turkey, Boiled, with Celery Sauce	646
with Oyster Sauce	647
Braized à l'Italienne	644
la Jardinière	645
Galantine of	706
Giblets of, Housewife Style	651
Roast à la Nopolitaine	649
Piémontaise	648
Stuffed, with Truffles	650
Turnips with Gravy	739
as a Garnish	284
Mashed	741
Purée	235
Soup	37
à la Savoisienne	740
Clear Soup	36

UXELLES, D' . . . 195
    Sauce . . . 195

VANILLA Cream Ice . 871
    Soufflé . . . 834
Veal, Blanquette of, . 524
    Boiled, Minced, with Poached Eggs . . . 387
    à la Napolitaine . . 388
    Braized Italienne . . 519
        Housewife Style . 518
    Breast of, Citizen Style . 536
        with Stuffing, Roast . 535
    Broth . . . 6
    Cushion of, Braized à la Jardinière . . 525
    Braized, with Glazed Onion . . 525
    à la Macédoine . 522

INDEX.

	No.
Veal, Cushion of, Braized, with New Carrots	525
Spinach	525
Stewed Mushrooms	525
Peas	525
Stuffed Tomatoes	525
à la Toulouse	525
with white Haricot Beans	525
Cutlets, Broiled	531
with Tomato Sauce	532
Ham	528
à l'Italienne	530
à la Milanaise	529
en Papillote	531
with Purée of Sorrel	527
and Ham, Galantine of,	705
and Ham Pie	690
Forcemeat of	270
Another	270a
Kidneys, Broiled à l'Indienne	349
Stewed à la Romaine	348
Remarks on, page 248	
Roast	534
Stewed, Country Style	520
Another	521
with Rice	522
Vegetable Broth	30
Another	31
Marrow, Butter Sauce	748
Housewife Style	749

	No.
Vegetable Marrow à l'Italienne	750
Purée of	230
Remarks on, page 356	
Velouté Sauce	153
Soup	141
Venison, Hashed	588
Jugged	584
Sauce	196
Remarks on, page 284	
Venetian Sauce	206
Soup	57
Victoria Cake	794
Sauce	214
WATER-HEN, Roast	683
Salmi of	687
Wheatears, Roast	682
Whitebait	742
Remarks on, page 219	
White Sauce	158
Whiting, Boiled	441
Broiled	442
Fillets of, Citizen Style	445
à l'Italienne	443
à la Venitienne	444
Fried	440
Remarks on, page 204	
Widgeon, Housewife Style	585
Roast	683
Salmi of	686
Woodcock, Roast	676

THE END.

www.ingramcontent.com/pod-product-compliance
Lightning Source LLC
Chambersburg PA
CBHW022115300426
44117CB00007B/718